# HUMAN RIGHTS IN THE WORLD

# HUMAN RIGHTS IN THE WORLD

*An introduction to the study of
the international protection of human rights*

*Fourth edition*

## A. H. ROBERTSON
B.C.L., S.J.D.

former *Professeur Associé*, University of Paris I
former Simon Visiting Professor at the University of Manchester
former Director of Human Rights, Council of Europe

## J. G. MERRILLS
B.C.L., M.A.

Professor of Public International Law at the University of Sheffield

MANCHESTER UNIVERSITY PRESS
Manchester and New York
*Distributed exclusively in the USA by St. Martin's Press*

Copyright © the estate of A. H. Robertson 1972, 1982, 1989
and J. G. Merrills 1989, 1992, 1996

*Published by*
Manchester University Press
Oxford Road, Manchester M13 9NR, UK
*and* Room 400, 175 Fifth Avenue,
New York, NY 10010, USA

*Distributed exclusively in the USA*
*by* St. Martin's Press, Inc., 175 Fifth Avenue,
New York, NY 10010, USA


*British Library Cataloguing-in-Publication Data*
A catalogue record for this book is available from the British Library


*Library of Congress Cataloging-in-Publication Data applied for*




ISBN 0 7190 4922 9 *hardback*
0 7190 4923 7 *paperback*



First published 1996

00 99 98 97 96          10 9 8 7 6 5 4 3 2 1




Printed in Great Britain by Bell & Bain Ltd, Glasgow

# Contents

# Preface

Since the third edition of this book was published in 1989 the existing arrangements for promoting and protecting human rights have been consolidated and extended and progress has been made on a number of other fronts. The ending of the Cold War has prompted the creation of the Organisation for Security and Co-operation in Europe and has had major consequences for the Council of Europe; the Inter-American Court of Human Rights has significantly developed its case law; and the African regional system has begun functioning. At the United Nations the Human Rights Committee and the other treaty bodies have been very active; there is now a High Commissioner for Human Rights; and the Security Council has taken a number of important initiatives in the humanitarian field, including the creation of criminal tribunals for former Yugoslavia and Rwanda. There have, of course, also been numerous new treaties including the Convention on the Rights of the Child, the Inter-American Conventions on Forced Disappearances and Violence against Women and the 1993 Chemical Weapons Convention.

In this new edition I have attempted to describe and analyse these and many other recent developments, while retaining the clear and concise outline of the legal background which was a feature of the editions of 1972 and 1982 for which the late Professor Robertson was responsible. The inclusion of so much new material has naturally required a good deal of rewriting and reorganisation. Thus significant portions of the text are entirely new and the protection of human rights in Europe is now divided between two chapters to permit both a more detailed account of the European Convention and a fuller survey of other arrangements in the region, including developments with regard to the

Convention for the Prevention of Torture and the European Social Charter. The present edition is based on material which was available at the end of 1995.

As with the previous edition, two points relating to what this book is and, no less important, what it is not, should also be mentioned. I have not tried to provide a detailed account of every human rights treaty, a comprehensive survey of human rights case law, or an exhaustive analysis of every institution and procedure. As its subtitle indicates, the book is an introduction, and as such is intended to complement more specialised studies. Secondly, this is a study of human rights law, not a review of the internal practice of States. The difference between what governments say and what they do is, of course, particularly marked in the field of human rights and cannot be overlooked. Account is taken of that discrepancy here, not by rehearsing a catalogue of human rights abuses, which others have painstakingly compiled, but by explaining how the formulation, the application and the enforcement of human rights law occurs in a political as well as a moral context.

My thanks are due to Mrs Jean Hopewell, who typed the manuscript, to other members of the secretarial staff of the Law Faculty for technical assistance, and, as always, to my wife Dariel for her encouragement and support.

J. G. Merrills
Sheffield
March 1996

# CHAPTER 1

# *International concern with human rights*

## I. The idea of international human rights

In 1993 the World Conference on Human Rights, meeting in Vienna, reaffirmed 'the solemn commitment of all States to fulfil their obligations to promote universal respect for, and observance and protection of, all human rights and fundamental freedoms for all in accordance with the Charter of the United Nations, other instruments relating to human rights, and international law'.[1] Concern with the protection of human rights, in the United Nations and elsewhere, has been one of the most striking developments in international law since the end of the Second World War. At the same time, widespread violations of human rights show that the attempts to provide international protection are not as effective as they ought to be and that a great deal remains to be done to improve the existing international procedures. But in order to improve them we need to know what they are and how they function. That is what this book is about.

The protection of human rights through international action is a revolutionary idea and traditional international law had no place for it at all. Thus Oppenheim, the leading authority on international law in the United Kingdom at the beginning of this century, wrote that the 'so-called rights of man' not only do not but cannot enjoy any protection under international law, because that law is concerned solely with the relations between States and cannot confer rights on individuals.[2] It was therefore the accepted doctrine that relations between individuals and the States of which they were nationals were governed only by the national law of those States, as a matter exclusively within their domestic jurisdiction. To move from this attitude to a position in which the fundamental rights of the individual are a matter of international law, with international remedies available if those standards are not respected, is clearly a major step. Currently we are in the middle of this process of transformation and, as we shall see, many governments seek to shelter behind the old view of international law and hide their actions behind the cloak of national sovereignty. But such regressive policies cannot alter the fact that today the protection of human rights has a place in international law which it never occupied in earlier times and there is widespread recognition of the need to render the system of international protection more effective.

A realistic view involves recognising that there are more countries in the world today where fundamental rights and civil liberties are regularly violated than countries where they are effectively protected. However, much is also changing: international opinion, as expressed in the United Nations and elsewhere; national opinion in many countries; and, for innumerable people throughout the world, individual opinion. Non-governmental groups such as Amnesty International and the International Commission of Jurists are tireless in their work and increasingly numerous and influential. All this has produced a new awareness of human rights – not everywhere, to be sure, but certainly enough to put the matter firmly on the international agenda. So, attitudes on this issue have changed in the last fifty years and will change further in the years to come. In the pages which follow we shall see how this concern for human rights is now being reflected in the institutions and principles of international law.

## II. Different cultures and their approach to human rights

### 1. *The liberal tradition of the Western democracies*

When we consider the philosophical foundations of the concept of human rights, it is clear that the mainstream has its origins in the liberal democratic tradition of Western Europe – a tradition which is itself the product of Greek philosophy, Roman law, the Judaeo-Christian tradition, the humanism of the Reformation and the Age of Reason.[3] It is the parliamentary democracies of Western Europe which are the direct heirs of this tradition. Other countries which have inherited this political philosophy have carried the tradition to other parts of the world. Others in turn have absorbed some of it but to varying degrees and incompletely.

A detailed formulation of that philosophy as applied to the specific problem of human rights may be found in the French Declaration of the Rights of Man and the Citizen of 1789 and particularly in its second article: 'The aim of all political association is the conservation of the natural and inalienable rights of man. These rights are: liberty, property, security and resistance to oppression.' The Declaration does not discuss why these rights are 'natural and inalienable' (in French: '*imprescriptibles*'). No doubt its authors would have considered that to be self-evident. Many believed that they can be deduced from the nature of man as a sentient and intelligent being; others, following Aristotle, from his nature as a political animal; yet others, drawing inspiration from the Bible, from the nature of man created by the Almighty in His own image. The doctrine of natural law, holding that there are laws of nature or laws of God above and beyond positive law laid down by man, also contributed to this belief. It is interesting incidentally that this belief in natural law as the basis of certain rights and duties finds expression in the twentieth century in the Constitution of Ireland of 1937, which recognises the family as 'a moral institution possessing inalienable and imprescriptible rights, antecedent and superior to all positive law'. It also acknowledges that man 'has the natural right, antecedent to positive law, to the private ownership of external goods'.

The French Declaration proclaimed a number of entitlements which are now generally called civil and political rights: the basic principle that all men are born and remain free and equal in their rights; also particular rights, including equality before the law, freedom from arrest except in conformity with the law, the presumption of innocence, protection against retroactivity of the law, freedom of opinion, freedom of expression, and the well known definition of liberty as freedom to do anything which is not harmful to others. The Declaration and the philosophy which it enshrined inspired liberals and romantics all over Europe and led the poet Wordsworth to write the famous lines:

> Bliss was it in that dawn to be alive,
> But to be young were very heaven.

Its political impact on the French nation and on other peoples
struggling against authoritarian governments was such that Lord
Acton, the historian, described it as 'a single confused page ...
that outweighed libraries and was stronger than all the armies of
Napoleon'. Its perpetual resonance is indicated by the fact that
one of the French political parties in 1977 reprinted the
Declaration of 1789 and distributed it all over France.

But if the French Declaration of 1789 constituted the
proclamation of rights which is the most widely known and the
most far-reaching in its consequences on the continent of Europe,
other historic texts fulfilled a similar role elsewhere. In England,
Magna Carta of 1215 guaranteed to the citizen freedom from
imprisonment or from dispossession of his property and freedom
from prosecution or exile 'unless by the lawful judgment of his
peers or by the law of the land'. It also included a primitive
formulation of the right to a fair trial in the famous words 'To
none will we sell, deny or delay right of justice'. These and other
provisions of the charter were of such importance that it was
confirmed and reissued no fewer than thirty-eight times by later
sovereigns in succeeding centuries. The civil war and the peaceful
revolution of the seventeenth century led to the Habeas Corpus
Acts and the Bill of Rights of 1689 (just a century before the
French Declaration) which assured the supremacy of Parliament,
the right to free elections, freedom of speech, the right to bail,
freedom from cruel and unusual punishments and the right to
trial by jury.

The independence of the judiciary and freedom of the press
were established shortly thereafter; and the philosopher John
Locke devised a seminal political theory to sustain constitutional
arrangements which had developed in a pragmatic fashion. He
held that sovereignty pertains not to the monarch but to the
people as a whole, and that government is an instrument for
securing the lives, the property and the well-being of the governed
without enslaving them in any way. 'Government is not their
master; it is created by the people voluntarily and maintained by
them to secure their own good.' The individual conveys to society
his own right to exercise certain functions; all other natural rights
he retains. The theory of reserved natural rights is the basis of the
maintenance of fundamental liberties; they belong to the
individual by nature, have not been surrendered to the

community and therefore cannot be limited or denied by the State.

This political philosophy was inherited by the colonists in North America. Their most eloquent spokesman was Thomas Jefferson, who had studied Locke and Montesquieu, and asserted that the Americans were a 'free people claiming their rights as derived from the laws of nature and not as the gift of their Chief Magistrate'. The first Continental Congress in its Declaration of Rights of 14 October 1774 considered 'the immutable laws of nature' as the principal source from which the colonies derived their rights. It is therefore not surprising that when Jefferson came to draft the Declaration of Independence in the summer of 1776 he referred to the necessity for a people 'to assume among the powers of the Earth the separate and equal station to which the Laws of Nature and of Nature's God entitled them'. That idea leads on directly to the belief in natural rights expressed in the second sentence: 'We hold these truths to be self-evident, that all men are created equal, that they are endowed by their Creator with certain unalienable rights, that among these are life, liberty and the pursuit of happiness.'

This has much in common with the second article of the French Declaration quoted earlier, particularly the idea that the rights of man are 'natural and inalienable'. Notice, however, that Jefferson selects as the three cardinal rights life, liberty and the pursuit of happiness, whereas the French Declaration chooses liberty, property and security. However, 'resistance to oppression', which also comes in the second article of the French Declaration, follows in the next paragraph of the Declaration of Independence. Immediately after the reference to the three cardinal rights we read: 'that to secure these rights Governments are instituted among men, deriving their just powers from the consent of the governed; that whenever any form of government becomes destructive of these ends, it is the right of the people to alter or abolish it'. The voice of Locke is thus unmistakable.

It is evident, then, that there is much in common between the two Declarations. Indeed, the demonstration could be carried further, because the American text refers to a number of other fundamental rights – not so much by proclaiming them as by complaining of their violation: independence of the judiciary, subordination of the military to the civil power, freedom of trade, freedom from taxation without consent, and the right to trial by jury. When to these are added equality before the law, and the rights to life, liberty and the pursuit of happiness, we have an extensive catalogue. But the Declaration, important as it was, did not form part of the positive law of the infant republic. It was not made part of the federal constitution drafted in 1787, which was criticised for not including a statement of fundamental rights. Two years later, therefore, twelve amendments to the Constitution were drafted by the first Congress in New York and approved on 25 September 1789 – just a month after the French Declaration. When ten were ratified by the states, they entered into force in 1791. They are generally known as the Bill of Rights and include the more important civil and political rights.

The fact that there is much in common – as regards the content, though not the drafting – between the American texts and the French Declaration is hardly surprising. On both sides of the Atlantic the objective was the same: to protect the citizen against arbitrary power and establish the rule of law. The French philosophers, including both Montesquieu and Rousseau, were studied in the Americas. Fifty years earlier Voltaire in his *Lettres philosophiques* had studied and described the English constitutional arrangements resulting from the peaceful revolution and the Act of Settlement. Lafayette was a member of the drafting committee of the Constituent Assembly which produced the French Declaration and submitted to it his own draft based on the Declaration of Independence and the Virginia Bill of Rights. The rapporteur of the Constitutional Commission proposed 'transplanting to France the noble idea conceived in North America' and Jefferson himself was present in Paris in 1789, having succeeded Benjamin Franklin as American Minister to France.

We therefore find in 1789 two parallel and broadly similar currents, the American and the French – the former largely inspired by English doctrines on the liberty of the subject – which together go to make up the mainstream of the philosophical and historical foundation for the modern idea of human rights, and there were, of course, similar developments in other European countries. And it is the same mainstream which, after the horrors of the Second World War, found expression in the Universal Declaration of Human Rights of 1948. Appropriately, it may be thought, the chair of the Human Rights Commission which drafted it was an American, Mrs Eleanor Roosevelt, while one of the principal authors was a Frenchman, M. René Cassin, and one of the most important documents considered by the Commission was the draft presented by the United Kingdom. Thus the Universal Declaration, accepted, as it was, without a dissentient vote, and with few abstentions, by all States which were members of the United Nations at that time, is a clear expression of the concept of human rights which evolved from the political and philosophical thinking outlined above. It is the human rights conception of one political culture, that of the parliamentary democracies.

## 2. *The universal tradition*

But there are other streams of thought and other cultures.

At the first International Conference on Human Rights in Tehran, in 1968, the Shah of Iran noted in his opening address that the precursor of the celebrated documents recognising the rights of man was promulgated in his country by Cyrus the Great about 2,000 years earlier.[4] Christian Daubie has drawn attention to the magnanimity and clemency of Cyrus to subject peoples – in marked contrast to the practice of earlier conquerors – and particularly his respect for their religion. The author deduced from the 'Charter of Cyrus' the recognition and protection of what we now call the rights to liberty and security, freedom of movement, the right of property and even certain economic and social rights.[5]

Cyrus was not the only ruler to manifest such sentiments. Ambassador Polys Modinos in '*La Charte de la Liberté de l'Europe*' quotes one of the pharaohs of ancient Egypt giving instructions to his viziers to the effect that 'When a petitioner arrives from Upper or Lower Egypt.... Make sure that all is done according to the law, that custom is observed and the right of each man respected'. He goes on to cite the Code of Hammourabi, King of Babylon 2,000 years before Christ, in which the monarch records his mission 'to make justice reign in the kingdom, to destroy the wicked and the violent, to prevent the strong from oppressing the weak ... to enlighten the country and promote the good of the people'.[6] Elsewhere the same author recalls that the essential problem of Sophocles' *Antigone* is the perennial conflict between the positive law of the sovereign maintaining order in his country and the unwritten law of the gods or of nature which commands respect for the dead and love of a brother.

The number of cultures which have made a contribution to the elaboration and dissemination of the rights of man is very large. In International Human Rights Year in 1968 UNESCO published a collection of texts gleaned from different cultural traditions and periods of history which sought to demonstrate the universality of the notion of individual rights or, as the title puts it, *The Birthright of Man*. Now, there is a certain risk in removing texts from their cultural context. It is not just time which separates the outlook of a pharaoh from that of a twentieth-century democrat. But although it is necessary to guard against the shallow and unhistorical view that at root human societies have always subscribed to similar values, it is equally clear that the moral worth of the individual is an idea which no culture can claim as uniquely its own.

The idea of individual worth can be found in the work of sages, philosophers, prophets and poets from different countries and many faiths in all continents, including India, China, Japan, Persia, Russia, Turkey, Egypt, Israel, several countries of black Africa and the pre-Columbian civilisations of South America. It is apparent, therefore, that the premise for human rights has been cherished through the centuries in many lands. The struggle for human rights is as old as history itself, because it concerns the need to protect the individual against the abuse of power by the monarch, the tyrant or the State. If we have referred above to a mainstream manifested in the political traditions of the parliamentary democracies of Western Europe, this is not because they have any monopoly of the subject; it is rather because they have produced its best-known formulations and instituted the most effective systems of implementation – both nationally and internationally.

This leads naturally to a further question: are human rights relevant only to a particular type of culture? This question concerns not the source of our ideas about human rights, but the practical problem of their current relevance. It is, for example, sometimes suggested that the rights proclaimed in the historic texts mentioned earlier and the majority of the rights proclaimed in the Universal Declaration are the product of a bourgeois or capitalist society with little or no relevance to socialist States based on Marxist principles. Alternatively, the argument is that rights which are considered important in the developed countries of the West reflect values which are alien to the cultures of Africa and Asia, or, if their value is admitted, that they are luxuries which the people of those continents cannot afford.

### 3. *The socialist concept*

In 1966, when Hungary and the rest of Eastern Europe were under Soviet hegemony, various members of the Hungarian Academy of Sciences explained what they termed the 'Socialist Concept of Human Rights'.[7] It is beyond the scope of this chapter to analyse this concept in any detail, and after the peaceful revolution which led to the break-up of the Soviet bloc and of the Soviet Union itself, no purpose would be served by attempting to do so. However, something should be said about the socialist concept because the issue here is a fundamentally different approach to human rights, and one moreover which is not just of historical interest, but still followed in China and a number of other States. What, then, are the features of this approach?

The point of departure is of course Marxist. Socialist theory 'rejects the natural-law origin of citizens' rights and is unwilling to deduce them from either the nature of man or from the human mind'. Equally, it rejects the idea that citizens' rights reflect the relationship between man and society or between an abstract 'man' and the State. The basis is rather society organised in a State; 'these rights should reflect the relationship between the state and its citizens'. This relationship in a socialist society is very different from that under bourgeois conditions and 'is tied up with the fact that the production and distribution process ... are owned by the state, and the socialist state is in charge of organising the national economy'. 'As national economy in a socialist economy becomes state-run, this creates the conditions for uniformly securing citizens' rights as state rights.' The State 'has to give expression to the class-will, the will of the working class, which will is ultimately determined by the socialist production relations'.

This emphasis on the primordial role of the State – which itself is seen as the guardian or incarnation of the interests of the workers – places human rights in an entirely different light from that in which it is perceived in liberal democracies. Since the State by definition represents the interests of the people, the citizens can have no rights against the State. At the same time, this emphasis on the role of the State as the source of citizens' rights leads to a belief in the absolute sovereignty of the State and a refusal to admit any form of international control over its actions. No conflict, it is said, can exist between individuals and the State, since the latter assures the economic well-being and the cultural development of the former. The individual must therefore behave as required by the State, because such behaviour corresponds to the interests of society as a whole. The socialist State expresses the will of the mass of the workers, and the individual owes it absolute obedience.

At the international level, we are told that 'co-operation of states in the field of human rights must be combined with unfailing observance of the principles of sovereign equality of states and non-interference in the affairs which are essentially within their domestic jurisdiction'. The 'UN Charter, as well as the post-war agreements in the field of human rights, refer the direct provision and protection of human rights and freedoms exclusively to the domestic jurisdiction of the states'. Exceptions to this rule are admitted only in certain clearly defined circumstances: under the trusteeship system (Chapter XII of the UN Charter) and in colonial territories; when violations of human rights are perpetrated on a mass scale, which endangers international peace and security, and brings Chapter VII of the Charter into play, and finally when UN organs decide to set up special bodies of investigation.[8] Even when there are systems of international control, as in the two UN Covenants of 1966, the organs of control, we are told, may only make 'general recommendations'. For the UN bodies:

> have no right to make concrete recommendations on specific measures to be taken to implement particular human rights and freedoms. The elaboration and implementation of such measures is the internal affair of states. International control over the activity of states in securing human rights and freedoms must be exercised with

strict observance of their sovereignty and non-interference in their internal affairs.

Here then we have a quite different approach to human rights from that of the liberal democracies, rejecting the view that they are 'natural' to human personality and 'inalienable', but asserting that they are the emanation of the State, which itself is the incarnation of the interests of the workers. This emphasis on the sovereignty and infallibility of the State is reminiscent of doctrines current in the West at an earlier period and particularly those of Machiavelli and Hobbes. It also has something in common with the postulate of English law that 'the King can do no wrong' – a doctrine which has now been largely abandoned.

The difficulty with the doctrine of infallibility of the State is plainly to be found in its consequences. In modern industrialised societies, whether capitalist or socialist, the State controls, directs or interferes with the daily lives of the citizens to a degree that would have been inconceivable 100 years ago. The practical problem which results from this concerns the relationship of the individual not with an abstract conception of the State but with the army of officials (including the police and gaolers) who represent it and who purport to apply laws and regulations promulgated in the name of the State by imperfect human beings. Even if, in theory, the State can do no wrong, in practice wrongs ranging from the errors of a tax inspector to the abomination of the concentration camps can be committed in its name. Hence there is a need to protect the individual, which is what human rights are all about.

This applies both nationally and internationally and leads to the question whether a system of international control violates the principle of non-interference in matters which are within the domestic jurisdiction of States, which will be discussed later. It must suffice for the present to say that matters with regard to which States have accepted international obligations by treaty thereby become subject to rules of international law and are no longer exclusively within the domestic jurisdiction of those States. Moreover, any system of international control becomes meaning-less if the matters to be controlled continue to be treated as exclusively subject to the sovereign will of the States concerned. Acceptance of the United Nations Charter, of the Universal

Declaration and of the United Nations Covenants therefore
involves moving beyond nineteenth-century conceptions of
national sovereignty and recognising a common set of basic
values.

## 4. *Developing countries and human rights*

We must now say something about another problem which arises
in relation to different cultures and their approach to human
rights: is it true that the rights which are considered important in
the developed countries of the West are inappropriate elsewhere
or, if they might be of value, that they are luxuries which the
people of the developing world cannot afford? This is a very large
issue which involves consideration of two distinct questions:
whether there is a set of human rights of universal applicability;
and what is the relationship between, and the comparative
importance of, the two main categories of human rights – civil
and political rights on the one hand, and economic, social and
cultural rights, on the other.

The first question was the subject of much debate at the 1993
World Conference on Human Rights, with Asian States in
particular suggesting that the Western version of human rights
fails to take account of distinctive elements in their religious and
political cultures and so cannot be fully accepted.[9] Earlier, as we
shall see in Chapter 7, rather similar sentiments were responsible
for the distinctive provisions of the 1981 African Charter on
Human and Peoples' Rights. The universality, or otherwise, of
human rights is clearly a matter of enormous importance, and
although it is scarcely possible to do more than scratch the
surface of the issue here, our thinking about it will be clearer if
the following features of the controversy are borne in mind.

In the first place, many of the governments which deny the
relevance of 'Western' standards of human rights do so not as
democratically chosen representatives of their people, but as
unelected elites, whose main concern is to stay in power. It is
obviously convenient for such governments to argue that freedom
of the press, the concept of the rule of law, and freedom from
torture and arbitrary imprisonment, reflect values alien to their
people, but as the latter are allowed no say in the matter, the
argument need not be taken seriously. The first point, then, is that

claims about distinctive cultural values are often just a smoke-screen behind which unrepresentative governments try to maintain their power and silence criticism.

Secondly, the argument that Western approaches to human rights are alien to non-European cultures cannot be evaluated without taking into account the complexity of the traditions under discussion. In reality there is no single African or Asian view of the position of the individual in society, but rather a wide variety of approaches and traditions. Likewise, the so-called Western view of human rights is composed of many historical strands, as we have seen, and contained within it are philosophies as diverse and contradictory as Catholicism and utilitarianism. Thus to assert, for example, that African and Asian cultures believe in the individual's responsibility to the family and society, whereas Western thinking does not, is a gross over-simplification of the respective philosophical traditions. Accordingly, when values are being discussed, particularly in political forums, we shall often find the protagonists merely caricaturing each other's positions and setting up straw men in order to knock them down.

Thirdly, and finally, we must recognise that despite what has just been said, there are genuine cultural differences between societies and that accepting universal human rights inevitably requires certain ideas and practices to change. The points to appreciate here, however, are first that the change required is general and not limited to any particular group of States, and secondly that there remains some scope for local variations. The first point is illustrated by the dramatic impact of the moves to outlaw race and sex discrimination in the Western world, and the second by the recognition by human rights decision makers that in many areas absolute uniformity is not required, provided that essential standards are respected.[10]

The view that human rights can be universal without obliterating national differences was the conclusion which eventually emerged at the World Conference in 1993, for after stating that all human rights are 'universal, indivisible, and interdependent and interrelated', the Vienna Declaration goes on to provide that 'while the significance of national and regional particularities and various historical, cultural and religious backgrounds must be borne in mind, it is the duty of States, regardless of their political, economic and cultural systems, to promote and protect all human rights and fundamental freedoms'.[11] This is plainly an endorsement of the concept of universal human rights. That there is some scope for different interpretations is indicated by the reference to 'regional peculiarities' and 'historical, cultural and religious backgrounds'. But this is quite different from the view that governments are entitled to adopt idiosyncratic approaches to human rights and ignore international standards.

As regards our second issue, the relation between different types of rights, we may again begin with some basic propositions. First, the traditional approach of the Western democracies has been principally (some would say excessively) concerned with civil and political rights, with much less attention to economic, social and cultural rights. Secondly, there is now widespread recognition of the importance of the second category. As already noted, the Vienna Declaration stressed that human rights are not only universal, but also indivisible, interdependent and inter-related, reiterating a point which had been made at the Tehran Conference in 1968.[12] Thirdly, as we have again already seen, States subscribing to the socialist view of human rights always attached much more importance to the second category than the first, which, in contrast to some of the less attractive features of Marxism, enabled them to act as advocates for human rights and champions of the underprivileged.

Turning to State practice, which will be more fully reviewed in Chapter 8, we find that the UN General Assembly decided in 1952 that there should be two separate international covenants dealing with the two separate categories of rights. However, although two separate covenants were approved by the General Assembly in 1966, and entered into force ten years later, almost all States which have ratified one covenant have also ratified the other. In other words, international practice appears to support treating both categories on an equal footing.

As regards the developing States specifically, most exhibit greater concern with economic and social rights than with their civil and political counterparts.[13] This is not surprising, having regard to their political and economic situation; nor is it cause for regret, provided – and this is an important qualification – that one category of rights is not sacrificed to the other. It is now in fact generally recognised that there is a crucial correlation between the enjoyment of human rights and economic development. Neither is possible without the other; rather there is an essential connection between them. Thus the Vienna Declaration, which had a great deal to say about the need for development, stated that 'Democracy, development and respect for human rights and fundamental freedoms are interdependent and mutually reinforcing.... The international community should support the strengthening and promoting of democracy, development and respect for human rights in the entire world.'[14]

This provides an appropriate conclusion to our brief review of the varying approaches of different cultures to human rights. There seems little point in trying to decide whether one category of rights is more important than the other and it is equally vain to hurl opprobrium at those who adopt a different system of priorities. Instead, we should recognise that the different categories of rights – civil and political, economic, social and cultural – are interrelated and that all are desirable, and actually necessary, to the full realisation of the human personality.

### III. The first international measures for the protection of human rights

#### 1. *The abolition of slavery*

The first international texts relating to what we would now call a human rights problem were formulated at the beginning of the nineteenth century. The problem they related to was slavery. Shocking as it now seems, the institution of slavery was generally legal under national law at the end of the eighteenth century; it remained legal in the United States until 1863, in Brazil until 1880, and in some countries into the twentieth century. In England it was illegal according to the decision in Somersett's case in 1772,[15] and at the turn of the century a humanitarian movement, largely inspired by Wilberforce, sought to prohibit it internationally. Since it was not possible to secure the immediate liberation of slaves in legal servitude in other countries, the first step was to secure the abolition of the slave trade, so as to prevent any increase in the number of slaves. The slave trade was prohibited in the British colonies in 1807. The institution of slavery was also abolished in France, and by the Treaty of Paris of

1814 the British and French governments agreed to co-operate in
the suppression of the traffic in slaves. This undertaking was
generalised and accompanied by a solemn condemnation of the
practice by the major European States at the Congress of Vienna
in 1815.

More than fifty bilateral treaties on the subject were concluded
between 1815 and 1880, and the Conference of Berlin on Central
Africa of 1885 was able to state in its General Act that 'trading in
slaves is forbidden in conformity with the principles of
international law as recognised by the signatory powers'. The
powers concerned, which were fifteen in number, also agreed that
the territories of the Congo basin should not serve as a market or
means of transit for the trade in slaves and that they would
employ all means at their disposal for putting an end to the trade
and punishing those engaged in it. Matters were taken a step
further at the Brussels Conference in 1890. An anti-slavery Act
was signed, and later ratified by eighteen States, including the
United States, Turkey and Zanzibar. It not only condemned
slavery and the slave trade, but also drew up a list of agreed
measures for their suppression both in Africa and on the high
seas, including the right of visit and search, the confiscation of
ships engaged in the trade and the punishment of their masters
and crew. In addition, the Act provided for the establishment of a
special office attached to the Belgian Foreign Ministry and for an
International Maritime Office in Zanzibar to assist in implementing these provisions – one of the earliest examples of
international measures of implementation.

The General Act of the Brussels Conference was the most
comprehensive instrument on the subject of slavery until the
outbreak of the First World War. Thereafter, the mandate system
established by Article 22 of the League Covenant declared that
the well-being and development of the peoples in the mandated
territories should form a 'sacred trust of civilization' and that the
mandatory powers should administer the territories under
conditions 'which will guarantee freedom of conscience and
religion ... and the prohibition of abuses such as the slave trade'.
And both the Convention of St Germain-en-Laye of 1919 and the
International Convention on the Abolition of Slavery and the
Slave Trade, concluded under the auspices of the League of
Nations in 1926, proclaimed as their object 'the complete

suppression of slavery in all its forms and of the slave trade by land and sea'.

There were more developments after the Second World War. Article 4 of the Universal Declaration reads: 'No one shall be held in slavery or servitude; slavery and the slave trade shall be prohibited in all their forms.' The institutional arrangements of the 1926 Convention were brought up to date in 1953 by a protocol amending the Convention, while a Supplementary Convention on the Abolition of Slavery, the Slave Trade and Institutions and Practices Similar to Slavery was concluded in 1956 and entered into force in the following year.[16] In 1958 the Geneva Convention on the High Seas laid down in Article 13 that the contracting States must take steps to prevent and, where necessary, punish any transport of slaves in their vessels and that any slave taking refuge thereon shall be free. Article 99 of the 1982 Law of the Sea Convention is to the same effect.

Condemnation of slavery and associated practices is also to be found in the various general human rights treaties concluded in the modern period. Article 8 of the 1966 United Nations Covenant on Civil and Political Rights follows the corresponding provision of the Universal Declaration. Slavery, along with servitude and forced or compulsory labour, is prohibited by Article 4 of the 1950 European Convention on Human Rights. The American Convention on Human Rights, which was concluded in 1969, is in similar terms and deals with these matters in Article 6, while a later regional instrument, the African Charter on Human and Peoples' Rights, which came into force in 1986, covers the issue in Article 5.

This evolution over almost 200 years shows that the right to freedom of the person and the concomitant prohibition of slavery and the slave trade are now the subject of established rules of international law. Indeed, such widespread and uniform State practice has unquestionably generated a rule of customary international law prohibiting slavery and the slave trade. The problem today – for unfortunately a problem still exists – is not agreeing the rules, but rather seeing that they are enforced. In other words, it is no longer a question of making the law, but through police action, in the widest sense, of seeing that it is observed.

## 2. Humanitarian law

The second development by which international law began to be concerned with human rights – or, as some would prefer to say, a closely related subject – was the evolution of humanitarian law. Though there have been notable exceptions through the ages, the vanquished in war was normally at the mercy of the victor, and frequently little mercy was shown. The atrocities which accompanied the Thirty Years' War, for example, were notorious. During the eighteenth century a more enlightened attitude appeared. After the Battle of Fontenoy in 1745, Louis XV ordered that the enemy wounded were to be treated in the same way as his own soldiers 'because once they are wounded they are no longer our enemies'. The English General Amherst applied the same rule at the siege of Montreal in 1762. Vattel advocated similar principles, while Rousseau wrote in his *Contrat social* in 1762:

> The object of war being the destruction of the enemy State, one has the right to kill its defenders only when they have weapons in their hands but immediately they put them down and surrender, thus ceasing to be enemies or agents of the enemy, they once more become ordinary men and one no longer has any right to their life. Sometimes one can extinguish a State without killing a single member of it; moreover, war confers no right other than that which is necessary for its purpose. These principles are not those of Grotius; they are not founded on the authority of poets, but they flow from the nature of things and are founded upon reason.[17]

The transformation of these principles into positive law was due to the work of the nineteenth-century Swiss philanthropist Henry Dunant. In 1859, having gone to Castiglione to see the Emperor Napoleon III, he witnessed the Battle of Solferino. Appalled at the slaughter and the suffering of the wounded, he personally helped more than a thousand casualties and called on the local inhabitants to assist him in the work. Determined as a result of this experience to institute a permanent system for humanitarian relief, he founded with the Geneva lawyer Gustave Moynier and others the Comité International et Permanent de Secours aux Blessés Militaires. Later the same year (1863) he organised a conference at which sixteen States were represented, and the delegates agreed to set up in their own countries private societies to supplement the work of the national army medical corps. They chose as their emblem the Swiss flag in reverse, that is, a red cross on a white background.

Official recognition of these arrangements was granted in the following year by the Geneva Convention of 1864, in which twelve States undertook to respect the immunity of military hospitals and their staff, to care for sick and wounded soldiers whatever their nationality, and to respect the emblem of the Red Cross. This Convention formed the basis of humanitarian activities during the Franco-Prussian War (1870), the Spanish-American War (1898) and the Russo-Japanese War (1904). It was revised and developed by a diplomatic conference in 1906, and further revised and improved in the light of the experience of the First World War, by the Geneva Convention of 1929.[18] The further development of humanitarian law during the last half century is summarised in Chapter 9.

It was, of course, necessary to extend a similar system of protection to the sick and wounded in naval warfare. This was achieved in a different framework, through the Hague Peace Conferences of 1899 and 1907. The Hague Convention No. III of 1899 extended the provisions of the original Geneva Convention to maritime warfare; when the latter was revised in 1906, its principles were extended to war at sea by the Hague Convention No. X of 1907. This remained in force for more than forty years, during both the First and the Second World Wars, and was not replaced until 1949.

Another branch of humanitarian law relates to a field of activity for which the Red Cross is particularly well known – the care of prisoners of war. This concerns in the first place their identification and the communication of information on their whereabouts and physical condition to their home countries; secondly, it involves arranging facilities for correspondence with their families and the despatch of parcels; thirdly, it covers visits to prisoner-of-war camps and the furnishing of medical supplies; and fourthly, it extends to the repatriation, usually on an exchange basis, of the seriously wounded.

The legal basis for this work was the Hague Convention No. IV of 1907, dealing with the Laws and Customs of War on Land. In accordance with its provisions, during the First World War the

International Committee of the Red Cross set up the International Agency for Prisoners of War in Geneva. This body established an index of over 5,000,000 cards, containing particulars of the identity and whereabouts of prisoners of war.

The humanitarian work of the Red Cross during the First World War was of such value for all the belligerents that the authors of the Covenant of the League of Nations included the following provision as Article 25:

> The Members of the League agree to encourage and promote the establishment and co-operation of duly authorized voluntary national Red Cross organizations having as purposes the improvement of health, the prevention of disease and the mitigation of suffering throughout the world.

Thus it was clearly established by a number of treaties, and finally by the explicit recognition of the Red Cross in the League Covenant, that the conditions of the sick and wounded and the care of prisoners of war had become matters of concern to international law. This laid the foundation for further legal developments in this field and also made a major contribution to the process whereby the protection of the individual became the concern of international law and respect for human rights in general an obligation on all members of the United Nations.[19]

## 3. The protection of minorities

The third development whereby international law came to be concerned with the rights of individuals relates to the protection of minorities. This was principally the result of the redrawing of frontiers which formed part of the peace settlement in 1919, though earlier, in the Treaty of Berlin (1878), Bulgaria, Montenegro, Serbia, Romania and Turkey had all assumed obligations to grant religious freedom to their nationals. The political changes of 1919 and 1920, including the restoration of Poland and the creation of successor States after the dissolution of the Austro-Hungarian Empire, sought to respect the principle of nationality, but the populations in many areas were so mixed that, wherever the frontiers were drawn, it was impossible to avoid the existence of minorities on the other side of the line.

The arrangements for protecting the new minorities took three main forms. First, there were five special treaties on minorities with the allied or newly created States: with Poland (Versailles, 1919), with Czechoslovakia and Yugoslavia (St Germain-en-Laye, 1919), with Romania (Trianon, 1920), and with Greece (Sèvres, 1920). Secondly, chapters on the rights of the minorities within their borders were included in the peace treaties with the ex-enemy States: with Austria (St Germain-en-Laye, 1919), with Bulgaria (Neuilly, 1919), with Hungary (Trianon, 1920), and later with Turkey (Lausanne, 1923). Thirdly, certain States made declarations before the Council of the League of Nations as a condition of their admission to the League: Finland (1921, as regards the Åland Islands), Albania (1921), Lithuania (1922), Latvia (1923), Estonia (1923), and later Iraq (1932).

Generally speaking, the various arrangements for the protection of the rights of minorities provided for equality before the law in regard to civil and political rights, freedom of religion, the right of members of the minorities to use their own language, and the right to maintain their own religious and educational establishments. It was also usual to provide for teaching in the language of the minority in State schools in districts where the minority constituted a considerable proportion of the population. Moreover, it was recognised that these various provisions protecting the rights of minorities constituted 'obligations of international concern', which were placed under the guarantee of the League of Nations and could not be modified without the consent of the Council of the League.

When violation of a State's obligations was alleged, minority groups could bring their complaints before the League. The usual procedure was that if the Secretary-General considered the case admissible, the Council would appoint an *ad hoc* minorities committee to investigate the matter and try to reach a friendly settlement; if this failed, the complaint was referred to the full Council. The Council in turn could refer the matter to the Permanent Court of International Justice. Although such references were rare, one well known case in which this occurred was that of the *Minority Schools in Albania*,[20] in which the Court insisted on the need to maintain equality in fact as well as equality in law and held that the closing of the minority schools was incompatible with equality of treatment.

Especially important – both for its practical effect at the time and for the precedent it created for the future – was the 1922 German–Polish Convention on Upper Silesia, a region which was divided into two parts, one on each side of the frontier between Germany and Poland. This Convention not only contained guarantees for the protection of the minorities on both sides of the frontier, but also set up an elaborate system of measures of implementation: a Minorities Office in each part of Upper Silesia, a Mixed Commission and an Arbitral Tribunal. The Commission and the Tribunal each had an independent president appointed by the League Council. The Mixed Commission dealt with more than 2,000 cases during the fifteen years of its existence (1922–37), and was essentially concerned with conciliation. The Arbitral Tribunal, on the other hand, was a judicial body, with competence to hear claims by individuals, and gave judgements which were binding on the courts and administrative authorities of the two countries. Either government could refer any difference of opinion relating to questions of law or fact to the Permanent Court of International Justice. One case so referred in 1928, after the failure of settlement before the Mixed Commission and the League Council, was that of the *Rights of Minorities in Upper Silesia*, in which the Court held that the question whether a person belonged to a racial, linguistic or religious minority, which was the criterion for admission to the German-speaking minority schools in Poland, 'is subject to no verification, dispute, pressure or hindrance whatever on the part of the authorities'.[21]

The arrangements for protecting national minorities worked better than might have been expected, but came under intolerable strain in the political turmoil of the 1930s. Even so, by the end of the interwar period it had been clearly established that with regard to several matters international law was concerned with the status or the treatment of the individual and not simply with relations between States. However, this was true in relation to only a limited number of topics – slavery, humanitarian questions, the rights of minorities – and it remained to generalise the field of application of this principle and extend it to all the basic rights of the individual. Moreover, it was only in the special situation regulated by the minority treaties that individuals possessed a remedy which would permit action on the international scene to protect their rights. The question of international enforcement measures had therefore barely been touched upon. International law was, however, ripe for development in both these respects. The cataclysm of the Second World War drove home the point and thus set the stage for the many developments which have occurred since 1945 and which are the subject of this book.

## Notes

1 See the Vienna Declaration and Programme of Action, 25 June 1993, section I, para. 1; text in *International Human Rights Reports*, I(1), 1994, p. 240.
2 A. H. Robertson, *Human Rights in Europe*, second edition, Manchester, 1977, p. 149, quoting a paragraph from the first edition of Oppenheim's *Treatise on International Law*, 1905. When Sir Hersch Lauterpacht prepared the eighth edition of Oppenheim in 1955 he modified this passage considerably.
3 For a more detailed account of the liberal democratic tradition see E. Kamenka and A. E-S. Tay (eds), *Human Rights*, London, 1978, Chapters 1 and 2, J. J. Shestack, 'The jurisprudence of human rights', in T. Meron (ed.), *Human Rights in International Law*, Oxford, 1984, pp. 69–113, and R. J. Vincent, *Human Rights and International Relations*, Cambridge, 1986, Chapter 2.
4 *The Final Act of the International Conference on Human Rights*, Tehran, 1968, is published in UN document A/Conf 32/41.
5 C. Daubie, 'Cyrus le Grand – un précurseur dans le domaine des Droits de l'homme', *Human Rights Journal*, V, 1972, p. 293.
6 P. Modinos, 'La Charte de la Liberté de l'Europe', *Human Rights Journal*, VIII, 1975, pp. 677–8.
7 I. Szabo, *et al.*, *The Socialist Concept of Human Rights*, Budapest, 1966, particularly pp. 53–81. See also V. Kartashkin, 'Human rights and peaceful coexistence', *Human Rights Journal*, IX, 1976, p. 5, F. Przetacnik, 'The socialist concept of human rights: its philosophical background and political justification', *Revue Belge de Droit International*, XIII, 1977, p. 238; A. E.-S. Tay, 'Marxism, socialism and human rights', in Kamenka and Tay, *Human Rights*, pp. 10–13, and R. N. Dean, 'Beyond Helsinki: the Soviet view of human rights in international law', *Virginia Journal of International Law*, XXI, 1980–81, p. 55.
8 For example, the *ad hoc* working groups concerned with southern Africa and Chile and the Special Committee concerned with human rights in the territories occupied by Israel. For discussion of these and similar special bodies see Chapter 3.
9 See J. T. H. Tang (ed.), *Human Rights and International Relations in the Asia-Pacific Region*, London, 1995, which contains an excellent group of essays on this issue, a useful collection of primary documents, including the 1993 Bangkok Declaration, in an appendix, and a wide-ranging bibliography.
10 See the discussion of the 'margin of appreciation' doctrine in Chapters 2, 4 and 10, and also J. G. Merrills, *The Development of International Law by the*

*European Court of Human Rights*, second edition, Melland Schill Monographs in International Law, Manchester, 1993, Chapter 7.

11 Vienna Declaration, section I, para. 5.

12 See Resolution XVII of the 1968 Conference stating, 'The enjoyment of economic and social rights is inherently linked with a meaningful enjoyment of civil and political rights, and ... there is a profound interconnection between the realisation of human rights and economic development.'

13 See K. M'Baye, 'Les réalités du monde noir et les droits de l'homme', *Human Rights Journal*, II, 1969, p. 382, and 'Le droit au développement comme un droit de l'homme', *Human Rights Journal*, V, 1972, p. 505. See also T. C. Van Boven, 'Some remarks on special problems relating to human rights in developing countries', *Human Rights Journal*, III, 1970, p. 383, and Y. K. Tyagi, 'Third world response to human rights', *Indian Journal of International Law*, XXI, 1981, p. 119. For further discussion of the right to development and other suggestions for new human rights, see Chapter 8.

14 Vienna Declaration, section I, para. 8.

15 20 *State Trials*, p. 1.

16 By 1 January 1995 there were 113 parties to this treaty.

17 Quoted by G. I. A. D. Draper, 'The Geneva Conventions of 1949', *Hague Recueil des Cours*, 114, 1965, p. 63.

18 For the history of the humanitarian conventions see H. Coursier, 'L'Evolution du droit international humanitaire', *Hague Recueil des Cours*, 99, 1960, p. 357, and Draper, 'The Geneva Conventions of 1949', p. 63.

19 The relationship between humanitarian law and human rights law is discussed in Chapter 9.

20 PCIJ, Series A/B, No. 64.

21 Series A, No. 15, pp. 46–7.

# CHAPTER 2

# The United Nations and human rights I: the International Covenant on Civil and Political Rights

## I. The Charter

As is well known, the Charter of the United Nations contains a number of references to the promotion of human rights. The first is in the preamble, which reads:

> We the peoples of the United Nations, determined ... to reaffirm faith in fundamental human rights, in the dignity and worth of the human person, in the equal rights of men and women and of nations large and small ... have resolved to combine our efforts to accomplish these aims.

Then, among the purposes of the United Nations set out in Article 1, is 'to achieve international co-operation ... in promoting and encouraging respect for human rights and fundamental freedoms for all'. The most important provisions are probably those contained in Articles 55 and 56 of the Charter. Article 55 provides that the United Nations shall promote 'universal respect for, and observance of, human rights and fundamental freedoms for all without distinction as to race, sex, language or religion'; while in Article 56 'all members pledge themselves to take joint and separate action in co-operation with the Organisation for the achievement of the purposes set forth in Article 55'. Other references in the Charter are in: Article 13, which authorises the General Assembly to make studies and recommendations about human rights; Article 62, which contains a somewhat similar provision relating to the Economic and Social Council; Article 68, which requires the Council to set up commissions in the economic and social fields and for the promotion of human rights; and Article 76, which makes the promotion of human rights and fundamental freedoms for all one of the basic objectives of the trusteeship system.

Less well known is the fact that the Charter very nearly gave to human rights only a passing reference. The Dumbarton Oaks proposals for the United Nations, prepared in 1944 by the four great powers, contained only one general provision about human rights. However, the delegations of several smaller countries and the representatives of a number of non-governmental organisations who attended the San Francisco conference as consultants to the United States delegation were able, by energetic lobbying, to secure the inclusion in the Charter of the much more positive provisions summarised above.[1] The obligation now contained in Article 56 was at one stage actually intended to be stronger. The first draft would have required member States 'to take separate and joint action and to co-operate with the Organisation for the promotion of human rights', which clearly implied an obligation for them to act individually, irrespective of the action, or failure to act, of other States. But this formulation was not approved, and the undertaking finally accepted was to 'take joint and separate action in co-operation with the Organisation'.

It is also worth pointing out that certain delegations at San Francisco considered that the phrase 'promoting respect for human rights' was too weak and so suggestions were made to substitute the words 'assuring' or 'protecting' for 'promoting', and to require the 'observance' of human rights rather than merely 'respect' for them.[2] These proposals were not accepted. However, in view of the fact that a number of delegations and influential non-governmental organisations considered that the human rights provisions of the Charter, though markedly stronger than the original Dumbarton Oaks proposals, were still too weak, it was agreed that a Bill of Rights should be drawn up separately and as soon as possible. There had, indeed, been suggestions, notably by Panama, for the incorporation of a Bill of Rights in the Charter itself. Although this proved impossible, partly for lack of sufficient support and partly for reasons of time, President Truman, in his closing speech to the conference, stated that:

We have good reason to expect the framing of an international bill of rights, acceptable to all the nations involved. That bill of rights will be as much a part of international life as our own Bill of Rights is a part of our Constitution. The Charter is dedicated to the achievement and observance of human rights and fundamental freedoms. Unless we can attain those objectives for all men and women everywhere – without regard to race, language or religion – we cannot have permanent peace and security.[3]

## II. The Universal Declaration

No time was lost in acting on the proposal for a more detailed document. The Charter was signed in June 1945 and entered into force in October of the same year. In the autumn of 1945 the Preparatory Commission recommended that the Economic and Social Council (ECOSOC) should immediately establish a Commission on Human Rights and direct it to prepare an International Bill of Rights. The General Assembly approved this recommendation on 12 February 1946 and ECOSOC acted on it four days later. The Commission on Human Rights was set up within a matter of months, initially with a nucleus of nine members.

In May 1946 the Commission recommended by majority vote that, since the Council consisted of representatives of governments, the members of the Commission should be elected by the Council from a list of nominees submitted by governments, but serve in an individual capacity. The USSR, however, opposed this proposal, and ECOSOC decided that the Commission should consist of eighteen members, appointed by the governments which were selected by the Council. Later in the same year the Council decided to leave it to the governments concerned to decide whether to appoint government officials or independent persons. In practice, therefore, it is governments which are members of the Commission, and its members attend as their representatives. In 1962 the membership was increased to twenty-one; in 1966 to thirty-two; in 1980 to forty-three; and in 1992 to fifty-three.

The first regular session of the Commission opened in January 1947, and its first task was the drafting of the International Bill of Rights. It decided later in the year that this should have three parts: a Declaration; a Convention containing legal obligations; and 'measures of implementation' – in other words, a system of international supervision or control. Work started immediately on the Declaration, for which purpose a drafting committee of eight members was appointed: the representatives of Australia, Chile, China, France, Lebanon, the United Kingdom, the United States and the USSR. The chair of the Commission and of the drafting committee was Mrs Eleanor Roosevelt.

The full Commission examined and revised the draft Declaration thus prepared, and submitted it through the Economic and Social Council to the General Assembly in 1948. At the same time it submitted a draft Covenant which the drafting committee had also prepared. However, the Assembly, at its third session, held in Paris in the autumn of 1948, decided to consider only the draft Declaration. The Third Committee devoted eighty-one meetings to examination of this text and to the 168 amendments which were tabled. In due course it submitted a revised version to the General Assembly. After a Soviet proposal to postpone further consideration of the matter until the following year had been defeated, the Declaration was adopted on 10 December 1948, with forty-eight votes in favour, none against and eight abstentions.[4]

The Universal Declaration was adopted by Resolution 217(III) of the General Assembly. It was not intended to impose legal obligations on States, but rather to establish goals for States to work towards. Thus, the operative part of the Resolution reads as follows:

> Now, therefore, the General Assembly proclaims this Universal Declaration of Human Rights as a common standard of achievement for all peoples and all nations, to the end that every individual and every organ of society, keeping this Declaration constantly in mind, shall strive by teaching and education to promote respect for these rights and freedoms and by progressive measures, national and international, to secure their universal and effective recognition and observance, both among the peoples of Member States themselves and among the peoples of territories under their jurisdiction.

Mrs Roosevelt stated in the General Assembly that the Declaration was 'first and foremost a declaration of the basic principles to serve as a common standard for all nations. It might well become the Magna Carta of all mankind'. She considered that its proclamation by the General Assembly 'would be of importance comparable to the 1789 proclamation of the Declaration of the Rights of Man, the proclamation of the rights of man in the Declaration of Independence of the United States of America, and similar declarations made in other countries'.[5] A leading commentator has observed that:

> There seems to be an agreement that the Declaration is a statement of general principles spelling out in considerable detail the meaning of the phrase 'human rights and fundamental freedoms' in the Charter of the United Nations. As the Declaration was adopted unanimously, without a dissenting vote, it can be considered as an authoritative interpretation of the Charter of the highest order. While the Declaration is not directly binding on United Nations Members, it strengthens their obligations under the Charter by making them more precise.[6]

Since 1948 the Universal Declaration has acquired a greatly reinforced status not only as 'a common standard of achievement for all peoples and all nations' but also as a statement of principles which all States should observe. It has been reaffirmed by the General Assembly on a number of occasions, of which the most striking were perhaps the adoption of the Declaration on Colonialism in 1960,[7] which provided 'All States shall observe faithfully and strictly the provisions of the Charter of the United Nations, the Universal Declaration of Human Rights and the present Declaration', and the unanimous adoption in 1963 of the Declaration on the Elimination of Racial Discrimination,[8] which contained a similar provision.

In the world outside the United Nations the influence of the Universal Declaration has been no less profound. It has inspired more than forty State constitutions, together with the regional human rights treaties of Europe, Africa and the Americas, and examples of legislation quoting or reproducing provisions of the Declaration can be found in all continents. Thus the impact of the Universal Declaration has probably exceeded its authors' most sanguine expectations, while its constant and widespread recognition means that the principles it contains can now be regarded as part of customary law.

### III. The International Covenant on Civil and Political Rights

Resolution 217(III) of 10 December 1948 not only approved the text of the Universal Declaration, it also decided that work should go ahead on the other two parts of the Bill of Rights: a Covenant containing legal obligations to be assumed by States, and measures of implementation. The Commission had already prepared and submitted a preliminary draft of the Covenant, but it was not yet ready for adoption and was referred back by the General Assembly.

#### 1. *The history of the Covenant*

There then began a period of discussion, drafting and negotiation which lasted eighteen years. The initial work of the Commission resulted in a text devoted to the classic civil and political rights, but when the General Assembly was consulted in 1950 for guidance on certain issues of policy, it decided that economic, social and cultural rights should also be included.[9] The Commission carried out this instruction, but when the Security Council considered the results, and particularly the differences in the two categories of rights, it recommended that the General Assembly should reconsider its decision. As a result, the Assembly, after a long debate, decided in 1952 that there should be two separate Covenants, with as many similar provisions as possible, and that both should include an article on 'the right of all peoples and nations to self-determination'.[10]

The articles on measures of implementation gave the Commission much more trouble than the normative provisions, largely because the views of its members were sharply divided on the basic question of how far governments could be expected to accept a system of international control. A number of far-reaching proposals were considered, including an Australian suggestion for an International Court of Human Rights, a proposal by Uruguay for the appointment of a United Nations High Commissioner for Human Rights, and a French proposal for an International Investigation Commission, coupled with the appointment of an Attorney-General of the Commission. India proposed that the Security Council should be informed of alleged violations, investigate them and enforce redress, while Israel suggested the creation of a new Specialised Agency for the implementation of the Covenants.[11]

The attitude of the United Kingdom and the United States was more cautious; they proposed that Human Rights Committees should be set up on an *ad hoc* basis, but only for inter-State disputes. The Soviet Union was consistently opposed to all arrangements of this sort on the ground that they would interfere in the internal affairs of States, contrary to Article 2(7) of the Charter, and would undermine their sovereignty and independence.[12] The Commission finally decided by seven votes to six, with one abstention, in favour of the establishment of a permanent Human Rights Committee to consider complaints of violations of human rights on an inter-State basis. However, it rejected by larger majorities the possibility of considering complaints by non-governmental organisations or petitions by individuals.[13]

Since there will be many references in this book to the problem of the meaning and effect of Article 2(7) of the Charter, it is worth examining this question more closely. Different governments have taken different positions at different times, according to the political context. A conspicuous feature of UN diplomacy is the facility with which some delegates argue that it is outside the competence of the UN to discuss human rights situations on their own territory or on that of their allies, but quite proper to discuss alleged violations by their political opponents. The whole issue was reviewed in the *Report of the UN Commission on the Racial Situation in South Africa* of October 1953. This discusses at length the meaning of Article 2(7) of the Charter, citing the views of such eminent jurists as Lauterpacht, Cassin and Kelsen, and contains the following statement:

> The United Nations is unquestionably justified in deciding that a matter is outside the essentially domestic jurisdiction of a State when it involves systematic violation of the Charter's principles concerning human rights, and more especially that of non-discrimination, above all when such actions affect millions of human beings, and have provoked grave international alarm, and when the State concerned clearly displays an intention to aggravate the position.

When this report was discussed in the General Assembly in 1953, South Africa sought to have it rejected on the ground that its racial policies were 'matters essentially within the domestic jurisdiction of a Member State' and therefore outside the competence of the United Nations. However, this argument was overwhelmingly rejected and subsequent attempts to invoke Article 2(7) with regard to matters of international concern have usually been no more successful.

Until 1945, the manner in which a State treated its own nationals was, apart from the limited circumstances in which humanitarian intervention was permissible, a question within its own jurisdiction and competence with which other States had no right to concern themselves. Since then, however, the legal position has clearly changed. Human rights, or any other matters with regard to which States have accepted international obligations, cease to be issues solely within their domestic jurisdiction. Other States have a legitimate interest in seeing that these undertakings are respected. The fact that the commitments in question concern a State's duty to respect the rights of its own citizens in no way qualifies the fundamental principle that a State must perform its international obligations and cannot invoke national sovereignty as a pretext for failing to do so.

The Commission on Human Rights completed its work on the draft Covenants in 1954, and submitted its texts to ECOSOC and the General Assembly.[14] In the following year the Secretary-General prepared an analysis of the texts and of the issues which had been discussed during their preparation, which is a valuable additional source for understanding their provisions.[15] When the draft Covenants were reviewed by the General Assembly's Third Committee, substantive issues naturally attracted the largest share of its attention. There was much discussion of the right of all peoples to self-determination, which resulted in Article 1, common to both Covenants. During the years 1956–58 the articles relating to economic and social rights were approved with a good deal of detailed revision but with little major amendment. From 1958 to 1961 the same was done for the civil and political rights. In 1962 and 1963 discussion centred mainly on the introductory articles, with particular reference to the question of whether the obligation to respect the rights set out is of immediate or progressive effect – a point discussed below.

In 1964 and 1965 comparatively little attention was devoted to the Covenants, as the Third Committee was principally concerned with the Convention on the Elimination of All Forms of Racial Discrimination. In 1966, however, a determined and successful attempt was made to finish the work on the Covenants and so it turned finally to the measures of implementation. Here the Third Committee made substantial changes to the proposals of the Commission. It agreed to the establishment of a Human Rights Committee, but enlarged its membership from nine to eighteen. It also decided that the members should be elected by the States parties, instead of by the International Court of Justice, as had been proposed by the Commission. As regards the Covenant on Economic, Social and Cultural Rights, the Committee retained the system of periodic reports by States to the Economic and Social Council, on the basis of which the Council could make recommendations of a general nature to the General Assembly. This is a subject we will return to in Chapter 8.

As regards the Covenant on Civil and Political Rights, the Committee decided in favour of a double system of implementation, namely, a compulsory system of reporting to the new Human Rights Committee to be established under the Covenant and an optional system of fact finding and conciliation, which would apply only in relation to States which had expressly agreed to this procedure. This was supplemented by a provision for *ad hoc* Conciliation Commissions, if the parties to a dispute agreed. The Netherlands proposed a further optional article providing for the possibility of individual petitions. This appeared to have more chance of success in 1966 than in previous years, since a provision of this kind had been included in the Racial Discrimination Convention the year before. The attempt, however, was unsuccessful and the Third Committee decided by a very narrow majority that arrangements for individual communications to the Human Rights Committee should be contained in a separate 'Optional Protocol' to the Covenant, and thus apply only to States which, by a separate act, ratified the Protocol.

The Covenants, as revised by the Third Committee, were finally approved unanimously by the General Assembly in December 1966.[16] This approval, the culmination of eighteen years' work, was in itself a remarkable achievement. Even the long time taken over the negotiations had one important advantage. Whereas about fifty States participated in the initial discussions, this number had more than doubled by the time the texts were completed, with the result that the treaties which finally emerged can be regarded, not as the work of a particular group of States, but as truly reflecting the views of the modern international community.

Each Covenant required thirty-five ratifications and both came into force in 1976. The Optional Protocol was approved in 1966 by majority vote and required ten ratifications. It came into force at the same time as the Covenant on Civil and Political Rights. In 1989 a Second Optional Protocol to this Covenant was concluded with the aim of abolishing the death penalty. This too needed ten ratifications, which were achieved in 1991. At the present time more than 100 States have ratified the two Covenants, over seventy have accepted the (First) Optional Protocol and more than twenty the Second Protocol.[17]

The contents of the two Covenants have already been the subject of much comment.[18] The Covenant on Economic, Social and Cultural Rights will be discussed in Chapter 8, and the Covenant on Civil and Political Rights in the remainder of this chapter.

## 2. The general provisions of the Covenant

In accordance with the decision of the General Assembly taken in 1952, both Covenants begin in identical terms, with an article on the right of self-determination. This right is stated as one which exists and is of immediate application ('All peoples *have* the right of self-determination') and which results in peoples' right freely to determine their political status. It is then elaborated in subsequent paragraphs which establish the right of peoples to dispose of their natural resources, and the obligation of States to 'promote the realisation of the right of self-determination'.

This article of both Covenants is, of course, in accordance with the political philosophy of the General Assembly. However, using such a philosophy to ground a legal obligation produces a number of problems. First, self-determination is a collective right and not an individual right, and so some would question whether it is appropriate in the present context – especially as it was proclaimed elsewhere, in the Declaration on the Granting of

Independence to Colonial Countries and Peoples of 1960.[19] Secondly, the right is stated as belonging to 'all peoples'. But what constitutes a 'people'? Without going outside Western Europe, one may ask, does the right of self-determination belong to the Scots and the Welsh, the Bretons, the Corsicans and the Alsatians, the Basques and the Catalans? Thirdly, what are the consequences of possessing this right? Specifically, does having a right to self-determination always mean having a right to full political independence? Not surprisingly, therefore, the transformation of this political principle into a legal right has generated an extensive debate as to the meaning and implications of self-determination.[20]

Articles 2–5 of both Covenants constitute Part II. They contain in each case an undertaking to respect, or to take steps to secure progressively, the substantive rights which follow in Part III, together with certain other provisions of a general nature.

In the Covenant on Civil and Political Rights, Article 2 provides that each State party 'undertakes to respect and to ensure to all individuals within its territory and subject to its jurisdiction the rights recognised in the present Covenant'. Does this impose on States an obligation of immediate implementation, or only an obligation to do something in the future? From the words just quoted, which are from the first paragraph of Article 2, one would conclude that the obligation is immediate. This would, indeed, appear to have been the intention as regards civil and political rights. At the same time it seems clear that some States cannot immediately accept all the obligations resulting from the Covenant, because the list of rights secured is, as we shall see shortly, very extensive. To encourage the largest possible number of ratifications, paragraph 2 of Article 2 creates an obligation to take 'the necessary steps ... to adopt such legislative or other measures as may be necessary to give effect to the rights recognised in the present Covenant', in cases where they are not already provided for in the national law. It thus appears that while the first principle is one of immediate obligation, the possibility of progressive application is also recognised. Moreover, it is significant that a proposal to set a time limit for taking 'the necessary steps', which was made during the negotiations, was not accepted. The immediate nature of the obligation is therefore somewhat weakened.

The first paragraph of Article 2 of the Covenant on Civil and Political Rights also contains a non-discrimination clause in what may now be considered the standard form, and the third paragraph an undertaking to make available an effective remedy to anyone whose rights set out in the Covenant are violated. The non-discrimination clause is amplified by Article 3, which contains an undertaking to respect the principle of equality of men and women in the enjoyment of the rights secured. Article 4 provides for the possibility of derogation 'in times of public emergency which threatens the life of the nation and the existence of which is officially proclaimed'; while Article 5 contains two separate provisions. The first is designed to prevent abuse of the rights and freedoms set out and is based on Article 30 of the Universal Declaration; and the second is a general saving clause which states that nothing in the Covenant may be interpreted as limiting the rights and freedoms already existing or recognised under national law or under other conventions.

## 3. *The rights protected*

Part III of the Covenant on Civil and Political Rights sets out the rights which the Covenant is designed to protect. They are as follows:

*Article*  6  The right to life.
        7  Freedom from torture and inhuman treatment.
        8  Freedom from slavery and forced labour.
        9  The right to liberty and security.
      10  The right of detained persons to be treated with humanity.
      11  Freedom from imprisonment for debt.
      12  Freedom of movement and of choice of residence.
      13  Freedom of aliens from arbitrary expulsion.
      14  The right to a fair trial.
      15  Protection against retroactivity of the criminal law.
      16  The right to recognition as a person before the law.
      17  The right to privacy.
      18  Freedom of thought, conscience and religion.
      19  Freedom of opinion and of expression.
      20  Prohibition of propaganda for war and of incitement to national, racial or religious hatred.

21  The right of peaceful assembly.
22  Freedom of association.
23  The right to marry and found a family.
24  The rights of the child.
25  Political rights.
26  Equality before the law.
27  The rights of minorities.

This is an extensive list, and there are more rights in the
Covenant than in the Universal Declaration or the European
Convention. A comparison with the latter will be found in
Chapter 4. As regards the Universal Declaration, it can be seen
that the rights set out in the Covenant are generally defined in
greater detail and include the following, which were not
contained in the Declaration:

10  The right of detained persons to be treated with humanity.
11  Freedom from imprisonment for debt.
20  Prohibition of propaganda for war and of incitement to hatred.
24  The rights of the child.
27  The rights of minorities.

On the other hand, the right of property, which was included in
Article 17 of the Universal Declaration, is not included in either
Covenant. This was because it proved impossible to reach
agreement between countries of widely different political
philosophies on a definition of this right.

The way the Covenant defines the various civil and political
rights has been the subject of extensive commentary and analysis
and need not be considered in detail here. However, two general
points should be made.

First, not only is the number of rights protected in the
Covenant greater than in comparable instruments, but also the
definitions given are frequently broader and more enterprising.
For example, Article 6, on the right to life, does not actually
prohibit the death penalty, but is clearly drafted with the
intention of indicating that it should be abolished.[21] As noted
earlier, it is now possible for States to take this further by
accepting the Second Protocol, which contains an obligation to
abolish the death penalty within their jurisdiction.[22] Similarly,
Article 10 provides that all detained persons shall be treated

humanely and with respect for the inherent dignity of the human person. This is a positive obligation going well beyond the mere prohibition of inhuman treatment found in other texts. Article 10 continues by laying down separate standards for accused persons and juveniles, who shall be separated from convicted persons; while paragraph 3 of this article provides that the aim of the penitentiary system shall be the reformation and social rehabilitation of prisoners.

Another example may be seen in Article 25, which sets out certain political rights. This appears to apply not only to the right to vote in national elections, but also to the same right in local elections and to the right to take part in the government of one's country and in the public service. A further illustration is Article 27, which protects the rights of minorities 'to enjoy their own culture, to profess and practise their own religion, and to use their own language'.

Article 14, on the right to a fair trial, is a provision of particular importance and wide scope. In addition to the usual guarantees of an independent and impartial tribunal, public hearings, the presumption of innocence and the rights of the defence, it also provides for protection against self-incrimination, the right of appeal, and compensation for miscarriage of justice, and lays down the principle that no one may be tried twice for the same offence.

A second general point is that some of the provisions are so general or imprecise as to make their interpretation a task of some difficulty. This point has already been made in relation to 'the right of self-determination of all peoples'. It could also be made as regards several other provisions, notably those relating to the aim of the penitentiary system (Article 10(3)), the right to recognition as a person before the law (Article 16), the prohibition of propaganda for war (Article 20) and the right to take part in the conduct of public affairs (Article 25(a)). Too much should not be made of this deficiency, however. In the last analysis, the effectiveness of the Covenant depends less on the definition of the rights to be protected than on its arrangements to ensure that governments respect the obligations they have assumed. The measures of implementation of the Covenant on Civil and Political Rights will therefore now be examined in a little more detail.

## 4. *The Human Rights Committee*

Article 28 of the Covenant provides for the setting up of the Human Rights Committee, which thus becomes the principal organ of implementation of the Covenant on Civil and Political Rights.[23] This contrasts with the Covenant on Economic, Social and Cultural Rights, where no new body was created and implementation was assigned to the existing Economic and Social Council.[24]

As already noted, the Third Committee doubled the number of members of the Human Rights Committee from the figure of nine, which had been proposed in the 1954 draft, to eighteen. This was well justified, as the number of members of the United Nations had doubled by 1966. As regards the qualifications of members of the Committee, in the first place they must be nationals of States which are parties to the Covenant; secondly, they must be 'persons of high moral character and recognised competence in the field of human rights'; and, thirdly, consideration shall be given 'to the usefulness of the participation of some persons having legal experience'. In 1954 the Commission had proposed 'some persons having a judicial or legal experience', but the Third Committee decided to delete the reference to judicial qualifications. The change in fact makes little difference, since consideration of persons with legal experience clearly does not exclude judges, and, in any event, the requirement is not mandatory.

Under Articles 29 and 30 of the Covenant the members of the Committee are elected by secret ballot by the States parties at a special meeting convened for the purpose by the Secretary-General of the United Nations. Each party may nominate no more than two candidates, who must be nationals of that State. The detailed procedure for the election is set out in Article 30. The following article provides that the Committee may not include more than one national of any State and that consideration shall be given to the principle of equitable geographical distribution and to representation of the different forms of civilisation and the principal legal systems.[25]

The term of office is four years, though that of nine members elected at the first election was only two years, in order to avoid a complete change of membership at any one time (Article 32).

Members of the Committee are eligible for re-election (Article 29). Articles 33 and 34 deal with the possibilities of incapacity and casual vacancies, while the following article provides that the members of the Committee shall be paid by the United Nations, reinforcing the principle already stated in Article 28 that they 'shall serve in their personal capacity', that is, not as representatives of their governments. This principle is further emphasised in Article 38, which requires each member of the Committee to make a solemn declaration to perform his or her functions impartially and conscientiously.

The Covenant provides that the Committee shall meet 'at such times as shall be provided in its rules of procedure' (Article 37(2)). In practice this means that there are usually three sessions annually, each of three weeks' duration. Thus the Committee, like most international human rights organs, is a part-time body. In accordance with Article 37(3), meetings are held either in New York or Geneva, although other venues would be possible. Article 36 provides that the Secretary-General of the United Nations shall provide the necessary staff and facilities for the functioning of the Committee. Since human rights work of all kinds in the United Nations is seriously underfunded,[26] administrative and other support for the Human Rights Committee has always been limited and on occasion cost-cutting measures, such as reducing interpretation or not producing summary records, have hampered its activity.

The Covenant on Civil and Political Rights and the Optional Protocol entered into force in March 1976, and the meeting of the States parties to elect the members of the Committee took place in September of the same year. This resulted in the election of five members from Western Europe, four from Eastern Europe, two from Asia, three from Africa, one from North America and three from Latin America. The newly elected Committee held its first two meetings in March and August 1977. The Committee was then principally concerned with organisational matters and, in accordance with Article 39 of the Covenant, with settling its rules of procedure, though at the second session it also considered the first periodic reports and individual petitions, to which we will return later.

A particularly important issue which had to be settled at the beginning concerned voting. The Covenant itself contains a provision dealing with this. Although Article 39 provides that the Committee shall establish its own rules of procedure, paragraph 2 stipulates that these shall provide (a) that twelve members shall constitute a quorum; and (b) that decisions shall be made by a majority vote of the members present. However, many United Nations bodies now make extensive use of consensus and when the rules of procedure were being drafted some members argued that the Human Rights Committee should adopt this method and thus 'underscore the resolve of members to work harmoniously and in a spirit of co-operation'. Other members maintained that while consensus is desirable if possible, to establish a rule to this effect 'might considerably restrict the Committee's power of decision-making' and would be inconsistent with Article 39, paragraph 2(b) of the Covenant, referred to above.

Finally, it was agreed to incorporate in Rule 51 the method of decision by a simple majority, but to add a footnote indicating that there was general agreement that the 'method of work normally should allow for attempts to reach decisions by consensus before voting'.[27] In practice the Committee has adopted consensus as the basis of its decision making. Thus, the qualification to Rule 51 has become extremely important. It should be noted, however, that in the procedures for the consideration of communications under the Optional Protocol, provision is made in Rule 94 for a summary of any individual opinion to be appended to the collective view of the Committee.

In 1979, after the tenth State had made a declaration under Article 41, bringing the inter-State complaints procedure into force, the Committee put into effect rules of procedure to govern such complaints. In general, these follow the provisions of Article 41, which are described in the next section. Preparation of the necessary procedural framework was relatively straightforward. No doubt it helped that most of the members of the Committee were nationals of countries that had not submitted to the Article 41 regime, and their governments were not threatened by it. The few members of the Committee from countries that had accepted the system were eager to see it work, and their governments, having submitted to it voluntarily, were not disposed to try to weaken or frustrate it.

## 5. Reporting procedures

The draft Covenant prepared by the Commission on Human Rights envisaged as the principal measure of implementation a procedure of inter-State complaints before the Human Rights Committee. A reporting procedure was added only at the end of the relevant chapter, and it is clear from the context that it was considered a less important and subordinate measure. In the final text of the Covenant, however, the position was reversed. The reporting procedure emerged as the principal measure of implementation, while the inter-State procedure is optional. Potentially, therefore, the submission of reports by States and their examination by the Human Rights Committee is of cardinal importance in the implementation of the Covenant, and so the practical and theoretical merits of such a system deserve careful study.

The obligation on States to report relates to 'the measures they have adopted' to give effect to the rights set out in the Covenant, to 'the progress made in the enjoyment of those rights' and also, under paragraph 2 of Article 40, to 'the factors and difficulties, if any, affecting the implementation of the present Covenant'. The reports are to be presented within one year of the entry into force of the Covenant for the States parties concerned, and thereafter when the Committee so requests (Article 40, paragraph 1). The Committee has decided that, as a general rule, reports should be submitted every five years, but in 1992 amended its rules of procedure to enable it to request a report whenever it deems appropriate, and to allow the chair to request a special report 'in the case of an exceptional situation' when the Committee is not in session.[28]

Reports presented to the Human Rights Committee are, of course, compiled by national officials, who naturally try to give the best account they can of the situation in their country. Plainly then reports in themselves are an unreliable method of control. What matters is how the reporting system functions in practice, and in particular whether a proper appraisal of States' reports is possible. To make a reporting system work several elements are needed: (1) the co-operation of governments in providing full information; (2) the possibility of obtaining further (and perhaps less flattering) information from other responsible sources; (3) the examination of the information obtained by independent persons who are not government officials; and (4) the right of the organ or body supervising the procedure to make suitable recommendations with a view to achieving improvements in the law or practice of the country concerned.

To encourage co-operation and provide an indication of what a report should contain, the Committee has set out general guidelines relating to their form and content. The guidelines for initial reports, which were devised in 1977, ask that they should be in two parts. The first should briefly describe the general legal framework within which civil and political rights are protected, including information as to whether they are protected in the constitution or by a separate 'Bill of Rights'; whether the provisions of the Covenant are directly enforceable in internal law, and what remedies are available to individuals who think that their rights have been violated. The second part should deal with the legislative, administrative or other measures in force in regard to each right and include information about restrictions or limitations on their exercise. By 1981, when many initial reports had been submitted and the Committee was well into its work, new guidelines were issued to assist the preparation of subsequent reports. Both sets of guidelines are designed to elicit information about the law of the reporting State and also its practice, which the Committee rightly sees as no less important. In accordance with the Committee's intention to keep itself up to date, it has also asked governments to provide information on significant new developments at any time.

When the first reports began to come in the Human Rights Committee quickly established its intention of following the example of the Committee on the Elimination of Racial Discrimination in requesting additional information from governments, if needed, and in inviting them to send representatives to discuss their reports with the Committee and answer questions. Of course, common sense requires such action and it may be thought superfluous to draw attention to the development of this procedure. However, some governments are extraordinarily sensitive about anything in the nature of international examination of their human rights record, invoking arguments about national sovereignty and Article 2(7) of the Charter, and it was therefore a distinct achievement to get them to accept even the modest measures just described. The argument was even being put forward that Article 40 of the Covenant does not contain an express provision like that in Article 9 of the Racial Discrimination Convention authorising the Committee to 'request further information from the States Parties', and that the Committee should therefore not make such requests. It is consequently a cause for satisfaction that these negative attitudes did not prevail.

In practice therefore when a State submits either an initial report, or a subsequent periodic report, examination of it usually extends over several meetings and may produce dozens, if not hundreds, of questions from the members of the Committee to the State's representatives.[29] Not infrequently, further information is requested and may be provided either orally or in writing to supplement the original report. This procedure, which is also used when the Committee has asked a State to submit a special report, is thus designed to promote constructive dialogue with governments and to elicit a more complete picture of the situation than might be obtainable from the report alone.

The Committee, however, can only go so far. Ultimately any reporting system relies on the willingness of governments to carry out their obligations under Article 40 and can therefore be sabotaged by a failure to co-operate. The record here is unfortunately rather mixed. Initially many States performed satisfactorily, leading a commentator in 1982 to note that 'Even the most sceptical observers have been impressed by the apparent seriousness that many states from different parts of the world, with diverse political systems, have taken toward their reporting obligations, as reflected by the quality of the reports and the calibre of the representatives, as well as their willingness to answer questions.'[30] On the other hand, as the number of parties to the Covenant has grown, the practice of an increasing number of States has been grossly inadequate.[31] Many have failed to produce reports and others have submitted them only when long overdue. The quality and presentation of some reports have also been defective. In 1993, for example, Libya submitted a report which was ten years late and criticised as excessively general,[32] while in the following year the Committee decided to suspend consideration of Yemen's report when it became apparent that the national delegation did not know what was in it![33] Governmental co-operation with the Committee is thus a matter on which there is enormous room for improvement.[34]

The second element in an effective reporting system, as already noted, is the possibility of obtaining further, and perhaps more critical, information from responsible sources other than governments. This is provided for in the systems established by the International Labour Organisation (ILO) for its international labour conventions and by the Council of Europe for the European Social Charter. The Covenant on Civil and Political Rights, however, does not contain any similar arrangements. The nearest it comes to doing so is the provision in paragraph 3 of Article 40, which was introduced as an amendment by the United Kingdom in the Third Committee, which authorises the Secretary-General of the United Nations, after consultation with the Committee, to 'transmit to the Specialised Agencies concerned, copies of such parts of the reports as fall within their field of competence'. Both the ILO and UNESCO expressed their willingness to co-operate with the Human Rights Committee in this respect, and appropriate provision has been made in the rules of procedure. The Committee has also decided that information concerning the Specialised Agencies' interpretation and practice with regard to the corresponding provisions of their instruments should be made available to the Committee. However, only the ILO has made much use of this opportunity, and in any case too much should not be expected of such arrangements because comparatively few of the rights protected by the Covenant on Civil and Political Rights relate to matters within the competence of the ILO and UNESCO. Moreover, the Specialised Agencies do not possess a right to comment on States' reports and may do so only if specifically requested by the Committee. As a result, the Specialised Agencies play only a marginal role in the reporting system at present.[35]

From what other responsible sources could the Committee obtain information to supplement, or possibly criticise, the information furnished by governments? The obvious answer is the non-governmental organisations (NGOs) having consultative status with the Economic and Social Council. But until very recently NGOs had no right to lay information before the Human Rights Committee when it was considering the reports of governments. This did not prevent NGOs from supplying information to members of the Committee in their individual capacity, and the influence of evidence supplied by Amnesty International and other NGOs was often evident in the questions put to State representatives. However, this behind-the-scenes influence was a second-best arrangement and NGOs' lack of official standing was a real defect in the system. It was therefore a major step forward when in 1993 the Committee formally recognised the role of NGOs by deciding that information sent by them to the Secretariat should be distributed to all members of the Committee as official documents.[36]

In 1993 the Committee also discussed the possibility of sending missions to States in order to obtain information,[37] and further measures to improve the position of NGOs and to involve the Specialised Agencies more closely in the Committee's work are currently being debated.[38] Another possibility for providing the Committee with the means to assess a State's report might be for it to receive evidence from individuals with expert knowledge of the particular country. There are no doubt still obstacles to some of these developments. However, as regards the possibility of obtaining independent information the situation is now considerably better than it was and may well improve further.

The third requirement which we have suggested is necessary in an effective reporting system is the independence of the persons who examine the reports. As we have seen in the previous section, the text of the Covenant is satisfactory in this respect. Article 28(3) states that the members of the Committee 'shall be elected and shall serve in their personal capacity'. Also important are Article 38, which requires each member to make 'a solemn declaration in open committee that he will perform his functions impartially and conscientiously'; and Article 35, which provides that the members of the Committee 'shall … receive emoluments from United Nations resources'. The rules of procedure reiterate the requirement of a solemn declaration of impartiality and require that in the event of a member of the Committee resigning, this must be notified by the member concerned to the chair or the Secretary-General, so guarding against the possibility that a government may decide to remove a member of the Committee and simply notify the chair or the Secretary-General of its decision.

The record to date indicates that the aim of ensuring that the Committee is in a position to discharge its functions competently and free from undue governmental pressure has largely been achieved. As elsewhere, however, independence is relative and the nomination and election to the Committee of diplomats, politicians and even government ministers inevitably compromises its character to some extent.[39] That said, the individual members of the Committee are usually well qualified, many being lawyers with expertise in human rights, and when scrutinising national reports and questioning State representatives they demonstrate a rigour which ensures that no government is safe from criticism. The individuals who make up the Committee do not agree on all matters relating to the application of the Covenant. There is, as we have seen, more than one way of approaching the issue of human rights, while the function and authority of the Committee, which lie at the heart of the Covenant system, are also controversial. These differences are naturally reflected in disagreements within the Committee. Such disagreements are, however, inevitable at this stage in the development of international human rights law. Much more important is the fact that despite these differences, the quality and independence of the Committee's members have generated mutual respect and an *esprit de corps* which augur well for the future.

The fourth requirement of an effective reporting system is the power to make recommendations about necessary improvements in the law or practice of the country concerned. In this respect the Covenant on Civil and Political Rights is rather vague. Article 40(4) requires the Committee to study the reports submitted by States and provides that when it has done so it 'shall transmit its reports, and such general comments as it may consider appropriate, to the State Parties'. When the Committee considered the scope of its powers under this provision in 1980 two radically different schools of thought emerged.[40]

One view was that the Committee's task is to study the national reports to satisfy itself that the reporting obligation has been fulfilled and, more importantly, to determine whether the reporting State has fulfilled its obligations. It follows that the Committee should prepare a report on each national report, thus monitoring each party's compliance and making appropriate recommendations to the State concerned. The other view was that the 'reports' referred to in Article 40 are simply the annual report which the Committee is required to supply to the General

Assembly under Article 45. On this interpretation the Committee's function was to assist States in promoting human rights, but not to pass judgement on them. Hence the Committee was not permitted to make an assessment of, or report on, each State's conduct.

Faced with these very different views of its functions, and committed to decision making by consensus, the Committee was for many years unable to issue reports on individual States, even though this view of the Committee's powers had majority support. Instead, in accordance with the minority view favoured by the Eastern European members, the Committee issued only annual reports containing general comments and did not assess the conduct of individual States. In 1992, however, there was a change. With the ending of the Cold War and the collapse of communism in Europe the Committee was at last able to agree on the wider interpretation of its powers under Article 40. It therefore began issuing concluding comments on each individual report, thereby fulfilling another essential requirement of an effective reporting procedure.

The Committee has adopted the practice of dividing its concluding comments into five parts. Part A is an introduction in which the Committee thanks the State for its report, comments on its timeliness, adequacy and comprehensiveness, and says something about the oral presentation. Part B deals with factors and difficulties affecting the implementation of the Covenant, mentioning any economic, social or political factors specific to the State concerned. Part C identifies positive aspects in the State's record such as adherence to human rights treaties, constitutional and political changes, and notable developments in domestic law. The two remaining parts are effectively the core of the report and show why concluding comments are so important, for Part D, entitled 'Principal subjects of concern', identifies elements in the State's practice which the Committee considers are unsatisfactory, while Part E contains suggestions and recommendations for improving matters.

Although it is not possible to examine the Committee's comments on individual reports in detail here, its practice already demonstrates that the Committee is making full use of the opportunity they provide to subject all reports to a critical appraisal. Thus States have been criticised for submitting reports that were late, insufficiently detailed, or misleading, in the frankest terms,[41] while subjects of concern to the Committee have ranged from gross violations such as torture, murder, disappearances, excessive use of the death penalty and abuse of emergency powers, to failure to incorporate the Covenant in domestic law, or to follow best practice in matters such as non-discrimination, pre-trial detention and minority rights. It is notable too that the Committee has not shied away from controversial and sensitive issues, being prepared, for example, to emphasise that human rights cannot be subordinated to religious and cultural precepts.[42] However, as well as criticising, the Committee has also sought to be constructive, recognising where progress has been made and invariably advancing suggestions for further improvement.

Commenting on States' reports individually, as the Committee now does, is extremely valuable as a way of commending good practice, highlighting problem areas and encouraging improvement. It is worth noting, however, that long before it adopted its present view of Article 40, the Committee had begun to issue general comments, that is comments addressed to all parties to the Covenant, with the aim of spelling out its meaning and implications. The first general comment was made in 1981 and, like others which quickly followed, concerned the reporting procedure itself (in this case the need for punctuality). Soon, however, the Committee turned its attention to substantive issues and by the end of 1994 had issued more than twenty general comments, of varying length, covering the most important of the Covenant's guarantees as well as other matters.[43] Comment 6, for example, addresses the right to life; comment 10 the right to freedom of expression; comment 12 the right to self-determination; comment 13 the right to a fair trial; comment 23 the rights of minorities; comment 24 the question of reservations; and so on. Some issues have been dealt with twice. Thus comments 20 and 21 of 1992 concern respectively torture and the treatment of detainees, and replace comments 7 and 9, which dealt with these topics in 1982.

The Human Rights Committee has said that the purpose of general comments is to give parties to the Covenant, and States preparing to become parties, the benefit of its experience in supervising the reporting system. Another way of putting this would be to say that they provide governments with a clearer idea of what their obligations under the Covenant are. Although in no sense a substitute for the appraisal of individual State's reports, the Committee's general comments therefore provide a further means of making the reporting system effective.

In summary, then, the provisions of the Covenant dealing with States' obligation to report are as they should be and although performance of those obligations has been extremely variable, it has proved possible to establish a constructive dialogue with many governmental representatives and to obtain additional information from them when necessary. Secondly, the opportunities for obtaining independent information were originally wholly inadequate, and this presented a particular problem for NGOs and an additional burden on members of the Committee. However, the position has recently improved and further means of providing the Committee with information are being considered. Thirdly, the provisions of the Covenant and rules of procedure concerning the independence of members of the Committee are adequate; in practice, however, not all governments respect them scrupulously and so the situation here could certainly be improved. Fourthly, as regards the possibility of recommending remedial action, the Committee's early practice of limiting itself to comments addressed to all parties to the Covenant was plainly defective. However, this inhibited approach has now been abandoned and the Committee's concluding comments currently enable it to provide an appraisal of every report, which is what is needed.

It is not surprising that the reporting system instituted by the Covenant on Civil and Political Rights contained weaknesses and deficiencies which even now have not been completely remedied. It is, after all, the product of a heterogeneous United Nations community, some of whose members were in complete disagreement on the fundamental question of setting up any system of international control at all. From this perspective the reporting system can be seen as a compromise conditioned, like all arrangements based on international agreement, by the background and circumstances of its creation. Like other procedures we shall consider, it should also be seen as an arrangement with the capacity to evolve and, as we have seen, has already developed beyond what might have been anticipated in its first decade. Since there is a genuine place for reporting procedures in the machinery of human rights protection, it is important that the Human Rights Committee maintains this progress in the future.

## 6. Proceedings between States parties

As already noted, a great variety of proposals for implementation of the Covenants was put forward in the Commission on Human Rights when it was engaged in preparing its drafts between 1947 and 1954. These included schemes for an International Court of Human Rights, an International Investigation Commission, a High Commissioner for Human Rights, a new Specialised Agency for the implementation of the Covenants, and the creation of a panel of independent experts from whom an *ad hoc* Human Rights Committee could be selected when required. These proposals were launched during the period of enthusiasm for a new world order following the shattering experience of the Second World War. Before long, however, the traditional methods of diplomacy and notions of sovereignty reasserted themselves and these ambitious new ideas failed to attract the necessary support. By 1950 the Commission had decided that there should be a permanent body of independent persons to examine alleged violations of human rights, but that it should be accessible only to States, not to individuals or NGOs. This position remained unchanged when the Commission finished its work on the draft Covenants in 1954.

The Third Committee of the General Assembly, instead of strengthening the powers of the Human Rights Committee in relation to inter-State disputes, did just the opposite. The most important change which it made was to render the competence of the Committee to examine inter-State complaints an optional procedure, instead of one applying automatically to all States parties, as the Commission had recommended. Thus, Article 41 of the Covenant, which sets out in detail the procedure for considering inter-State 'communications', starts off with the words: 'A State Party ... may at any time declare ... that it recognises the competence of the Committee to receive and consider communications to the effect that a State Party claims that another State Party is not fulfilling its obligations under the present Covenant.' A separate declaration recognising this competence, in addition to the act of ratification, is therefore required. Moreover, it is not enough for the State alleged to be responsible for a violation to have made such a declaration. Communications can be considered by the Committee only if the complaining State has also done so. Thus, it is only States which have agreed to expose themselves to this procedure which have the right to use it against another party.[44]

Another way in which the Third Committee diluted the Commission's proposals is that the Human Rights Committee no longer has the right to express an opinion on the question of violation. The procedure set out in Article 41 of the Covenant envisages, in the first place, bilateral negotiations between the two States concerned. Then, if the matter is not settled, either State may refer it to the Human Rights Committee, which must examine the question in closed meetings, provided that domestic remedies have been exhausted. The Committee may call for all relevant information and the States parties may be represented and make oral and written submissions.

As the next step, the Committee is to make available its good offices with a view to a friendly settlement of the matter based on respect for human rights. Finally, if a friendly settlement is not achieved, the Committee is required to submit a report which must be confined to a brief statement of the facts, with the written and oral submissions of the States parties attached. It is apparent, therefore, that the functions of the Committee in relation to inter-State disputes are limited to establishing the facts, proposing its good offices and exercising them if the offer is accepted. As certain representatives stated in the Third Committee, the Human Rights Committee is 'no longer the same as the quasi-judicial body originally proposed by the Commission on Human Rights' but 'more in the nature of a functional organ'.[45]

There is, however, another procedural possibility, offered by Article 42 of the Covenant. This provides that if a matter referred to the Committee under Article 41 is not resolved to the satisfaction of the States concerned, the Committee may, if those States consent, appoint an *ad hoc* Conciliation Commission. This will in turn make available its good offices 'with a view to an amicable solution of the matter on the basis of respect for the present Covenant'. The Commission is to consist of five members who are nationals of States which have accepted the Article 41 procedure, but not nationals of the States parties to the dispute. Article 42 deals in some detail with the composition, method of election and procedure of the Conciliation Commission. In particular, it provides that the information obtained by the Human Rights Committee shall be made available to the Commission, which may also call on the States concerned for further information.

When it has completed its work, and in any event within a year of taking the matter up, the Conciliation Commission is to draw up its report. If the matter has been resolved amicably, the report will contain a brief statement of the facts and the solution. If there has been no amicable solution, the report will contain a full statement of the facts and the Commission's views on 'the possibilities of an amicable solution of the matter'. Within three months of the receipt of the report, the States parties must indicate whether or not they accept the contents of the Commission's report.

The procedures laid down in Articles 41 and 42 of the Covenant have been aptly described as 'complex, delicate and long-winded'.[46] They can be summarised by saying that in inter-State disputes the function of the Human Rights Committee is one of good offices, while that of the Conciliation Commission is good offices and conciliation. However, neither function can be exercised except in relation to two States which have both made an express declaration accepting the competence of the Committee to exercise this function and, as regards the Conciliation Commission, consented to its appointment.

The inter-State procedure became available in 1979, when ten States had made the necessary declarations. So far, however, only about thirty others have done so,[47] which clearly limits its potential. This conclusion is strengthened by the fact that many of the States which accept the Committee's competence are parties to the European Convention on Human Rights and, as we shall see in Chapter 4, will not normally refer to the United Nations matters which can be considered by the European Commission. Furthermore, a number of States have made it clear that they will never accept this optional procedure, as they are opposed to the basic principle on which it rests. Indeed, it is hard to believe that many governments, other than those of democracies with genuine guarantees of freedom of expression and association, free elections, protection against arbitrary arrest and due process of law, will be willing to expose themselves to the possibility of complaints by other States that they are violating civil and political rights. The prospects of Articles 41 and 42 of the Covenant being used very much in practice are therefore not substantial.[48]

## IV. Individual communications: the Optional Protocol

### 1. *Background*

The real test of the effectiveness of an international system for the protection of human rights is whether it permits individuals who believe that their rights have been violated to seek a remedy from an international institution. According to the classic conception, as we have seen, international law was the law which governed relations between States, and individuals had no place. Their interests were supposed to be protected by the State of which they were nationals, and they had no *locus standi* before international tribunals or international organisations. It is immediately obvious, however, that this simply does not work in the area of human rights.

If an individual's rights are violated, in the great majority of cases it will be the result of acts by organs or agencies of the State of which he or she is a national. It is therefore absurd to pretend that individuals' rights will be championed by the State of which they are nationals when that State is *ex hypothesi* the offender. Furthermore, Article 1 of the Charter states that one of the purposes of the United Nations is 'to achieve international co-operation ... in promoting and encouraging respect for human rights and fundamental freedoms for all', and there are several other references in the Charter to human rights. If, as was once the case, the organisation takes no action with regard to the communications it receives, it is failing to fulfil one of its principal functions. Considerations both of common sense and of the job of the United Nations under the Charter therefore make it necessary to adopt a constructive and positive attitude to the question of the individual's access to international remedies.

An additional argument for allowing individuals who believe that their rights have been violated to seek an international remedy is that once it is admitted that an international body can consider inter-State complaints, then if no right of individual petition exists the only possibility is the inter-State procedure. This means that aggrieved individuals will be tempted to look for another government that will take up their cause by bringing a case against the government of which they are nationals. Thus, Greek citizens whose rights were violated by the military regime in their country in 1967 were led to appeal to the Scandinavian governments for help. It is plainly in the interests of peaceful relations between States that what is essentially an individual or national problem should be dealt with as such and should not be transformed into an international dispute between States, with all the consequences which that entails.

When the Covenant on Civil and Political Rights was being drafted, one of the many questions that had to be decided was whether the measures of implementation should include the right of individual petition to the Human Rights Committee. The Third Committee discussed the matter at length.[49] After it had approved the two articles on inter-State procedures, it considered an amendment by the Netherlands proposing the addition of a new article providing for the competence of the Human Rights Committee to receive and consider individual petitions on an optional basis – a text which was largely inspired by the corresponding provisions of the European Convention. Jamaica and France tabled further amendments, the French proposal being aimed at limiting the functions of the Committee to the simple receipt and transmission of communications. There followed a ten-power revised amendment, which followed the general lines of the earlier proposal of the Netherlands, but set out the procedure in greater detail. This would have authorised the Committee, when examining individual communications, to 'forward its suggestions, if any, to the State Party concerned and to the individual'.

During the discussion in the Third Committee all the old arguments for and against the right of individual petition were rehearsed. Finally the debate turned on the question whether such a procedure should be included in the Covenant itself, on an optional basis, or in a separate protocol, which would also be optional. The representative of Lebanon made a formal proposal for the latter, which was adopted in a roll call vote by forty-one

votes to thirty-nine, with sixteen abstentions. It was thus decided
by a very narrow majority to incorporate the right of individual
petition in a separate legal text.[50]

In one way it is a pity that such an important measure of
implementation had to be omitted from the Covenant itself. On
the other hand, this may have been a wise decision, because its
inclusion would no doubt have discouraged ratification by
countries suspicious of these arrangements. There is also perhaps
a certain psychological advantage in the fact that the measure is
included in a separate Optional Protocol, because this serves to
emphasise the existence of the procedure of individual petition
more than if it were set out in Article 43. The Protocol is now
included separately in the list of United Nations treaties, and
ratifications are published and to some extent publicised. It is
therefore an object of greater attention than the optional
procedure in Article 41 of the Covenant. The importance of this
point should not be exaggerated, but given that the procedure
could not be made compulsory, nothing seems to be lost and
probably something is gained by the fact that the Optional
Protocol exists as an independent text.

The Optional Protocol provides that any State party to the
Covenant which ratifies the Protocol thereby 'recognises the
competence of the Committee to receive and consider communications from individuals subject to its jurisdiction who claim
to be victims of a violation by that State Party of any of the rights
set forth in the Covenant'. Articles 2 and 3 of the Protocol
incorporate the rule of exhaustion of domestic remedies and
provide that communications shall be considered inadmissible if
they are anonymous, abusive or incompatible with the provisions
of the Covenant. Article 5(2) introduces a further condition of
admissibility, excluding communications which relate to a matter
which is being examined under another procedure of international
investigation or settlement. This is a reasonable requirement
which has been extended by some States to cover cases examined
under another international procedure which has been completed.[51] Article 5(2) also repeats the rule of exhaustion of
domestic remedies, adding that the rule shall not apply if the
domestic remedies are unreasonably prolonged.

Article 4 and the remaining paragraphs of Article 5 deal with
the procedure of the Committee when dealing with individual

communications. They must be communicated to the State party concerned, which shall within six months 'submit to the Committee written explanations or statements clarifying the matter and the remedy, if any, that may have been taken by that State'. Nothing is said about oral hearings of the case, and Article 5(1) indicates that the proceedings are to be based on 'all written information made available ... by the individual and the State Party concerned', which has been interpreted as excluding oral hearings and information from other sources. Article 5(3) lays down that communications under the Protocol must be considered at closed meetings and Article 5(4) provides that when the proceedings have been completed the Committee 'shall forward its views to the State Party concerned and to the individual'.

The Protocol supplies the framework for considering individual communications and is now supplemented in practice by procedures which the Committee has developed to enable it to process its cases efficiently and respond promptly in situations of urgency.[52] As soon as communications are received by the UN Centre for Human Rights they are sent to the Committee's Special Rapporteur for New Communications, who screens them, seeks the observations of the State party and then passes them to the five-member Working Group on Communications. The latter meets for one week before each session and can declare a communication admissible so long as the Working Group is unanimous. Otherwise, the issue of admissibility is considered by the whole Committee. Cases found to be admissible are in due course then considered on their merits after further consultation with the State and the author of the communication.

Although the Protocol says nothing about requests for interim measures, the Committee has decided that it can consider such requests in urgent cases. Moreover, in cases involving persons under sentence of death, the matter can be dealt with immediately by its Special Rapporteur. Interim measures are most frequently sought in cases of this type, where the object, of course, is to ensure that the death penalty is not carried out before the Committee has been able to consider the issue of admissibility. Although interim measures are not binding, they have a moral force and in cases involving an immediate threat to the rights of a petitioner, provide a way of preserving the Covenant's effectiveness.

## 2. The work of the Committee

The Human Rights Committee began its work under the Optional Protocol in 1977 and in the next sixteen years considered more than 300 individual communications.[53] Just over half were found to be inadmissible, while the remainder were concluded with decisions. Of the latter about three-quarters were found to involve violations of the Covenant. Bearing in mind also that in the same period consideration of nearly 100 further cases was discontinued, it is clear both that significant use is being made of the Protocol and that the Committee is very busy. Since the work of the Committee cannot be examined in detail here,[54] we shall instead mention some decisions which may be regarded as representative, in order to give an impression of its practice.

As the figures just quoted indicate, much of the Committee's work is taken up with issues of admissibility. In the recent *Sara case*,[55] for example, an application by Finnish reindeer herders, alleging a violation of Article 27, was held to be inadmissible because domestic remedies had not been exhausted, and many cases have to be rejected on similar grounds. Cases are also dismissed: if they relate to events before the State concerned accepted the Optional Protocol, as in the case of *AS and LS v. Australia*;[56] if the author of the communication seeks to act on behalf of another without authorisation, as in *R and MH v. Italy*;[57] and, as noted earlier, if the matter is already being considered in another international forum, or if the State concerned has extended this limitation to cover any case referred elsewhere, even if the other procedure has been completed.[58]

A particularly important condition of admissibility is the requirement in Article 1 of the Optional Protocol that the author of a communication must claim to be the victim of a violation of one of the rights protected by the Covenant. This has a double effect. In the first place it rules out cases in which the claimant invokes a right which is not protected. In *KJL v. Finland*,[59] for example, the claim was ruled inadmissible *ratione materiae* on the ground that it concerned the right to property, which is not protected. Secondly, the requirement that the author must be a 'victim' means that it is not enough for a complaint to relate to matters of public interest; to be admissible it must affect the author's rights directly. Thus in *EW v. Netherlands*,[60] where the authors complained that the decision to deploy nuclear missiles in the respondent's territory infringed their right to life, the Committee held the communication inadmissible on the ground that the Optional Protocol does not provide an *actio popularis*.

When a communication meets the criteria of admissibility, the Committee is required to consider it on its merits. In 1979 the Committee for the first time 'forwarded its views to the State Party concerned and to the individual' (Article 5(4)) and made public what was, in effect, its first 'decision' on a private communication under the Protocol. The Committee had received a 'communication' from a Uruguayan citizen alleging mistreatment of herself and three members of her family. Each had been charged with 'subversive association' or 'assistance to subversive association', and was allegedly detained without trial, held incommunicado and tortured. The Committee brought the communication to the attention of the government of Uruguay (Article 4(1)). The government of Uruguay objected to the admissibility of the claim on the grounds that domestic remedies had not been exhausted, and that the alleged violations against the principal complainant had occurred before the Covenant entered into force for Uruguay. The Committee agreed that acts occurring before the Covenant's entry into force were outside its jurisdiction. As regards violations alleged to have occurred after that date, however, the Committee found that no further domestic remedy was available. It decided also that the 'close family connection' permitted the author of the communication to act on behalf of herself and the other victims.

When, after six months (Article 4(2)), the government of Uruguay failed to give a satisfactory explanation of its actions, the Committee formulated its views on the basis of the facts as alleged. It expressed the view that the facts disclosed several violations of the Covenant, including: torture and detention in unhealthy conditions, contrary to Articles 7 and 10(1); imprisonment after a release order, contrary to Article 9(1); failure to inform the prisoners of the charges against them, contrary to Article 9(2); denial of a prompt and fair trial, contrary to Articles 9(3) and 14; inadequate possibilities of appeal, contrary to Article 9(4); imprisonment incommunicado, contrary to Article 10(1); and denial of political rights, contrary to Article 25. The Committee expressed the view that the government of Uruguay was obliged to 'take immediate steps to ensure strict observance of the provisions of the Covenant and to provide effective remedies to the victims'.[61]

This first case is typical of many which the Committee has considered. Indeed, of the first sixty-four cases in which the Committee gave a decision on the merits, no less than forty-one, or sixty-four per cent, related to Uruguay and involved violations of the Covenant's most basic provisions. In the *Conteris case*,[62] for example, the victim was a former Methodist pastor, journalist and university professor, who was arrested by the security police on account of previous connections with the Tupamaros movement. He was held incommunicado for three months in various military establishments where he was hung by the wrists, burned and subject to other forms of torture too horrible to describe. After signing a confession he was sentenced by a military court to fifteen years in prison, but following a change of government in Uruguay was subsequently released.

The communication in this case was submitted by the victim's sister and declared admissible in 1984. In the course of its study of this case the Committee emphasised the State's duty under Article 4(2) of the Optional Protocol to investigate alleged violations of the Covenant and to provide the Committee with any information in its possession. Finding, however, that the government had failed to shed any light on the matter, the Committee did what it normally does in such situations and based its views on the evidence submitted by the author. Not surprisingly, the Committee concluded that the treatment endured by Mr Conteris involved violations of many articles of the Covenant, including Article 7 (prohibition of torture), Article 9(1) (prohibition of arbitrary arrest), 9(2) (right to be informed promptly of reasons for arrest), 9(3) (right to be brought promptly before a judge), 9(4) (habeas corpus), and Articles 10(1), 14(1) and 14(3), which have already been mentioned. While severely critical of the conduct of the Uruguayan authorities in this case, the Committee also expressed its satisfaction with the measures of the new government, especially the release of political prisoners.

Not all the early cases involved Uruguay. In 1982, for example, the Committee decided an unusual case involving Colombia. The *Suarez de Guerrero case*[63] concerned the application of a law providing members of the police force with a defence to certain criminal charges. A police patrol was ordered to raid a house which it was believed was being used by kidnappers. Nothing was found, but the police decided to hide and await the suspects' arrival. Seven people subsequently came to the house and as each person arrived he or she was shot dead, at point-blank range, some in the back. Criminal proceedings were begun against the policemen involved, but all were acquitted because the law provided a defence where the act which was the subject of a criminal charge was committed in the course of operations to prevent kidnapping.

The author of the communication in this case, who was acting on behalf of the husband of one of the victims, alleged that the application of this law violated the right to life, which is guaranteed by Article 6(1) of the Covenant. The Committee agreed. Pointing out that the facts were not in dispute and that the emergency which, according to the government, had made special measures necessary could not justify a derogation from the right to life, the Committee ruled that the Covenant had been violated and that Colombia should take measures to compensate the victim's husband and amend the law in question.

Communications alleging flagrant violations of the Covenant which have been considered more recently include the *Bwalya case*,[64] which concerned the persecution of a political activist in Zambia; the *Youssef El-Megreisi case*,[65] which concerned incommunicado detention in Libya; and the *Mojica case*,[66] which concerned the disappearance of a labour leader's son in the Dominican Republic. In all three cases the State refused to cooperate, but the Committee found that there had been a violation of the right to liberty and security of person guaranteed by Article 9. In the Zambian case it also identified violations of Articles 12 (freedom of movement), 19 (freedom of expression), 25 (right to take part in public affairs) and 26 (non-discrimination); while in the Libyan case it held that there had been violations of Articles 7 and 10, and in the Dominican case of Articles 6 and 7. In the light of its findings the Committee reminded the States concerned that they were obliged under Article 2 of the Covenant to provide the victims with an appropriate remedy, which the Committee specified,[67] and asked them to indicate within ninety days what action had been taken.

Although a large part of the Committee's work has been taken up with consideration of serious abuses of one sort or another, these types of cases are by no means the whole of its work. In addition to cases involving torture, arbitrary detention and the grosser violations of human rights, the Committee is sometimes called upon to consider issues similar to those which arise under the European Convention. We shall see in Chapter 4 that almost all the cases which come to the European Commission of Human Rights concern either maladministration or the kinds of conflicts of interests which are features of any complex society. Cases of this type demonstrate that human rights are not just an issue in undemocratic societies, and from time to time they also come to the Human Rights Committee. Indeed, because many of the world's democratic States have accepted the Optional Protocol, whereas most undemocratic States have not, such cases are more prominent than might be expected.

Typical of the cases in this second group is the *Toonen case*,[68] in which the Committee was required to decide whether legislation criminalising male homosexual activity in Tasmania constituted a violation of Article 17 of the Covenant, which prohibits arbitrary or unlawful interference with privacy. An unusual feature of the case was that the government of Australia conceded that this provision had been violated, but incorporated into its submission the observations of the Tasmanian authorities, which sought to justify the legislation on the grounds of health and morals. The Committee, however, found this to be unconvincing and considered also that no weight should be given to the fact that for the previous ten years the law against homosexual activity had not actually been enforced in Tasmania.[69] It therefore decided that the disputed legislation was incompatible with Article 17, considered in conjunction with Article 2(1) of the Covenant, and indicated that the Act in question should be repealed.

Also representative of the cases in this second group is the *Hartikainen case*,[70] which concerned the State's obligation under Article 18(4) of the Covenant 'to have respect for the liberty of parents ... to ensure the religious and moral education of their children in conformity with their own convictions'. The author of the communication, who was a schoolteacher in Finland, complained that children who did not receive formal religious instruction were required to enrol in a course on the history of religions and ethics. The latter, according to the complaint, was biased towards Christianity and as such violated the rights of parents under the Covenant. An obvious objection to the communication was that as the author was a teacher, not a parent, he lacked standing to bring the complaint. However, since Finland had not sought to argue that the communication was inadmissible, the Committee reviewed the case on its merits. The Committee decided that the law requiring the alternative course was not itself incompatible with the Covenant, provided 'such alternative course of instruction is given in a neutral and objective way and respects the convictions of parents and guardians who do not believe in any religion'. Noting that even the alternative course was not obligatory in all circumstances, and that the State was taking steps to deal with difficulties which had arisen over its implementation, the Committee decided that in all the circumstances there was nothing here incompatible with Article 18(4).

The issue in this case was rather similar to that considered in 1976 by the European Court in the *Danish Sex Education cases*,[71] and the Committee's reasoning is virtually identical. This shows the way in which, when similar issues arise, decisions under one human rights instrument can be influential elsewhere. In 1983, moreover, the Finnish government informed the Committee that it had amended its legislation and taken steps to monitor the teaching of the course complained of, so demonstrating that even a complaint which is formally unsuccessful may nevertheless be effective.

Another case of the same type is the *Aumeeruddy-Cziffra case*,[72] which was brought by a number of Mauritian women, some of whom had married foreigners and who now complained that their husbands' rights to residency and citizenship were subject to review. Since the same measures of control were not applicable to foreign wives, they complained of interference with the family contrary to Article 17(1) of the Covenant, and discrimination on grounds of sex, contrary to Articles 2(1), 3 and 26. Finding that the grounds for discriminatory treatment, which related to national security, were inadequate, the Committee upheld the complaint of the married petitioners on all counts. Soon afterwards Mauritius informed the Committee that in the light of its decision the legislation in question had been amended so as to remove the element of sex discrimination. Again it is interesting to note that a case raising rather similar issues has been considered by the European Court,[73] which also found the element of discrimination objectionable.

When dealing with the question of the protection of the family under the Covenant, the Committee observed that 'the legal protection or measures a society or a State can afford to the family may vary from country to country and depend on different social, economic, political and cultural conditions and traditions.' This point, that there is often room for different ways of applying international obligations, is one of general importance in human rights law. We shall see in Chapter 4 that on numerous occasions the European Court has employed the concept of a 'margin of appreciation' as a way of accommodating national differences. Since the Human Rights Committee is dealing not with a single region, but with States from all over the world, it is not surprising that in its work also the concept of a national margin of discretion has sometimes proved extremely useful.[74]

Although it is common to find different human rights organs using the same approaches or reaching identical conclusions on similar facts, this need not always be so. Indeed, because the terms of the various human rights treaties are not identical, and the organs concerned are differently composed, one would expect to find differences also in their decisions. A case which illustrates the point is the Human Rights Committee's decision in the *Kindler case*,[75] in which the question was whether it would be a violation of the Covenant for Canada to extradite an escaped murderer to the United States, where he faced the death penalty. The main issue in the case was not the status of the death penalty itself, which is permitted by Article 6 of the Covenant, but the so-called 'death row phenomenon', that is, the long delays which can ensue while appeals against the death sentence are going through the American courts. In the *Soering case*,[76] the European Court of Human Rights held that such delays may be relevant when the question is whether a person will be exposed to inhuman treatment if extradition takes place. The Human Rights Committee, however, preferred to follow its own case law and decided that the death row phenomenon *per se* did not entail treatment contrary to the standards in Article 7 of the Covenant.[77]

Not all the cases under the Optional Protocol concern rights which are also protected in other instruments and on these matters the Committee has no choice but to develop its own jurisprudence. Thus some of its most interesting cases have raised an issue under Article 27, which concerns the rights of minorities and which, as we have seen, is unique to the Covenant. In the *Lovelace case*,[78] for example, the petitioner was a Canadian Indian woman who married a non-Indian and thereby lost her status under Canadian law. When her marriage broke up she tried to return to the Indian reserve, but found that she was not admitted by the authorities. The Committee decided that although the Covenant does not guarantee the right to live on an Indian reserve, it does guarantee the members of a minority access to native culture and language, which in the circumstances of this case had been unjustly denied. Following the Committee's decision, the Canadian government amended the legislation so as to restore the petitioner's status.

In the *Ballantyne case*,[79] on the other hand, the petitioner was a member of the English-speaking community in Quebec and complained that the local law, which was designed to promote the use of French, made it a criminal offence for him to advertise in English. He argued that this constituted a violation of his rights as a member of a minority under Article 27, but the Committee rejected the complaint, holding that as English speakers are not a minority in Canada as a whole, their rights are not protected by this provision. This was a controversial conclusion and four members of the Committee appended an individual opinion in which they suggested that the majority had interpreted Article 27 too narrowly.

Although the Committee rejected the claim under Article 27 in *Ballantyne*, it upheld an alternative argument based on Article 19 (freedom of expression). Here the Committee decided that although the Covenant authorises the limitation of freedom of expression in certain circumstances, none of the limitations was relevant on the facts of the case. However, this conclusion too was not unanimous, as one member of the Committee held that the ban on advertising in English could be justified as a means of protecting the French language and thereby furthering the objectives of Article 27. Whatever one's view of these arguments about minority rights, they provide a striking demonstration of the complexity of such issues and the adjudicator's dilemma when incompatible claims come into collision.

## 3. *Appraisal*

An evaluation of what has been achieved under the Optional Protocol and how the work of the Human Rights Committee may develop in the future calls for consideration of several aspects of its record to date.

First, there is the scale of the Committee's activity. The twenty or so decisions on merits which the Committee now gives each year is a respectable number by international standards, but means that it has a growing backlog of cases[80] and in wider perspective seems insignificant when set against the deplorable state of human rights in many parts of the world. When it is also recalled that more than half of the early decisions relate to a single State, the selective nature of the Committee's work, and hence the limited contribution of the Protocol to the protection of human rights, is further emphasised.

The factors which shape the Committee's case-load are not difficult to identify. The majority of members of the United Nations have not accepted the Optional Protocol. Indeed, only about half the parties to the Covenant have done so. In addition, the States which have not accepted the right of individual petition include many of those with the worst records on human rights. This situation, which is, of course, not accidental, means that many of the most serious cases lie outside the Committee's jurisdiction. Acceptances of the Optional Protocol are steadily increasing, which is encouraging, but it is unlikely that the range of the Committee's competence will be enlarged radically in the foreseeable future. Thus the fact that so many States cannot be the object of petitions seems bound to remain a major limitation.

When the States which have accepted the Protocol are considered, other factors become apparent. Some States are notorious violators of human rights yet rarely have cases brought against them,[81] which suggests that fear and ignorance are highly significant. Conversely, many of the States which have accepted the Committee's jurisdiction have an excellent record and already provide domestic means of dealing with complaints. While this does not make international procedures irrelevant, it does reduce the number of complaints which reach the international level. The fact that the Committee is never going to have a large number of complaints against, say, Canada or Norway, is therefore another influence on the nature of its work.

It is also necessary to remember that many of the States with good human rights records, and some whose records are less good, are already parties to regional treaties on human rights. These may provide an alternative forum for consideration of individual complaints. The participation of a State in a regional system does not in itself prevent an individual from referring a case to the Human Rights Committee if the State concerned has also accepted the Optional Protocol. However, as we have seen, it is frequently not possible to have a complaint considered in both systems. Consequently, the number of cases referred under the Optional Protocol is to some extent a reflection of the vigour and attractiveness of regional systems. Since the European and Inter-American systems are conspicuously active, and have now been joined by an African system, the relation between the Committee's work and regional schemes of protection is another factor of continuing importance.

The second element to be considered in assessing the Optional Protocol is how the Committee has discharged the task of deciding the cases which have been referred to it and the contribution its decisions have made to the law. No organ of the type represented by the Human Rights Committee can be counted a success unless it deals competently with matters which fall within its jurisdiction. A body which is incompetent will not only antagonise States, which is particularly damaging for an organ which lacks compulsory jurisdiction and depends on co-operation, but will also lose the confidence of individuals on whose communications its work depends. The importance of such confidence can scarcely be overstated. After all, the Covenant is not the only human rights treaty, and, as we have mentioned, individuals who consider that their rights have been violated may have avenues of complaint available elsewhere. If, therefore, the Human Rights Committee is to be regarded as an effective forum for ventilating complaints, it is essential that it should be proficient.

Judged by the criterion of competence, the Human Rights Committee can certainly be rated a success. It is true that about half the communications to the Committee are rejected on grounds of admissibility, but this is not unusual for a body dealing with human rights complaints, and is actually low by international standards. The Committee's decisions on admissibility are now published and, since they are reasoned, constitute a body of case law indicating the scope of the Committee's powers. Analysis of this record suggests that the Committee has interpreted its jurisdiction quite broadly and has certainly adopted a less restrictive approach to admissibility than the European Commission of Human Rights in its early years.[82] The latter often used to reject claims at the stage of admissibility on grounds which it would have been more appropriate to consider as part of the merits. Although a similar tendency has been detected in certain decisions of the Human Rights Committee,[83] its handling of issues of admissibility in general has been exemplary.

Cases which proceed to a consideration of the merits call for the Committee to attempt to establish the facts, and here, as noted earlier, it has sometimes encountered problems. When governments co-operate, as they generally do in cases involving the less serious type of complaint, there is no difficulty. In the many cases involving allegations of flagrant violations of human rights, on the other hand, the governments concerned are often much less helpful, with the result that the Committee can face formidable evidentiary problems. In such situations, as we have seen, the Committee has taken the view that the test is not whether a complaint has been proved beyond all reasonable doubt, a test which would frequently be impossible to satisfy, but rather whether a complaint which is consistent with the evidence available to the Committee has been successfully refuted by the State. If it has not, the Committee will regard the facts as proved, and the absence of an adequate explanation as indicative. As regards the facts, then, the Committee does its best but, using an approach which has also been adopted by the Inter-American Commission of Human Rights for such situations,[84] will not allow non-co-operation to prevent a decision.

As regards its approach to the law, the Committee again emerges with credit. Although it is important to remember that the Committee is not an international court, but rather a quasi-judicial body, its decisions demonstrate the advantages of entrusting the interpretation and application of the Covenant to a body of independent experts rather than to government representatives. Because its decisions are reasoned, the Committee's work constitutes an important body of case law in which, as indicated above, fundamental issues of life and liberty and philosophically interesting problems of human rights have all been considered. In dealing with these questions the Committee has made little explicit reference to the wider body of human rights law, but its decisions, as might be expected, are nonetheless a reflection of a tradition to which its own jurisprudence is now contributing. When some of the most controversial issues in human rights law have to be considered it is true that differences of opinion among the members of the Committee are likely to surface and to be reflected in its decisions. That, however, is inevitable. While matters would be simpler if everyone saw the Covenant in the same way, the Committee, like other international organs, can provide a forum where differences can be articulated and the possibility of a common understanding of human rights explored.

The third and final factor to be considered in assessing the work of the Human Rights Committee under the Optional Protocol is the effect of its decisions on States which are found to be in breach of their obligations. From our review of a representative sample of the Committee's case law it will be obvious that the reception of decisions is something which can vary widely. Governments which co-operate with the Committee at the stage of investigation are normally those involved in the less serious cases and, as a rule, are anxious to take whatever steps are needed to correct any deficiency which the Committee has identified. Thus, as we have seen, Canada amended its legislation following the decision in the *Lovelace case*, Mauritius changed its law in response to the *Aumeeruddy-Cziffra case*, while Finland changed its law in the light of the *Hartikainen* decision, even though no violation of the Covenant had been found. These cases show that use of the Optional Protocol can have a direct effect on the protection of rights within a State and demonstrate a point which we shall find confirmed in Chapter 4, that governments which have the least to be ashamed of are usually also the first to correct their mistakes.

When we turn from these cases to those in which the allegation is of gross violations of human rights, the record is much less satisfactory. Steps may be taken to deal with a problem identified by the Committee, as in the *Suarez de Guerrero case*, but compliance with the letter and, more important, the spirit of the Committee's decision certainly cannot be guaranteed. Just as governments which routinely abuse rights will do their best to obstruct investigation of their practices, so when an international decision is handed down, it is unlikely that much will be done in the way of either compensating the victim or dealing with the general problem. If the parallel with the first type of case is the ready compliance of States with decisions under the European Convention on Human Rights, the parallel with the second is the experience of the Inter-American Commission which, as we shall see in Chapter 6, has the thankless task of supervising a very different regional system.

Recognising the importance of systematically monitoring the implementation of its decisions, in 1990 the Committee appointed a special rapporteur with the following functions:

1    to recommend to the Committee action upon all letters from individuals who have been found by the Committee to be victims of a violation of their rights and who contend that no appropriate remedy has been afforded to them;

2    to communicate with States parties and, if he or she deems it appropriate, with victims, in respect of such letters received by the Committee;

3    to seek to obtain information on any action taken by States parties in relation to views adopted by the Committee, when such information has not otherwise been made available;

4    to assist the Committee's rapporteur in the preparation of the relevant sections of the annual report of the Committee;

5    to advise the Committee on appropriate deadlines for the receipt of information on remedies adopted by States parties found to have violated provisions of the Covenant; and

6    to submit regularly to the Committee recommendations on possible ways to make the follow-up procedure more effective.[85]

Since the rapporteur's appointment, requests for follow-up information have been sent to every State found by the Committee to have violated the Covenant. By the beginning of 1993 just over 100 States had been asked for information, and about two-thirds had replied. Of the replies, however, the Committee considered only about a quarter to be satisfactory, the remainder being vague or irrelevant, or in some cases indicating rejection of the Committee's recommendations.

The Committee's experience with its monitoring system has thus confirmed that implementation of its decisions is at best spasmodic and that, as the Committee itself has acknowledged,[86] the absence of an explicit provision on enforcement is a major weakness in the Optional Protocol. Initially the Committee considered follow-up information on a confidential basis, but in 1993 it decided that such information should be made public, with States which are unwilling to co-operate listed in its annual report, and the Committee ready to issue an official response, if, for example, a State challenges its findings. These steps are welcome and, as a means of enhancing the Committee's authority and encouraging States to comply with its decisions, will serve to further the interests of victims. Other ways of increasing the effectiveness of the follow-up procedure, such as broadening the mandate of the special rapporteur and amending the Optional Protocol to include an undertaking to comply with the Committee's decisions, are also being considered.

The problems encountered with follow-up are a reminder of the single most important factor about the Optional Protocol, that the Human Rights Committee is not like a domestic court, issuing judgements and equipped with the power to enforce them, but a body which 'forwards its views' to the individual and government concerned and reports to the General Assembly through the ECOSOC. In relation to States with a poor record on human rights, the significance of the Optional Protocol is that, when it has been accepted, it provides a way of publicising abuses and putting pressure on the State to improve in much the same way as the compulsory reporting procedure. As a way of ensuring that States respect the rights of the individual, this is indirect, not always visible and may turn out to be ineffective. However, since political pressure is sometimes the best, and often the only, way of encouraging governments to improve their practice, the procedure under the Optional Protocol has a value which should be recognised.

If we think of the Human Rights Committee as a sort of Supreme Court of Human Rights, we shall inevitably be disappointed by the scale and effect of its activity. If, on the other hand, we see the Committee for what it is, as one of several bodies charged with responsibility for human rights, then the procedure under the Optional Protocol appears in its true light – as just one of a number of ways in which States can be encouraged to respect their obligations. The Committee, then, is significant and certainly to be encouraged, but it is not alone. Arrangements which need to be taken into account if the role of the Committee is to be seen in perspective will therefore now be considered.

## Notes

1 The leading work on the provisions of the Charter relating to human rights is Sir H. Lauterpacht, *International Law and Human Rights*, London, 1950. Part III contains the author's own proposals for an International Bill of Human Rights.

2 L. B. Sohn, 'A short history of United Nations documents on human rights', in *The United Nations and Human Rights*, eighteenth report of the Commission to Study the Organisation of Peace, New York, 1968, pp. 51–2.

3 Quoted by Sohn, *ibid.*, p. 55.

4 The eight abstentions were from the Soviet bloc, South Africa and Saudi Arabia. For the text of the Declaration see I. Brownlie, *Basic Documents on Human Rights*, third edition, Oxford, 1992, p. 21, and P. R. Ghandhi, *International Human Rights Documents*, London, 1995, p. 21. For analysis of the Declaration and discussion of its significance see A. Eide (ed.), *The Universal Declaration of Human Rights*, Oslo, 1992.

5 Quoted in Sohn, 'A short history', p. 70.

6 *Ibid.*, p. 71.

7 Resolution 1514(XV), which was passed with ninety votes in favour, none against and nine abstentions.

8 Resolution 1904(XVIII).

9 Resolution 421(V) of 4 December 1950.

10 Resolutions 543(VI) and 545(VI) of 5 February 1952.

11 Sohn, 'A short history', pp. 103, 105, 125, 132, 137.

12 *Ibid.*, pp. 127, 132, 154, 163.

13 *Ibid.*, pp. 143–4, 161.

14 *Report of the Tenth Session of the Commission*, UN document E/2573, pp. 62–72.

15 UN document A/2929 of 1 July 1955.

16 Resolution 2200 of 16 December 1966. For the texts of the Covenants see Brownlie, *Basic Documents*, pp. 114, 125, and Ghandhi, *Human Rights Documents*, pp. 51, 68.

17 On 1 January 1995 there were 129 parties to the Covenant on Civil and Political Rights, seventy-nine parties to the (First) Optional Protocol, and twenty-five parties to the Second Optional Protocol.

18 The following works and articles on the Covenants are particularly recommended: C. M. Eichelberger (ed.), *The United Nations and Human Rights*, New York, 1968; E. Schwelb, 'Civil and political rights: the international measures of implementation', *American Journal of International Law*, LXII, 1968, p. 827, and A. G. Mower, 'The implementation of the UN Covenant on Civil and Political Rights', *Human Rights Journal*, X, 1977, p. 271. Further

references relating to the Covenant on Economic, Social and Cultural Rights will be found in Chapter 8.

19  Resolution 1514(XV) of 14 December 1960.

20  For an attempt to rely on the right to self-determination in proceedings before the Human Rights Committee see the *Mikmaq case*, Communication No. R. 19/78. Text of the decision of the Human Rights Committee in *Human Rights Law Journal*, V, 1984, p. 194.

21  Thus Article 6 refers to countries which have not abolished the death penalty as if this is a temporary situation which should be changed, and states specifically that nothing in this provision may be invoked to prevent or delay the abolition of capital punishment.

22  See further G. J. Naldi, 'The United Nations seeks to abolish the death penalty', *International and Comparative Law Quarterly*, XL, 1991, p. 948. It should be noted that Article 2(1) of the Protocol permits States to make a reservation permitting the death penalty to be used in time of war following 'conviction for a most serious crime of a military nature committed during wartime'.

23  Excellent accounts of the Committee and its work will be found in D. McGoldrick, *The Human Rights Committee*, Oxford, 1991, and T. Opsahl, 'The Human Rights Committee', in P. Alston (ed.), *The United Nations and Human Rights, A Critical Appraisal*, Oxford, 1992, pp. 369–444.

24  However, ECOSOC subsequently delegated this function to the Committee on Economic, Social and Cultural Rights, which is described in Chapter 8.

25  Compare Article 9 of the Statute of the International Court of Justice, which requires that 'the representation of the main forms of civilisation and of the principal legal systems of the world should be assured'.

26  See Opsahl, 'The Human Rights Committee', pp. 380–1.

27  *First Annual Report of the Human Rights Committee to the General Assembly*, UN document A32/44 (1977), paras 28–32.

28  In 1992 the Committee called for special reports from Bosnia-Herzegovina, Croatia and the Federal Republic of Yugoslavia; in 1993 from Angola and Burundi; and in 1994 from Haiti and Rwanda.

29  See Opsahl, 'The Human Rights Committee', pp. 402–6.

30  See D. D. Fischer, 'Reporting under the Covenant on Civil and Political Rights: the first five years of the Human Rights Committee', *American Journal of International Law*, LXXVI, 1982, pp. 142, 145.

31  See A. F. Bayefsky, 'Making the human rights treaties work', in L. Henkin and J. L. Hargrove (eds), *Human Rights: An Agenda For the Next Century*, Washington, 1994, p. 229. Tables A to F at pp. 286–90, which provide a statistical overview of the reporting situation, are particularly illuminating.

32  See *Human Rights Monitor*, XXIII, 1993, p. 9.

33  See *Human Rights Monitor*, XXVII, 1994, p. 15.

34  At its forty-ninth session in 1993 the Committee decided to list in its annual reports those States which had accumulated the longest delays in the submission of their reports. In the report adopted at its fifty-first session in July 1994 seventeen States were named in this category. See *Human Rights Monitor*, XXIII, 1993, p. 10, and XXV/XXVI, 1994, p. 38.

35  See Opsahl, 'The Human Rights Committee', pp. 392–4.

36  See *Human Rights Monitor*, XXIII, 1993, p. 11.

37  *Ibid.*, p. 10.
38  See *Human Rights Monitor*, XXVII, 1994, p. 16.
39  See Opsahl, 'The Human Rights Committee', pp. 375–6.
40  See T. Meron, *Human Rights Law Making in the United Nations*, Oxford, 1986, pp. 124–5.
41  For example, commenting on the second periodic report of El Salvador, the Committee expressed its regret that the report 'neither accurately nor candidly represents the actual human rights situation in El Salvador in the period covered by the report'; see UN document CCPRC/C/79/Add 34, also in *International Human Rights Reports*, I(3), 1994, p. 203.
42  See, for example, the concerns expressed by the Committee over the position of the Evangelical-Lutheran religion, the Catholic Church and Islamic influences in its recent comments on, respectively, the reports of Norway, Costa Rica and Iran. These reports can be found in *International Human Rights Reports*, I(2), 1994, p. 272; I(3), 1994, p. 196; and II, 1995, p. 201.
43  The text of General Comments Nos 1–24 can be found in *International Human Rights Reports*, I(2), 1994, p. 1; I(3), 1994, p. 1; and II, 1995, p. 10.
44  It is interesting to compare the Covenant with the other general human rights treaties as regards the optional or obligatory nature of the control systems. Whereas the Covenant makes both the inter-State and the individual complaint procedures optional, the European Convention makes the former compulsory and the latter optional; the American Convention takes the opposite approach; and the African Charter on Human and Peoples' Rights makes both procedures compulsory.
45  UN document A/6546 (1966), para. 308.
46  P. R. Ghandhi, 'The Human Rights Committee and the right of individual communication', *British Year Book of International Law*, LVII, 1986, pp. 201, 203.
47  On 1 January 1995 forty-four States had made declarations under Article 41.
48  At the beginning of 1995 the inter-State procedure had not yet been used.
49  *Report of the Third Committee*, UN document A/6546 (1966), paras 474–85.
50  *Ibid.*, para. 485. Most of the Soviet bloc and the Asian and African States voted in favour. Most of the Western group and the Latin American States voted against. Among the abstentions were: Brazil, China, Cyprus, Greece, Israel and Turkey. When it came to the vote in the General Assembly on 16 December 1966, the Optional Protocol was approved by sixty-six votes to two, with thirty-eight abstentions.
51  For example, a number of European States have accepted the Optional Protocol subject to a reservation excluding cases which have been referred to, or considered under, another international procedure.
52  See H. Hannum (ed.), *Guide to International Human Rights Practice*, second edition, Philadelphia, 1992, pp. 46–7.
53  The figures in this paragraph are taken from the Human Rights Committee's *Follow-Up on Views Adopted under the Optional Protocol to the International Covenant on Civil and Political Rights*, UN document A/CONF 157/TBB/3, 9 June 1993, reproduced in *International Human Rights Reports*, I(2), 1994, p. 345.
54  See the works cited in note 23.

55 Communication No. 431/1990, decision of 23 March 1994. Text in *International Human Rights Reports*, I(3), 1994, p. 14.
56 Communication No. 490/1992, decision of 30 March 1993. Text in *International Human Rights Reports*, I(1), 1994, p. 55.
57 Communication No. 565/1993, decision of 8 April 1994. Text in *International Human Rights Reports*, I(3), 1994, p. 52.
58 As in *VEM v. Spain*, communication No. 467/1991, decision of 16 July 1993. Text in *International Human Rights Reports*, I(2), 1994, p. 36.
59 Communication No. 544/1993, decision of 3 November 1993. Text in *International Human Rights Reports*, I(2), 1994, p. 74.
60 Communication No. 429/1990, decision of 8 April 1993. Text in *International Human Rights Reports*, I(1), 1994, p. 67.
61 *Report of the Human Rights Committee, 1979*, document A/34/40, Annex VII.
62 Communication No. R. 139/1983, decision of 17 July 1985. See M. Nowak, *Human Rights Law Journal*, VII, 1986, p. 295.
63 Communication No. R 11/45, decision of 31 March 1982. Text in *Human Rights Law Journal*, III, 1982, p. 168.
64 Communication No. 314/1988, decision of 14 July 1993. Text in *International Human Rights Reports*, I(2), 1994, p. 84.
65 Communication No. 440/1990, decision of 23 March 1994. Text in *International Human Rights Reports*, I(3), 1994, p. 65.
66 Communication No. 449/1991, decision of 15 July 1994. Text in *International Human Rights Reports*, II, 1995, p. 86.
67 In the *Bwalya case* the Committee urged Zambia to provide the victim with appropriate compensation; in the *El-Megreisi case* it urged Libya to secure the victim's immediate release from detention and to provide financial compensation; and in the *Mojica case* it urged the Dominican Republic to investigate the victim's disappearance, to bring those responsible for it to justice, and to provide his family with compensation.
68 Communication No. 488/1992, decision of 31 March 1994. Text in *International Human Rights Reports*, I(3), 1994, p. 97.
69 Cf. the *Dudgeon case*, ECHR, Series A, No. 45 (1981) and the *Norris case*, Series A, No. 142 (1988), in which the European Court of Human Rights reached a similar conclusion with regard to laws in, respectively, Northern Ireland and the Irish Republic.
70 Communication No. R. 9/40, decision of 9 April 1981. Text in *Human Rights Law Journal*, II, 1981, p. 133.
71 Series A, No. 23 (1976).
72 Communication No. R. 9/35, decision of 9 April 1981. Text in *Human Rights Law Journal*, II, 1981, p. 139. The complaints of the unmarried petitioners, however, were rejected on the ground that their rights had not been interfered with.
73 See *Abdulaziz, Cabales and Balkandali case*, Series A, No. 94 (1985).
74 A further illustration is provided by the decision in the *Hertzberg case*, Communication No. R. 141/61, decision of 2 April 1982. Text in *Human Rights Law Journal*, III, 1982, p. 174.
75 Communication No. 470/1991, decision of 30 July 1993. Text in *International Human Rights Reports*, I(2), 1994, p. 98.

76 Series A, No. 161 (1989).

77 It should be noted, however, that although the European Court might well have reached a different conclusion on the legal consequences of the 'death row phenomenon', the Human Rights Committee followed the Court in holding that where treatment in a foreign State would infringe human rights, extradition to that State engages the responsibility of the extraditing State and is therefore prohibited.

78 Communication No. R 6/24, decision of 30 July 1981. Text in *Human Rights Law Journal*, II, 1981, p. 158. For discussion see A. F. Bayefsky, 'The Human Rights Committee and the case of Sandra Lovelace', *Canadian Yearbook of International Law*, XX, 1982, p. 244.

79 Communication No. 359/1989, decision of 31 March 1993. Text in *International Human Rights Reports*, I(1), 1994, p. 145.

80 Thus in 1992 it took an average of four to five years to deal with a communication compared with two years when the Committee began. See M. G. Schmidt, 'Individual human rights complaints procedures based on United Nations treaties and the need for reform', *International and Comparative Law Quarterly*, XXXXI, 1992, p. 648.

81 See Bayefsky, 'Making the human rights treaties work', p. 237, and Table J, p. 292.

82 For an excellent review of the Committee's treatment of admissibility see Ghandhi, 'The Human Rights Committee'.

83 See M. Nowak, 'UN-Human Rights Committee. Survey of decisions given up to July 1986', *Human Rights Law Journal*, VII, 1986, p. 303.

84 See Chapter 6.

85 See the Committee's *Follow-Up* document, p. 345, and Schmidt, 'Individual human rights complaints procedures', pp. 650–1.

86 *Ibid.*

# CHAPTER 3

# The United Nations and human rights II: other instruments and procedures

## I. Standard setting

There are many other United Nations texts and procedures which concern human rights in addition to the Universal Declaration and two Covenants, but space does not permit consideration of all of them in detail. The Convention against Torture (1984) and the Convention on the Rights of the Child (1989) are two such instruments which are further discussed below. Earlier conventions of this type include the Convention on the Prevention and Punishment of the Crime of Genocide (1948); the Supplementary Convention on the Abolition of Slavery and the Slave Trade (1956); three Conventions on Nationality and Statelessness, which deal with the Nationality of Married Women (1957), the Reduction of Statelessness (1961) and the Status of Stateless Persons (1954); the Convention on the Status of Refugees (1951) and its Protocol (1966); the Convention on the Political Rights of Women (1952); and the Convention on the Non-applicability of Statutory Limitations to War Crimes and Crimes against Humanity (1968).

As is well known, the United Nations has been particularly concerned with the prevention of discrimination. This concern is reflected in the 1966 International Convention on the Elimination of All Forms of Racial Discrimination, the 1973 International Convention on the Suppression and Punishment of the Crime of Apartheid, and the 1979 Convention on the Elimination of All Forms of Discrimination against Women, which are all discussed below. Also relevant here are the 1981 Declaration on the Elimination of All Forms of Intolerance and Discrimination based on Religion or Belief, and the Declaration on the Rights of Persons Belonging to National or Ethnic, Religious and Linguistic Minorities of 1992.[1] The Specialised Agencies, for their part, have produced conventions for the elimination of discrimination in employment (ILO) and in education (UNESCO), which we will examine in Chapter 8.

This considerable volume of international legislation is the product of what may be called the promotional or standard-setting function of the United Nations, that is to say, the creation of rules of international law which lay down the standards of human rights which States must observe. This was the main activity of the organisation in relation to human rights until 1966, when the Covenants were adopted, and as the list above indicates, the Commission on Human Rights has continued to produce texts on a variety of important issues. There has, however, now been something of a change of emphasis resulting in more attention to the protection of human rights, that is, to the prevention or remedying of violations. Certain procedures designed to provide a remedy for violations were included in the Covenants and have already been described. Other procedures of this nature form the subject of this chapter.

## II. The Resolution 1503 procedure

From the time the United Nations was first established the Secretary-General has received thousands of communications annually from individuals or non-governmental organisations, complaining of violations of human rights. For many years, however, the Commission on Human Rights considered that it had no power to take any action in regard to any complaints concerning human rights. This attitude was approved by the Economic and Social Council in 1947 and reaffirmed by the Council in 1959.[2] Various attempts to adopt a more positive approach were made, but were regularly countered by the argument from the Soviet Union and others, that consideration of individual complaints would constitute 'intervention in matters which are essentially within the domestic jurisdiction of States', in violation of Article 2(7) of the Charter.

After 1965, however, the situation changed. The principal reason was the large increase in Afro-Asian members of the

United Nations and the increase in the membership of the Commission on Human Rights. The enlargement of the Commission was intended to encourage the participation of new members, who soon showed they were particularly concerned with such problems as racial discrimination and apartheid, colonialism and economic development.

The new orientation of the Commission, and the organisation as a whole, produced a refreshing change of attitude towards the role of the United Nations with regard to human rights. In 1966 the General Assembly in Resolution 2144(XX) invited the Economic and Social Council and the Commission 'to give urgent consideration to ways and means of improving the capacity of the United Nations to put a stop to violations of human rights wherever they might occur'. One of the consequences was a proposal by the Commission that it should be permitted to examine 'communications, together with replies of governments, if any, which appear to reveal a consistent pattern of gross violations of human rights'. In 1970 this step was approved by the Economic and Social Council in its Resolution 1503, which authorised the Commission to perform this function. The system is therefore known as 'the Resolution 1503 procedure'.[3]

Following the Council's authorisation, the Commission set up an elaborate procedure for processing communications involving a body called the Sub-Commission on Prevention of Discrimination and Protection of Minorities.[4] The Sub-Commission is a body of twenty-six independent experts which was created by the Commission in 1947 to assist it in its work. Under the Resolution 1503 procedure a Working Group of the Sub-Commission, containing one member from each of the five regional groups, screens all communications for admissibility before the meeting of the full Sub-Commission, which takes place in Geneva every August. Communications which pass the Working Group are reviewed by the Sub-Commission, which decides in each case whether to keep the matter under review, to pass it to the Commission, or to take no action. The Sub-Commission's proceedings are normally public, as is its voting; however, this item of the agenda is considered in closed session and voting is by secret ballot.

Although the Resolution 1503 procedure is confidential, in 1978 the chairperson of the Commission began the practice of

announcing which countries have been the subject of consideration. We therefore know that the Sub-Commission normally
sends its parent body six to ten cases each year from a
significantly larger number that are considered. Communications
which reach the Commission go first to its Working Group on
Situations and are then examined by the full Commission. The
Commission's Working Group makes recommendations as to how
situations should be dealt with, but has no screening function.
Thus all situations referred by the Sub-Commission are
considered by the Commission, which is free to accept or reject
its Working Group's recommendations.[5]

When deciding what action, if any, should be taken the
Commission has a number of options available. At one extreme it
can simply decide to discontinue consideration;[6] at the other, it
can decide to transfer the case to the public Resolution 1235
procedure, described below, or, with the consent of the State
concerned, it can appoint an *ad hoc* conciliation committee with
the aim of finding a friendly solution. Intermediate possibilities
are to appoint an independent expert or special rapporteur for the
country concerned, to request further information from the
government, or to keep the situation under review, all of which
decisions lead to the situation being considered again in the
following year. How the Commission decides to deal with a given
situation in practice is likely to depend on political considerations.

When the Resolution 1503 procedure was set up, many saw it
as an important breakthrough and a move away from a neglect of
human rights which had been described by the Secretary-General
as 'bound to lower the prestige and authority not only of the
Commission on Human Rights but of the United Nations in the
opinion of the general public'.[7] How far have the expectations
invested in this procedure been realised?

Criticism of the procedure has tended to focus on two of its
prominent features: its confidential nature and its apparent lack
of effectiveness.[8] Critics of the confidentiality of the procedure
seem to assume that the best way to change behaviour is by
confrontation, but in international affairs, as in personal
relations, this is not always the case. Significantly, confidentiality
is a feature of the initial stage of proceedings under the European
Convention on Human Rights and, as we shall see shortly, the

United Nations Commission has a public procedure available in situations where this is appropriate. Moreover, although the procedure under Resolution 1503 is confidential, it is certainly not secret. Communications relating to the States under review are seen in summary by the twenty-six experts of the Sub-Commission and the fifty-three government representatives on the Commission. These bodies are naturally also informed of the government's response and as a result have access to the available information on the situation in the country concerned. A procedure which was both confidential and secret would clearly be open to objection on the ground that governments would have no compelling reason to improve their behaviour. Under the Resolution 1503 procedure, however, there is a sufficient degree of openness for the desire to avoid embarrass-ment to be significant.

This brings us to the second point, which concerns the effectiveness of the system. Here the criticism is that the procedure is not only highly politicised, but also cumbersome and slow. As a result, and because in addition the whole procedure is confidential, for long periods of time nothing appears to be happening. Is this then a system which achieves results, or is it one which promises more than it can deliver?

Any procedure for protecting human rights must ultimately be judged by its results and it is right that the Resolution 1503 should be assessed from this point of view. Before rejecting the confidential procedure as ineffective, however, we should be clear about what this kind of arrangement is meant to achieve. The objective is not, as is sometimes assumed, to register convictions against a State and then pass the decision elsewhere for enforcement. If this were so, criticism of the slowness and complexity of the procedure would certainly be justified. But this is not the aim. Rather the aim is to establish a dialogue with the government concerned and to make it clear, on the one hand, that if there is no improvement consideration of the case will continue, and on the other that co-operation will be rewarded.

Since the object of the procedure is not to produce a judgement but to maintain discreet political pressure, the complexity of the procedure is actually an advantage, for as a member of the Sub-Commission has observed:

Everything which induces a government to cooperate is particularly
important because the efficacy of United Nations procedures in the
field of human rights depends to a large extent, on the measure of
dialogue which can be established between the United Nations and
the government of the country concerned. The procedure is useful as
long as it is a means of exercising pressure on the country concerned.
By expressing regrets when communications are kept pending ...
instead of being forwarded to the superior organ, human rights
friends overlook the point that there is no real solution to the
problem at the end of the procedure. The succession of steps
composing the procedure is more influential than the actual step
itself.[9]

Because the procedure is confidential it is, of course, difficult to
know precisely what effect it has on governments' behaviour. As
we pointed out earlier, however, governments are sensitive to
criticism on human rights matters. As a result, arrangements
which have the effect of drawing attention to their shortcomings,
whether publicly or through the Commission's confidential
procedure, can all be regarded as useful. Although it would be
wrong to exaggerate the significance of the Resolution 1503
procedure, we can therefore conclude that it fulfils a modest but
constructive role. Specifically, three advantages of dealing with
human rights complaints through this procedure may be
identified.

First, it provides a way of bringing abuses of human rights to
the attention of international bodies in circumstances where this
might not otherwise occur. Governments, as we have seen, are
often reluctant to take up human rights cases and the procedure
under the Optional Protocol to the Covenant on Civil and
Political Rights, which allows individuals to initiate proceedings,
is binding on only a limited number of States. Anyone, however,
can write to the United Nations and ask to have a case considered
by the Sub-Commission. There is naturally no guarantee that a
complaint will be taken up, but the evidence suggests that
complaints which are numerous and serious are unlikely to be
ignored, which was certainly not the position before the
confidential procedure became available.

The second advantage of the Resolution 1503 procedure is that
once a human rights issue is on the international agenda, the
government concerned has an incentive to do something about it.

As we saw in Chapter 2, this is true of human rights procedures generally, but the distinctive features of the confidential procedure are that, being confidential, it may sometimes be more effective than more dramatic methods and that, because it is so elaborate, it provides a way of maintaining pressure on a government almost indefinitely.

The third advantage is that dealing with the human rights situation in a country through the confidential procedure may make it easier for the Commission to take the next step and deal with it through its public procedure. As we shall see shortly, many of the Commission's public investigations of the situation of human rights in a particular country have been preceded by consideration of communications under the confidential procedure. Although therefore the Resolution 1503 procedure may not in itself bring about a change of practice, it can sometimes prepare the way for the use of other procedures which may have the desired effect.

## III. Investigation of particular countries

In June 1967 the Economic and Social Council adopted Resolution 1235, in which it approved the Commission's decision to give annual consideration to an item entitled 'Questions of the violation of human rights and fundamental freedoms, including policies of racial discrimination and segregation and of apartheid, in all countries, with particular reference to colonial and other dependent countries and territories'.[10] Like Resolution 1503, this was the result of the renewed interest in human rights shown by General Assembly Resolution 2144 and, like the confidential procedure, has been extensively used.

The Resolution 1235 procedure, which is public, can be initiated by a member State, or group of States, or by the Sub-Commission on Prevention of Discrimination and Protection of Minorities. The Sub-Commission's role is particularly important as resolutions relating to individual countries which it passes in August are considered by the Commission when it meets in the New Year, along with any situations raised by member States. As a result, when the Sub-Commission reaches this item on its agenda its members are subjected to intensive lobbying by NGOs and governments, the former anxious to see that resolutions relating to specific countries are passed, the latter, on the other hand, trying to tone them down, or avoid condemnation altogether.

The Commission itself decides whether or not to act on any proposal that is made, and its decision, as might be expected, is generally influenced by political considerations. If the Commission decides to make a thorough study of a particular situation, it may appoint a working group or a special rapporteur to study and report, or ask the Secretary-General to do so. It may also adopt a resolution condemning a situation and notify the government concerned. A milder alternative is to appoint an expert to provide 'advisory services'. This is normally used when the situation in a particular country is improving, perhaps on account of a change of government, but the Commission wishes to oversee the situation. In all cases it will report, through the Council, to the General Assembly.

Consideration of human rights abuses in particular countries through the public procedure is now one of the major items on the Commission's agenda. In 1995 no less than fourteen experts were reporting to the Commission as special rapporteurs or special representatives, including two appointed at emergency sessions of the Commission on former Yugoslavia (1992) and Rwanda (1994).[11] In addition, the Secretary-General was preparing reports at the Commission's request on a further four countries and five others were receiving advisory services.[12] Moreover, at its 1994 session the Sub-Commission had adopted resolutions, declarations or presidential statements in relation to several more countries which the Commission also had to consider. This scale of activity, however, is relatively new. An outline of earlier practice may therefore be useful to show how the present position was arrived at and demonstrate the procedure in action.

The earliest examples of the public investigation of the situation in a particular country were the Ad Hoc Working Group of Experts on the situation of human rights in Southern Africa and the Special Committee to investigate Israeli practices in the Occupied Territories. The Working Group was created by the Commission in 1967 originally to report on the treatment of prisoners in South Africa, although its mandate was subsequently broadened to include Namibia and the remaining colonial territories. The Special Committee was created by the General Assembly in 1968, in response to Israel's occupation of various Arab territories in the war of the previous year. Neither body was able to visit the areas it was concerned with as the States concerned refused to co-operate, but both prepared regular reports based on visits to neighbouring countries and other sources which were considered by the Commission. With the ending of apartheid the Working Group presented its final report in 1995, but the Special Committee continues to report to the Commission and the General Assembly.[13]

Although the investigations just mentioned were concerned with particular countries, neither was based on Resolution 1235. The first investigation of that type was carried out by the Ad Hoc Working Group on the situation of human rights in Chile, following the coup d'état in that country in 1973. The situation was discussed at the Commission at the beginning of 1974 and in the summer the Sub-Commission requested the Commission to study the situation in detail at its next session, at the same time inviting governments and NGOs with information about torture and inhuman treatment in Chile to submit it to the Commission. In the autumn of 1974 the General Assembly supported this request and asked the Commission to undertake an investigation. At its session in February 1975 the Commission decided to do so, appointed an Ad Hoc Working Group of five members, and asked the Chilean government to grant to it all necessary facilities. At first the government promised to do so, but then had second thoughts and refused to admit the Group. They were therefore unable to visit the country and obliged to use information from other sources. On this basis the Working Group, whose mandate was renewed annually, submitted several reports to the General Assembly and the Commission in which they concluded that flagrant violations of human rights continued to take place in Chile. In 1978 the government finally agreed to a two-week visit by the Ad Hoc Working Group, during the course of which it had meetings with government officials and judges, and representatives of the churches and private organisations. It also visited detention centres and interviewed prisoners. In its reports to the General Assembly and the Commission it stated that the human rights situation had improved to a certain extent, but that there were still frequent and serious violations.

In 1979 the Commission again demanded that the Chilean government take measures to restore human rights in Chile, decided to continue to follow the situation in that country and appointed a special rapporteur for the purpose. This put an end to the mission of the Ad Hoc Working Group itself, but not to the interest of the United Nations, for successive rapporteurs continued to report annually to the Commission and the General Assembly. Though the proceedings of the Working Group had been slow and fraught with difficulties, they were the first case of a United Nations mission of inquiry carried out on the territory of a member State and, as such, were to prove an important precedent.

The appointment of a special rapporteur to examine the situation of human rights in a particular country was next used in the case of Equatorial Guinea.[14] Originally the examination of complaints against the Macias dictatorship in that country was undertaken as a confidential procedure under Resolution 1503. But in 1978 the Commission decided to make a public inquiry under Resolution 1235 and appointed a special rapporteur. In August 1979 Macias was overthrown in a coup d'état, following which the special rapporteur was able to visit the country and investigate the situation. The Commission considered his report in 1980. It indicated a considerable improvement as regards respect for human rights, and appealed to the Commission to provide Equatorial Guinea with assistance which the new government wished to receive in order to restore human rights on its territory. In 1981 the Commission requested the Secretary-General to draw up a draft plan of action. This was done and in 1984 the Commission asked the Secretary-General to appoint an expert to advise on its implementation. The expert, who was in fact the former rapporteur, visited the country again and reported that although progress had been made, other measures, including modifications to the constitution, were needed. The Commission took note of this and requested the Secretary-General to appoint a further expert to assist the government in implementing the plan of action.

The investigations undertaken by the Commission during the same period in Bolivia, El Salvador and Guatemala followed a broadly similar pattern.[15] In each case, study of the situation was begun under the Resolution 1503 procedure and subsequently broadened. In each case also the Commission was assisted by information obtained through visits to the territory. Here, as in the Equatorial Guinea case, the Commission benefited from co-operation from the government with the result that the procedure lost its adversarial character and became more of a consultative exercise. Later cases, however, have underlined the lessons of the Commission's earlier experience with Chile, that governments are not usually anxious to have their record on human rights investigated, and so the Commission's representatives may find themselves working under severe handicaps.

A case in point is the Commission's attempt to deal with the situation in Afghanistan. In February 1980 the Commission condemned the Soviet invasion of that country which had taken place two months earlier and began to review the situation there under the confidential procedure. In 1984 this review was discontinued when the Commission decided to appoint a special rapporteur and the chairperson of the Commission appointed Professor F. Ermacora of Austria to the post later in the same year. The special rapporteur received no co-operation from the authorities in Afghanistan, but, after visiting Pakistan, made the first of a series of reports to the Commission at the beginning of 1985.

In a long and detailed report,[16] running to nearly 200 paragraphs, the rapporteur examined the political and historical background to the situation, the impact of recent events on civil and political rights, economic and social rights, and self-determination, and considered the state of human rights in the armed conflict which was in progress. Among the recommendations of the report were: that the government of Afghanistan should respect its international obligations and stop torturing its political opponents; that all the parties to the conflict should meet with a view to restoring normality; that all parties to the conflict should also respect their obligations under humanitarian law and accept the supervision of an organisation such as the Red Cross; and finally that the rights of the 4,000,000 Afghan refugees to return to their homes should be recognised and that a general amnesty should be declared for everyone, regardless of their political opinions.

In spite of his inability to visit Afghanistan, the special rapporteur succeeded in producing a remarkably comprehensive report which contributed to the pressure on the Soviet Union, as the key protagonist, in the Commission on Human Rights and elsewhere. The mandate of the special rapporteur was regularly reviewed, terminating only in 1995 when the Soviet occupation of Afghanistan was a matter of history. The part which the pressure of monitoring by the Commission played in the eventual Soviet decision to withdraw can only be a matter of speculation. It is a cause for satisfaction, however, that in a situation in which the co-operation of the State under review was non-existent, it was nevertheless possible to conduct investigations which shed valuable light on the situation and may have influenced subsequent events.

Lack of co-operation from the government whose activities are under investigation is one obstacle to the Commission's work. Another, which has already been mentioned, is the intrusion of political considerations into the Commission's decisions. The essential point here is that it is only when a majority in the General Assembly or the Commission on Human Rights are prepared to offend a given State that action will be taken. Thus relatively friendless States such as Chile following the military coup, Israel and South Africa in the days of apartheid are vulnerable, whereas proposals to investigate human rights in China or the Uganda of Idi Amin have been rejected for reasons which have nothing to do with the country's human rights record, but simply reflect the voting strength of the different regional groups in the United Nations.

The political character of the work of the Commission may be illustrated by considering its treatment of specific countries in a typical year. In 1994 the Commission adopted resolutions concerning eighteen countries under this item.[17] These, however, did not include China, as a resolution relating to that country and sponsored by the United States and the European Union was defeated on a procedural motion. Among the eighteen resolutions were six relating to African States, an unusually high number. However, two of these concerned only advisory services (Burundi and Angola), two (on Equatorial Guinea and Togo) were diluted by amendments, while the resolution on Sudan was adopted after a debate in which the government accused the special rapporteur of being an enemy of Islam. Other States which were considered included Cuba, where a resolution was passed but the government announced that it would not co-operate with the special rapporteur, Iran, where lobbying by the government failed to defeat the resolution, but ensured that it received less support than the previous year, and Jammu-Kashmir, where a resolution was proposed by Pakistan, but withdrawn owing to strenuous opposition from India.

The controversy occasioned by the Commission's annual consideration of resolutions on specific countries, which, as indicated earlier, is also present in the Sub-Commission, suggests that governments care enough about avoiding criticism for the Resolution 1235 procedure, and the monitoring arrangements it can generate, to be worthwhile. Getting a particular country considered under the public procedure and then maintaining momentum are a matter of securing and retaining the necessary political support. If this can be done, as in the cases mentioned earlier, the effect of the Commission's activity will depend on a government's concern for its reputation. An intransigent government will at least be inconvenienced, while a co-operative government can seek and be provided with assistance. In either case, a public investigation, like the confidential procedure which it often follows, can provide governments with an incentive to improve their conduct.

### IV. Investigation of particular issues

The last type of Commission procedure which needs to be considered is the appointment of special working groups, or individual rapporteurs, to examine a particular type of human rights issue.[18]

In 1980 the Commission on Human Rights established a Working Group on Enforced and Involuntary Disappearances to deal with a problem which, as we shall see in Chapter 6, has also exercised the Inter-American Commission. Disappearances occur when governments adopt the practice of seizing people, or condoning their seizure by others, and then refuse to acknowledge the seizure and subsequent detention. The Working Group, which consists of five persons acting in an individual capacity, can receive information from governments, intergovernmental and non-governmental organisations, and individuals. Its chairperson may transmit reports of enforced or involuntary disappearances which are received between sessions of the Group and which call for urgent action directly to the government concerned, accompanied by a request for information.

In its annual reports to the Commission the Working Group discusses disappearances in specific named countries and puts forward recommendations. The scale and importance of the problem of enforced and involuntary disappearances are made starkly evident in these reports. In 1993, for example, the Working Group received more than 5,500 new cases of disappearances from over thirty countries, and after verification transmitted more than half to the governments concerned for comment. Urgent appeals were addressed to fifteen countries, while the report mentions fifty-four countries as having un-resolved cases from previous years. In December 1992 the General Assembly adopted the Declaration on Enforced Disappearances[19] and the Working Group, with the support of the Commission, now monitors the implementation of the Declaration as part of its mandate.

As with the investigation of particular countries, the Com-mission sometimes prefers to appoint a special rapporteur to conduct a thematic investigation, instead of a working group. This happened in 1982 when the Commission requested its chairperson to appoint a special rapporteur on summary and arbitrary executions. Soon afterwards Mr Amos Wako of Kenya was appointed and submitted his first report in 1983. In it he assembled data extending back over the previous twenty years and used this as the basis for both a general analysis of the phenomenon and a more detailed study of its recent manifest-ations. The special rapporteur's mandate was then extended and in subsequent reports he dealt with current developments. The rapporteur, whose mandate covers abuse of the death penalty, death in detention, genocide and extradition if life would be endangered, employs working methods similar to those of the Working Group on Disappearances – receiving communications, making visits and reporting to the Commission.

Again, such reports reveal an alarming situation. Thus in 1993 the rapporteur addressed more than 200 appeals concerning 1,300 persons to the governments of fifty-two countries, while communications concerning no less than seventy-four countries were examined. The rapporteur also reported on visits to Rwanda and Peru. In the former he confirmed massive disregard of the right to life during the civil war and put forward a series of recommendations to the authorities. In the latter he criticised the use of military courts and of impunity and emphasised that political instability could not excuse murder and kidnappings by the government.

Torture is another fundamental issue of human rights to call for the services of a special rapporteur. The Convention against Torture and Other Cruel, Inhuman or Degrading Treatment or Punishment was adopted in 1984 and establishes a special procedure for investigating complaints of torture which will be described later. However, the Convention did not come into force immediately and in any case only creates obligations for the parties. In 1985 therefore the Commission decided to expedite matters and authorise a comprehensive treatment of the problem by appointing a special rapporteur. Accordingly, a rapporteur was appointed whose function is to respond to allegations of torture and to investigate how and where it occurs.

The work of the special rapporteur involves the same kinds of activities as those of the special rapporteur on summary executions. Information is sought from governments about cases which are presented and an urgent appeal will be sent where a person has been arrested and there is reason to fear that he or she may be tortured. An urgent appeal will also be made when there is a possibility of extradition to a country where a person may be tortured. In 1993 the rapporteur presented his own observations on the responses of several governments; he can also make visits and formulate recommendations. Although his mandate refers only to 'torture', the special rapporteur has indicated that he will not interpret this term strictly and is prepared to consider practices in the 'grey area' between torture and other forms of serious ill-treatment. It is also worth noting that since 1982 the United Nations has had a Voluntary Fund for Victims of Torture,[20] although this does not come within the remit of the special rapporteur.

Studies of particular issues of human rights have also been undertaken by the Sub-Commission on Prevention of Discrimination and Protection of Minorities. In 1981 the Sub-Commission set up a Working Group on Indigenous Populations.[21] The Group, which held its first meeting in August 1982, has the task of following developments with regard to the rights of indigenous peoples and identifying and formulating standards relating to such rights, which has included finding a way of defining the relevant populations and protecting them from physical destruction and threats to their culture. In 1994 the Working Group completed its preparation of a draft Declaration on the Rights of Indigenous Peoples and passed it on to the Commission. The Working Group, which reports to the Sub-Commission, holds annual sessions which are attended by NGOs and the representatives of indigenous groups and provides the main forum for discussing indigenous issues in the UN. Although the Working Group does not consider individual complaints, it accepts oral and written information from those attending and has indicated that it will give special attention to gross and persistent violations of human rights.

The Sub-Commission has also established a Working Group on Contemporary Forms of Slavery.[22] This is concerned with a practice which, as we have seen, has been the subject of international attention since the last century, but which in various forms is unfortunately still prevalent in some parts of the world. Contemporary forms of slavery which fall within the Working Group's remit include the sale and prostitution of children, child pornography, debt-based servitude, forced labour, street children, child soldiers, trafficking in human organs, incest, exploitation of migrant labour and sex tourism. Like the Working Group on Indigenous Populations, the Group reports to the Sub-Commission and can receive information from NGOs with consultative status, which may also attend its meetings, where they make an indispensable contribution to its work.

The question of religious intolerance and discrimination has the distinction of being the subject of investigations by both the Sub-Commission and the Commission. In 1981, as we have mentioned, the General Assembly adopted its Declaration on the Elimination of All Forms of Intolerance and of Discrimination based on Religion or Belief. This established certain standards, but contains no implementation provisions; accordingly, in 1986 the Commission appointed a special rapporteur, who since 1987 has examined incidents of religious intolerance and discrimination, reported on compliance with the Declaration and recommended remedial measures. The Sub-Commission's involvement was somewhat earlier, for in 1983 it had appointed a special rapporteur with a very similar mandate. It is interesting to note that one of the points made by both rapporteurs was that consideration should be given to producing a convention on the subject of religious discrimination to consolidate the principles set out in the Declaration. However, the first attempt to draft such a convention had to be abandoned in the face of problems which seemed insuperable. With the current rise of religious extremism, a fresh look at this project would be well justified.[23]

Another significant development of the thematic approach took place in 1991 when the Commission created a Working Group on Arbitrary Detention.[24] Composed of five independent experts, the Group can investigate all forms of arbitrarily imposed detention, including administrative detention, and reports annually to the Commission. As with the other thematic procedures, the Group receives individual communications, which are passed for comment to the government concerned, but can also take decisions on the nature of the disputed detention, so giving it a quasi-judicial role. Urgent appeals can be made to governments on humanitarian grounds and the Group has indicated its readiness to carry out visits where this might be useful. Discussion of the Group's report provides NGOs with an opportunity to put further pressure on governments at the Commission. The mandate of the Working Group on Arbitrary Detention was originally for three years, but has been extended.

In recent years the Commission has widened the scope of its thematic procedures by a number of further initiatives. In 1992 a representative of the Secretary-General was asked to report on strengthening the protection of persons displaced within their own country, often as a result of internal armed conflicts.[25] In the following year a special rapporteur was appointed for an initial period of three years to study racism, racial discrimination, xenophobia and other forms of intolerance. Several initiatives of this kind have been prompted by timely urging from the Sub-Commission. Thus in 1990 the Commission appointed a special rapporteur on the sale of children, child prostitution and child pornography, following the highlighting of these subjects by the Sub-Commission's Working Group on Contemporary Forms of Slavery, and in 1993 and 1994 appointed special rapporteurs on freedom of expression and the independence of the judiciary to

follow up work on these topics by individual members of the Sub-
Commission. In 1994 the Commission also turned its attention to
the issue of violence against women and here too appointed a
special rapporteur, the step being prompted on this occasion by
the emphasis on women's rights at the World Conference on
Human Rights in 1993 and the General Assembly's adoption of
the Declaration on the Elimination of Violence against Women[26]
in the same year.

Although there is an obvious difference between investigating the
state of human rights in a particular country and undertaking a
worldwide study of an issue such as torture or slavery, the purpose
of the two types of procedure is essentially the same. Both are
concerned with the collecting of information, not as an end itself,
but as a means of keeping questions of human rights on the
international agenda and enabling pressure to be put on
governments to remedy abuses. Since the aim is to change
governmental behaviour, the country type of investigation with its
sharper focus may seem superior to the thematic approach we have
been describing. In fact this is not so, and the thematic approach
has several advantages, which account for its increasing popularity.

First and most obviously there is the point that thematic
surveys can cover a much larger number of countries than could
ever be dealt with in country-type investigations. Since the United
Nations is concerned with the protection of human rights
everywhere, it is clearly important to have the geographical net
spread as widely as possible, and this is something only thematic
investigations can do.

The point about geographical spread is reinforced by a second
consideration, which is political. There is, as we have seen, an
unwillingness on the part of the Commission to investigate
certain countries. If, then, human rights practices in these places
are to be investigated at all, it has to be by means of the thematic
approach. Naturally, political considerations can come into play
here also, but the nature of the exercise means that they have
much less scope. The fact that in many cases the thematic type of
investigation and the country type of investigation are not true
alternatives therefore constitutes another advantage of the
thematic approach.

Finally there is the point that for some human rights issues the
thematic approach is essential if the issue is to be tackled sensibly.

Mass exoduses,[27] for example, which involve a worldwide movement of populations, can be dealt with properly only by considering the problem as a whole. The same may be said of slavery and related practices, which can also involve the crossing of frontiers, and the rights of indigenous peoples, where comparative review is particularly instructive. Even issues such as torture or arbitrary executions, which can be exposed by a country-oriented investigation (if it is permitted), can be illuminated by the thematic approach.

While there are therefore circumstances in which the country type of investigation is undoubtedly useful, the thematic approach offers a way of investigating specific issues which is already being used extensively, and which students of the United Nations are likely to see even more of in the future.

## V. Monitoring treaty compliance

A number of the human rights treaties adopted by the United Nations include arrangements for monitoring the way the standards they contain have been implemented by the States parties. There are currently seven treaties of this type in force. One, the UN Covenant on Civil and Political Rights, has already been described; another, the Covenant on Economic, Social and Cultural Rights, will be examined in Chapter 8. The other five will be described in this section. As we shall see, each convention is different. However, the supervisory bodies face a number of common problems. Before considering the treaties concerned individually, it may therefore be useful to draw attention to these problems and to say something about what is being done to resolve them.

All five conventions use a reporting system like that of the Covenant on Civil and Political Rights as the main, and in some cases the only, method of supervision. It has already been explained that such arrangements require the co-operation of States if they are to work and that in the case of the Covenant this has not always been forthcoming, with many States submitting late or inadequate reports and others failing to report at all. The experience of the other treaty bodies has been similar.[28] While there are differences in the reporting record among the various conventions, and some States discharge all their obligations conscientiously, the problem of overdue reports has been a major one for all the treaty bodies.

A second problem concerns resources. The underfunding of human rights activities which hampers the Human Rights Committee has a similar effect on the other treaty mechanisms. Sessions must be kept short, which makes it difficult to get through the business in the time available, and on occasion have had to be cancelled in order to save money. None of the treaty bodies has the kind of administrative support which would be taken for granted in a government department or commercial organisation and the treaties themselves do not always provide the best or most efficient arrangements.

A third general problem concerns the obligations which States have assumed for, when ratifying the various conventions, many have attached far-reaching reservations to their acceptances. Reservations are normally permitted and when they relate to minor matters are not in principle objectionable. However, some reservations are so extensive as to make the State's assumption of obligations under the convention concerned more nominal than real. The legal validity of reservations of this kind can, of course, be questioned.[29] However, there is as yet no obligatory procedure through which this can be tested. Accordingly, when the treaty bodies are exercising their supervisory functions, they are frequently presented with situations in which a State invokes a reservation to deny or limit its obligations.

The problems just described reflect the limited commitment of many States to human rights, and so improvement is a long-term project. However, some progress has been made. Since 1984 the chairpersons of the seven treaty bodies have been meeting periodically to consider these and other issues and have formulated a number of recommendations in an effort to move things forward.[30] To encourage the submission of reports they have recommended that each treaty body should, as a last resort, consider the situation in States whose reports are long overdue, and some are now doing this. They have constantly pressed for more resources and, although there is a long way to go, they have succeeded in improving some of the more unsatisfactory funding arrangements.[31] As regards reservations, they have urged the individual treaty bodies to indicate when reservations are contrary to the object and purpose of the treaty and have themselves condemned such reservations in unequivocal terms.

Other matters on which the chairpersons have made constructive recommendations include the adoption of a common set of guidelines for national reports,[32] the closer involvement of NGOs and the specialised agencies in the work of the treaty bodies, succession to human rights treaties, early-warning measures and public information. What the chairpersons are doing to co-ordinate the work of the treaty bodies is clearly useful. It is now therefore time to examine the conventions in question separately.

### 1. *The International Convention on the Elimination of All Forms of Racial Discrimination*

This Convention, which was adopted by the General Assembly in December 1965, restates in a precise and more developed form the principles set out in the Declaration on the Elimination of All Forms of Racial Discrimination approved by the General Assembly in 1963.[33] In particular, the parties to this Convention: commit themselves to a policy of eliminating racial discrimination (Article 2); condemn racial segregation (Article 3); undertake to make it an offence to disseminate ideas based on racial superiority or hatred and to incite racial discrimination, and promise to declare illegal and prohibit organisations which engage in such activities (Article 4); guarantee the enjoyment of a wide range of specific rights on a non-discriminatory basis (Article 5); promise effective protection and remedies (Article 6); and undertake to adopt educational and other measures to combat prejudice (Article 7). These far-reaching commitments are then backed up by elaborate measures of implementation, which supplied the model for other UN instruments.

Supervision is the responsibility of the Committee on the Elimination of Racial Discrimination (CERD), which is provided for in Article 8.[34] The Committee consists of eighteen independent experts, elected for a four-year term, with three main functions. Article 9 requires the parties to report to the Committee 'on the legislative, judicial, administrative or other measures which they have adopted and which give effect to the provisions of the Convention'; Article 11 allows any State party to bring an alleged violation of the Convention to the attention of the Committee; and Article 14 enables it to receive individual complaints. The reporting obligation is mandatory, as is submission to the inter-State procedure. However, the procedure under Article 14 is optional and, like the arrangements under the Optional Protocol to the Covenant on Civil and Political Rights, requires separate acceptance from the State concerned.

The Convention entered into force on 4 January 1969 and has now been ratified by more than 140 States, making it, for many years, the most widely ratified of all UN Conventions.[35] The Committee usually holds two sessions annually, each of three weeks. Consequently, although sessions have occasionally had to be cancelled for financial reasons, it has now accumulated a significant amount of experience, particularly with the reporting system. This is not only important as a means of supervising the Convention, but, as we saw in Chapter 2, has also influenced the practice and procedure of the Human Rights Committee.

The Convention requires reports to be submitted within one year of its entry into force for the State concerned and thereafter every two years or on request. The Committee has decided that comprehensive reports should be submitted every four years with brief updating reports in the intervening two-year periods. In 1972 the Committee was the first human rights organ to invite States to send a representative to take part in its proceedings when a report is under examination. Almost all States have accepted these invitations and in this way it has been possible to develop a constructive dialogue between the Committee and the governmental representatives, who can answer questions, give explanations and provide additional information. To assist States in preparing their reports CERD has now adopted the consolidated guidelines proposed by the treaty body chairpersons.

In its first twenty years CERD received nearly 900 reports, which indicates that many States are performing their reporting obligations. Others, however, are not, submitting reports which are late or lack the information required, or failing to submit reports at all. When a report is submitted late the Committee treats it as discharging the State's obligation in respect of all its overdue reports, which has the merit of enabling a single report to clear any backlog, but can scarcely be said to encourage diligent reporting. CERD does, however, also now follow the practice recommended by the chairpersons and reviews the situation in States whose reports are long overdue. In 1994, for example, it undertook a study of six States which fell into this category.[36] It has also recently begun to request special reports in urgent cases and in 1994 adopted findings with regard to five States in this category.[37]

On completion of its examination of the situation in a particular State, CERD issues concluding observations in which it comments on the report and the party's implementation of the Convention. In addition to these individual observations, it has for many years also issued General Recommendations addressed to all the parties.[38] Seventeen such Recommendations were made between 1972 and 1993, most dealing with matters the Committee wished to see States addressing in their reports, or emphasising provisions the Committee sees as particularly significant. The majority are quite short, but No. 15 of 1993 is rather longer and of particular interest as it deals with the obligation under Article 4 to penalise the dissemination of racist ideas, and specifically with the relation between this obligation and the rights to freedom of association and freedom of expression, a controversial issue with important implications.[39]

As already noted, Article 14 of the Convention contains an optional provision for individual complaints. A State party may at any time declare that it recognises the competence of the Committee to consider communications from an individual or a group of individuals within its jurisdiction who claim to be the victim of a violation by that State of any of the provisions of the Convention. The procedure for dealing with such petitions is somewhat complicated. It involves investigation by the Committee, subject to certain safeguards including the exhaustion of domestic remedies, and although it does not lead to a binding decision, the Committee is authorised to make suggestions and recommendations. The procedure, which seems to have been partly inspired by the way the European Convention on Human Rights deals with the right of individual petition, required acceptance by ten States to bring it into force. This was not achieved until December 1982 and even now only a small number of States have made the necessary declarations.[40]

The limited acceptance of Article 14 means that so far the Committee has dealt with very few individual complaints.

However, two recent cases involving different aspects of the Convention show the procedure in operation. In the *Narrainen case*[41] in 1994, a Norwegian citizen of Tamil origin had been convicted by a court in Oslo of drug trafficking and complained that one of the members of the jury had been racially biased. Although there was some evidence to support the allegation, the Committee found that the matter had been fully investigated by the Norwegian court and dismissed the claim. At the same time, however, it recommended that the State give due attention to the impartiality of jurors, in accordance with Article 5(a) of the Convention and the requirement of equal treatment in the administration of justice.

In *LK v. Netherlands*[42] in 1993, on the other hand, the dispute concerned Article 6, which requires a victim of racial discrimination to be provided with effective protection and remedies through the tribunals of the States parties. The author of the communication was a Moroccan who lived in the Netherlands and was subject to racial abuse and threats when he visited a house which he was thinking of leasing, in Utrecht. Although he complained to the authorities, no action was taken under the article of the Criminal Code dealing with racial discrimination and the Committee found that in all the circumstances there had been a violation of Article 6. The Committee therefore recommended that the State party should review its handling of the decision to prosecute in cases of alleged racial discrimination in the light of its obligations under Article 4 of the Convention, and further recommended that it should provide the applicant with relief commensurate with the non-pecuniary loss he had suffered.

The inter-State procedure set out in Article 11 of the Convention has not so far been used. All that need be said about it therefore is that the Convention provides for any such complaint to be communicated to the State concerned, which then has three months to provide the Committee with a written explanation or statement clarifying the matter. If the matter is not resolved to the satisfaction of both parties, either State has the right to refer it to the Committee again and the chairperson must then appoint an *ad hoc* conciliation commission. Although States have been unwilling to use Article 11, they have on occasion criticised the conduct of other States in their periodic reports.[43]

Such 'disguised inter-State disputes' would be better raised under Article 11 but if the State concerned is unwilling to invoke that provision, the Committee must decide how far it is able to deal with the matter under Article 9.

As well as considering reports and individual communications, CERD has recently begun to take various other initiatives. In 1993, following its consideration of the special reports submitted by Croatia, Bosnia-Herzegovina and the Federal Republic of Yugoslavia, the Committee accepted an invitation to send one of its members on a 'good offices' mission to Croatia and persuaded the authorities in Yugoslavia to accept a similar mission. The results were discussed in private meetings in 1994. In that year CERD also reached decisions on terrorism, following attacks on Jewish organisations in London and Buenos Aires, took up the issue of State succession by urging republics of the former USSR that had not yet confirmed their adherence to the Convention to do so, and, following its study of the situation in Burundi, urged the Secretary-General to establish an international tribunal with jurisdiction over genocide and crimes against humanity.[44]


## 2. *The Convention on the Elimination of All Forms of Discrimination against Women*

This Convention was adopted by the General Assembly in December 1979. Although it is not the first convention to deal with women's rights, it is the first universal instrument to address the issue of discrimination and this, together with the fact that it contains arrangements for monitoring compliance, makes it of special interest in the present context.[45] The substantive provisions of the Convention cover a wide area of State conduct, but as they have been reviewed elsewhere,[46] they need not be examined in detail here.

Article 1 defines discrimination against women as:

> any distinction, exclusion or restriction made on the basis of sex which has the effect or purpose of impairing or nullifying the recognition, enjoyment or exercise by women, irrespective of their marital status, on a basis of equality of men and women, of human rights and fundamental freedoms in the political, social, cultural, civil or any other field.

This follows the approach of the Convention on the Elimination of All Forms of Racial Discrimination and, as in the earlier instrument, States undertake to adopt measures to promote the principle. Activities of this kind which are specifically mentioned include measures to suppress the exploitation of prostitution (Article 6); measures to eliminate sex discrimination in political and public life (Article 7); and equal rights in relation to nationality (Article 9), education (Article 10), employment (Article 11) and health care (Article 12). The Convention also provides for equality of the sexes with regard to marriage and family relations (Article 16), while recognising the legitimacy of 'special measures ... aimed at protecting maternity'.

The Convention deals with an issue of human rights of fundamental importance and the decision to supplement the very general provisions on discrimination to be found in such instruments as the Covenant on Civil and Political Rights was a positive step. Before moving on, however, we must mention that both the application and the interpretation of the Convention present certain difficulties. The fact that in some form or other sex discrimination is to be found in almost every country in the world makes this a vitally important issue, but means that persuading governments to implement their obligations fully is proving a long and difficult task. That is the problem of application. The problem of interpretation involves deciding how the rights created by the Convention relate to different and apparently conflicting rights under other human rights treaties. Article 5, for example, requires States to take 'all appropriate measures':

> (a) To modify the social and cultural patterns of conduct of men and women, with a view to achieving the elimination of prejudices and customary and all other practices which are based on the idea of the inferiority or the superiority of either of the sexes or on stereotyped roles for men and women.

It has been perceptively noted that this:

> might permit States to curtail to an undefined extent privacy and associational interests and the freedom of opinion and expression. Moreover since social and cultural behaviour may be patterned according to factors such as ethnicity or religion, state action ...

which is directed towards modifying the way in which a particular ethnic or religious group treats women may conflict with the principles forbidding discrimination on the basis of race or religion.[47]

While it is true that both the application and the interpretation of other treaties can give rise to similar problems, the subject matter of the present Convention is such as to pose them in a particularly acute form.

The Convention came into force on 3 September 1981 and has now been accepted by more than 100 States.[48] Supervision is the responsibility of the Committee on the Elimination of Discrimination against Women (CEDAW).[49] This consists of twenty-three experts elected by the parties and, like their counterparts on the Committee on the Elimination of Racial Discrimination, they sit in an independent capacity, not as representatives of their nominating States. The main functions of the Committee are set out in Articles 18 and 21 of the Convention. Under Article 18 the parties are to submit reports on the measures they have adopted to give effect to the provisions of the Convention. As in the Convention on Racial Discrimination, the first report must be submitted one year after the entry into force of the Convention for the State concerned, but then subsequently at four-year, rather than two-year, intervals. Article 21 authorises the Committee to make 'suggestions and general recommendations based on the examination of reports and information from the States parties'.

The Committee was convened for the first time shortly after the Convention came into force and soon began its work of reviewing State reports. Shortage of time, however, severely constrained its activities. Meeting as it normally does for only two weeks each year,[50] the Committee can review no more than ten reports annually and to achieve even this it must concentrate on initial reports and treat periodic reports very superficially. To speed up its work the Committee has a pre-sessional working group to prepare questions on periodic reports, but only so much can be achieved through such arrangements. It is fortunate that here, as elsewhere, many States fail to submit their reports, or the situation would be even more difficult. But a system which relies upon States ignoring their obligations is plainly unsatisfactory and without the resources and authority to hold longer meetings the impact of the reporting system will remain limited.

In addition to its annual report to the General Assembly,[51] the Committee, like most of the other treaty bodies, issues General Recommendations from time to time based on its experience in studying States' reports, or its desire to emphasise particular topics. More than twenty such Recommendations have been made since the first in 1986, and they have covered a wide range of subjects.[52] Several deal with the form and content of reports and indicate matters on which the Committee needs information. Many, on the other hand, concern substantive issues such as violence against women (Nos 12 and 19); equal pay (No. 13); female circumcision (No. 14); and equality in marriage and family relations (No. 21). Two Recommendations (Nos 4 and 20) deal with the important issue of reservations. This was necessary because many of the reservations which States have made to this Convention are of a particularly far-reaching character.[53] The Committee has therefore indicated that this situation is not acceptable and has urged the States concerned to consider withdrawing them.

The Committee's General Recommendations, together with its supervision of the reporting system, make a useful contribution in a key area of human rights. However, the control machinery provided in the Convention has aptly been described as 'modest'[54] and it is a matter for regret that there is as yet no provision authorising the Committee to deal with complaints by States, nor any procedure permitting claims by individuals, although the latter is now under consideration.[55] This, though, would be little use at present. As already indicated, what the Committee on the Elimination of Discrimination against Women needs most is more time, if it is to promote the objectives of this valuable Convention effectively.

### 3. The Convention against Torture and Other Cruel, Inhuman or Degrading Treatment or Punishment

This Convention was adopted by the General Assembly in December 1984 and provides a more detailed treatment of a subject which was first addressed in the Declaration on the Protection of All Persons from being subjected to Torture and Other Cruel, Inhuman or Degrading Treatment or Punishment, adopted by the General Assembly in 1975. Following the adoption of the Declaration, the General Assembly requested the Commission on Human Rights to draw up a draft convention in the light of its principles. In 1983 the Assembly urged the Commission to complete this work as a matter of urgency and added that it should include provisions for its effective implementation. This was carried out by a Working Group of the Commission and the final text, which the General Assembly called upon all governments to consider signing and ratifying 'as a matter of priority', was opened for signature in the following year.[56]

The first part of the Convention, which consists of Articles 1 to 16, establishes the scope of the Convention and the nature of the parties' obligations. Article 1 defines torture in a way which follows the earlier Declaration and rectifies an omission in the Covenant on Civil and Political Rights and other human rights agreements. The obligations which the Convention creates are quite extensive and include a duty on the part of each State to take measures to prevent acts of torture in any territory under its jurisdiction; a duty not to return people to countries where they may be subjected to torture; a duty to make torture a criminal offence and establish jurisdiction over it; a duty to prosecute or, where relevant, extradite persons charged with torture; a duty to co-operate with other States and ensure appropriate education and training for its own personnel; a duty to exclude evidence obtained by torture; and a duty to make a prompt investigation of allegations of torture and to provide a remedy for those who have been tortured. Many of the above obligations also extend to 'other acts of cruel, inhuman or degrading treatment or punishment' (Article 16), although these concepts, understandably, are not defined.

Articles 17 to 24, which make up the second part of the Convention, provide for the creation of a Committee against Torture to supervise its implementation.[57] Like the committees already considered, this Committee is made up of independent experts elected by the parties and for a term of four years. The Committee, which has ten members, performs three main functions. Under Article 19 it receives and considers reports from the parties as to the measures they have taken to give effect to their undertaking under the Convention. Under Article 21 a State may complain to the Committee that another State is not fulfilling its obligations. And under Article 22 the Committee is empowered to consider complaints from individuals. However, both the inter-State procedure and the power of the Committee to receive individual complaints require a declaration from the State or States concerned that it recognises the Committee's competence in this area.

Article 20 of the Convention provides that if the Committee receives 'reliable information' that torture is being systematically practised in the territory of a party it may invite the State to co-operate in examining the information, and whether co-operation is forthcoming or not, initiate a confidential inquiry. This procedure, unlike those laid down in Articles 21 and 22, is not subject to specific acceptance by the State concerned. However, Article 28 permits States which do not wish to be subject to the inquiry procedure to opt out by making a reservation to that effect when ratifying the Convention. Fortunately, only a handful have so far taken advantage of this opportunity. It is therefore open to the Committee to initiate an inquiry with regard to the majority of parties to the Convention, which means that Article 20 provides the Committee with a further power which can be useful.

The Convention came into force in June 1987, when it had been ratified by twenty States. The arrangements for inter-State complaints and individual complaints required acceptance by five States and came into force at the same time. There are now more than eighty parties to the Convention, of which about half have accepted the optional arrangements.[58] A protocol which would extend the powers of the Committee and enable it to make preventive visits to places of detention is currently under discussion.

The Committee against Torture was set up in November 1987 and although it is one of the newer supervisory bodies, it has a vigorous and developing practice. The Committee normally holds two sessions annually, each of two weeks' duration. Its main activity to date has been concerned with the reporting system. Here it has followed the practice of the other treaty bodies and has sought to establish a dialogue with States and, where necessary, supplementation of the report with further information. As with the other treaties, not all States have been willing to co-operate, some producing reports that are late or inadequate, others failing to produce reports at all. As far as possible, however, the Committee subjects reports to rigorous scrutiny and makes concluding comments on each report in which it evaluates the State's performance of its obligations under the Convention and puts forward recommendations. A notable feature of the Committee's recent practice has been the extensive use made of information provided by NGOs, not only in the remarks of individual experts, but also in the Committee's concluding comments.

The Committee's power to deal with complaints from individuals under Article 22 has not been widely used and so far only a handful of cases have been considered. To be eligible for examination, a communication must satisfy conditions of admissibility similar to those of the Covenant on Civil and Political Rights and the State concerned must, of course, have recognised the Committee's competence.[59] In one respect the admissibility requirements of the Convention are stricter than those of the Covenant because Article 21(5)(a) excludes claims which have been examined under another international procedure, and not just those which are currently being examined. As many of the States with declarations under Article 21 are parties to the European Convention on Human Rights this is a significant limitation. Cases found to be admissible are considered on their merits, although the Convention permits the Committee to do no more than 'forward its views' to the State and the individual; there is no provision for sanctions.

The earliest cases submitted to the Committee under Article 21 were all found to be inadmissible, but two recent cases which were decided on the merits indicate the value of the procedure. In the *Halimi-Nedzibi case*[60] in 1993, a Yugoslav citizen imprisoned in Austria claimed that he had been convicted on the basis of evidence obtained by torture contrary to Article 15 of the Convention and that the authorities had failed to investigate his allegations of torture, as required by Article 12. The Committee rejected the first claim on the facts, but upheld the second, requesting the State to avoid such violations in the future and to inform it of the measures adopted.

The *Bulabou Mutombo case*[61] in the following year was quite different. Here the petitioner had fled from Zaire and was living in Switzerland. The authorities wished to send him back to Zaire, but the petitioner claimed that if he was returned he would be tortured. Article 3 of the Convention expressly prohibits the return of a person in such circumstances and the Committee, after reviewing the petitioner's situation, upheld his claim. Interesting features of this case are that while the case was pending the Committee used its power to grant interim protection and asked Switzerland not to expel the petitioner, and that in justifying its conclusion the Committee referred to investigations of the situation in Zaire involving the thematic procedures of the Commission on Human Rights mentioned earlier.

The record with regard to Articles 20 and 21 of the Convention can be described very briefly. To date there have been no inter-State cases under Article 21; however, in 1993 the Committee announced that it had carried out its first confidential inquiry under Article 20. The State concerned was Turkey, where the Committee began an investigation in 1990 after receiving reports about torture there from NGOs. In its report on the situation,[62] which was presented to the General Assembly, the Committee confirmed that a systematic practice of torture had been carried out. Noting that legal measures to discourage the practice had been adopted, the Committee found that these had not yet been effectively implemented and put forward a series of far-reaching recommendations, relating both to long-term legal and administrative arrangements and to improvements in the treatment of detainees, requiring immediate implementation.

## 4. *The Convention on the Rights of the Child*

This Convention was adopted by the General Assembly in November 1989. Like the Convention against Torture, it deals with a subject which had earlier been the subject of a declaration, in this case the Declaration on the Rights of the Child, adopted by the General Assembly as long ago as 1959.[63] However, whereas the Declaration is quite short, the Convention is much more elaborate and also, of course, provides arrangements for supervising its obligations. This is the newest human rights treaty, but is already the most widely accepted, having been ratified with remarkable speed. It came into force in September 1990, when it had been ratified by twenty States, and now has more than 160 parties.[64]

The substantive provisions of the Convention are set out in the first part, which contains Articles 1 to 41. This is considerably longer than the corresponding sections of the other UN conventions, including the two Covenants, which is explained by the fact that the Convention not only includes numerous provisions which confer new rights, but also lists existing rights which are owed to everyone, in order to emphasise that children are entitled to them too. In the new rights category we find, for example, rights relating to fostering and adoption (Articles 20 and 21); rights to protection from sexual and other exploitation (Articles 32 to 36); and recognition of the special position of children in the legal process (Article 40). Rights of a more general character that are mentioned in the Convention include the right to life (Article 6); freedom of expression (Article 13); respect for privacy (Article 16);[65] and the right to education (Article 28).

For the purposes of the Convention the term 'child' means everyone below the age of eighteen, 'unless, under the law applicable to the child, majority is attained earlier' (Article 1). The obligation of the States parties, as one would expect, is to respect and ensure the rights set out in the Convention for each child within their jurisdiction without discrimination (Article 2). With regard to civil and political rights this obligation is unqualified; however, the Convention contains many guarantees relating to health, social security, welfare and other economic, social and cultural rights, and here the States' obligation is to undertake the necessary measures 'to the maximum extent of their available resources and, where needed, within the framework of international co-operation' (Article 4). Underlying the whole Convention is the proposition that children are entitled to human rights in their own capacity and its corollary, laid down in Article 3, that in all official actions concerning children 'the best interests of the child shall be a primary consideration'.

The second part of the Convention, containing Articles 42 to 45, deals with implementation. These provide for the creation of the Committee on the Rights of the Child, which, like the other treaty bodies, is made up of independent experts elected by the States parties.[66] The Committee is ten in number and its members' term of office is four years, with a possibility of re-election. As with CEDAW, the Committee has only one function, namely to consider the reports submitted by the parties (Article 44). Given the subject matter this limitation is understandable, while the near universal acceptance of the Convention means that in any case the Committee has found itself fully occupied with reviewing States' reports. It is therefore probably just as well that the Convention makes no provision for inter-State cases or individual petitions.

The Committee held its first session in October 1991, when it dealt with various procedural matters. These were discussed further at its second session the following year and it began reviewing reports at its third session in January 1993. It was initially thought that one three-week annual session would be all that was necessary, but as the Convention gained more and more parties it soon became clear that more would be needed. The Committee therefore held an extra session in 1991 and in the following year held three sessions, which the General Assembly has now accepted as the general pattern. Nevertheless, even allowing for the failure of some States to produce their reports, the Committee is likely to be hard pressed to avoid accumulating a backlog.

The Convention requires reports to be submitted within two years of its entry into force and thereafter every five years (Article 44(1)). The Committee in turn reports on its activities to the General Assembly every two years. The method of reviewing reports is similar to that used by the other Committees, with representatives of the reporting State invited to attend and answer questions. To speed things up lists of questions prepared by a pre-sessional Working Group are given to the State representatives before they present their reports. A feature of this process is that when the questions are being prepared, the Working Group invites views from NGOs, thus ensuring that the Committee has independent information to appraise reports, which as we have seen is so important.[67]

When the Committee has completed its review of each report it expresses its findings in the form of Concluding Observations. These use the same format as those of the Human Rights Committee, commenting first on the adequacy and timeliness of the report and going on to identify the positive aspects of the State's record, any difficulties in implementing the Convention, followed by subjects of concern to the Committee, and ending with its suggestions and recommendations. Like the Human

Rights Committee, the Committee on Children's Rights often criticises reports as being insufficiently informative and has performed its task in a dispassionate and constructive manner, finding room for improvement in every State's practice.[68]

In the relatively short period it has been in existence, the Committee has been extremely active and, as well as reviewing States' reports, has already taken a number of noteworthy initiatives in furtherance of children's rights. One of its earliest decisions was to devote one day each year to a general discussion of a specific issue. The first such discussion took place in 1992 on the subject of children in armed conflict; the second, in 1993, was on the economic exploitation of children; and the third, in 1994, on the role of the family.[69] Again, NGOs played a prominent part, as did UNICEF, UNHCR and a number of specialised agencies. The 1993 discussion led to the formulation of a series of recommendations on prevention and protection. Members of the Committee have undertaken missions to various countries and a procedure for early warning and urgent action has been developed. Finally, two proposals for optional protocols to the Convention have been put to the Commission: one on children in armed conflicts, based on the 1992 discussion; and the other on the question of child prostitution and pornography.[70]

### 5. The International Convention on the Suppression and Punishment of the Crime of Apartheid

This Convention was adopted by the General Assembly in November 1973.[71] It declares that apartheid is a crime against humanity entailing international responsibility. The parties to the Convention undertake to adopt measures to prevent and discourage apartheid and similar segregationist policies and to punish it as a crime wherever committed. The Convention came into force in July 1976 and currently has almost 100 parties.[72]

The arrangements for supervising this Convention are unusual because, unlike the other treaties, there is no committee of independent experts. Instead, Article 9 directs the chairperson of the Commission to appoint three of its members, who are also parties to the Convention, to supervise its implementation. The so-called Group of Three, which was active for almost twenty years, had the function of receiving reports required by Article 7 in which the parties described how they were implementing the Convention.[73] The work of the Group of Three was essentially a way of exerting pressure on South Africa during the period of white minority rule. As such, the activities of the Group are now only of historical interest. In recognition of its reduced importance the Commission decided in 1991 that annual meetings of the Group, which had been the practice hitherto, were no longer necessary, and in 1995 decided to suspend its meetings indefinitely.[74] This winding up of the supervisory arrangements, of course, leaves the Convention itself unaffected.

## VI. The Commissioner for Human Rights

In December 1993 the General Assembly approved Resolution 48/141, creating the post of UN High Commissioner for Human Rights.[75] As we have seen, the idea of a UN Commissioner had been suggested forty years earlier, during the drafting of the Covenants, and resurfaced from time to time subsequently.[76] But it was not until the World Conference on Human Rights in 1993 endorsed the suggestion in the Vienna Declaration and Pro- gramme of Action that the necessary support was forthcoming.[77] Even then, settling the details was not easy and when the question was discussed in the General Assembly's Third Committee in November differences of opinion appeared between the Western and the developing States, reflecting their different priorities in the field of human rights. Eventually, however, a compromise was agreed, specifying the High Commissioner's functions and laying down that he or she should be appointed by the Secretary- General subject to approval by the General Assembly. In January 1994 Mr José Ayala Lasso, Ecuador's ambassador to the United Nations and the chairman of the group which had drafted Resolution 48/141, was appointed to the post.

Under the terms of appointment the High Commissioner serves a four-year term with the possibility of renewal for one additional term. The High Commissioner's responsibilities can be sum- marised as promoting and protecting human rights, co-ordinating human rights activities within and outside the United Nations, and assisting other UN organs by performing delegated tasks and putting forward recommendations. Thus Resolution 48/141 refers to the Commissioner's responsibilities as including: promoting and protecting the effective enjoyment by all of all civil, cultural, economic, political and social rights and realisation of the right to development; rationalising, adapting, strengthening and stream-lining the human rights machinery of the United Nations, supervising the Centre for Human Rights, and providing advisory services; and carrying out the tasks assigned by the competent UN bodies. Although the Western countries would have favoured giving the High Commissioner a somewhat stronger mandate,[78] these are clearly wide-ranging responsibilities.

If the task of the High Commissioner had to be expressed in a single phrase it would be to provide leadership in human rights, which the UN unquestionably needs.[79] The activities Mr Ayala has already undertaken, and which he described in his first reports,[80] point to several areas in which such leadership is likely to be particularly important. One is the provision of early warning and the ability to activate other organs in emergencies. Thus it was on the High Commissioner's initiative that the Commission on Human Rights held a special session in May 1994 to consider the serious human rights situation in Rwanda. As noted earlier, this led to the appointment of a special rapporteur, who the Commission decided should be assisted by a team of field officers under the direction of the High Com-missioner.

A second area is advisory, technical and financial assistance to governments in building democratic institutions, improving the administration of justice, training the police, drafting national plans of action for human rights and similar activities. To this end the High Commissioner in his first months of office visited Estonia, Latvia and Lithuania to discuss action plans, Nepal to discuss a programme for technical assistance, and Cambodia and Malawi, where offices were opened to provide technical assistance.

A third area where leadership is needed is the co-ordination of UN activity in the field of human rights. This aspect of the High Commissioner's work is unsensational but extremely important. We have seen that something has been achieved through regular meetings of the chairpersons of the treaty bodies, but much remains to be done as regards both the treaty bodies and the variety of Commission procedures. Co-ordination between UN bodies and the regional human rights organisations should also receive attention. Dealing with these matters will be an enormous task, but the High Commissioner has made a start by initiating a restructuring of the Centre for Human Rights and meeting with the special rapporteurs, chairpersons of working groups and treaty bodies, the specialised agencies, and regional and non-governmental organisations. The measures introduced as a result of the High Commissioner's consultations will be an early test of his effectiveness.

## VII. Appraisal

This summary account of developments in the United Nations aimed at securing a more effective respect for human rights indicates that in the half century or so that the organisation has existed much of significance has been achieved. From the Universal Declaration in 1948 to the appointment of the first Commissioner for Human Rights in 1994, in one form or another the issue of human rights has always been on the agenda and efforts to advance on a variety of fronts are constantly being made. At the same time, however, no dispassionate observer could pretend that the position we have arrived at is ideal, or would deny that progress so far has been extremely uneven.

In the field of standard setting and promotion, excellent work has been done with the two Covenants and the Universal Declaration, numerous conventions dealing with specific topics and a variety of declarations and soft-law instruments. As regards actual protection and measures of implementation, on the other hand, the record is less impressive. Some instruments contain no procedures for supervision and those that do rely primarily on reporting, which the treaty bodies can only go so far in making an effective means of implementation. There are, of course, the optional procedures for individual or inter-State cases and the various procedures of the Commission, notably those under Resolutions 1235 and 1503. However, all of these, as we have seen, are limited in various ways.

To recognise that serious violations of human rights are occurring in many countries and that at present there is only so much that can be done through the United Nations to provide redress, and even less by way of prevention, is not to deny the great and genuine efforts made by certain governments, by rapporteurs and independent experts, by the High Commissioner and officials of the Centre, and by NGOs working for the protection of human rights. The political reality, however, is that an international organisation cannot do more than its member governments are prepared to accept, and the majority of members of the United Nations are not willing to accept a strong system of international control over actions which may affect the human rights of their citizens. Though the progress made has been remarkable as regards standard setting, it has been modest as regards measures of implementation, and governments' unwillingness to accept more effective measures is the explanation.

We may therefore conclude that the United Nations has achieved a great deal in developing the international law of human rights, particularly as regards international standards, which are increasingly significant as conventional or customary rules of law. If it has been less successful in securing the 'universal and effective recognition of those standards', as the Universal Declaration puts it, that is because the organisation cannot exercise greater powers than its member States are prepared to give it, and to change the practice of governments in almost every part of the world is a monumental task. Many governments are prepared to vote for idealistic texts in New York or Geneva, yet ignore these ideals in their daily conduct of affairs. Despite the difficulties, however, procedures for exposing hypocrisy and defending human rights have evolved and are being used. As we said in Chapter 1, although international law is not yet capable of preventing violations of human rights, it can be made more effective, and both inside the United Nations and outside it many are working with that aim.

## Notes

1 The texts of most of the instruments cited in this section can be found in I. Brownlie, *Basic Documents on Human Rights*, third edition, Oxford, 1992, and P. R. Ghandhi, *International Human Rights Documents*, London, 1995.
2 See Resolutions 75(V) and 728(f). An excellent account of the history and development of the treatment of human rights petitions can be found in T. J. M. Zuijdwijk, *Petitioning the United Nations*, New York, 1982.
3 For the text of Resolution 1503 see Ghandhi, *Human Rights Documents*, p. 121.
4 See A. Eide, 'The Sub-Commission on Prevention of Discrimination and Protection of Minorities', in P. Alston (ed.), *The United Nations and Human Rights. A Critical Appraisal*, Oxford, 1992, p. 211.

5 For a fuller description of the Commission's procedure, including the criteria of admissibility, see N. S. Rodley, 'United Nations non-treaty procedures for dealing with human rights violations', in H. Hannum (ed.), *Guide to International Human Rights Practice*, second edition, Philadelphia, 1992, pp. 64–70.

6 Since 1984 the chairperson of the Commission has announced at the end of each session the names of the countries no longer being considered.

7 *Report on Communications Concerning Human Rights*, UN document E/CN.4/165 of 2 May 1949.

8 For other criticisms see P. Alston, 'The Commission on Human Rights', in Alston, *The United Nations*, pp. 145–55.

9 See M. J. Bossuyt, 'The development of special procedures of the United Nations Commission on Human Rights', *Human Rights Law Journal*, VI, 1985, pp. 183–4.

10 For the text of Resolution 1235 see Ghandhi, *Human Rights Documents*, p. 120. For the background to this resolution and discussion of its significance in practice see Alston, 'The Commission on Human Rights', pp. 155–73.

11 The twelve countries on which the other experts were reporting were: Equatorial Guinea, Afghanistan, Burma, Cuba, Guatemala, Iraq, Iran, Haiti, Palestine, South Africa, Sudan and Zaire.

12 The Secretary-General was preparing reports on Albania, East Timor, Burundi and Togo; and the countries receiving advisory services were Cambodia, Angola, Georgia, El Salvador and Somalia.

13 It should be noted, however, that in 1993 the Commission appointed its own special rapporteur for the territories occupied by Israel, including Palestine.

14 See Bossuyt, 'Development of special procedures', p. 184.

15 *Ibid.*, pp. 183–4.

16 *Report on the Situation of Human Rights in Afghanistan*, UN document E/CN.4/1985/21 of 19 February 1985. Text in *Human Rights Law Journal*, VI, 1985, p. 29.

17 For an excellent account of this and other aspects of the Commission's activity see J. R. Crook, 'The Fiftieth Session of the UN Commission on Human Rights', *American Journal of International Law*, LXXXVIII, 1994, p. 806.

18 See Alston, 'The Commission on Human Rights', pp. 173–81, N. S. Rodley, 'United Nations non-treaty procedures', in Hannum, *Guide*, pp. 70–5, Bossuyt, 'Development of special procedures', pp. 194–9, and D. Weissbrodt, 'The three "theme" Special Rapporteurs of the UN Commission on Human Rights', *American Journal of International Law*, LXXX, 1986, p. 685.

19 Text in *International Legal Materials*, XXXII, 1993, p. 903.

20 See T. van Boven, *Study Concerning the Right to Restitution, Compensation and Rehabilitation for Victims of Gross Violations of Human Rights, Final Report*, UN document E/CN.4/Sub.2/1993/8 at p. 53, para. 133. In 1994 the Fund's Board of Trustees approved projects to a total value of $3,700,000; see *Human Rights Monitor*, XXVIII, 1995, p. 33.

21 See Eide, 'The Sub-Commission', pp. 235–9, H. Hannum, 'New developments in indigenous rights', *Virginia Journal of International Law*, XXVIII, 1988, p. 649, and R. L. Barsh, 'United Nations Seminar on Indigenous Peoples and States', *American Journal of International Law*, LXXXIII, 1989, p. 599.

22 See Eide, *ibid.*, pp. 232–5.

23  For discussion of this issue and the developments described in the text see D. J. Sullivan, 'Advancing freedom of religion or belief through the UN Declaration on the Elimination of Religious Intolerance and Discrimination', *American Journal of International Law*, LXXXII, 1988, p. 487, and B. Dickson, 'The United Nations and freedom of religion', *International and Comparative Law Quarterly*, XXXXIV, 1995, p. 327.

24  See R. Brody, 'The United Nations creates a Working Group on Arbitrary Detention', *American Journal of International Law*, LXXXV, 1991, p. 709.

25  See R. Cohen, 'International protection for internally displaced persons', in L. Henkin and J. L. Hargrove (eds), *Human Rights: An Agenda for the Next Century*, Washington, 1994, p. 31.

26  Text in *International Legal Materials*, XXXIII, 1994, p. 1049.

27  The Commission appointed a special rapporteur on this issue in 1981 and, though the appointment has lapsed, the issue is still on the Commission's agenda. For discussion of the contribution of the special rapporteur see the third edition of this book, pp. 85–6.

28  See A. F. Bayefsky, 'Making the human rights treaties work', in Henkin and Hargrove, *Human Rights*, p. 229.

29  See C. Redgwell, 'Universality or integrity? Some reflections on reservations to general multilateral treaties', *British Year Book of International Law*, LXIV, 1993, p. 245, and the references in note 53.

30  For a summary of the fourth (1992) and fifth (1994) meetings of the chairpersons see *Human Rights Monitor*, XIX, 1992, p. 4, and XXVII, 1994, p. 11.

31  For example, since 1994 the Committee on the Elimination of Racial Discrimination and the Committee on Torture have been financed from the UN budget, instead of by the parties to the respective conventions, as previously. See *Human Rights Monitor*, XVII/XVIII, 1992, p. 41.

32  See UN document A/45/636, para. 65 (1990). These guidelines have been adopted by all the treaty bodies.

33  For the text of this Convention see Ghandhi, *Human Rights Documents*, p. 42. For analysis of its provisions see T. Meron, 'The meaning and reach of the International Convention on the Elimination of All Forms of Racial Discrimination', *American Journal of International Law*, LXXIX, 1985, p. 283.

34  A detailed description of the Committee and its work will be found in K. J. Partsch, 'The Committee on the Elimination of Racial Discrimination', in Alston, *The United Nations*, p. 339.

35  On 1 January 1995 there were 142 parties to this Convention, less than to the 1989 Convention on the Rights of the Child.

36  Afghanistan, Mauritius, Mali, Barbados, United Arab Emirates and Chad.

37  Burundi, Rwanda, Israel, Papua New Guinea and Sudan.

38  For the text of these recommendations see *International Human Rights Reports*, I(3), 1994, p. 4.

39  See, for example, the decision of the European Court of Human Rights in the *Jersild case*, ECHR, Series A, No. 298 (1994).

40  On 1 January 1995, twenty-one States had made such declarations. Several contain reservations excluding from the Committee's jurisdiction matters which are being, or have been, examined under another international procedure.

41  Text in *International Human Rights Reports*, I(3), 1994, p. 30.

42  Text in *International Human Rights Reports*, I(1), 1994, p. 32.
43  See Partsch, 'The Committee on the Elimination of Racial Discrimination', p. 361.
44  See *Human Rights Monitor*, XXV/XXVI, 1994, p. 46.
45  For the text of the Convention, see Ghandhi, *Human Rights Documents*, p. 82.
46  See, for example, J. Loranger, 'Convention on the Elimination of All Forms of Discrimination against Women', *Canadian Yearbook of International Law*, XX, 1982, p. 349, and T. Meron, *Human Rights Law-Making in the United Nations*, Oxford, 1986, Chapter 2 (with references to earlier literature).
47  Meron, *ibid.*, p. 66.
48  On 1 January 1995 there were 138 parties to this Convention.
49  See R. Jacobson, 'The Committee on the Elimination of Discrimination against Women', in Alston, *The United Nations*, p. 444, and M. A. Freeman and A. S. Fraser, 'Women's human rights: making the theory a reality', in Henkin and Hargrove, *Human Rights*, p. 103.
50  However, according to Freeman and Fraser (*ibid.*, p. 114), several days' additional meeting time has been obtained in recent years. Article 20 of the Convention provides for meetings 'normally' of two weeks' duration only.
51  Article 21(2) of the Convention requires the Secretary-General also to transmit the reports of the Committee to the Commission on the Status of Women. For discussion of the latter, which is not to be confused with CEDAW, see L. Reanda, 'The Commission on the Status of Women', in Alston, *The United Nations*, p. 265.
52  The text of Recommendations Nos 1 to 20 can be found in *International Human Rights Reports*, I(1), 1994, p. 15, and of Recommendation No. 21, in II, 1995, p. 1.
53  See R. Cook, 'Reservations to the Convention on the Elimination of All Forms of Discrimination against Women', *Virginia Journal of International Law*, XXX, 1990, p. 643, and B. Clark, 'The Vienna Convention reservations regime and the Convention on Discrimination against Women', *American Journal of International Law*, LXXXV, 1991, p. 281.
54  Meron, *Human Rights Law-Making*, p. 53.
55  At the World Conference on Human Rights in 1993 the conclusion of an optional protocol providing for a right of petition was seen as a matter of urgency. See D. Sullivan, 'Women's human rights and the 1993 World Conference on Human Rights', *American Journal of International Law*, LXXXVIII, 1994, p. 152. As a result, a draft of such a protocol was prepared by an expert group in the autumn of 1994. On the issue of procedures generally see T. Meron, 'Enhancing the effectiveness of the prohibition on discrimination against women', *American Journal of International Law*, LXXXIV, 1990, p. 213.
56  For the text of the Convention see Ghandhi, *Human Rights Documents*, p. 93.
57  See A. Byrnes, 'The Committee against Torture', in Alston, *The United Nations*, p. 509. Article 17(2) of the Convention envisages and encourages some overlap of membership with the Human Rights Committee; however, as Byrnes notes (p. 511), this has been largely ignored in practice.
58  On 1 January 1995 there were eighty-five parties to this Convention, of which thirty-seven had made declarations under Article 21 and thirty-five declarations under Article 22.

59  See S. Lewis-Anthony, 'Treaty-based procedures for making human rights complaints within the UN system', in Hannum, *Guide*, pp. 49–52.

60  Text in *International Human Rights Reports*, I(2), 1994, p. 190.

61  Text in *International Human Rights Reports*, I(3), 1994, p. 122.

62  See *Human Rights Monitor*, XXIII, 1993, p. 12.

63  For the texts of the Declaration and the Convention see Ghandhi, *Human Rights Documents*, pp. 38, 102. See also S. Detrick (ed.), *The United Nations Convention on the Rights of the Child. A Guide to the Travaux Préparatoires*, Dordrecht, 1992, and M. S. Pais, 'Rights of children and the family' in Henkin and Hargrove, *Human Rights*, p. 183.

64  On 1 January 1995 there were 168 parties to this convention.

65  See P. Alston, 'Interpreting a child's right to privacy in the UN context: the influence of regional standards', in D. Gomien (ed.), *Broadening the Frontiers of Human Rights*, Oslo, 1993, p. 125.

66  See S. Coliver, 'International reporting procedures', in Hannum, *Guide*, pp. 184–6.

67  Non-governmental organisations also made a major contribution to the drafting of this Convention and have also been consulted by the Committee about its procedures; see Coliver, *ibid.*, p. 185.

68  See, for example, the Committee's concluding observations of January and April 1994, reported in *International Human Rights Reports*, I(3), 1994, p. 162.

69  See *Human Rights Monitor*, XIX, 1992, p. 4; XXIII, 1993, p. 6; and XXVII, 1994, p. 24.

70  *Ibid.*, XXVII, 1994, pp. 4, 24, and XXVIII, 1995, pp. 24, 25.

71  For the text of this Convention see Ghandhi, *Human Rights Documents*, p. 78.

72  On 1 January 1995 there were ninety-nine parties to this Convention.

73  See Coliver, 'International reporting procedures', p. 186.

74  See *Human Rights Monitor*, XXVII, 1994, p. 12, and XXVIII, 1995, p. 16.

75  For the text of Resolution 48/141 see *International Legal Materials*, XXXIII, 1994, p. 303.

76  For the historical background see R. S. Clark, *A United Nations High Commissioner for Human Rights*, The Hague, 1972, and R. St. J. Macdonald, 'A United Nations High Commissioner for Human Rights: the decline and fall of an initiative', *Canadian Yearbook of International Law*, X, 1972, p. 40. The matter was also the subject of an inconclusive discussion in the Commission on Human Rights in 1979.

77  See the Vienna Declaration and Programme of Action, 25 June 1993, para. 18. *International Human Rights Reports*, I(1), 1994, p. 240.

78  The Western version would have made the High Commissioner responsible for the 'elimination and prevention' of human rights violations. A requirement that the Commissioner 'respect the sovereignty, territorial integrity and domestic jurisdiction of States' was added at the insistence of the developing States.

79  See R. Brody, 'Improving UN human rights structures', in Henkin and Hargrove, *Human Rights*, p. 303.

80  See the High Commissioner's Report to the General Assembly on 11 November 1994, A/49/36 and his Report to the Commission on Human Rights of 15 February 1995, E/CN.4/1995/98.

# CHAPTER 4

# Human rights in Europe I: the European Convention on Human Rights

## I. The origin and history of the Convention

The factors which led the United Nations to concern itself with the protection of human rights had a similar effect in Europe.

One such factor was a natural reaction against the Nazi and Fascist systems which had provoked the Second World War and wrought such havoc on millions of lives during the course of that conflict. The denial of human rights was not merely an incidental result of these systems; it was a deliberate instrument of policy and even a precondition of their ascendancy. If the dictators had built their empires by suppressing individual freedoms, then an effective system for the protection of human rights would, it was thought, erect a bulwark against any recrudescence of dictatorship.

Another stimulus was that in the post-war years it soon became evident that the democratic systems of Western Europe needed protection, not only against a possible revival of the pre-war dictatorships, but also against the Soviet style of despotism which had captured control of half the continent. The principles championed by the French Revolution, some of which were enshrined in the English 1689 Bill of Rights and earlier in Magna Carta, were menaced by a new political philosophy in which the so-called dictatorship of the proletariat gave all power to the State and reduced the individual to insignificance. The preservation of democracy and the maintenance of the rule of law required, as Robert Schuman put it, foundations 'on which to base the defence of human personality against all tyrannies and against all forms of totalitarianism'. Those foundations were the effective protection of human rights and fundamental freedoms.

As early as August 1941 the Atlantic Charter proclaimed the historic Four Freedoms and also (which is sometimes forgotten) the right of self-determination. These principles were reaffirmed in the Declaration of the twenty-six 'United Nations' on 1 January 1942, and three years later came the well known provisions of the United Nations Charter. These texts, however, were proclamations of a very general nature. It was left to the Congress of Europe at The Hague in May 1948 to announce:

> We desire a united Europe, throughout whose area the free movement of persons, ideas and goods is restored;
>
> We desire a Charter of Human Rights guaranteeing liberty of thought, assembly and expression as well as the right to form a political opposition;
>
> We desire a Court of Justice with adequate sanctions for the implementation of this Charter;
>
> We desire a European Assembly where the live forces of all our nations shall be represented.

The essence of this message lay in the words 'guaranteeing' and 'sanctions'. Something more was required than declarations of intention. An organised system was needed to ensure the collective guarantee of human rights in the proposed 'European Union'.

The task of designing such a system was taken up by the Consultative Assembly of the Council of Europe during its first session, in August and September 1949. The Statute creating the Council of Europe had been signed earlier in the year. It laid down that the maintenance and further realisation of human rights and fundamental freedoms were one of the means for achieving the aim of the Council, which is a greater unity between its members, and Article 3 of the Statute reinforced this commitment by making respect for human rights a condition of membership. In August 1949 the Assembly's Committee on Legal and Administrative Questions met to study a proposal for the establishment of 'an organisation within the Council of Europe to ensure the collective guarantee of human rights' and before the end of the session presented its conclusions in the famous Teitgen Report of September 1949.

The Committee proposed that a list of ten rights from the Universal Declaration should be the object of a collective guarantee; that the member States should bind themselves to respect the fundamental principles of democracy and to hold free elections; and that a European Commission for Human Rights and a European Court of Justice should be established, the former to hear complaints of alleged violations and attempt conciliation, the latter to take decisions as to whether a violation had occurred.

This is not the place to describe in detail the negotiation of the Convention on Human Rights.[1] It is enough to note that the Committee of Ministers of the Council of Europe appointed two separate governmental committees which met during the first half of 1950. After further consultation of the Assembly in the summer of that year, the Convention was signed in Rome by the foreign ministers in November. The rights guaranteed are substantially the same as those proposed by the Assembly in the previous year and the organs of control are a Commission and a Court of Human Rights. However, the right of individuals to lodge complaints with the Commission was made conditional on the express acceptance of this procedure by the State concerned. Moreover, the possibility of bringing a case before the Court was made conditional on the State concerned agreeing to accept the Court's jurisdiction, and the Committee of Ministers of the Council of Europe was brought in as the final arbiter in cases which are not referred to the Court.

The Convention entered into force on 3 September 1953, when ten ratifications had been deposited. It has now been accepted by three times that number, including Iceland, Malta and Cyprus as well as the democracies of mainland Europe.[2] With the ending of the Cold War many of the States of the former communist bloc have recently joined the Council of Europe and become parties to the Convention and more, including Russia itself, are likely to do so in the future.

The Convention records in its preamble that it was concluded in order 'to take the first steps for the collective enforcement of certain of the rights stated in the Universal Declaration'. Further steps were envisaged and were not long in coming. In the summer of 1950, even before the Convention was signed, the Assembly had proposed the inclusion of three additional rights, which were subsequently included in Protocol No. 1, signed in March 1952, and which entered into force two years later.

Four further protocols were concluded between the years 1963 and 1966. Protocol No. 2, of May 1963, grants the Court a limited competence to give advisory opinions, while Protocol No. 3, of the same date, modified the procedure of the Commission. Since they affect the institutions of the Strasbourg system, these protocols required ratification by all parties to the Convention and came into force in 1970. Protocol No. 4, securing four additional rights, required only five ratifications to enter into force, and this was achieved in May 1968. The Agreement Relating to Persons Participating in the Proceedings of the Commission and the Court came into force in 1971, and Protocol No. 5, concerning the procedure for the election of members of the Commission and the Court, which required ratification by all contracting parties, entered into force in 1974.

Subsequently several more protocols were added. Protocol No. 6, which concerns the abolition of the death penalty, was concluded in April 1983 and entered into force on receiving its fifth ratification in March 1985. Protocol No. 7 was agreed in November 1984. It confers five additional rights and came into force in November 1988, when it had received seven ratifications. Protocol No. 8 deals with the procedure of the Commission and the Court and was concluded in March 1985. Like the earlier protocols of this type, it required ratification by all the parties to the Convention and came into force in January 1990.

The three most recent protocols all concern the institutional machinery and have a number of unusual features. Protocol No. 9, concluded in 1990, enables individuals to take cases to the Court in certain circumstances and is further discussed below. Protocol No. 10, opened for signature in 1992, modifies the voting arrangements in the Committee of Ministers, while Protocol No. 11, concluded in 1994, is intended to reconstruct the whole system of control. Protocols Nos 10 and 11 need general endorsement and are not yet in force. Protocol No. 9, on the other hand, required only ten acceptances, which were achieved in 1994.

The States which drew up the Convention in 1950 initiated a legislative process which is clearly still continuing. In due course, no doubt further protocols will be negotiated, while those which have not yet been accepted by all States will secure progressively wider adherence. Against this general background, the scope of the Convention as it stands today can now be considered in more detail.[3]

## II. The rights guaranteed

The first article of the Convention provides: 'The High Contracting Parties shall secure to everyone within their jurisdiction the rights and freedoms defined in Section 1 of the Convention.' The obligation assumed by each State is therefore not limited to protecting the rights of its own nationals, nor even to protecting those of the nationals of the other contracting parties. The obligation extends to all persons within the jurisdiction, whatever their nationality or legal status, and however short their length of stay.[4] It will be noted, however, that the obligation, though extensive as regards the category of the beneficiaries, is strictly limited to the rights and freedoms defined in the first part of the Convention.

The rights defined include, as we shall see shortly, the civil and political rights which are the hallmark of a democratic society. Yet they do not include every right one might wish to see guaranteed in an ideal community. As a result, many individual applications to the Commission have to be rejected because the applicant alleges the violation of a right which, however necessary or desirable, is not covered by the Convention or its protocols. This has happened with applications based on the denial of the right to a pension, the right to a nationality, the right to practise as a lawyer, the right to reside in one's own country, the right to a career in the public service, the right to political asylum, the right to be compensated for Nazi persecution, the right to a passport, the right to social security benefits, and many others.

Part I of the Convention sets out twelve rights and freedoms which are specifically guaranteed. These are:

1   the right to life (Article 2);
2   freedom from torture and inhuman or degrading treatment or punishment (Article 3);

3     freedom from slavery and servitude (Article 4);

4     the right to liberty and security of the person (Article 5);

5     the right to a fair trial (Article 6);

6     protection against retroactivity of the criminal law (Article 7);

7     the right to respect for private and family life, the home and correspondence (Article 8);

8     freedom of thought, conscience and religion (Article 9);

9     freedom of expression (Article 10);

10    freedom of assembly and association (Article 11);

11    the right to marry and found a family (Article 12);

12    the right to an effective remedy if one's rights are violated (Article 13);

Protocol No. 1 adds three further rights:

13    the right to property (Article 1);

14    the right of parents to ensure the education of their children in conformity with their own religious and philosophical convictions (Article 2);

15    the right to free elections (Article 3);

Protocol No. 4 adds four more rights:

16    freedom from imprisonment for debt (Article 1);

17    liberty of movement and freedom to choose one's residence (Article 2);

18    freedom from exile and the right to enter the country of which one is a national (Article 3);

19    prohibition of the collective expulsion of aliens (Article 4).

Protocol No. 6 adds one further right:

20    prohibition of the death penalty in time of peace (Articles 1 and 2);

Protocol No. 7 adds five further rights:

21    the right of an alien not to be expelled from a State without due process of law (Article 1);

22    the right to appeal in criminal cases (Article 2);

23    the right to compensation for a miscarriage of justice (Article 3);

24    immunity from being prosecuted twice for the same offence (Article 4);

25     equality of rights and responsibilities of spouses as regards
       matters of a private law character between them and in their
       relations with their children (Article 5).

The twenty-five rights and freedoms are, of course, defined,
sometimes in considerable detail. In many articles the first
sentence or paragraph contains a general affirmation of the right,
often based on the text of the Universal Declaration, and the
following paragraphs set out the limitations to which that right
may be subjected. For example, the right to liberty can be
restricted after conviction by a competent court, or in the event of
lawful arrest or detention. Several other rights, such as freedom
of expression, freedom of assembly and freedom of association,
may be limited in the interests of national security, public safety,
protection of the rights and freedoms of others, and so on.
However, the limitations are carefully formulated and, in general,
permitted only when they are prescribed by law and necessary in
a democratic society to safeguard some aspect of the public
interest.

Articles 14–18 of the Convention relate to the exercise of the
rights guaranteed. Article 14 contains a widely drawn prohibition
against discrimination. Article 15 permits the suspension of some,
though not all, rights 'in time of war or other emergency
threatening the life of the nation', but only 'to the extent strictly
required by the exigencies of the situation' and after a notice of
derogation has been filed with the Secretary-General of the
Council of Europe. Article 16 permits restrictions on the political
activities of aliens. Article 17 provides that 'nothing in this
Convention shall be interpreted as implying ... any right to
engage in any activity or perform any act aimed at the destruction
of any of the rights and freedoms set forth herein'. And Article 18
stipulates that the restrictions which are permitted under the
Convention may not be applied for any purpose other than those
for which they have been prescribed.

The rights and freedoms just described are all civil and political
rights. As we saw in Chapter 1, however, there are other rights
which the State should protect and which many regard as no less
important, namely economic, social and cultural rights. The
Council of Europe 'began at the beginning', as M. Teitgen had
proposed in 1949,[5] but when the Convention and Protocol No. 1

had been concluded, turned its attention to what he had called 'the generalisation of social democracy'. The result was the European Social Charter of 1961, to which we will return in Chapter 5.

## III. The system of international control

The rights discussed above are secured by the contracting parties undertaking to ensure them to 'everyone within their jurisdiction'. However, the authors of the Convention did not consider that by itself this obligation was sufficient. They therefore provided something more, an institutional guarantee. For this purpose they decided to create a Commission of Human Rights and a Court of Human Rights, and also to make use of the existing governmental organ of the Council of Europe, the Committee of Ministers.

### 1. *The European Commission of Human Rights*

The Commission consists of as many members as there are high contracting parties. In fact there is normally one national of each State, although this is not mandatory. They act in an individual capacity and, in contrast with the members of the UN Commission on Human Rights, not as governmental delegates. The Commission elects its own President. Under Article 24 of the Convention any party may refer to the Commission an alleged breach of the Convention by any other party.

The system of control established by Article 24 is valuable, but if it stood alone would not be adequate. As we pointed out when discussing the Optional Protocol to the UN Covenant on Civil and Political Rights, if a violation occurs the real party in interest is the person whose rights have been denied, and in most cases this will be the result of acts by organs or agencies of that person's own government. It is therefore vital to give the individual access to an international organ which is competent to provide a remedy even against a person's own government. The European Convention on Human Rights contains just such a procedure. When the Convention was negotiated this was a remarkable innovation, so much so, indeed, that some governments hesitated to accept it. The right of individual petition was therefore made optional, and so applies only to States which have expressly declared they accept it, in accordance with Article 25 of the Convention. It is pleasing to report that this provision has now been generally endorsed, with the result that the remedy is currently available to nearly 500 million people.[6]

Since its creation in 1954 the Commission has been competent to examine cases brought by one State against another. However, only a handful of such cases have been brought so far, almost all in situations of political tension.[7] The Commission acquired its competence to consider individual applications in July 1955, when six States had recognised the right of redress given by Article 25 to 'any person, non-governmental organisation or group of individuals claiming to be the victim of a violation by one of the High Contracting Parties of the rights set forth in this Convention'. The overwhelming importance of this right, as compared with the inter-State procedure, may be seen from the fact that in 1993 alone the Commission registered more than 2,000 individual applications.[8]

The first task of the Commission when it considers an application is to decide whether it is admissible. Here strict rules apply. Article 26 of the Convention lays down two conditions which apply both to inter-State cases and to individual applications. The Commission may deal with a case only after all domestic remedies have been exhausted, unless no such remedies are available or they are unreasonably delayed, and within six months of the date of the final decision at the national level. Moreover, under Article 27, which applies only to individual cases, the Commission must reject as inadmissible any application which is anonymous, substantially the same as a matter already examined by the Commission or through another international procedure, incompatible with the provisions of the Convention or manifestly ill-founded, or which constitutes an abuse of the right of petition. There are therefore seven separate grounds on which an application may be declared inadmissible, and bearing in mind that it is open to anyone to attempt to set the machinery of the Convention in motion by writing to Strasbourg, it is hardly surprising that the great majority of individual applications are rejected at this stage.

A ground of inadmissibility which has caused particular problems in practice is that of 'manifestly ill-founded'. The Commission is not competent to decide that an application is ill-founded on the merits because that is a decision for the Committee of Ministers or the Court. However, it must reject an application as inadmissible if the fact that it is ill-founded is 'manifest'. Where is the line to be drawn between these two concepts? This is clearly a difficult and important question. In its early days the Commission was very cautious and a high proportion of applications was rejected on this ground. Today, however, it is less restrictive and so more survive this initial scrutiny and pass to the next stage.

A rather different problem of admissibility arises when a matter is brought to the Commission having already been submitted to another procedure of international settlement. This issue assumed increased importance when the United Nations Covenant on Civil and Political Rights and its Optional Protocol came into force in 1976, since a respondent State which has accepted both the Covenant and the Convention along with their optional provisions, can now be faced with a claim from an individual who wishes to use both procedures. Article 27(2) deals with just this type of situation. If a matter has already been submitted to the Human Rights Committee, then the European Commission must declare an application to Strasbourg based on the same facts inadmissible, unless, of course, it contains new information. In the other direction, that is if the applicant tries first in Strasbourg and then in New York, Article 5(2)(a) of the Optional Protocol will render the application inadmissible in New York for as long as it is under examination in Strasbourg, but not thereafter. However, to avoid what would look like an 'appeal' from the Commission, several parties to the Convention have made their acceptance of the Optional Protocol subject to a reservation which has had the desired effect.[9]

If the Commission declares a case to be admissible, Article 28 of the Convention requires it to undertake an examination of the application 'with a view to ascertaining the facts'. This examination is carried out 'together with the representatives of the parties', which means in practice a hearing of a judicial nature with the individual applicant and the respondent government represented by counsel on a footing of complete equality. The difference between the procedure of the European Commission and that of the Human Rights Committee, described in Chapter 2, is thus striking.

Article 28 of the Convention also authorises the Commission, when necessary, to undertake an investigation, for which the State or States concerned are obliged to 'furnish all necessary facilities, after an exchange of views with the Commission'. It should be noted that the consultation concerns the modalities of the investigation, that is the date, the place, and the detailed arrangements, but not the major question of whether an investigation is needed. On that point there is no discussion. By ratifying the Convention, the States concerned have accepted the obligation to agree to an investigation if the Commission so desires. Again, the difference between the European procedures and those of the United Nations is striking.

When the Commission has completed its investigation, Article 28(1)(b) of the Convention requires it to try to secure a friendly settlement of the matter 'on the basis of respect for human rights as defined in this Convention'. About ten per cent of the individual applications found to be admissible are settled by this method, which was also used in the inter-State case against Turkey in 1985. In the event of a friendly settlement the Commission draws up a report, which is published, containing a brief statement of the facts and of the solution reached (Article 30). If a friendly settlement is not achieved, the Commission draws up a detailed report, setting out the facts and stating its opinion as to whether its findings disclose a violation of the Convention. Article 31 entitles the Commission to include whatever proposals it thinks fit and the report is then transmitted to the Committee of Ministers of the Council of Europe.[10]

## 2. *The Committee of Ministers*

The Committee of Ministers consists of the ministers for foreign affairs, or their deputies, of the member States of the Council of Europe. It is essentially a political organ, yet judicial or quasi-judicial functions were conferred on it by the Convention. Article 32 provides that if a case is not referred to the Court of Human Rights, the Committee of Ministers shall decide whether or not a violation has occurred. It takes this decision by a two-thirds majority, although its important decisions in other spheres require unanimity.[11]

In the majority of cases which are referred under Article 32 the Committee of Ministers simply endorses the conclusions in the report of the Commission. Sometimes, however, the parties succeed in reaching a settlement before a case reaches the Committee of Ministers or while it is actually under consideration. In cases of this kind the Committee will usually discontinue its examination without actually taking a decision as to whether the Convention has been violated. If the Committee finds that a violation has occurred, Article 32(2) provides that it must prescribe a period during which the State must do whatever is necessary to correct the violation. However, in almost all cases in which the Commission identifies a violation the respondent quickly works out what is needed and informs the Committee of Ministers before it takes its decision. When this happens the usual practice of the Committee is to note the measures and decide that no further action is called for.

The Committee of Ministers does not have the power to order a State to take specific remedial action, but can make recommendations to the respondent, which may then be taken into account when deciding whether Article 32(2) has been complied with. If it has not, in other words if the State has failed to correct a violation, Article 32(3) requires the Committee to decide 'what effect shall be given to its original decision', that is to review the matter again, and to publish the Commission's report. When the Convention was drawn up this probably appeared to be an effective sanction because the expectation was that the Commission's reports would normally remain confidential. Today, however, almost all the Commission's reports are published and so whatever force lay in this threat has now been lost. To see what sanctions are available it is therefore necessary to look outside the Convention.

The desire of a responsible government not to be seen to be violating its human rights obligations is as a rule normally all that is needed to achieve compliance. But there is a legal as well as a political sanction because Article 8 of the Statute of the Council of Europe empowers the Committee of Ministers to suspend or expel from membership any State which has seriously violated Article 3 of the Statute. This, as mentioned earlier, is the article which makes respect for the rule of law and for the enjoyment of human rights a condition of membership of the organisation.

Thus the ultimate sanction is expulsion. It is clear, therefore, that the Committee of Ministers disposes of strong means of pressure, should this be necessary, to ensure compliance with its decisions.[12]

### 3. *The European Court of Human Rights*

The Court contains as many judges as there are members of the Council of Europe (Article 38). Its current membership is therefore more than thirty. The judges act in complete independence, and must possess the same personal and legal qualifications as the members of the International Court of Justice at The Hague (Article 39(3)). The Court, like the Commission, elects its own President.[13]

The Court's jurisdiction extends to all cases concerning the interpretation or application of the Convention which are referred to it under the conditions described below. However, such jurisdiction is not automatic, but exists only in relation to States which have made a general declaration accepting it in accordance with Article 46, or an *ad hoc* acceptance for a particular case under Article 48. Almost all the members of the Council of Europe have now made general declarations and so the contingent element in jurisdiction, which reflects the consensual basis of international adjudication, is in practice not a significant limitation on the Court's activity.[14]

Under the original Convention only the Commission or a State could refer a case to the Court – an individual applicant could not (Article 44). This was an unsatisfactory situation from the point of view of applicants because it meant that an individual who took a case to the Commission and was unsuccessful had no opportunity to have the matter reviewed by the Court; but if the position was reversed and a State was unsuccessful before the Commission, it could, in effect, appeal against the ruling to the Court. To deal with this problem and to put individuals and States on a footing of equality, Protocol No. 9 was concluded in 1990 with the aim of enabling individuals to take cases to the Court in certain circumstances.

Protocol No. 9 came into force in 1994, when ten States had ratified it, but many of the parties to the Convention have yet to do so.[15] For the latter, therefore, the original arrangements continue and cases can be referred to the Court only by the

Commission or a contracting State. In relation to States which have ratified Protocol No. 9, on the other hand, the provisions dealing with the Court's jurisdiction are modified and there is the additional possibility of an individual taking a case to the Court, using a special procedure set out in Article 5(2) of the Protocol. This adds a new paragraph to Article 48 of the Convention (Article 48(2)) and creates a special panel of three judges to examine individual references and to decide which cases of this type shall actually be considered by the Court.

As one would expect, the new Article 48(2) lays down that the relevant national judge shall sit as an *ex officio* member of the panel. It then goes on to provide that the panel's function is to decide by a unanimous vote that a case shall not be considered by the Court if it 'does not raise a serious question affecting the interpretation or application of the Convention and does not for any other reason warrant consideration by the Court'. These criteria are very broad and allow the panel to consider the kinds of factors which no doubt already influence the Commission when deciding which cases to refer to the Court. If, for example, a case turns mainly on the facts, or the State indicates that it accepts the conclusions of the Commission, the panel may well decide that it is better dealt with by the Committee of Ministers. However, it is worth noting that to decide that a case should not be considered by the Court the panel must be unanimous. Thus, while a filtering procedure is appropriate as a way of preventing the Court from becoming over-burdened, any case in which its decision would be beneficial is likely to be taken forward.

To be considered by the Court, all cases must be submitted to it within three months after the report of the Commission has been transmitted to the Committee of Ministers (Article 47). Article 2 of Protocol No. 9 amends Article 31(2) of the Convention so as to ensure that the Commission's report shall also be transmitted to the applicant, which is obviously essential if an individual is to be in a position to decide whether to take a case to the Court. However, it is important to notice that the panel procedure laid down in Protocol No. 9 is not used if a case is referred to the Court by the Commission or a contracting State. Consequently, the three-month period provided for in Article 32(1) and Article 47 must be allowed to expire before a panel can consider the matter.[16]

Whether a case comes to the Court via a panel under Protocol No. 9, or directly as a result of a referral by the Commission or a State, Article 43 of the Convention provides that for each case the Court shall consist of a chamber of nine judges, which shall include as *ex officio* members the President or the Vice-President and the judge who is a national of any State party concerned, with the remaining judges chosen by lot. This is the normal procedure. However, under Rule 51 of the rules of procedure a chamber may relinquish jurisdiction in favour of a grand chamber of nineteen judges if the case pending before it 'raises one or more serious questions affecting the interpretation of the Convention'. Moreover, such relinquishment is obligatory if there is a possibility of conflict with a previous judgement of the Court. In exceptional cases the grand chamber may itself relinquish jurisdiction in favour of the plenary Court. The provision for grand chambers was introduced in 1993, when the Court became so large that referring important cases to the plenary Court, which was the former practice, ceased to be feasible. Under the old arrangements, when the Court's workload was smaller, a relatively large number of cases were heard by the plenary Court. However, use of the plenary Court was already declining when the concept of the grand chamber was introduced and so far little use has been made of the new facility. In practice therefore almost all the Court's cases are now decided by chambers.

Any disputes relating to jurisdiction are decided by the Court, as are questions of admissibility, propriety and similar matters. The Court's main work is, of course, the interpretation and application of the rights set out in the Convention and its protocols, a task which, as we shall see shortly, raises a wide range of issues of law and policy. If a violation has occurred, the Convention does not say whether the Court has the power to order remedial measures. This contrasts with the American Convention on Human Rights, which specifically confers such powers on the Inter-American Court. In the absence of an equivalent provision, the European Court has concluded that it lacks this power and in a number of cases has made the point that it is for the respondent State, not the Court, to decide upon the measures needed to implement its obligations. Article 50 of the Convention, on the other hand, specifically empowers the Court to give 'just satisfaction' to an injured party if the internal law of the country concerned does not provide an adequate remedy. This has proved very important and, although a decision upholding a complaint does not invariably include an award of compensation, if loss can be proved the Court will generally award an applicant damages, as well as reimbursement of any costs and expenses.

The contracting parties undertake to abide by the decision of the Court in any case to which they are parties (Article 53). Moreover, the judgement of the Court is transmitted to the Committee of Ministers of the Council of Europe, which has the responsibility of supervising its execution (Article 54). This means in practice that the representative of the government concerned will explain to the Committee what action that government has taken in order to give effect to the judgement – for example, by amending its legislation or paying damages to an injured party – and the Committee will decide whether such action satisfies the requirements of the situation. In this respect the powers of the European Court of Human Rights are less extensive than those of the Inter-American Court or the European Court of Justice, both of which can make an order for compensation which is directly enforceable in the country concerned. Nevertheless, the Strasbourg system works quite well in practice and the requirement that governments should explain to the Committee of Ministers how they are implementing the Court's judgements is certainly of value.

## IV. The application of the Convention

Many substantial volumes have been published reproducing decisions and reports of the European Commission of Human Rights, decisions of the Committee of Ministers and judgements of the Court. It is obviously impossible to summarise this voluminous case law in the present chapter. To indicate the kinds of cases which arise and convey the flavour of Strasbourg jurisprudence, we shall therefore outline the two most important inter-State cases and review a number of typical individual applications. We shall then suggest some issues for consideration in the future in the light of experience with the Convention to date.

## 1. *The Greek case*

In April 1967 there was a coup d'état in Greece. The following month the Greek government addressed a letter to the Secretary-General of the Council of Europe invoking Article 15 of the Convention and stating that various articles of the constitution had been suspended in view of internal dangers threatening public order and the security of the State. In subsequent letters, in May and September, the Greek government gave further information in regard to Article 15.

In September 1967 the governments of Denmark, Sweden, Norway and the Netherlands made applications to the European Commission in which they challenged the new government's reliance on Article 15 and submitted that by various legislative measures and administrative practices it had violated Articles 5, 6, 8, 9, 10, 11, 13 and 14 of the Convention. The Greek government denied these allegations, but in January 1968 the Commission found the four applications admissible[17] and in May reached the same conclusion in relation to allegations concerning Articles 3 and 7 of the Convention and Articles 1 and 3 of Protocol No. 1 which the three Scandinavian governments had made in a further joint memorial in March.

The hearings which followed lasted some eighteen months and more than eighty witnesses were heard in Strasbourg and Athens. An investigation *in situ* was made and photographs were taken of the security police building in Athens. More than 300 pages of the Commission's report were devoted to the question of torture and many victims were heard as witnesses. Acting throughout with scrupulous objectivity, the Commission required corroboration of the allegations made, and offered the government every opportunity to rebut them. After carefully reviewing the evidence the Commission concluded that torture had been inflicted in a number of cases and that there was evidence in several others in which it had been prevented from completing its investigation. It also found that there was a practice of torture and ill-treatment by the Athens security police of persons arrested for political reasons and that the Greek authorities, confronted with numerous and substantial complaints and allegations of torture and ill-treatment, had failed to take any effective steps to investigate them or remedy the situation.

The Commission, of course, also examined the other allegations made by the applicant governments. It concluded that in
April 1967 there had not been a public emergency threatening the
life of the nation; as a consequence the Greek derogations under
Article 15 were invalid. Moreover, it identified violations of nine
other articles of the Convention and Protocol No. 1, including the
right to liberty, the right to a fair trial, freedom of association,
and the right to free elections. Its conclusions were contained in a
report which was transmitted to the Committee of Ministers of
the Council of Europe in November 1969.[18]

Consideration of the *Greek case* was complicated by the fact
that two parallel procedures were being pursued in the Council of
Europe at the same time. On the one hand, there was the case
brought before the Commission under Article 24 of the Convention. On the other, the Consultative Assembly of the Council of
Europe, relying on Articles 3 and 8 of the Statute, had
recommended that the Committee of Ministers should expel the
Greek government from the organisation. While the lengthy
proceedings under Article 24 of the Convention were still in
progress, the Assembly considered that there was already a strong
case for holding that the Greek government had violated Article
3. It therefore concluded that the Committee of Ministers should
act under Article 8 and suspend Greece from membership without
waiting for the result of the proceedings before the Commission.[19]
When the ministers met in London in May 1969, strong pressure
was put upon them to do this. Knowing that the report of the
Commission was nearly ready, they promised a decision at their
next session.

This was held in Paris in December, when the ministers
discussed both the situation in Greece and whether it could
remain a member of the organisation. At a dramatic session,
during which a draft resolution for the suspension of Greece
was circulated and received a wide measure of support, the
Greek Foreign Minister announced that his government had
decided to withdraw from the Council of Europe and
denounce the Convention on Human Rights. However, the
denunciation of the Convention could take effect only after
six months and the denunciation of the Statute at the end of
the following year. Moreover, as regards proceedings under
the Convention, Article 65(2) makes it clear that denunciation

has no effect on duties or obligations arising out of events occurring before the denunciation becomes effective. Consequently, the Committee of Ministers adopted a resolution in which they took note of the Greek declarations and agreed that Greece would cease to participate in the work of the Council of Europe immediately.

The Committee of Ministers was still required by Article 32 of the Convention to take a decision on the report of the Commission. This they did at their next session, in April 1970. They endorsed the opinion of the Commission and decided that Greece had violated ten articles of the Convention and Protocol No. 1. At the same time they expressed the hope that democratic liberties would be restored in the near future and that Greece would then rejoin the Council of Europe. Happily the situation in Greece was restored with the return to democratic government in 1974, after which Greece resumed its membership of the Council of Europe and once more ratified the European Convention.

The *Greek case* is certainly the most serious situation the Convention institutions have had to deal with and demonstrates both the strengths and the limitations of the Strasbourg system. The fact that Greece was a party to the Convention did not prevent the coup d'état, or the large-scale violations of human rights which were among its consequences. Human rights agreements can reinforce and consolidate democracy; what they cannot do is guarantee that liberty will always prevail when powerful forces are ranged against it. But if the Convention, like other human laws, is vulnerable to overwhelming social or political forces, its existence is far from meaningless. In the *Greek case* it supplied both a standard against which the conduct of the government could be measured and an objective procedure for assessment. Even more important, it made the conduct of affairs within Greece a legitimate subject for international concern. The withdrawal of Greece from the Council of Europe, which was the direct result of that organisation's commitment to human rights, had the effect of isolating the State and strengthening its democratic forces. Thus, following the coup, the inter-State procedure worked just as intended, to expose oppression in a way that left no room for doubt and to bring pressure to bear for a return to democratic values.

## 2. *The Irish case*

Physical maltreatment was also one of the issues raised in the case of *Ireland v. United Kingdom*. The Irish government lodged this application in December 1971 and filed two supplementary memorials in March 1972. The Commission decided to treat the first supplementary memorial as part of the original application, but to register the second as a new application.

The Irish government referred to the Civil Authorities (Special Powers) Act, Northern Ireland, 1922, and alleged *inter alia* that persons taken into custody under this legislation were subjected to treatment which constituted torture and inhuman and degrading treatment and punishment contrary to Article 3 of the Convention. The government also claimed that internment without trial, as carried out in Northern Ireland subsequent to 9 August 1971, constituted a violation of Article 5 (the right to liberty and security of the person) and Article 6 (the right to a fair trial). In addition, the applicant government alleged that the powers of detention and internment were exercised in a discriminatory manner, contrary to Article 14 of the Convention.

On the question of torture or inhuman treatment, the Irish government complained particularly about the methods of interrogation used by the British security forces in Northern Ireland, including hooding, noise, standing against a wall, deprivation of sleep and limited diet. These methods, known as 'interrogation in depth', had in fact already aroused concern in the United Kingdom and in March 1972, following two official reports,[20] the Prime Minister announced in the House of Commons that the government had decided that the use of the techniques in question would be discontinued. This action to stop the use of questionable methods of interrogation was clearly commendable. However, it put a powerful argument in the hands of the Irish government, which could now quote official British sources describing these practices and condemning their use.

In October 1972 the Commission declared the first application admissible, but decided to strike the second application off the list. Examination of the merits then began. After an exchange of memorials, hearings on the merits took place in October 1973, and again in December of that year. Witnesses called by the Irish government were heard by three delegates of the Commission in

December 1973 and February 1974, and those put forward by the British government on several occasions in 1974. For reasons of security some witnesses were heard at an air force base at Stavanger in Norway, and others in London in February 1975. In all, 118 witnesses were heard by the delegates of the Commission in the course of this case.

The Commission sent its report to the Committee of Ministers in February 1976.[21] It expressed the opinion that the measures for detention without trial were not in violation of the Convention, because they were 'strictly required by the exigencies of the situation' and were therefore covered by the derogation made by the British government under Article 15. Moreover, the Commission found that the powers of detention and internment had not been applied in a discriminatory manner. On the other hand, it considered that the use of the five techniques for 'interrogation in depth' constituted a violation of Article 3 of the Convention, prohibiting torture and inhuman treatment.

In March 1976 the Irish government referred the case to the Court, the first, and so far the only, inter-State case to be so referred. Oral hearings took place in two stages in the following year and judgement was given in January 1978.[22] In it the Court made a distinction between torture, on the one hand, and inhuman and degrading treatment, on the other. It held that the techniques of interrogation which had been used in Northern Ireland constituted inhuman and degrading treatment, in violation of Article 3, but that they did not occasion suffering of the degree of intensity and cruelty implied by the word 'torture'. The Court agreed with the Commission that the measures of detention and internment without trial were covered by the derogation made under Article 15 of the Convention and that these measures had not been exercised in a discriminatory manner.

Despite certain similarities, the *Irish case* shows the inter-State procedure functioning in an altogether different situation from that which prompted the *Greek case*. In the latter, as we have seen, totalitarian forces had taken over and use of the Convention was a way of encouraging a return to democracy. In the *Irish case*, on the other hand, the question was how far a government may go when it is committed to democratic values, but confronted with the intractable problem of terrorism. By exonerating the respondent's actions under Article 15, the Court and the Commission recognised that an exceptional situation can justify measures which would not otherwise be permissible. However, by upholding the claim under Article 3 the Strasbourg institutions again demonstrated the value of the inter-State procedure and underlined one of the Convention's basic principles, that in a democracy the end does not always justify the means.

## 3. *Some individual applications*

Since the European Commission of Human Rights began work in 1954 it has declared admissible more than a thousand individual applications. About one-tenth formed the object of a friendly settlement within the meaning of Article 28 of the Convention, and as many more have been settled by some informal arrangement.[23]

The remainder, apart from some cases still under examination, have been the object of reports to the Committee of Ministers under Article 31 of the Convention. Many of these cases have been decided by the Committee of Ministers and more than 300 have been referred to the Court by the Commission or a government. There are no rules setting out the criteria on which such decisions are made. Generally speaking, however, one may say that if the Commission is unanimous or nearly unanimous in expressing the opinion that no violation has occurred, the tendency is to leave the case with the Committee of Ministers. On the other hand, the Commission or the government concerned, or both of them, will tend to refer a case to the Court in three circumstances: if the Commission is narrowly divided in its opinion, if the Commission considers that a violation has occurred, or if the case raises an important question of interpretation.

As a result, if we wish to obtain a general view of the application of the Convention but have to be selective in doing so, we can find the best examples in the case law of the Court. And since space precludes an examination of that case law in detail, we shall limit ourselves to outlining the issues in some of the more significant applications.[24]

The first case considered by the Court was the *Lawless case*, decided in 1961. It concerned the detention without trial in

Ireland of a suspected member of the Irish Republican Army in
the exercise of special powers conferred by the Offences Against
the State Act, 1940. The Irish government had made a derogation
under Article 15 of the Convention, claiming the existence of a
state of emergency. The Court held that the derogation was
justified and there was no violation.[25] The issues in *Lawless* were
very similar to those arising under Articles 5 and 6 in the *Irish
case*. There, as we have seen, the Court held that British measures
against the IRA could be justified under Article 15 and more
recently came to a similar conclusion in the case of *Brannigan
and McBride* (1993).[26] Cases like these, involving emergency
situations, are fortunately rare, but when they occur present the
Court with particularly delicate problems.

Most of the Court's early cases concerned the right to personal
liberty in situations where there was no emergency. Here the
Court had to decide the precise scope of the right and, in
particular, whether conduct which would certainly be unacceptable in some States could nevertheless be regarded as within the
Convention.[27] In contrast, the *Golder case* in 1975 concerned the
right of access to a court of law. The applicant, who was serving
a sentence of imprisonment in the United Kingdom, wished to see
a lawyer with a view to bringing a civil action against one of the
prison warders. Permission to do so was refused. The Court
found a violation of the Convention, because the right to a fair
trial was held to imply the right of access to a court.[28]
Subsequently, the Home Secretary announced to Parliament a
change in the prison rules in order to comply with the judgement.

*Golder* is one of the Court's most important cases because,
apart from its immediate consequences, it demonstrated the
possibility of extending the scope of the Convention by an
imaginative interpretation of its provisions. Shortly afterwards, in
the *Airey case*, the Court went even further and held that the
Convention had been violated because the prohibitive costs of
obtaining a judicial separation in Ireland meant that, although
there was no formal barrier, the applicant had been deprived of
an effective right of access to a court.[29] As bold pieces of judicial
legislation, both decisions were controversial, and while the right
of access to the courts is now firmly established in the Strasbourg
jurisprudence, the proper approach to interpretation of the
Convention can still give rise to controversy.

As might be expected, judicial proceedings and the scope of the right to a fair trial have provided the subject of many other cases. The case of *Luedicke, Belkacem and Koç* involved the obligation to provide free interpretation for defendants in a criminal case if they do not understand the language used in court. The requirement that the applicants should reimburse the cost of interpretation in the Federal Republic of Germany was here held to constitute a violation.[30] In the *Winterwerp case* there was violation by the Netherlands because there was no possibility of recourse to a court for a person confined to a psychiatric hospital,[31] and in the *Borgers case*[32] because a government official, the *avocat général*, had participated in the deliberations of the Belgian Court of Cassation. On the other hand, in the *Schiesser case* it was decided that the applicant's detention in Switzerland by order of the district attorney, on suspicion of having committed a series of aggravated thefts, was not a violation of the Convention.[33]

Another important group of cases has concerned the right to respect for private and family life, home and correspondence. The *Klass case* concerned the clandestine control of correspondence and telephone calls in the Federal Republic of Germany. While such action clearly interferes with the right to respect for correspondence and for private life, the Court held that in the circumstances it was justified in the interests of safeguarding national security and preventing disorder or crime.[34] On the other hand, in the *Keegan case*[35] an Irish applicant was successful when his daughter was placed for adoption without his knowledge, and in the *Gaskin case*[36] the Court decided that Article 8 had been violated because a British applicant was denied details of the foster homes in which he had grown up.

In the *Marckx case*,[37] which also concerned Article 8, the Court held that certain provisions of Belgian law relating to children born out of wedlock, particularly as regards rights of inheritance, put them at a disadvantage as compared with legitimate children, and therefore violated the Convention. A notable feature of this decision was the emphasis which the Court placed on its duty to interpret the Convention in the light of current attitudes towards illegitimacy rather than ideas which were prevalent when the Convention was drawn up. The Court also made the point that the Convention is not just concerned with restraining interference with rights, but in certain circumstances requires governments to take positive steps to promote them. Like the concept of implied rights which proved so significant in *Golder*, these principles reflect an approach to interpretation with enormous creative potential, and while the Court has recognised that it can only go so far, it has often used them to extend the scope of the Convention.[38]

Trade union freedoms were first considered by the Court in several early cases[39] and the Court returned to the question in 1981 when it decided the case of *Young, James and Webster*, which raised the difficult issue of the 'closed shop'. The applicants complained that they had been dismissed for refusing to join a union, which was a condition of employment in the British railway industry. The Court held that they were entitled to compensation for violation of their rights under Article 11, despite the fact the Convention does not expressly provide for 'freedom of non-association'.[40] This was taken further in 1993, when the Court held in the *Sigurdur A. Sigurjónsson case* that requiring the applicant to belong to a taxi drivers' organisation in Iceland had violated Article 11 because a negative right of association is impliedly guaranteed.[41] Like the *Golder case*, these judgements show the Court's ability to develop the law in the individual's interests, as well as the impact of its decisions on the domestic plane.

Freedom of expression is one of the most basic rights in a democratic society, but obviously cannot be unlimited. In almost all the cases in which this freedom has been invoked the Court has had to decide whether the action complained of indicates that it has been infringed, or whether what is clearly a limitation of freedom of expression can be justified on one of the grounds set out in the Convention. In dealing with this issue, which is typical of the way adjudication in the field of human rights often requires individual rights to be assessed against the background of the general interest, the Court has made use of a concept called 'the margin of appreciation'. In the *Müller case*, for example, the applicant complained that his conviction in Switzerland for exhibiting obscene paintings violated his right to freedom of expression. However, the Court decided that in the absence of a uniform approach to issues of sexual morality among the members of the Council of Europe, the question was not whether the Court agreed with the conviction, but whether the actions complained of had exceeded the bounds of reasonableness. Deciding that the authorities were entitled to regard the paintings as morally pernicious, the Court held that in view of their margin of appreciation no violation of the Convention had occurred.[42]

The margin of appreciation is a useful concept and has been applied in many other areas.[43] Its relevance and application, however, depend very much on the Court's view of the particular issue. An important case in which it did not help the government was the *Sunday Times case*, decided in 1979. The applicants claimed that a court order prohibiting the publication of an article concerning 'thalidomide children' (children who were born deformed by reason of their mothers having taken thalidomide as a tranquilliser during pregnancy) constituted a violation of the right of freedom of expression. The order had been made on the ground that the article in question might prejudice the court proceedings then pending against the manufacturers of the drug. The European Court held that where the authority of the judiciary is concerned the margin of appreciation is much narrower than in cases involving morality, such as *Müller*. It concluded that the United Kingdom had violated the Convention and subsequently ordered payment of a substantial sum to the applicants for their costs.[44] The United Kingdom then enacted legislation to bring English law into line with the judgement.

Subsequent cases on Article 10 exhibit the same approach. Thus in the *Sunday Times No. 2 case* the Court held that neither maintaining the authority of the judiciary nor national security could justify measures to suppress material in the book *Spycatcher* once it had been published in the United States.[45] Similarly, in the *Open Door and Dublin Well Woman case* an injunction to prevent the applicants from assisting Irish women to travel abroad to obtain abortions was found to violate Article 10;[46] and in the *Jersild case* the Court held that punishing a Danish journalist for making a television programme which contained interviews with racist bigots violated his right to freedom of expression, notwithstanding the government's margin of appreciation.[47]

Some of the Court's most interesting cases have concerned an issue touched on in *Jersild* and central to the work of a human rights tribunal, discrimination. The Convention's prohibition on discrimination is complementary to the other substantive provisions in the sense that it can be applied only where the facts fall within the ambit of one or more of the other articles. Moreover, even when this condition is fulfilled, a difference of treatment can be justified by showing that it has an 'objective and reasonable justification'. Here, not surprisingly, there is often scope for a margin of appreciation, although, as in the cases on freedom of expression, the scope for this will vary. In the case of *Abdulaziz, Cabales and Balkandali*, for example, the question was whether the United Kingdom was justified in having different admission requirements for the wives and husbands of immigrants, and the Court, emphasising that sex discrimination can be justified only in the most exceptional circumstances, decided that, despite the margin of appreciation, the Convention had been violated.[48]

The cases mentioned so far were mainly concerned with the rights and freedoms protected by the original Convention. However, there have also been numerous cases involving the provisions of Protocol No. 1. The right to property, for example, which is protected by Article 1, has been considered by the Court on several occasions. For example, the Court held in the *James case* that the compulsory transfer of property under the Leasehold Reform Act did not give rise to a violation,[49] and shortly afterwards in the *Lithgow case* reached the same conclusion as regards the nationalisation of shipyards in the United Kingdom.[50] In both of these cases the Court pointed out that the power of the State to take measures in the public interest, which is expressly preserved by Article 1, means that it is harder to establish a violation of this provision than of most articles of the Convention.

Another right guaranteed by Protocol No. 1 is the right of parents to ensure education and teaching in conformity with their religious and philosophical convictions (Article 2). Like most of the Convention's provisions, this article requires a balance to be struck between the powers of the State and the rights of the individual and so can give rise to difficult questions of interpretation. In the *Danish Sex Education cases* in 1976 the Court held that the Danish legislation on this subject, which provided for information to be given to schoolchildren in an objective manner, did not violate the Convention, even though some parents objected.[51] In *Campbell and Cosans* in 1982, on the other hand, it held that in similar circumstances the use of corporal punishment in a Scottish school did violate Article 2.[52]

The *Campbell and Cosans case* also raised the question of whether the corporal punishment which was objected to could be regarded as 'inhuman or degrading treatment or punishment', thereby contravening Article 3. The Court held that in the circumstances it could not, although in its earlier decision in the *Tyrer case* (1978) it had decided that the birching of a juvenile which had been ordered by a court in the Isle of Man did constitute a violation of this provision.[53] The *Soering case* (1989) raised an even more important point. There the Court not only decided that prolonged detention on 'death row' may involve inhuman treatment for the purposes of the Convention, but also held that if the United Kingdom were to extradite the applicant to the United States, where he could be sentenced to death, and subjected to such detention, the British government would violate its obligations under Article 3.[54] It reached this conclusion by emphasising the well established principle that the Convention must be interpreted and applied so as to make its safeguards practical and effective,[55] and noting in this connection that the 'absolute prohibition of torture and of inhuman and degrading treatment or punishment under the terms of the Convention shows that Article 3 enshrines one of the fundamental values of the Council of Europe'.[56]

Those who drafted the Convention would probably have been as surprised by the ruling in *Soering* as to see Article 3 being relied on by the applicants in *Campbell and Cosans*. As with some of the other issues we have considered, however, the cases on this provision show that the Convention can sometimes be used in unexpected ways, and reinforce the point made earlier, that in interpreting its provisions the Strasbourg organs do not regard themselves as circumscribed by the ideas of 1950, but are prepared to treat the Convention as a living and changing instrument.

## V. The Convention and the future

Having seen how the Convention functions at the present time, we shall conclude this review of the Strasbourg system by considering its future and the lessons to be learned from its evolution. Specifically, the questions needing attention are how the Convention and its working can be improved and the significance of the European experience for other schemes of regional protection.

## 1. *The system of international control*

Since the Convention was signed in 1950 membership of the Council of Europe has tripled and there has been a corresponding increase in the number of parties to the Convention. This expansion, and in particular the general acceptance of the right of individual application under Article 25, has generated an ever-increasing workload for the Strasbourg institutions. Contributing factors have been the dynamic approach of the Commission and the Court to the interpretation of the Convention, which, along with the conclusion of new protocols, has widened its protection, and the dissemination of knowledge about the Convention, which has encouraged more and more people to explore its possibilities. These developments are, of course, an indication of the Convention's success. But they have also put its institutional machinery under increasing strain and raised the question of how it can be adapted to cope with the new situation.

A number of steps to relieve the pressure have already been taken. The Commission and the Court, though not yet permanent organs, have extended their sessions significantly and the main purpose of Protocol No. 8 was to streamline the Commission by enabling it to work in chambers and to handle issues of admissibility through committees. These changes have been beneficial and make it possible for the Strasbourg organs to deal with cases more efficiently. However, they are plainly not enough. When Protocol No. 8 came into force in 1990 it was already clear that more drastic changes would be needed. Accordingly, the Committee of Ministers, which had initiated a review of the control mechanisms of the Convention some time earlier, decided that work on this project should be speeded up with a view to making further and more radical changes.

The negotiation of a new protocol with that object was, as may be imagined, not entirely straightforward, for while there was general recognition of the need for reform, there were different views as to how this should be achieved and a number of proposals had to be considered. Finally, however, in April 1994 agreement was reached on the text of Protocol No. 11, which was opened for signature in the following month.[57]

The main effect of the new protocol is to replace the present Commission and Court of Human Rights with a single full-time Court which will perform all the functions of the present organs. Although the new Court will have the same name as the existing institution, it will be a quite different organ. The provisions of Protocol No. 11 will therefore replace Articles 19–56 of the Convention, which govern the present institutions, with a new set of articles, dealing with the composition and powers of their successor. They will also replace the provisions of Protocol No. 2, which concerns advisory opinions, and those of the recent Protocol No. 9, which, as noted earlier, provides for individual access to the Court.

The number of judges on the new Court will be equal to the number of parties to the Convention. Their term of office will be six years, with the possibility of re-election, but they must retire at seventy. The terms of office of the present judges and commissioners will expire when the new protocol comes into force but, as a transitional arrangement, the Commission will continue to deal with cases which are in progress, for up to one year.

The business of the new Court will be conducted through various sub-units in a manner analogous to the practice of the present organs. Thus the Court will sit in committees of three judges to decide on admissibility. A case may be declared inadmissible if the committee is unanimous, but if it is not, the issue will be decided by a chamber of seven judges. Such chambers will also decide cases on the merits, unless a chamber decides to relinquish jurisdiction in favour of a grand chamber of seventeen judges. Grand chambers will also review decisions given by a chamber, if a case raises an important issue and a panel of five judges of the grand chamber decides that it is appropriate to do so. Grand chambers will also deal with all inter-State cases and requests for advisory opinions.

For each case that is registered, a judge rapporteur will be appointed to prepare the case and sit on the committee which will examine its admissibility. When a case is found to be admissible, the judge rapporteur may also take steps with a view to a friendly settlement, for which purpose the Court's facilities are to be at the parties' disposal. Committees will be established for one year and chambers for three years. The judge elected in respect of the State concerned will sit as an *ex officio* member of the chamber and, where relevant, the grand chamber; if necessary, an *ad hoc* judge may be appointed. The Presidents of the chambers and President and Vice-Presidents of the Court will also be members of grand chambers.

States will be able to bring cases, as at present, but, in an important innovation, the right of individual application will become mandatory. There will therefore be no need for this to be accepted separately, as is currently the position under Article 25. On the other hand, the existing conditions of admissibility will continue to apply and will presumably be given the same interpretation as at present. In all but exceptional cases the Court's hearings will be in public. Reasons will be given for decisions on admissibility and on the merits and the final judgement, which will be published and may, where appropriate, award just satisfaction, will be binding.

Although the most striking innovation of Protocol No. 11 is the replacement of the present Commission and Court with an entirely new institution, it also has major significance for the role of the Committee of Ministers. At present, as we have seen, the Committee performs two functions in the human rights system: supervising the execution of judgements in accordance with Article 54, and dealing with cases which are not referred to the Court under Article 32. The first function will continue, but as the new Court will be competent to handle all cases which are taken to Strasbourg, the second function will be abolished. The Committee of Ministers will therefore still be able to supply the necessary political backing for the Court, but will no longer be required to decide whether the Convention has been violated. That question will be exclusively one for the new Court, which is where, as a legal decision, it belongs.

As it is an amending protocol, Protocol No. 11 requires ratification by all the parties to the Convention and will come into force a year later. The new protocol, as noted earlier, was opened for signature in May 1994 and, since general ratification always takes some time, may not come into effect in the immediate future.[58] Until it does so, the supervisory arrangements of the original Convention, as modified by the earlier protocols, will continue to apply. Protocol No. 11, however, aims to effect a radical overhaul of the machinery of control to equip the Strasbourg system to face the future and seems well designed to do so.

## 2. *The rights protected*

The second issue which must be considered concerns the range of rights protected. We have seen that the list of rights and freedoms guaranteed in the Convention itself has been significantly extended in the four substantive protocols. The protocols have been widely, but not universally, accepted and so an important objective must be to encourage States which have not yet done so to accept them, thereby extending the Convention's protection. It is, of course, also important to ensure that new parties to the Convention accept the right of individual application and the jurisdiction of the Court, and to encourage support for Protocol No. 9. As regards the scope of the obligations undertaken, it is worth noting that many acceptances of the Convention and its protocols are subject to reservations which limit their effect. Accordingly, every effort should be made to dissuade new parties from making reservations and States which already have reservations should be urged to reconsider them.

What of the possibility of extending the Convention by the conclusion of new protocols? A useful reference point here is the Covenant on Civil and Political Rights to which many members of the Council of Europe are already parties. The Covenant contains a number of provisions with no counterpart in the Convention[59] and although considerable progress in bringing the two instruments into line was achieved with the conclusion of Protocol No. 7, there are still a number of discrepancies. Not all of these are important – there would, for example, probably be little purpose in a protocol guaranteeing the right of self-determination, even if it could be agreed. In other cases, however, an extension of the Convention would be valuable and in these areas there does appear to be scope for development.

One such area, which has recently been addressed, is the protection of minorities. Article 27 of the Covenant provides that persons belonging to ethnic, religious or linguistic minorities 'shall not be denied the right in community with other members of their group, to enjoy their own culture, to profess and practise their own religion, or to use their own language'. The Convention has no corresponding article, although when Protocol No. 4 was being drafted in 1965 the Assembly proposed the inclusion of a far-reaching provision on this issue which the governments did not feel able to accept.[60] The protocol was therefore completed without any reference to the rights of minorities. However, the Assembly continued to press the issue and in October 1991 the Steering Committee for Human Rights was asked to consider how the Council of Europe could take action to protect national minorities, taking into account the work on this subject of the United Nations and the Conference on Security and Co-operation in Europe, as well as deliberations within the Council of Europe. The Committee's report, which was available in September 1993, led to further discussions, the outcome of which just over a year later was the adoption of the Framework Convention for the Protection of National Minorities.[61]

The Convention is called a 'Framework Convention' because it is mainly a statement of objectives which the parties undertake to pursue, but does not specify in detail how they are to be implemented. Articles 1–3 set out the general principles which underlie the Convention, and Articles 4–19 the parties' undertakings, including protection from discrimination and recognition of cultural and language rights. Articles 20–23 contain provisions relating to the scope and interpretation of the Convention, and Articles 24–26 create supervisory arrangements, which utilise the Committee of Ministers, assisted by an advisory committee. The Convention, which was opened for signature in February 1995, will come into force when it has been ratified by twelve members of the Council of Europe[62] and is a significant step forward. For minority rights to be examined by the Commission and Court it will, of course, be necessary to go further and add a new protocol to the Convention. Work on this project is now proceeding.

Another provision of the Covenant which has no counterpart in the European Convention is Article 10, which provides that 'All persons deprived of their liberty shall be treated with humanity and with respect for the inherent dignity of the human person'. It continues by providing for the separation of accused persons from

convicted persons and of juveniles from adults, and asserts that
the essential aim of the penitentiary system shall be the
reformation and social rehabilitation of prisoners. The principles
to be observed in the treatment of prisoners broadly correspond
to those set out in the Standard Minimum Rules for Prisoners
adopted by the United Nations in 1955. Many of these principles
have been further developed in Council of Europe texts, while the
1987 European Convention for the Prevention of Torture,
described in the next chapter, contains a novel form of
supervisory machinery. The difference between the Convention
and the Covenant is therefore less important here than on the
issue of minorities. The inclusion of a general provision
corresponding to Article 10 would, nevertheless, enable the
Strasbourg institutions to review the treatment of prisoners on a
broader basis than that currently provided by Article 3 and, by
emphasising the positive obligations of the State authorities,
further encourage the best penalogical practice. This would
therefore be another useful development.

In the case of two other matters included only in the Covenant,
the value of adding obligations to the Convention is less evident.
Article 20 of the Covenant provides that 'any propaganda for war
shall be prohibited by law', and continues by demanding a similar
prohibition of 'any advocacy of national, racial or religious
hatred that constitutes incitement to discrimination'. However,
Article 10(2) of the Convention already authorises the limitation
of freedom of expression on grounds of public interest, and so
restrictions designed to further the objectives of the Covenant
would not usually be difficult to justify. The question is therefore
not whether a right which the Convention guarantees needs any
further qualification, but whether it would be useful to add a
positive obligation to prohibit the various forms of inflammatory
activity mentioned in the Covenant. This might be worth
considering. However, the machinery of the Convention is not
well suited to enforcing this kind of obligation and so, as many
European States are already parties to the Covenant, a protocol
dealing with these matters would largely be of symbolic
significance.[63]

In the case of Article 24 of the Covenant, which deals with the
rights of the child, the objection is rather different. It is true that
the Covenant provides for special measures of protection, the

requirement of registration immediately after birth, the right to a name and the right to acquire a nationality, and so goes well beyond the Convention, which does not deal with these matters explicitly. However, the rights in the Convention are guaranteed to 'everyone', which includes children, and in numerous cases, especially under Article 8, the rights of children and young people have been recognised. In addition, it is now open to States to become parties to the 1989 United Nations Convention on the Rights of the Child[64] and many have done so. The new Convention deals with children's rights in far more detail than would be possible in a modification to the European Convention. Here also, therefore, a new protocol would seem to be unnecessary.

In addition to changes which would extend the Convention's coverage of civil and political rights, suggestions have also been made from time to time for adding a protocol or protocols guaranteeing social, economic and cultural rights. Thus in 1978, when the Convention had been in force for twenty-five years, the Committee of Ministers reaffirmed its confidence in the Commission and the Court and decided to give priority to this issue.[65] However, this initiative has yet to produce results. The issues here are not easy, as there are bound to be differences of opinion not just about which rights should be included and how they should be defined, but also over the fundamental question of whether a system which functions on the basis of individual complaints is appropriate for dealing with economic and social rights. As we shall see in Chapter 5, the European Social Charter uses a quite different procedure and was intended to be the counterpart to the Convention. If the Charter can be overhauled and made to work more successfully, there will be less need to consider extending the Convention in this direction.

### 3. The significance of the Convention

The synopsis of leading cases given earlier cannot pretend to present a complete picture of the extraordinarily rich case law of the Commission and Court, but may at least convey an impression of the Convention in action. It can therefore provide a basis for answering our third and final question relating to the future, which concerns the inferences which may be drawn from

experience with the European Convention as regards the value of
a system for protecting human rights in this part of the world and
the conditions which have made it possible.

Any assessment of the record must begin by recognising the
crucial importance of co-operation by governments which has
been instrumental in enabling the Strasbourg institutions to work
effectively. It is also interesting to note the great variety of
problems which have arisen, involving nearly all the rights and
freedoms protected by the Convention and its protocols.
Moreover, the case law of the Court and Commission indicates
that no State should be immune from scrutiny to check that its
domestic arrangements comply with the obligations it has
accepted under treaties for the protection of human rights. Every
State which has accepted the right of individual petition has seen
cases against it brought before the Commission and the majority
have also had cases referred to the Court. No administration is
free from the possibility of error, even in countries which are
unquestionably among those with the best record for protecting
civil liberties.

This appraisal suggests two conclusions: first, that a system of
international supervision like that of the European Convention is
necessary and desirable, even for States which respect the rule of
law and possess constitutional guarantees of human rights and
fundamental freedoms; secondly, that, as has often been pointed
out, the Convention is the most effective international system for
protecting human rights that has yet been introduced anywhere in
the world. It is scarcely necessary to add that neither the
guarantees provided, nor the supervisory arrangements, are
perfect. Indeed, as we have seen, both have been periodically
revised and are bound to change further. The fact remains,
however, that the Convention functions in a way that would have
delighted its founders and seems set for a promising future.

But if there are grounds for satisfaction, there is an important
corollary which should not be forgotten. The European system
has been able to function effectively because the governments
concerned have been willing to co-operate with the Strasbourg
organs, and the States to which the system applies genuinely wish
to secure the effective exercise of human rights on their
territories.[66] The problems which come to Strasbourg, important
as they may be for the individuals concerned, are with few

exceptions of only marginal significance when compared with the massive and flagrant violations of human rights which occur in other parts of the world. The systematic torture of political prisoners, arrest of persons who then 'disappear', persecution of political opponents, imprisonment of human rights activists, and other practices which are prevalent elsewhere pose problems which are immeasurably more serious than those which constitute the day-to-day business of the European organs.

It follows that a member of the Inter-American Commission on Human Rights would be impressed by the functioning of the European system, but might reflect that it has comparatively little relevance to the problems of massive violations in certain Latin American countries with which that Commission has to deal. What is true for Latin America applies with even greater force elsewhere. If an analogy may be drawn without trivialising the issue, it is fine to have a referee in a football match when all the players know what game is being played and intend to respect the rules. But if there is no agreement on these matters, what is needed is not a referee but a fundamental change in outlook and political culture. Thus, much work remains to be done before we can expect to see regional arrangements for the protection of human rights, comparable to the European system, in other parts of the world.

## Notes

1 The negotiations are described more fully in A. H. Robertson and J. G. Merrills, *Human Rights in Europe*, third edition, Manchester, 1993, Chapter 1, and A. H. Robertson, 'The European Convention for the Protection of Human Rights', *British Year Book of International Law*, XXVII, 1950, p. 145.
2 On 1 January 1995 there were thirty parties to the Convention.
3 Among the many studies of the Convention are A. H. Robertson and J. G. Merrills, *Human Rights in Europe*, J. G. Merrills, *The Development of International Law by the European Court of Human Rights*, second edition, Melland Schill Monographs in International Law, Manchester, 1993, and P. van Dijk and G. J. H. van Hoof, *Theory and Practice of the European Convention on Human Rights*, second edition, Deventer, 1990. The text of the Convention, its protocols and related instruments can be found in Council of Europe, *European Convention on Human Rights: Collected Texts*, Dordrecht, which is regularly updated, I. Brownlie, *Basic Documents on Human Rights*, third edition, Oxford, 1992, p. 326, and P. R. Ghandhi, *International Human Rights Documents*, London, 1995, p. 125.

4 In many member States the provisions of the Convention are part of national law and can be applied by the domestic courts. See A. Z. Drzemczewski, *European Human Rights Convention in Domestic Law*, Oxford, 1982.

5 See Consultative Assembly, *Official Reports*, 7 September 1949, p. 127.

6 On 1 January 1995 declarations under Article 25 had been made by thirty States, i.e. by all parties to the Convention.

7 Only eleven inter-State applications have been made to date: two cases brought by Greece against the United Kingdom in 1956 and 1957 over Cyprus; a case brought by Austria against Italy in 1960 over a murder trial in the South Tyrol; two cases brought by Denmark, Norway and Sweden against Greece in 1969 and 1970, the Netherlands being a joint applicant in the first case; two cases brought by Ireland against the United Kingdom in 1971 and 1972 over the situation in Northern Ireland; three cases brought by Cyprus against Turkey in 1974, 1975 and 1977, following the Turkish intervention; and a case brought by Denmark, France, the Netherlands, Norway and Sweden against Turkey in 1982.

8 See European Commission on Human Rights, *Survey of Activities and Statistics 1993*.

9 For discussion of this issue see P. R. Ghandi, 'The Human Rights Committee and the right of individual communication', *British Year Book of International Law*, LVII, 1986, pp. 201, 229–32. For decisions in 1994 involving the French reservation see the *Thierry Trébutien case*, Communication No. 421/1990, and the *Jean Glaziou case*, Communication No. 452/1991, in *International Human Rights Reports*, II, 1995, pp. 16 and 25. As regards inter-State cases Article 62 of the Convention provides for exclusive use of the latter's procedures.

10 The functions and procedure of the Commission are described in more detail in Robertson and Merrills, *Human Rights in Europe*, Chapter 7.

11 When Protocol No. 10 comes into force this will be changed to a simple majority.

12 The role of the Committee of Ministers under the Convention is examined more fully in Robertson and Merrills, *Human Rights in Europe*, Chapter 9.

13 The functions and procedure of the Court are described in more detail in Robertson and Merrills, *ibid.*, Chapter 8.

14 On 1 January 1995 declarations under Article 46 had been made by thirty States, i.e. by all the parties to the Convention.

15 On 1 January 1995 fifteen States had ratified Protocol No. 9.

16 See *Explanatory Report* to Protocol No. 9, para. 21. Text in *Human Rights Law Journal*, XII, 1991, p. 51.

17 *Yearbook*, XI, 1968, pp. 690–728.

18 *Yearbook*, XII, *bis*: the *Greek case*.

19 Recommendation 547, *Texts Adopted by the Assembly*, January 1969, *Yearbook*, XII, 1969, p. 126.

20 The Compton Report (Cmnd 4823) and the Parker Report (Cmnd 4901).

21 *Yearbook*, XIX, 1976, p. 512.

22 ECHR, Series A, No. 25 (1978).

23 A convenient source of information on the practice of the Commission is its annual *Survey of Activities and Statistics*.

24 For a comprehensive review of the Court's jurisprudence see Merrills,

*Development of International Law*. A survey of the latest decisions of the
European Court is published each year in the *British Year Book of International
Law*.

25  Series A, Nos 1, 2 and 3 (1960–61).
26  Series A, No. 258 B (1993).
27  See, for example, the *Wemhoff case*, Series A, No. 7 (1968) (no violation), and
the *Ringeisen case*, Series A, No. 13 (1971) (violation).
28  Series A, No. 18 (1975).
29  Series A, No. 32 (1979).
30  Series A, No. 29 (1978).
31  Series A, No. 33 (1979).
32  Series A, No. 214 A (1991).
33  Series A, No. 34 (1979).
34  Series A, No. 28 (1978).
35  Series A, No. 290 (1994).
36  Series A, No. 160 (1989).
37  Series A, No. 31 (1979).
38  See Merrills, *Development of International Law*, pp. 98–124.
39  See the *National Union of Belgian Police case*, Series A, No. 19 (1975), the
*Swedish Engine Drivers' Union case*, Series A, No. 20 (1976), and the *National
Union of Belgian Police case*, Series A, No. 21 (1976).
40  Series A, No. 44 (1981).
41  Series A, No. 264 (1993).
42  Series A, No. 133 (1988).
43  See Merrills, *Development of International Law*, pp. 151–76.
44  Series A, No. 30 (1979). For the legislative response see S. H. Bailey, 'The
Contempt of Court Act 1981', *Modern Law Review*, XXXXV, 1982, p. 301.
45  Series A, No. 216 (1991).
46  Series A, No. 246 (1992).
47  Series A, No. 298 (1994).
48  Series A, No. 94 (1985); contrast the *Rasmussen case*, Series A, No. 87 (1984).
49  Series A, No. 98 (1986).
50  Series A, No. 102 (1986).
51  Series A, No. 23 (1976).
52  Series A, No. 48 (1982).
53  Series A, No. 26 (1978).
54  Series A, No. 161 (1989).
55  *Ibid.*, para. 87.
56  *Ibid.* para. 88.
57  For the text of Protocol No. 11 and the accompanying *Explanatory Report*, see
*International Human Rights Reports*, I(3), 1994, p. 206. For discussion of its
significance with references to earlier literature, see R. Bernhardt, 'Reform of
the control machinery under the European Convention on Human Rights',
*American Journal of International Law*, LXXXIX, 1995, p. 145.
58  On 1 January 1995 Protocol No. 11 had been ratified by four States.
59  A detailed comparison of the two instruments will be found in the third edition
of this book at pp. 131–41.
60  The Assembly's proposal was made in Recommendation 285 of 28 April 1961

but was rejected in the *Sixteenth Report of the Committee of Ministers, 1965,* paras 301–2.

61 The text of the Convention and the accompanying *Explanatory Report* can be found in *International Human Rights Reports,* II, 1995, p. 217. See also the 1992 European Charter for Regional or Minority Languages, text in Council of Europe, *Human Rights Information Sheet* No. 31, Strasbourg, 1994, p. 198.

62 It should be noted, however, that under Article 29 of the Convention States which are not members of the Council of Europe may accede to it on invitation.

63 It should also be noted that the 1966 Convention on the Elimination of All Forms of Racial Discrimination covers some of the same ground.

64 See Chapter 3.

65 Declaration on Human Rights of 27 April 1978, *Yearbook,* XXI, 1978, p. 82. See also F. G. Jacobs, 'The extension of the European Convention on Human Rights to include economic, social and cultural rights', *Human Rights Quarterly,* III, 1978, p. 166, and A. Berenstein, 'Economic and social rights: their inclusion in the European Convention on Human Rights – problems of formulation and interpretation', *Human Rights Law Journal,* II, 1981, p. 257.

66 It should be noted, however, that one party to the Convention, namely Turkey, has a particularly poor record in this respect. Its occupation of northern Cyprus has already given rise to four inter-State cases; Turkey has only recently made declarations under Articles 25 and 46 and, as noted in Chapter 5, the European Committee for the Prevention of Torture has been extremely critical of the government. These shortcomings make Turkey something of an 'odd man out' among Council of Europe States.

# CHAPTER 5

# Human rights in Europe II: other instruments and procedures

## I. The promotional activities of the Council of Europe

The first article of the Statute of the Council of Europe provides that the aim of achieving a greater unity between its members shall be pursued in a number of different fields (economic, social, cultural, scientific, legal and administrative) and also in the maintenance *and further realisation* of human rights and fundamental freedoms. In other words, the Council is required to work not only for the protection of such rights and freedoms as already exist, but also for their development and for the realisation of further rights. This was also recognised by the authors of the Convention. The Teitgen Report,[1] mentioned in the previous chapter, proposed that the Convention should protect 'those rights and freedoms [which] are the common denominator of our political institutions' and that other rights 'must also, in the future, be defined and protected'. In 1950 the governments added a preamble to the Convention indicating that in concluding it they were taking 'the first steps for the collective enforcement of certain of the rights stated in the Universal Declaration'. This also implied that further steps were to follow.

The work of 'further realisation', or protection of additional rights, requires intergovernmental agreement on new measures. It is therefore usually referred to as 'promotion' of human rights, in order to distinguish it from 'protection' of human rights, which involves judicial or quasi-judicial application of standards which have already been agreed. The UN Commission on Human Rights, for example, is primarily an organ of promotion, whereas the European Commission and Court, since they are concerned with the application of an existing treaty, are organs of protection. In the Council of Europe, since the promotional function is not within the competence of the two Convention organs, it has been necessary to provide for that function in another way. Accordingly, the Council has developed a kind of legislative procedure.

There are two types of instruments which the Council can employ: treaties (or conventions) and recommendations.[2] Treaties, of course, become legally binding only when they are ratified by States, while recommendations, as the name indicates, are instruments which do not purport to have binding effect. In both cases then the effectiveness of a given measure depends on the response of States and reflects the fact that the Council of Europe was conceived as, and has remained, a loose confederation of States, not a supranational organisation. Consequently, it would be wrong to take references to the 'legislative' activities of the Council of Europe too literally; nevertheless, measures to promote human rights have to originate and be negotiated somewhere and by providing a forum in which such initiatives are now routine, the Council has amply demonstrated its value.

Proposals for new measures usually stem from the Parliamentary Assembly, having been prepared by its Legal Affairs Committee. They are then transformed into action by the Committee of Ministers, assisted by its own committees of governmental experts. Thus there has developed a regular procedure by which a parliamentary committee studies the action required to promote human rights and submits its conclusions to the Assembly. The latter then addresses recommendations to the Committee of Ministers who, if they support the issue in principle, as they usually do, instruct their experts to prepare the necessary legal texts, which then come back to the ministers for final approval. Treaties and recommendations proceed through the Council system in much the same way, but at the last stage in the Committee of Ministers there is a difference which reflects their different legal character. Both types of instrument require unanimous approval;[3] however, in the case of draft treaties the effect of approval is to open the instrument for signature and ratification by the member States, whereas with recommendations no further steps are required.

By making use of the procedures just described, the Council of Europe has been able over the years to take a series of measures which have extended its human rights programme far beyond the 'first steps' represented by the conclusion of the Convention in 1950. Some of these measures, namely the various protocols to the Convention, the 1994 Framework Convention for the Protection of National Minorities and the 1969 Agreement Relating to Persons Participating in Proceedings of the European Commission and Court of Human Rights, have already been described. Two further measures, the 1987 European Convention for the Prevention of Torture and the 1961 European Social Charter and their recent protocols, will be examined in the next two sections. But these are not all. More than a hundred conventions and agreements sponsored by the Council of Europe have come into force, and these and a comparable number of recommendations are being added to at a steady rate. A considerable number of these measures concern aspects of European co-operation other than human rights. However, as the following review of recent instruments indicates, many, like those already mentioned, relate directly to issues with which we are concerned.[4]

As regards the protection of privacy, for example, a number of early initiatives culminated in Convention No. 108 of 1981, designed to provide protection with regard to the automatic processing of personal data. This in turn was followed by a whole series of recommendations covering the use of such data for scientific research, direct marketing, social security and other specific purposes.[5] Similarly, in 1987 as part of a preventative strategy to fight HIV infection, the Committee of Ministers passed a recommendation which supported voluntary testing for HIV, and rejected as unacceptable compulsory screening and restrictions on freedom of movement, while at the same time emphasising the importance of confidentiality in relation to reporting, notification and education.[6]

As regards protection against discrimination, recommendations designed to support the United Nations Convention on the Elimination of All Forms of Racial Discrimination of 1966 have been followed by others relating to equality of spouses in the criminal law and sex discrimination in general.[7] Also relevant in this connection are Convention No. 93 on the status of migrant workers, a recommendation concerning the problems which can arise when individuals with different nationalities marry, and another relating to the nationality of children.[8] Several of the measures taken, such as the last two, concern the family. Thus Convention No. 85 seeks to eliminate discrimination against children born out of wedlock and has already influenced the jurisprudence of the European Court of Human Rights and the Commission,[9] while Convention No. 105 is intended to ensure that decisions relating to custody are uniformly recognised and enforced. On a different aspect of family law, a recommendation of 1981 is designed to regulate the right of spouses to occupy the family home.[10]

Other promotional measures relate to the broad area of the administration of justice, criminal law and the legal process. The European Convention on Extradition No. 24 of 1957 has been supplemented by additional protocols (No. 86 and No. 98). There has been a recommendation on prosecutions *in absentia*[11] and two recommendations on compensation for the victims of crimes[12] and a Convention, No. 116, on the subject. Following the Heysel stadium disaster of 1985, Convention No. 120 was produced with the aim of bringing spectator violence within a common administrative and penal framework, and earlier, in 1977, Convention No. 90 on the suppression of terrorism had addressed another contemporary problem. In the field of punishment Convention No. 112 provides for persons convicted of a crime abroad to serve their sentences in their own country and a large number of recommendations have addressed the issue of prison conditions and the treatment of convicted persons. These include, for example, recommendations relating to prison labour, the treatment of long-term prisoners and foreign prisoners, the use which may be made of a person's criminal record and the question of rehabilitation.[13]

Measures such as these constitute an impressive body of international legislation, although conventions, of course, require acceptance and implementation. However, almost all the conventions sponsored by the Council of Europe, whether on issues of human rights or on other matters, eventually come into force and a high proportion have been ratified by more than half the member States.[14] It is worth noting in this connection that some conventions allow accession by States which are not members of the Council and that the European Union (EU), exercising its treaty-making power, has also become a party to certain conventions. Although it often takes some time for a new convention to be widely accepted, the matter is not left entirely to States, because the progress of particular conventions is regularly reviewed through procedures within the Council, which is therefore able both to encourage and to facilitate ratification.

In the case of recommendations the issue of ratification does not arise. However, although recommendations are not binding they are usually the result of long discussion and reflect a broad consensus. It would therefore be surprising if they were not influential. Moreover, to encourage compliance, the Committee of Ministers periodically exercises its power under the Statute to request governments to inform it of measures they are taking to implement specific recommendations. This makes it possible for the process of implementation to be monitored by an expert committee. The same committee also reviews the implementation of conventions. Moreover, several conventions contain their own monitoring mechanisms. Thus Convention No. 108, which was mentioned earlier, provides for the creation of a committee to facilitate and improve the application of the Convention and we shall see shortly that the same is true of the Social Charter.

Before moving on it is worth pointing out that conventions and recommendations are by no means the only ways in which the organs of the Council of Europe contribute to the promotion of human rights. The Council attends sessions of the UN Commission on Human Rights and its Sub-Commission on Prevention of Discrimination and Protection of Minorities and takes part in many similar activities. In Order No. 456 (1990) the Parliamentary Assembly decided to organise a symposium on the rights of minorities and to play a role of mediation and conciliation in minority conflicts.[15] The Council continues to encourage and support the fledgling democracies of Eastern Europe in a variety of ways. In 1994, for example, the Committee of Ministers decided that it will consider any question relating to the implementation of member States' commitments concerning democracy, human rights and the rule of law, which is referred to it by a member of the Council of Europe, by the Secretary-General, or by the Parliamentary Assembly, and, having considered the matter, will take such specific action as may be appropriate within its statutory powers.[16] Many similar initiatives of the Council in the field of human rights could be mentioned.

## II. The European Convention for the Prevention of Torture

In January 1981 the Consultative Assembly of the Council of Europe recommended that the Committee of Ministers should invite member States to hasten the adoption and implementation of the draft Convention against Torture which was being prepared by the United Nations Commission on Human Rights. As we saw in Chapter 3, the Convention was adopted by the General Assembly in December 1984 and subsequently opened for signature. In the meantime, however, the Legal Affairs Committee of the Council of Europe had approved a draft European Convention on Torture and, after extensive consultations, produced a final text. After consulting the Assembly, the Committee of Ministers adopted this text and the result, the European Convention for the Prevention of Torture and Inhuman or Degrading Treatment or Punishment, was opened for signature on 27 November 1987, came into force on 1 February 1989 and has now been widely accepted.[17]

The purpose of the Convention is to create a procedure for supervising the treatment of persons deprived of their liberty, with a view to strengthening, where necessary, the protection of such persons from torture and from inhuman or degrading treatment or punishment. To this end the Convention creates a Committee which may visit any place within the jurisdiction of the parties where persons are deprived of their liberty by a public authority. The first part of the Convention, which consists of Articles 1–3, defines the function of the Committee and lays down the parties' obligation to co-operate with it. The second part, Articles 4–6, deals with the membership and procedure of the Committee. The European Committee for the Prevention of Torture and Inhuman or Degrading Treatment, as the new body is known, has as many members as there are parties to the treaty. They must be suitably qualified and serve in their individual capacity. They are elected by the Committee of Ministers for four years and may be re-elected.[18] The Committee meets in camera and draws up its own rules of procedure.

The heart of the Convention is the third section, which consists of Articles 7–14 and which deals with the organisation of visits and the specific responsibilities of the Committee. It is important to appreciate that although the Committee is given wide powers to visit prisons and other places of detention and can, if necessary, be assisted by experts, it does not perform any judicial functions. It is therefore not its task to judge whether violations of treaty obligations have occurred, but rather to study the situation in the place visited, draw up a report on the facts found and make appropriate recommendations. As the explanatory report to the Convention puts it, 'The purpose of the Committee is not to condemn States, but, in a spirit of co-operation and through advice, to seek improvements, if necessary, in the protection of persons deprived of their liberty'.[19]

In accordance with the above aim, the information gathered by the Committee in relation to a visit, its reports and its consultations with the State concerned are confidential. However, a report can be published at the request of a party and, more important, if a State fails to co-operate or refuses to improve the situation in the light of the Committee's recommendations, 'the Committee may decide by a majority of two-thirds of its members to make a public statement on the matter' (Article 10(2)). In addition, and as a way of ensuring that the Committee's work becomes known, notwithstanding its confidential nature, the Committee must annually submit 'a general report on its activities' to the Committee of Ministers for publication.

The remaining provisions deal with the privileges and immunities of members of the Committee and various technical matters. Article 17 contains a saving clause in the usual form, providing that the Convention cannot be invoked as a justification for restricting the protection granted under other international instruments, or at the domestic level. Article 17(3), however, lays down that: 'The Committee shall not visit places which representatives or delegates of Protecting Powers or the International Committee of the Red Cross effectively visit on a regular basis by virtue of the Geneva Conventions of 12 August 1949 and the Additional Protocols of 8 June 1977 thereto'. This recognises that although the new Convention is not limited to time of peace, in cases of armed conflict the Geneva Conventions have priority of application.[20] The Convention required seven ratifications to bring it into force (Article 19) and is not subject to reservations (Article 21).

The Committee began visiting the States which have accepted the Convention in 1990 and has been very active.[21] The

Convention provides for both periodic visits, for which notice is given, and *ad hoc* visits, which are not announced, and can be made whenever the Committee deems necessary. Both types of visit have been made. In 1993, for example, the Committee made periodic visits to Greece, Liechtenstein, Luxembourg, Norway, Belgium, Ireland and Iceland, and an *ad hoc* visit to Northern Ireland.[22] When deciding where it should go when on a periodic visit, or whether an *ad hoc* visit is needed, the Committee utilises information supplied to its Strasbourg-based secretariat by NGOs, which also help by disseminating information about the Convention and the Committee among detainees and those responsible for places of detention.[23]

When making a visit members of the Committee can speak privately to detainees and interview any other person with relevant information. The report on a visit, as mentioned earlier, is normally confidential. However, it is interesting that in practice the State concerned often asks the Committee to publish the report so as to be able to make known the government's response. The United Kingdom, for example, requested publication of the report on the periodic visit which was made in 1991 and subsequently published its own follow-up report, and Finland and the Netherlands took similar action in relation to their visits in 1992.[24] One of the Committee's aims is to maintain a dialogue with the countries visited and such openness with regard to the process is to be welcomed.

Turkey, which has been a country of particular concern to the Committee, was the subject of *ad hoc* visits in 1990 and 1991 and a periodic visit in 1992. In its reports the Committee, having identified a number of serious deficiencies, made various recommendations concerning the treatment of detainees which were then discussed with the Turkish government. At the end of 1992 the Committee reviewed the action taken by the authorities and concluded that they had failed to strengthen the legal safeguards against torture and other forms of ill-treatment in police and gendarmerie establishments, or to deal with abuses in the anti-terror department of two police forces, as the Committee had recommended. It therefore decided to invoke the sanction provided for in Article 10(2) of the Convention and make a public statement on Turkey.[25] The statement documented the concerns of the Committee in considerable detail and shows that when recommendations are persistently ignored, which should be very rare, the Convention provides a useful means of applying pressure which the Committee is prepared to use.

Although the Convention is relatively new, the value of an instrument of this kind is already clear. As we have seen, the supervisory system established by the European Convention on Human Rights operates on the basis of inter-State complaints under Article 24 and individual complaints under Article 25. Important as these are for ensuring that States respect their obligations under Article 3, they require an alleged violation to have occurred and so operate after the event. There is therefore value in non-judicial machinery of an essentially preventative character, which is what this Convention provides. When the United Nations Convention was being drawn up a similar mechanism was proposed,[26] but, as noted earlier, the text which was adopted creates a Committee against Torture with other functions. It is thus not surprising that the members of the Council of Europe, several of whom are parties to the United Nations Convention, considered it appropriate to produce a regional Convention.

To develop the European Convention further two protocols have recently been negotiated and were opened for signature in November 1994.[27] Protocol No. 1 widens the geographical scope of the Convention by enabling States which are not members of the Council of Europe to accede to it by invitation, and Protocol No. 2 makes technical changes to the arrangements for elections. Both protocols require acceptance by all the parties to the Convention.

### III. The European Social Charter

#### 1. *Background*

We saw in the previous chapter that when the members of the Council of Europe were drafting the Convention on Human Rights they decided to concentrate on the protection of civil and political rights and to leave the question of economic and social rights for later consideration. Once the Convention had entered into force in 1953, closely followed by Protocol No. 1 in the following year, the Council turned its attention to the second category.

The issues here were far more difficult. One reason was the wide difference in social and economic conditions in the member States. It is only necessary to compare the resources and social services of Britain and the Scandinavian countries, on the one hand, with those of Greece and Turkey on the other to appreciate the problem of achieving agreement on common standards. A further difficulty stemmed from the very nature of the rights to be protected. If people are wrongly imprisoned they can apply for a writ of *habeas corpus*. If they do not receive a fair trial, they can appeal to a higher court, and so on. With economic and social rights, however, it is different. Implementing the right to work depends on the general economic situation and if someone is unable to find a job, an order from a court of law will not change matters. Similarly, a decent standard of living for all is a proper aim of social policy, but depends more on economic prosperity than on legislation. This does not mean that legal measures to give effect to social and economic rights serve no purpose, but it did mean that the approach to protecting those rights had to be different from that of the European Convention, and this was also true of the two United Nations Covenants.

The first step was the political decision that a new instrument should be prepared. During the winter of 1953–54 the Committee of Ministers prepared a programme of work for the Council of Europe which envisaged, among many other matters, the preparation of a Social Charter.[28] The task of preparing this was assigned to a new Social Committee which was set up at the same time, as a permanent body, to facilitate co-operation between the member States on social issues, under the overall authority of the Committee of Ministers.

When the Committee's decision was transmitted to the Assembly in May 1954 the latter welcomed the new development and instructed its own Committee on Social Questions to prepare a draft setting out its views.[29] By October this had been done and a complete draft Charter, proposing the creation of a European Economic and Social Council and other far-reaching provisions, was submitted to the Assembly.[30] In the Assembly the draft received a mixed reception and so a revised and less radical draft was produced for the following April. Further discussion resulted in the preparation of a third draft, which was discussed by the Assembly in October 1956.[31] However, as there were still differences of opinion on many points, the Assembly did not endorse the draft, but simply encouraged the Committee of Ministers to continue its work.[32]

It was now the turn of the Social Committee to take matters forward. In December 1958 the Committee of Ministers published another draft Charter[33] and at the same time encouraged the International Labour Organisation to convene a conference which resulted in a report recording the views of a wide range of participants on the text.[34] After receiving a further opinion from the Assembly in January 1960,[35] the Social Committee then worked out the final draft of the Charter, which was signed at a ceremony in Turin on 18 October 1961.[36] These long negotiations, extending over seven years, have been described here because they show the complexity of this type of law making, the contribution which was made by the different organs of the Council of Europe, parliamentary and governmental, and how, as a happy illustration of co-operation between international organisations, the ILO also played a part.

Certain basic features of the Social Charter are worth pointing out before we study its provisions in detail. The first is its treatment of the fact that a number of 'rights' which it asserts are really objects of social policy rather than rights which are legally enforceable. The difficulty here was that if these 'rights' were merely proclaimed as objectives, the Charter would have little value as an effective guarantee of economic and social standards. The solution was to divide the Charter into several distinct parts. Part I sets out nineteen separate rights, the realisation of which the contracting parties accept as the aim of their policy. This permits general affirmations of a far-reaching character, but as statements of policy without precise legal commitments. Part II then contains the legal obligations which the parties undertake so as to ensure the effective exercise of the rights proclaimed in Part I. With this double formulation it is thus possible to combine the general statement of long-term objectives with particular and more limited commitments of immediate application.[37]

The second basic characteristic of the Charter is its approach to the problem raised by variations in the economic and social development of the different member States. It was clearly unrealistic to expect that the less developed countries in Europe could assume the same obligations as their more fortunate partners. Equally, it would have been contrary to the general policy of the Council of Europe to draft an instrument to which only the more developed countries could subscribe. It was therefore provided that a member State would not be obliged to accept all the provisions of the Charter before ratifying it, but that it could initially be bound only by a stated minimum, in the expectation that it would find itself able to accept additional obligations with the passage of time. In this way it was hoped to achieve the progressive implementation of a Charter which, when fully applied, would guarantee a high standard of economic and social rights for everyone.

The third basic feature of the Charter is the attention given to the question of supervising its implementation. As already mentioned, the Assembly had suggested an Economic and Social Council which would have had representatives of employers, workers and consumers, rather like the ILO. The governments did not favour this approach, but set up instead an elaborate system of control based on reports by governments as to how they are implementing the Charter. This system, which makes supervision a task for the various committees and organs of the Council of Europe, will be examined after we have considered the scope of the Charter's protection.

## 2. *The rights protected*

Part I of the Charter begins by providing that 'the Contracting Parties accept as the aim of their policy, to be pursued by all appropriate means, both national and international in character, the attainment of conditions in which the following rights and principles may be effectively realised...'. These 'rights and principles' are then listed:

1    the right to work, which is formulated as: 'Everyone shall have the opportunity to earn his living in an occupation freely entered upon';
2    the right to just conditions of work;
3    the right to safe and healthy working conditions;
4    the right to a fair remuneration;
5    the right to organise;
6    the right to bargain collectively;
7    the right of children and young persons to protection against 'physical and moral hazards';

8     the right of employed women to special protection in case of maternity, and in other situations as appropriate;
9     the right to vocational guidance;
10    the right to vocational training;
11    the right to protection of health;
12    the right to social security;
13    the right to social and medical assistance;
14    the right to benefit from social welfare services;
15    the right of the disabled to special facilities;
16    the right of the family to social, legal and economic protection;
17    the right of mothers and children to social and economic protection;
18    the right to earn one's living on a footing of equality in the territory of another contracting party;
19    the right of migrant workers who are nationals of a contracting party and their families to protection and assistance.

Part II of the Charter, as already noted, then contains more precise commitments which the contracting parties assume with a view to ensuring the effective exercise of these rights. The provisions vary considerably, according to the nature of the right to be protected. The right to just conditions of work, for example, involves, among other things, limitation of working hours, public holidays with pay, two weeks' annual holiday with pay and a weekly rest period. Similarly, the right to a fair remuneration includes additional pay for overtime, equal pay for men and women, and so on. The right of children and young persons to protection includes ten separate provisions for their benefit. The undertakings designed to secure the right to protection of the family and of mothers and children, on the other hand, are rather more general and imprecise.

A number of the rights covered in the Social Charter were already the subject of the other conventions and agreements concluded earlier by the members of the Council of Europe. Though cross-references are, understandably, not given in the Charter, it is clear that its authors had these other instruments in mind. The right to organise, for example, is already guaranteed by Article 11 of the Convention on Human Rights. The right to social security in its international aspects forms the subject of two Interim Agreements on Social Security signed in Paris in December 1953,[38] and standards of social security are dealt with in the European Code of Social Security, concluded in April 1964.[39] Moreover, the right to social and medical assistance, also in its international aspects, forms the subject of the European Convention on Social and Medical Assistance of December 1953,[40] and the right to earn one's living in another country is one of the matters covered in the European Convention on Establishment of December 1955.[41]

Part III of the Charter contains the provisions which permit progressive implementation. They are rather complicated, but their key element is as follows. Seven rights were regarded as particularly important:

1    the right to work;
2    the right to organise;
3    the right to bargain collectively;
4    the right to social security;
5    the right to social and medical assistance;
6    the right of the family to special protection;
7    the right of migrant workers and their families to protection and assistance.

Under the provisions of Article 20 any contracting party must agree to be bound by the Articles of Part II of the Charter relating to at least five of these rights. In addition, it must agree to be bound by the provisions relating to at least five other rights as set out in Part II. It is possible, however, instead of accepting ten articles in their entirety, to accept a larger number in part.[42]

Also relevant to the scope of States' obligations are the final clauses of the Charter, which constitute Part V. Article 30 permits derogation 'in time of war or other public emergency threatening the life of the nation' and thus corresponds to Article 15 of the Convention on Human Rights, while Article 31, dealing with permissible restrictions, corresponds to Article 18 and the qualifications attached to the Convention's substantive provisions. Article 32 of the Charter, like Article 60 of the Convention, preserves any more favourable treatment that may already be provided in domestic law or other international treaties and Article 34, like Article 63, allows the Charter to be extended to non-metropolitan territories. Article 33, which has no equivalent in the Convention, deals with the implementation of certain obligations through collective agreements.

The Charter came into force in February 1965 on deposit of the fifth instrument of ratification and has now been accepted by just over half the members of the Council of Europe.[43] Almost all the States which have ratified the Charter have accepted considerably more than the minimum number of obligations under the arrangements in Part III, although, as yet, only a minority have accepted all its provisions. An Additional Protocol was adopted by the Committee of Ministers in November 1987 and opened for signature in May 1988.[44] It extends and improves the protection of certain rights already included in the Charter, guaranteeing, for example: the right to equal opportunities in employment without discrimination based on sex; workers' right to information and consultation in the workplace; workers' right to take part in deciding and improving their working conditions and working environment; and the right of the elderly to measures of social protection. The Additional Protocol came into force in September 1992, when it had been ratified by three States, but as yet has not been widely accepted.[45] Its application by the contracting States is monitored by the same international machinery as the Charter.

### 3. *The system of international control*

Part IV of the Charter provides for an elaborate system of control and supervision. Article 25 sets up a Committee of Experts, appointed by the Committee of Ministers from a list of independent experts 'of the highest integrity and of recognised competence in social questions', nominated by the contracting parties. The term of office is six years and members may be reappointed. Article 26 provides for the ILO to nominate a representative to assist the Committee in a consultative capacity.

The function of the Committee of Experts is to receive and examine reports which Articles 21 and 22 require the contracting parties to provide. These reports are of two kinds. Article 21 requires a report every two years concerning the application of all provisions in Part II which the State concerned has accepted. Article 22, on the other hand, requires reports 'at appropriate intervals' relating to the provisions of Part II which the State has not accepted. In relation to this second type of report it is for the Committee of Ministers to determine the particular provisions on which such reports shall be requested, and the form which they should take.

As well as being sent to the Committee of Experts, copies of each State's report must also be sent to national organisations of employers and trade unions, whose comments the governments must transmit to the Council of Europe (Article 23). This provides an opportunity to obtain information from independent sources which, as we have explained earlier, is essential if a reporting system is to be effective. After being considered by the Committee of Experts, the reports and the Committee's conclusions are next considered by the Governmental Social Committee of the Council of Europe, which represents the contracting parties and is assisted by selected organisations of employers and trade unions. Article 28 provides that the conclusions of the experts must also be sent to the Parliamentary Assembly, which then passes its views to the Committee of Ministers. Finally, the latter examines the results of all these deliberations and under Article 29 may by a two-thirds majority make appropriate recommendations to the contracting parties.

As the Charter has now been in force for more than a quarter of a century, it is possible to see how these complicated monitoring arrangements have worked in practice and to draw some conclusions about the effectiveness of the Charter generally. The supervision cycle provided for in Article 21, as mentioned earlier, covers a period of two years and the contracting States accordingly submit regular reports on the application of those provisions of the Charter which they have accepted. When it has considered a report the Committee of Experts divides its conclusions into sections, listing separately provisions of the Charter which it considers are being complied with, those which are not being complied with, and those where it is unable to say whether there is compliance. As might be expected, the independent experts have been more critical of the governments' reports than the Governmental Social Committee. Similarly, the Parliamentary Assembly has been quicker to detect shortcomings than the Committee of Ministers. The latter, moreover, for many years merely transmitted the reports of the various organs to the governments concerned, instead of using its power to make recommendations under Article 29.[46]

Nevertheless, practical results have been achieved. Thus the record indicates that numerous discrepancies have been corrected as a result of the operation of the reporting system. In 1990, for example, the Parliamentary Assembly noted that Cyprus had recently adopted a maternity protection law modelled on Article 8, while Austria had modified its legislation relating to the need for foreigners to obtain a work permit.[47] Many other examples of States changing their laws to comply with the Charter could be cited.[48] As with other human rights treaties, however, the effect of the Charter goes beyond the number of errors corrected, for the existence of the instrument is itself significant. The reporting obligation makes governments accountable for their laws and practices and provides all who are concerned with the economic and social aspects of human rights, whether as officials or citizens, with an international yardstick against which local practices can be measured. Thus with the Charter, as with the Convention on Human Rights, its indirect effect, in the sense of measures which are introduced to comply with obligations and to forestall criticism, is at least as important as the correction of deficiencies which are formally identified.

## 4. *The future of the Charter*

Although the Charter has undoubtedly been useful, it has been clear for some years that it can be improved. The supervisory machinery in particular came in for criticism as it became clear that the Committee of Experts was overworked and underfunded and that what one observer called a 'counter-productive rivalry'[49] between that body and the Governmental Social Committee had developed. Rectifying these deficiencies, like achieving institutional reform in other areas of human rights, was ultimately a matter of the States concerned summoning the necessary political will and it was only long after the deficiencies in the Charter had become apparent that this matter received attention. By the end of 1990, however, as the impact of legal and political developments elsewhere became evident,[50] the issue of reform could no longer be postponed. The Committee of Ministers therefore created an *ad hoc* committee of experts to make 'proposals for improving the functioning of the Social Charter and particularly the functioning of its supervisory machinery'.[51] The first fruit of this initiative was the Amending Protocol to the Charter, which was opened for signature in October 1991.[52]

The Amending Protocol is wholly concerned with improving the system of supervision and to that end makes a number of changes to the present arrangements. Perhaps the most significant change concerns the role of the Governmental Social Committee and its relation to the Committee of Experts. The 'rivalry' mentioned above stemmed from the practice which the Governmental Social Committee had developed of reviewing the findings of the experts and passing on to the Committee of Ministers only those findings that it agreed with. This naturally diminished the experts' influence and by creating what was in effect a political filter reduced the cases which reached the final stage. The new Protocol removes this element, not by eliminating the Governmental Social Committee altogether, but by removing its power to interpret the Charter and making its main function one of advising the Committee of Ministers of the cases in which it should exercise its power to make recommendations. As an ancillary function, the Governmental Social Committee may also propose to the Committee of Ministers that studies be carried out on social issues and articles of the Charter which might be updated, a task for which, as a political organ, it is well suited.

To enable the Committee of Experts to deal with its increasing workload, its membership is enlarged from the maximum of seven laid down in Article 25 of the Charter to a minimum of nine. Instead of being appointed by the Committee of Ministers, as at present, the experts will, like judges of the European Court of Human Rights, be elected by the Parliamentary Assembly from a list of nominations by the contracting parties. And to enable it to scrutinise reports more effectively, the Committee will be able to request additional information from the parties and conduct oral hearings. The Parliamentary Assembly will no longer receive the report of the Committee of Experts and pass its comments to the Committee of Ministers. Instead, it will simply hold periodic debates on the Charter when the Committee of Ministers has completed its work. This change, which was suggested by the Parliamentary Assembly, will simplify the present arrangements and speed the whole process up.

Other important changes made in the Amending Protocol concern the role of the Committee of Ministers and the contribution of employers' organisations, trade unions and NGOs. As regards the Committee of Ministers, the States eligible to vote will be limited to the parties to the Charter (rather than all the members of the Council of Europe, as previously) and the Committee is to adopt individual recommendations to the contracting parties, instead of non-specific resolutions, as hitherto. As regards the role of outside organisations, the Protocol provides for a 'modest extension'[53] of their involvement by requiring the comments of employers' organisations and trade unions to be sent directly to the Secretary-General, providing for NGOs to be consulted also, and improving the latter's position in the Governmental Social Committee. In a further move towards openness national reports, formerly treated as confidential, are to be made available on request.

To come into force the Amending Protocol must be accepted by all the parties to the Charter, which is likely to take some time.[54] However, the Final Resolution of the Turin Conference at which the Protocol was agreed requested the contracting States and the supervisory bodies to bring certain of the new measures into force immediately, insofar as this was not inconsistent with the Charter. In accordance with that request, the Governmental Social Committee is now performing its more limited role, while the Committee of Ministers decided in 1993 to adopt the revised voting arrangements and in accordance with the Protocol to make individual recommendations to the contracting parties.[55] In the following year it decided to enlarge the Committee of Experts to nine. It can therefore be seen that even before the acceptances needed to bring the Protocol into force have been obtained, many of its provisions are already in effect.

A number of other steps to improve the operation of the Charter have also been taken recently, or are under consideration. In 1992 the Committee of Ministers adopted on a trial basis a new set of rules concerning the periodicity of reports, under which States are to report every two years on the 'hard core' articles of the Charter identified in Article 20(1)(b) and on provisions in respect of which negative or adjourned conclusions have been adopted, and every four years on the remaining provisions.[56] In accordance with the Final Resolution of the Turin Conference a study was made of the possibility of introducing a system which would permit collective complaints similar to that operated by the ILO, and an optional protocol to provide for this was agreed in 1995.[57]

Attention is also being given to the extension of the Charter's substantive guarantees. As already noted, an Additional Protocol with that object was adopted as recently as 1988, but as the Charter itself was negotiated more than thirty years ago, there is much that might be added to reflect today's ideas. Issues under consideration include the protection of children in employment, the protection of parenthood and the family and equality between the sexes.[58] A further protocol addressing these and other issues may therefore emerge in due course.

Currently, then, efforts are being made to revitalise the Social Charter by both extending the scope of its provisions and improving its institutional arrangements. These measures are important and, as we have seen, have already had an effect. For them to be fully effective, however, it is also necessary for governments to play their part. This requires more contracting parties to agree to be bound by all of the Charter's provisions, for those members of the Council of Europe which have not ratified it to do so and for the various protocols and any subsequent instruments to be accepted. While the Social Charter already occupies a significant place in the development of international protection for economic and social rights, there is much to be done if, as its drafters intended, it is to be an effective guarantee of 'the bread and butter rights of the working man' in democratic Europe.

## IV. The Organisation for Security and Co-operation in Europe

### 1. *The Helsinki Agreement and its aftermath*

The Conference on Security and Co-operation in Europe (CSCE) opened in July 1973 and concluded at Helsinki two years later.[59] The thirty-five participants included all the European States from East and West, with the exception of Albania, together with the United States and Canada. The final session was attended by the heads of State or government of nearly all the participating States and the Final Act was signed on 1 August 1975.[60] It comprised four sections concerning respectively: (1) questions relating to security in Europe, (2) co-operation in the fields of science, technology and of the environment, (3) co-operation in humanitarian and other fields, (4) the 'follow-up' to the Conference. As this list indicates, the Final Act covered a great deal of ground and, among other things, was the first step in a process with enormous significance for human rights in Europe.

The main concern of the Final Act is not with human rights, but with international security and relations between States. During the period of détente which followed the most intense phase of Cold War the Soviet Union had been seeking recognition of its European frontiers established in 1945 and this had become a central goal of Soviet foreign policy. The difficulty was that there was little that the Western powers were likely to receive in return. They had no territorial claims to make – apart from the Germans, who knew that reunification was not then on offer – and it appeared that major political changes in the East in the immediate future were very unlikely. What the Western powers therefore tried to obtain were certain rather modest concessions as regards respect for human rights in the hope that these might eventually contribute to liberalisation.

The first three sections of the Final Act are generally referred to as the three 'baskets'. The most important for our purpose is 'Basket I', which begins with a 'Declaration on Principles Guiding Relations Between Participating States'. This sets out ten fundamental principles including, as Principle No. 7, 'Respect for human rights and fundamental freedoms, including freedom of thought, conscience and religion and belief' and, as Principle No. 8, 'Equal rights and self-determination of peoples'. Each principle is then explained in more detail. Principle No. 7 has eight paragraphs of explanatory text and is wide in its scope because the second paragraph refers to the effective exercise of all rights and freedoms. However, its effect is limited because the commitment is to 'promote and encourage' rather than to 'respect' human rights. Some of its provisions cover the same ground as treaties such as the UN Covenants, but are nevertheless significant because the whole point of this part of the Final Act was to try to secure a political commitment from Moscow to do something for human rights.

Basket III, entitled 'Co-operation in Humanitarian and Other Fields', is also relevant. It contains four sections. The first relates to 'human contacts' and deals with reunification of families, marriages between citizens of different States, travel, tourism, meetings of young people and sport. The second section concerns the free flow of information. The participating States 'make it their aim to facilitate the freer and wider dissemination of information of all kinds', and this section sets out a number of steps to be taken, relating to oral, printed, filmed, and broadcast information. Basket III concludes with two short sections about co-operation and exchanges in the fields of culture and education.

Although the Final Act is usually referred to as the 'Helsinki Agreement', it is not a treaty. Consequently, like subsequent instruments in what came to be known as 'the CSCE process', the Helsinki Agreement does not create legal obligations, but sets out essentially political undertakings. This does not mean that the Agreement and later documents are unimportant, or can be violated with impunity. Indeed, as events were to demonstrate, the signature of the Soviet Union and the communist governments of Eastern Europe to the Final Act was a great deal more significant in practice than their ratification of the UN Covenants, for it put the issue of human rights firmly on the agenda and, by demonstrating Western concern, encouraged dissidents such as Youri Orlov and Andrei Sakharov in the Soviet Union, and movements such as Solidarity in Poland and Charter 77 in Czechoslovakia to press their governments for action.

At first, however, little in the way of positive change was achieved and the communist authorities responded to human rights activists with a policy of repression. In accordance with the provisions of Basket IV of the Helsinki Agreement a follow-up meeting to the 1975 Conference was held in Belgrade between October 1977 and March 1978, but was not a success.[61] A further conference was held in Madrid in 1980. When that year opened, the international atmosphere was sombre. Détente had been wrecked by the Soviet invasion of Afghanistan in December 1979 and human rights activists everywhere in the Soviet bloc were being persecuted. The climate could scarcely have been worse for attempting to make progress in the observance of human rights. Despite this, however, a concluding document was eventually agreed which contained several new commitments in the three main baskets and arrangements to further meetings to provide continuity.[62]

## 2. The Vienna follow-up conference

A further follow-up conference began in Vienna in November 1986. Although East–West relations were now much improved, the proceedings, like those of the Madrid conference, were initially held up by disagreements in which the issue of human rights was again prominent. The conference therefore overran and instead of finishing, as planned, in the middle of 1987, was not concluded until 1989. On this occasion, however, the final document represented a very significant advance. Following their established strategy of offering economic co-operation and progress on security issues in exchange for progress on human rights, the Western States succeeded in obtaining a document with a much more elaborate statement of, and commitment to, human rights than any of its predecessors. The Concluding Document, which also contains provisions on security, trade, culture, education and the environment, is too long to summarise here.[63] However, a number of key features of its provisions on human rights must be mentioned.

As regards human rights in general, the participating States agree to ensure that their laws are in conformity with their obligations under international law and their CSCE commitments. They also agree to develop their laws in the field of human rights so as to guarantee their effective exercise, including the provision of effective remedies. Furthermore, they undertake to respect the right of citizens to contribute to the promotion and protection of human rights, and to that end agree to publish and disseminate information on CSCE documents. They also state that they will consider acceding to human rights treaties and undertake to continue their efforts to realise economic, social and cultural rights.

As regards specific rights, there is a detailed commitment on freedom of religion, with a list of rights which are specifically recognised, including freedom to establish and maintain places of worship, freedom to create religious organisations and freedom to give and to receive religious education in the language of one's choice. In addition, there is a guarantee of freedom of movement both within the State and in the sense of the freedom to leave and return, and a number of commitments on security of the person, including the protection of individuals from psychiatric or other medical practices that violate human rights, and an undertaking that States will consider acceding to the UN Convention against Torture.

An important part of the document deals with the difficult and sensitive issue of national minorities.[64] There is thus an undertaking to refrain from discrimination and to implement the provisions of the Helsinki Agreement and the Madrid Concluding Document. However, the Vienna Concluding Document goes further by promising the creation of conditions for the free exercise of minority rights and the full equality of minorities with others. As we shall see, these undertakings were soon to be taken even further. The Document also contains commitments relating to the monitoring of the CSCE commitments by individuals and groups, which the States undertake not to interfere with, and specific undertakings to facilitate dissemination of information.

In a long section entitled 'Human Contacts', the Concluding Document reaffirms the right to leave and return and addresses particular issues relating to the implementation of these rights, including the procedure to be adopted when an application is refused, and the right to be informed of remedies against the decision. While it is recognised that there can be legitimate reasons for refusing a person permission to leave, there are provisions designed to ensure that such decisions are regularly reviewed and others which seek to ensure that in all cases the initial decision is given within a reasonable time, for which purpose specific time limits are laid down.

A particularly important feature of the Concluding Document is the inclusion for the first time in a CSCE text of a human rights monitoring procedure.[65] This is a diplomatic, not a legal procedure, with four possible stages. The first stage involves exchanging information and responding to requests and representations; the second, holding bilateral meetings concerning situations and cases with a view to resolving them; the third, drawing the attention of other CSCE States to those situations and cases; and the fourth and final stage, bringing the matter to one of the conferences in the CSCE process. The separate stages are clearly envisaged as a way of putting a defaulting State under increasing pressure. Thus what begins as a discreet diplomatic exchange can be escalated, if necessary, to a major political confrontation. As with any system for protecting human rights, success cannot be guaranteed, but the 'Human Dimension' mechanism, as it is known, encouraged governments to take up and to rectify human rights complaints and was soon being used.[66]

### 3. *The Copenhagen meeting and Paris Summit*

The Vienna Concluding Document was adopted in January 1989 and was followed in June by the first meeting of the Conference on the Human Dimension of the CSCE in Paris, and in June 1990 by a second meeting, in Copenhagen.[67] At the Paris meeting there was much said on the subject of human rights, but no final document was adopted. By the time of the Copenhagen meeting, however, a political revolution had taken place in the East, with liberalisation in the Soviet Union, the overthrow of the Ceausescu regime in Romania, the impending reunification of Germany and the withdrawal of Soviet power from Eastern Europe, clearing the way for the emergence of popular governments. In this dramatically changed situation the Copenhagen meeting was able to agree that there had been a 'fundamental improvement' in compliance with commitments in the field of the Human Dimension since the Paris meeting and to adopt a wide-ranging Concluding Document which constitutes a further significant step in the CSCE process.

The Copenhagen Document has five parts, or chapters. The first chapter is concerned with the rule of law and the essential features of democracy. Thus it contains commitments to free and honest elections with universal suffrage, to freedom to organise political parties and to campaign with non-discriminatory access to the media, to a clear separation between the State and political parties, to the accountability of the police and the military to civil authorities and to constitutional and representative government. A number of commitments in this chapter correspond closely to provisions in the European Convention on Human Rights and were clearly inspired by it. For example, there is a guarantee of the right to take proceedings to challenge detention similar to Article 5(4), a guarantee of the right to a fair trial corresponding to Article 6(1), together with recognition of the presumption of innocence and the rights of the defence equivalent to Articles 6(2) and (3). Not the least significant feature of this part of the Concluding Document is that it recognises the value of treaties on human rights and commits States which are not already parties to consider accession to instruments such as the European Convention which provide a procedure for individual complaints.

Chapter 2 of the document reaffirms and advances previous CSCE commitments to freedom of expression, freedom of assembly and association and freedom of movement. It also restates and confirms a large number of other rights, including the rights of the child, the protection against torture and other forms of ill-treatment, the right of conscientious objection, the question of abolition of the death penalty, free movement and contacts among citizens and the rights of migrant workers. Particularly interesting features of this chapter are a commitment to the promotion of economic, social and cultural rights, and the acceptance, as a confidence-building measure, of the presence of observers from outside States and NGOs at court proceedings in the participating States.

The third chapter of the Document concerns the promotion of democracy and human rights through co-operation and the sharing of ideas, expertise and information. A number of areas appropriate for such co-operation are listed and the expertise of the Council of Europe in the field of human rights is mentioned specifically. This acknowledgement is then reinforced by an undertaking to consider ways of enabling the Council of Europe to contribute to the Human Dimension of the CSCE process in the future.

Chapter 4 is entirely devoted to the question of national minorities. Thus it returns to one of the main themes of the Vienna Concluding Document, but with a significant elaboration of States' commitments. It begins by stating that minorities issues need to be resolved within a democratic framework and goes on to proclaim the right of minorities to the free exercise of their human rights without discrimination. Policies of forcible assimilation are rejected and the Document provides a long list of specific minority rights, including the right to use their own language, to set up their own religious and educational institutions, to freedom of association and expression and to freedom of movement. The Document states that these commitments do not imply any right to contravene the United Nations Charter, or other principles of international law, or, significantly, the provisions of the Helsinki Agreement, 'including the principle of the territorial integrity of States'. Measures envisaged for the future included action by States to combat discrimination and persecution and a future meeting of experts (held in Geneva in 1991).

The fifth and final chapter is concerned with the monitoring procedure, or 'Human Dimension' mechanism, which we have noted was a key innovation in the Concluding Document of the Vienna conference. The Copenhagen Concluding Document recognised the value of this mechanism and developed it by incorporating two useful improvements. A four-week time limit was introduced for responses to requests for information and representations at the first stage; then at the second stage a three-week time limit was agreed for the holding of the required bilateral meeting, along with an undertaking, presumably based on experience, not to raise extraneous matters at such meetings, except with prior agreement. Other proposals for strengthening the mechanism which were considered included the sending of observers to investigate situations and cases, the appointment of rapporteurs to conduct inquiries and conciliation and the setting up of a Committee on the Human Dimension of the CSCE. However, these and a number of other suggestions were reserved for later consideration.

The Copenhagen meeting was quickly followed by the Paris Summit of Heads of State and of Government in November 1990. The outcome of that meeting was the Paris Charter for a New Europe.[68] Unlike the documents we have been considering, the Charter contains little in the way of new substantive commitments and its first two chapters largely repeat and emphasise earlier commitments as regards human rights and other matters. What distinguishes the Paris Charter, however, is that it creates a comprehensive institutional framework for the CSCE to replace the *ad hoc* arrangements which had been followed previously. For in the third chapter of the Charter and in a supplementary document a regular schedule of meetings is laid down and three central offices are established to facilitate communication among the participating States.[69]

## 4. *Recent developments*

In accordance with the schedule set out in the Charter, regular meetings have been held since the Paris Summit, at which there have been further developments in relation to human rights. In September 1991 the third meeting of the Conference on the Human Dimension of the CSCE was held in Moscow. This had several important features.[70] There was an extensive debate on the implementation of established standards in the former communist States, an elaboration of commitments in the Copenhagen Document and a series of new commitments with regard to matters such as the rights of women, disabled people, minorities and migrant workers which had not previously been covered. In addition, NGOs were given an increased role in the CSCE process for monitoring human rights, both nationally and at meetings relating to the Human Dimension.

The Human Dimension mechanism, which we have seen was introduced at Vienna and modified in the Copenhagen Document, was further refined, but a more dramatic development was the introduction of a new, third-party procedure, which had been hinted at in the Paris Charter. This utilises a list of experts, nominated by the participating States, which is maintained by one of the offices set up by the Charter, the Office for Democratic Institutions and Human Rights (ODIHR). The new scheme became operational in 1992 and is rather complicated. In essence, however, it can be thought of as a combined mediation, fact-finding and conciliation mechanism which can function in three different ways.

Under the 'voluntary mechanism', a State can invite a CSCE mission of up to three experts to 'address or contribute to the resolution of questions on its territory relating to the human dimension of the CSCE'.[71] The mission submits its observations to the inviting State and the latter then reports to the ODIHR. Under the 'mandatory procedure' a State which has used stages 1 and 2 of the original mechanism can ask the ODIHR to invite the other State to use the voluntary mechanism, and if it does not, or the mechanism is unsuccessful, the requesting State can, with the support of at least five other States, obtain the appointment of up to three CSCE rapporteurs, whose function is to investigate the question and report to the ODIHR. Finally, under the 'super-mandatory mechanism', stages 1 and 2 can be missed out and mandatory involvement begun immediately. For this to happen, however, nine, rather than five, co-sponsoring States are required.

The fourth follow-up meeting was held at Helsinki in 1992. As at Copenhagen, there was a new political situation. The Soviet Union and Yugoslavia had both disintegrated and with the admission of nearly all the successor States the number of participants had increased from the thirty-five States which were present in 1975 to more than fifty. A further effect was to change the nature of proceedings from the traditional confrontation between rival political blocs to a looser and more open process of negotiation in which States were free to press their individual interests. An additional and extremely ominous factor was that whereas the break-up of the Soviet Union had been relatively painless, Yugoslavia seemed about to descend into all-out civil war. As a result, much of the Helsinki meeting was taken up with that situation.

The Helsinki meeting, which lasted three months, produced a long document containing an extensive set of decisions.[72] As on previous occasions, much of the business of the meeting was concerned with security, the settlement of disputes and other issues in addition to human rights. However, a number of matters of present relevance were dealt with and are covered in the Concluding Document. Thus it is confirmed that commitments relating to the human dimension cannot be considered to fall exclusively within States' domestic jurisdiction, and there are enhanced undertakings on a number of specific matters including indigenous populations, minorities, non-discrimination and democracy. No changes are made to the Human Dimension mechanism, but the ODIHR becomes the 'main institution of the Human Dimension', with a broad range of competencies. Moreover, in a further significant institutional development, the Helsinki Document establishes the office of CSCE High Commissioner on National Minorities, with the function of early warning and conflict prevention with regard to minority issues.

The Helsinki Document provided for a review of Human Dimension issues at annual meetings and issues of human rights are now regularly taken up either through the Human Dimension mechanism or in other ways. In September 1992, for example, Estonia invited a mission of experts to visit the country and measure its legislation against human rights standards, and in January of the following year a similar mission visited Moldova to study its handling of inter-ethnic relations. During this period the CSCE also had a rapporteur mission in Croatia to investigate reports of atrocities against civilians. In addition to missions under the Human Dimension mechanism, activities with human rights implications have included CSCE missions to Kosovo, Georgia and Bosnia-Herzegovina, election observation in Romania, Lithuania and elsewhere, and the sending of personal representatives designated by the current Chairman-in-Office to Moldova and Tajikistan.[73]

At the end of 1994 it was decided to rename the CSCE the 'Organisation for Security and Co-operation in Europe', in recognition of its transformation from a series of conferences to a fully fledged organisation with permanent organs and arrangements.[74] Within the structure which has now evolved it is clear that measures to promote and protect human rights occupy a prominent place. The original Human Dimension mechanism was useful in enabling East–West issues to be raised in the final days of the Cold War, but as membership of the Council of Europe has widened and many former communist States have accepted the European Convention on Human Rights, the Moscow procedures and the other activities mentioned above are now more significant. The OSCE is, of course, a political method of dealing with human rights and, as such, may be constrained by the factors noted in Chapter 3, when we were considering the United Nations Commission.[75] However, as we saw then, there are advantages in having a political institution which considers questions of human rights routinely and through a variety of procedures, and that is what the OSCE now provides.

In assessing the significance of these developments it is important to remember that the process which produced the OSCE was and still is about much more than human rights. As we have seen, the Helsinki Agreement grew out of security proposals put forward by the Soviet Union during the period of détente and while the political landscape has changed enormously, much of the importance of the OSCE is still to be found in these and related considerations. It is significant that the Paris Summit was immediately preceded by the twenty-two countries which had participated in the negotiations on Conventional Armed Forces in Europe signing a treaty on arms reduction and a declaration on the use of force.[76] The institutions created by the Charter for a New Europe include a Conflict Prevention Centre, and there are, of course, numerous undertakings in the CSCE documents relating to economics, science, technology and the environment, which we have not mentioned.

A second point is that if one considers what has been achieved in the specific field of human rights, it is clear that the process described above should not be looked at in isolation but must be seen in the context of legal and political developments elsewhere. Legally, it is clear that the inspiration for the norms articulated in the various CSCE documents is to be found in the UN Covenants, the European Convention and other human rights instruments. On the institutional side the Human Dimension mechanism does break new ground, although it is also recognised that this is an addition to, and not a substitute for, the protection offered by the various treaty mechanisms. Politically, the Helsinki Agreement put the issue of human rights firmly on the agenda of East–West relations and ensured that it stayed there. By doing so it not only raised expectations, but also initiated a dialogue about human rights leading to commitments capable of expansion. Despite the changes of recent years, the dialogue and the commitments are still important. While the Council of Europe will continue to welcome new members, diplomatic arrangements for handling the problems of an increasingly fragmented continent at the political level may be no less significant for human rights than the legal procedures of the European Convention. By surviving the final phase of the Cold War and contributing to its demise, the CSCE process passed its first test. Its contribution to human rights in Europe in the next decade, a second and quite different test of its value, is potentially enormous.

## V. Conspectus

In this chapter we have outlined a range of institutions and procedures that are now available for promoting and protecting human rights in Europe. Bearing in mind that these arrangements function alongside the elaborate machinery of the European Convention on Human Rights, described in Chapter 4, it is evident that Europe is a region in which an unusually rich variety of international human rights activity takes place. Yet there is more, for the European Court of Justice has declared that fundamental rights are part of Community law[77] and the 1992 Treaty of Maastricht contains extensive provisions on economic and social matters. Consequently, in addition to the arrangements described above, there is also the possibility of securing protection for human rights through the institutions of the EU, at least in some circumstances. Although therefore the place of human rights in Community law is a complex topic which cannot be examined here,[78] no account of human rights in Europe would be complete without mentioning the fact that over large areas of economic and social activity within the Union human rights are well protected.

The existence of so many arrangements for dealing with rights of different types and at different levels raises the question whether the situation within Europe could be simplified and a single institution created to deal with all human rights. This question was posed more than twenty years ago by Professor Max Sørensen, former President of the European Commission of Human Rights and later to be a judge of the European Court of Justice, who wrote in 1972:

> Plans for a 'Grand Design' with a view to the reorganisation and amalgamation of European institutions have been conceived, but never realised. The rational urge of the human mind and the hard realities of governing Europe will some day breathe new life into these plans and overcome the political obstacles of various kinds which have delayed their realisation.
>
> One element in such a 'Grand Design' might very well be an amalgamation of existing judicial bodies on the European level and a corresponding extension of the jurisdiction of a new European Court of Justice to all subject-matters and all persons covered by the separate judicial bodies existing at present. Unity of jurisdiction is to some extent an important element of a fair and adequate administration of justice, and the very ideal of human rights may in this way be harnessed to future moves for the reform of European institutions.[79]

At the present time, when a radical recasting of the Strasbourg institutions is about to take place and the prospects for further European integration are being debated, it cannot be said that uniting the institutions of the EU with those of the European Convention is an immediate possibility. Widening the debate to include the institutions of the European Social Charter and those of the OSCE makes the prospect of a 'Grand Design' in which human rights in Europe are administered under one roof recede even further.

The fact that the protection of human rights in Europe forms an historical patchwork rather than a single undifferentiated composition should not, however, be a source of unease. The different arrangements have developed to satisfy different requirements and both the rate and direction of their growth have been determined by social, political and moral forces whose influence has varied materially, geographically and over time. Moreover, underlying the various systems which have been developed, and are developing, there is to be found a single philosophical impulse, the idea of the individual as a being of moral worth whose rights, whether in the civil and political sphere, or in the economic, social and cultural sphere, merit international protection.

## Notes

1  *Documents of the Assembly*, 1949, Document 77.
2  See F. E. Dowrick, 'Council of Europe juristic activity 1974–86, Part I', *International and Comparative Law Quarterly*, XXXVI, 1987, p. 633.
3  But see Dowrick, *ibid.*, p. 636 note 13 and p. 641 note 51 for explanation of how this requirement is interpreted in practice.
4  For an excellent survey of the Council's recent work see Dowrick, *ibid*. For an outline of earlier initiatives by the Council see the same author's 'Juristic activity in the Council of Europe – 25th year', *International and Comparative Law Quarterly*, XXIII, 1974, p. 610.
5  For example, Recommendation (83)10, Protection of Personal Data used for Scientific Research; Recommendation (85)20, Protection of Personal Data used for Direct Marketing; Recommendation (86)1, Protection of Personal Data used for Social Security.
6  Recommendation R(87)25, Concerning a Common European Public Health Policy to Fight the Acquired Immunodeficiency Syndrome (AIDS).
7  Recommendation (78)37, On Equality of Spouses in Criminal Law; Recommendation (85)2, On Legal Protection against Sex Discrimination.
8  Recommendation (77)12, On Nationality of Spouses of Different Nationalities; Recommendation (77)13, On Nationality of Children born in Wedlock.
9  See the *Inze case*, ECHR, Series A, No. 126, discussed in J. G. Merrills, *The Development of International Law by the European Court of Human Rights*, second edition, Manchester, 1993, pp. 225–6. The same Convention was also referred to in the *Marckx case*, Series A, No. 31, and the *Johnston case*, Series A, No. 112.
10  Recommendation (81)15, On the Right of Spouses to the Occupation of the Family Home and Use of Household Contents.
11  Recommendation (75)11, On the Criteria Governing Proceedings in the Absence of the Accused.
12  Recommendation (77)27, On the Compensation of Victims of Crimes; Recommendation (85)11, Victim's Position in the Framework of Criminal Law and Procedure.
13  See Recommendation (75) 25, On Prison Labour; Recommendation (76)2, On the Treatment of Long-Term Prisoners; Recommendation (84)12, On the

Treatment of Foreign Prisoners; Recommendation (84)10, On the Criminal Record and Rehabilitation of Convicted Persons.

14 See Dowrick, 'Juristic activity 1974–86', pp. 636–7.

15 See Council of Europe, *Human Rights Information Sheet*, No. 27, Strasbourg, 1991, p. 214.

16 See Declaration on Compliance with Commitments Accepted by Member States of the Council of Europe, adopted by the Committee of Ministers on 10 November 1994, text in *International Human Rights Reports*, II, 1995, p. 250.

17 For the text of the Convention see I. Brownlie, *Basic Documents on Human Rights*, third edition, Oxford, 1992, p. 383, and P. R. Ghandhi, *International Human Rights Documents*, London, 1995, p. 141. For a detailed analysis see A. Cassese, 'A new approach to human rights: the European Convention for the Prevention of Torture', *American Journal of International Law*, LXXXIII, 1989, p. 128. On 1 January 1995 the Convention had been ratified by twenty-nine States.

18 Protocol No. 2 to the Convention, which is not yet in force, will enable members of the Committee to be re-elected twice, instead of once as at present.

19 Council of Europe, *Explanatory Report*, 1987, para. 20. But see note 24.

20 It should be noted, however, that the Committee may visit any places of detention if the International Committee of the Red Cross does not visit them 'effectively' or 'on a regular basis'; see *Explanatory Report*, para. 93.

21 See M. Evans and R. Morgan, 'The European Convention for the Prevention of Torture: operational practice', *International and Comparative Law Quarterly*, XXXXI, 1992, p. 590.

22 See Council of Europe, *Human Rights Information Sheet*, No. 32, Strasbourg, 1994, p. 92, and No. 33, 1994, p. 116.

23 See K. Boyle, 'Europe: The Council of Europe, the CSCE and the European Community', in H. Hannum (ed.), *Guide to International Human Rights Practice*, second edition, Philadelphia, 1992, pp. 151–2.

24 For information on these responses see note 22. A useful analysis of the first three reports to be published can be found in Evans and Morgan, 'Operational practice', pp. 610–14. The UK report identified prison conditions which in the Committee's view amounted to inhuman and degrading treatment. As Evans and Morgan point out (p. 592), this finding raises problems as regards both the relation between the Committee and the institutions of the European Convention on Human Rights, and the standards the Committee is applying in its work.

25 For the text of the statement see *International Human Rights Reports*, II, 1995, p. 251.

26 Costa Rica submitted a draft optional protocol to this effect which was not adopted. See *Explanatory Report*, para. 2.

27 For the text of the protocols and the Secretariat's Introductory Note, see *International Human Rights Reports*, I(2), 1994, p. 339.

28 Special Message of the Committee of Ministers transmitting to the Consultative Assembly the Programme of Work of the Council of Europe, *Documents of the Assembly*, 1954, document 238, para. 45.

29 Opinion No. 9, *Texts Adopted by the Assembly*, May 1954.

30 *Documents of the Assembly*, 1955, document 403.

31  *Documents of the Assembly*, 1956, document 536.
32  Recommendation 104, *Texts Adopted by the Assembly*, October 1956.
33  *Documents of the Assembly*, 1959, document 927.
34  ILO, *Record of the Proceedings of the Tripartite Conference Convened by the ILO at the request of the Council of Europe*, Geneva, 1959.
35  Opinion No. 32, *Texts Adopted by the Assembly*, January 1960.
36  For the text of the Charter see Brownlie, *Basic Documents*, p. 363. For an excellent analysis see D. J. Harris, *The European Social Charter*, Charlottesville, 1984.
37  See F. Tennfjord, 'The European Social Charter – an instrument of social collaboration in Europe', *European Yearbook*, IX, 1961, p. 71.
38  *European Treaty Series*, Nos 12 and 13.
39  *Ibid.*, No. 48.
40  *Ibid.*, No. 14.
41  *Ibid.*, No. 19. These five Conventions and Agreements may be found in the collection published by the Council of Europe, *European Conventions and Agreements* I (1949–61) and II (1961–70).
42  The nineteen articles in Part II of the Charter contain seventy-two numbered paragraphs. A State may ratify the Charter if it agrees to be bound by no fewer than forty-five numbered paragraphs, provided that it accepts no fewer than five of Articles 1, 5, 6, 12, 13, 16 and 19.
43  On 1 January 1995 twenty members of the Council of Europe had ratified the Charter.
44  For the text of the Additional Protocol see *International Legal Materials*, XXVII, 1988, p. 575.
45  On 1 January 1995 five parties to the Charter had also ratified the Additional Protocol.
46  Discussion of the application of the Charter can be found in Harris, *European Social Charter*, and the earlier history in F. Sur, 'La Charte Sociale Européenne: dix années d'application', *European Yearbook*, XXII, 1974, p. 88, and H. Wiebringhaus, 'La Charte Sociale Européenne et la Convention Européenne des Droits de l'homme', *Human Rights Journal*, VIII, 1975, p. 527.
47  See Opinion No. 149, *Texts Adopted by the Assembly*, May 1990.
48  See the examples given in the third edition of this book at pp. 253–5.
49  See the comments of the Secretary-General of the Council of Europe to the Informal Ministerial Conference on Human Rights, held at Rome in November 1990, reported in Council of Europe, *Human Rights Information Sheet*, No. 27, Strasbourg, 1991, p. 217.
50  In particular, the end of communist rule in Eastern Europe, leading to applications to join the Council of Europe from that region, and the renewed emphasis on social rights in the EU during the negotiation of the Treaty of Maastricht. See D. J. Harris, 'A fresh impetus for the European Social Charter', *International and Comparative Law Quarterly*, XXXXI, 1992, p. 659.
51  Decision of the ministers' deputies, 449th meeting, December 1990.
52  For the text of the Protocol see *International Legal Materials*, XXXI, 1992, p. 155.
53  See Harris, 'A fresh impetus', p. 669.
54  On 1 January 1995 seven States had accepted the Amending Protocol.

55 For examples of the Committee's present practice see its Resolution and Recommendations of 7 September 1993 in respect of Greece, Norway and the United Kingdom, in *International Human Rights Reports*, I(1), 1994, p. 264.

56 See Harris, 'A fresh impetus', p. 675, and Council of Europe, *Human Rights Information Sheet*, No. 31, Strasbourg, 1994, p. 73.

57 See Harris, *ibid.*, p. 673, and Council of Europe, *Human Rights Information Sheet*, No. 32, Strasbourg, 1994, p. 92. The protocol providing for collective complaints is not yet in force.

58 See Harris, *ibid.*, p. 675, and Council of Europe, *Human Rights Information Sheet*, No. 32.

59 For a contemporary view of the Conference, see D. G. Scrivner, 'The Conference on Security and Co-operation in Europe: implications for Soviet–American détente', *Denver Journal of International Law and Policy*, VI, 1976, p. 122. For discussion of the Final Act of the Conference, with particular reference to its treatment of human rights, see H. S. Russell, 'The Helsinki Declaration: Brobdingnag or Lilliput?' *American Journal of International Law*, LXX, 1976, p. 242.

60 The full text of the Final Act, which is very long (about 80,000 words), may be found in various official publications. Extensive extracts are given in Brownlie, *Basic Documents*, p. 391, and Ghandhi, *Human Rights Documents*, p. 186.

61 See W. W. Bishop and others, 'Human rights and the Helsinki Accord – a five year road to Madrid', *Vanderbilt Journal of Transnational Law*, XIII, 1980, p. 249.

62 See G. Edwards, 'The Madrid Follow-Up Meeting to the CSCE', *International Relations*, VIII, 1984, p. 49.

63 For the text of the Concluding Document see *Human Rights Law Journal*, X, 1989, p. 283, Brownlie, *Basic Documents*, p. 450, and Ghandhi *Human Rights Documents*, p. 226. The Concluding Document was also published in the United Kingdom as Cm 649 in March 1989. For discussion of the treatment of human rights in the Document, see A. Bloed and P. van Dijk, *The Human Dimension of the Helsinki Process*, Dordrecht, 1991, and D. McGoldrick, 'Human rights developments in the Helsinki process', *International and Comparative Law Quarterly*, XXXIX, 1990, p. 923.

64 See F. Ermacora, 'Rights of minorities and self-determination in the framework of the CSCE', in Bloed and van Dijk, *Human Dimension*, p. 197.

65 For detailed discussion see A. Bloed and P. van Dijk, 'Supervisory mechanism for the Human Dimension of the CSCE' in Bloed and van Dijk, *Human Dimension*, p. 74, and R. Brett, 'The development of the Human Dimension Mechanism of the Conference on Security and Co-operation in Europe (CSCE)', *Papers in the Theory and Practice of Human Rights*, No. 1, Human Rights Centre, University of Essex, 1992.

66 In the first fifteen months in which it was available the new mechanism was used about 100 times in many different circumstances; see McGoldrick, 'Human rights developments', pp. 924–7, and F. Coomans and L. Lijnaad, 'Initiating the CSCE supervisory procedure', in Bloed and van Dijk, *Human Dimension*, p. 109.

67 See McGoldrick, 'Human rights developments', pp. 935–9, and A. Bloed, 'A new human rights catalogue: the Copenhagen Meeting of the Conference on

the Human Dimension of the CSCE', in Bloed and van Dijk, *Human Dimension*, p. 54.

68  For the text of the Paris Charter see *Human Rights Law Journal*, XI, 1990, p. 379, Brownlie, *Basic Documents*, p. 474, and Ghandhi, *Human Rights Documents*, p. 264.

69  For a useful account see E. Schlager, 'The procedural framework of the CSCE: From the Helsinki consultations to the Paris Charter, 1972–1990', *Human Rights Law Journal*, XII, 1991, pp. 233–7.

70  For the text of the Document produced by the Moscow meeting see Ghandhi, *Human Rights Documents*, p. 273. For discussion see D. McGoldrick, 'The development of the Conference on Security and Co-operation in Europe – from process to institution', in B. S. Jackson and D. McGoldrick, *Legal Visions of the New Europe*, Dordrecht, 1993, pp. 148–51.

71  See McGoldrick, *ibid.*, p. 149.

72  See McGoldrick, *ibid.*, pp. 159–75, and D. McGoldrick, 'The development of the Conference on Security and Co-operation in Europe (CSCE) after the Helsinki 1992 Conference', *International and Comparative Law Quarterly*, XXXXII, 1993, p. 411, and R. Brett, 'The challenges of change', *Papers in the Theory and Practice of Human Rights*, No. 2, Human Rights Centre, University of Essex, 1992.

73  On the various activities mentioned in the text and others see, Council of Europe, *Human Rights Information Sheet*, No. 31, Strasbourg, 1994, p. 95, and No. 32, 1994, p. 116.

74  See M. Sapiro, 'Changing the CSCE into the OSCE: legal aspects of a political transformation', *American Journal of International Law*, LXXXIX, 1995, p. 631.

75  In June 1993, for example, it was decided to send a rapporteur mission under the Human Dimension mechanism to Serbia to investigate reports of human rights violations. However, the Serbian authorities refused to allow the CSCE representatives entry, with the result that the mission was unable to carry out its mandate.

76  See Schlager, 'The procedural framework', p. 234.

77  See M. H. Mendelson, 'The European Court of Justice and human rights', *Yearbook of European Law*, I, 1982, p. 125, and M. B. Akehurst, 'The application of general principles of law by the Court of Justice of the European Communities', *British Year Book of International Law*, LII, 1981, p. 29.

78  For discussion of this issue see A. H. Robertson and J. G. Merrills, *Human Rights in Europe*, third edition, Manchester, 1993, pp. 368–78, with references to earlier literature.

79  M. Sørensen, 'The enlargement of the European Communities and protection of human rights', *European Yearbook*, XIX, 1972, pp. 3–17. See also H. Lannung, 'Human rights and the multiplicity of European systems for international protection', *Human Rights Journal*, V, 1973, p. 651.

# CHAPTER 6

# *The American Convention on Human Rights*

## I. The origin and history of the Convention

The movement for Latin American unity began in the early years of the nineteenth century, when the Latin American republics achieved their independence. By 1825 they had been recognised by the United States and then by Britain, and the proclamation of the Monroe Doctrine was effective in discouraging European intervention in American affairs.

As early as 1822 Simon Bolivar proposed a 'meeting of plenipotentiaries of the Americas' with a view to establishing a confederation of the newly independent republics. As a result of further proposals which he made in December 1824, the 'First Congress of American States' was held in Panama in June and July 1826. It produced a 'Treaty of Perpetual Union, League and Confederation' between the participating States, but this ambitious project was stillborn, because it was ratified by only one State. Subsequently, the 'First International American Conference', held at the invitation of the United States and attended by seventeen American republics, was held in Washington from October 1889 to April 1890. It was here that the International Union of American Republics was founded. Commonly known as the Pan American Union, its principal functions were to encourage economic co-operation and the peaceful settlement of disputes.

Between the beginning of the twentieth century and the outbreak of the Second World War eight conferences of American States were held at irregular intervals, but with increasing frequency, in various Latin American capitals. This period also saw the opening in 1910 of the 'House of the Americas' in Washington, as the headquarters of the Pan American Union. During the Second World War meetings of consultation of foreign ministers took place in 1939, 1940 and 1942 to discuss the problems confronting the American republics as a result of the war, and to protect them from subversion in what came to be known as 'the political defence of the hemisphere'. The third of these meetings recommended that the American republics should sever diplomatic relations with the Axis powers.

The Inter-American Conference on Problems of War and Peace was held in Mexico in February and March 1945 to consider, among other matters, the organisation of the Inter-American system in the post-war world. Its conclusions were instrumental in the adoption at the San Francisco conference a few months later of Chapter VIII of the UN Charter on 'Regional Arrangements'. The Inter-American Conference in Rio de Janeiro in 1947 was principally devoted to the question of the maintenance of continental peace and security, and its outcome, the Inter-American Treaty of Reciprocal Assistance, signed in Rio on 2 September 1947, is still the basic instrument of collective security of the Inter-American system.

At the ninth Inter-American Conference at Bogotá in 1948, the American States undertook a review of their methods of co-operation and reorganised the whole system. The 'Charter of Bogotá' adopted on this occasion furnished the new constitutional instrument that was needed and thereby established the Organisation of American States (OAS). The Charter announces in its first article that the OAS is a regional agency within the United Nations. It then continues by laying down the essential purposes of the Organisation, which include: to strengthen peace and security, to ensure the peaceful settlement of disputes, to provide for common action in the event of aggression, and to promote economic, social and cultural development.

Next come two important chapters on 'Principles' and 'Fundamental Rights and Duties of States'. These affirm the significance of international law and fundamental human rights, declare that an act of aggression against one constitutes aggression against all American States, and emphasise the principle of non-intervention, to which the American republics have traditionally attached great importance. The Charter then provides separate chapters on the pacific settlement of disputes, on collective security, and on economic, social and cultural standards.

Another basic text adopted at Bogotá was the American Declaration on the Rights and Duties of Man. While it is, for the most part, on rather similar lines to the Universal Declaration of the United Nations, it is worth noting that it was adopted in May 1948, that is to say, seven months before the Universal Declaration, and that it contains no less than ten articles setting out the duties of the citizen, in addition to twenty-eight articles proclaiming individual rights.

The Bogotá Conference gave new life, as well as new institutions, to the Inter-American system. The Inter-American Conference was established as the supreme policy-making organ. New councils (Economic and Social, Cultural, Juridical) were organised and started their work, while the existing Council of Permanent Representatives in Washington continued as the organ of direction for current business.

A meeting of consultation of the ministers for foreign affairs, held at Santiago in 1959, resulted in further initiatives in the field of human rights. The Ministers adopted a 'Conclusion' containing the following statement:

> eleven years after the American Declaration of the Rights and Duties of Man was proclaimed, the climate in the hemisphere is ready for the conclusion of a Convention – there having been similar progress in the United Nations Organisation and in the union known as the Council of Europe in the setting of standards and in the orderly study of this field, until today a satisfactory and promising level has been reached.

The same document instructed the Inter-American Council of Jurists to prepare a draft Convention on Human Rights and a draft Convention for the creation of an Inter-American Court for the Protection of Human Rights, along with other appropriate organs. It also resolved to create an Inter-American Commission on Human Rights of seven members elected as individuals by the Council of the OAS from panels of three candidates presented by the governments. Accordingly, the Inter-American Council of Jurists met in Santiago later in the year and prepared a draft Convention, which was largely based on the European model.

This draft Convention was considered at the Second Special Inter-American Conference held in Rio de Janeiro in 1965. In fact the Conference considered three drafts: one prepared by the Inter-American Council of Jurists in 1959, and two revised drafts presented by Chile and by Uruguay which took account of recent European developments. The Chilean text added a striking innovation in its Article 19, designed to prevent military coups d'état – the right of the electorate to be represented and governed by their legally elected representatives. The Uruguayan draft, on the other hand, gave particular attention to economic and social rights. It was soon evident, however, that the competent committee of the Rio Conference could not produce a new draft Convention in the short time at its disposal. The three drafts were therefore referred to the Council of the OAS so that, after hearing the views of the Inter-American Commission on Human Rights, it could produce a new draft Convention. This would then be sent to the governments for their comments, after which the Council would call a special conference to produce a final text and open it for signature.

The Rio Conference resolved that, pending the conclusion of the new Convention, the existing Commission on Human Rights should be authorised to consider complaints from individuals alleging violation of certain basic rights, namely the right to life and liberty, freedom of opinion and expression, the right to a fair trial, protection from arbitrary arrest, due process of law, equality before the law without discrimination, and freedom of religion. The Commission would have the right, when considering such complaints, to request information from and make recommendations to governments and, in certain cases, to publish reports on the action taken.

The Third Special Inter-American Conference was held in Buenos Aires in February 1967, with the object of revising the Charter of the OAS. Most of its decisions do not concern the subject matter of this book[1] but one which does relates to the Inter-American Commission on Human Rights.

The Inter-American Commission, which, as we have seen, was originally created by a resolution of the foreign ministers at Santiago in 1959, became in the amended Charter a statutory organ of the OAS 'whose principal function shall be to promote the observance and protection of human rights and to serve as a consultative organ of the Organisation in these matters'. The revised Charter went on to say that the structure, competence and procedure of the Commission would eventually be set out in an Inter-American Convention on Human Rights. Pending the conclusion of the new Convention, the existing Commission on Human Rights would discharge the functions set out in the Charter (Article 150).

In accordance with the decisions taken at Rio de Janeiro in 1965, the Council of the OAS requested the Inter-American Commission on Human Rights to examine the various drafts for the proposed Convention and submit its own proposals on the matter. This was duly done. In the meantime the General Assembly of the United Nations, in December 1966, approved the text of the UN Covenants. The Council of the OAS then asked its member governments whether they still wished to go ahead with the preparation of a separate Inter-American Convention. The majority of member governments said that they did. Accordingly, at the beginning of October 1968 the Council of the OAS submitted the revised draft Convention prepared by the Inter-American Commission on Human Rights, inviting comments from governments. When these had been received a Special Conference on Human Rights was held in San José, Costa Rica, in November 1969 to produce a final text.

Nineteen of the twenty-four member States of the OAS were represented at the Conference, the absentees being Bolivia, Barbados, Haiti, Jamaica and Cuba. There were observers from various non-member States and from certain international organisations, including the United Nations, UNESCO, and the ILO. The members of the Inter-American Commission on Human Rights also attended, together with three 'special advisers', who were invited as expert consultants on account of their knowledge of the European Convention and its system.[2]

The American Convention on Human Rights, otherwise known as the 'Pact of San José', was drafted at this Conference and signed on 22 November 1969.[3] It entered into force on 18 July 1978, on the deposit of the eleventh instrument of ratification, and has now been widely accepted.[4] In 1988 an Additional Protocol was concluded which extended the range of rights protected, and two years later a further protocol was added to abolish the death penalty. The OAS Charter itself has also been further amended, first by the 1985 Protocol of Cartagena de Indias,[5] which extended the objectives of the Organisation and modernised its institutional machinery, and then in 1992 and 1993 by the Protocols of Washington and Managua, which enhanced its treatment of human rights. The protocols to the Convention are further described in the survey of the rights protected immediately following, and the latest Charter amendments in the final section of this chapter.

## II. The rights protected

The undertaking of the States in Article 1 of the American Convention is to 'ensure to all persons subject to their jurisdiction the free and full exercise' of the rights and freedoms recognised therein. The limitation 'within their territory', which is found in the UN text, is thus not included in the American Convention. The obligation is otherwise very similar to that contained in the UN Covenant, as it was intended, in principle, to be of immediate application. Article 2 provides that contracting parties will adopt such legislative or other measures as may be necessary in cases where the rights and freedoms are not already ensured in their domestic law.

Twenty-six rights and freedoms are protected by the American Convention. Twenty-one of these are included in the UN Covenant on Civil and Political Rights. They are:

1  the right to life;
2  freedom from torture and inhuman treatment;
3  freedom from slavery and servitude;
4  the right to liberty and security;
5  the right to a fair trial;
6  freedom from retroactivity of the criminal law;
7  the right to respect for private and family life;
8  freedom of conscience and religion;
9  freedom of thought and expression;
10  freedom of assembly;
11  freedom of association;
12  freedom to marry and found a family;
13  freedom of movement;
14  the right to free elections;
15  the right to an effective remedy if one's rights are violated;
16  the right to recognition as a person before the law;

17   the right to compensation for miscarriage of justice;
18   the right to a name;
19   the rights of the child;
20   the right to a nationality;
21   the right to equality before the law.

The five rights and freedoms included in the American Convention but not in the United Nations Covenant are:

22   the right of property;
23   freedom from exile (though the Covenant provides in Article 12 that 'No one shall be arbitrarily deprived of the right to enter his own country');
24   prohibition of the collective expulsion of aliens;
25   the right of reply;
26   the right of asylum.

On the other hand, the provision in the UN Covenant on the rights of minorities (Article 27) has no counterpart in the American Convention.

A comparison of the provisions of the American Convention with those of the European Convention and its protocols reveals that the principal rights included in the American but not in the European text are: the right of reply, the rights of the child, the right to a name and to a nationality, and the right of asylum. On the other hand, the right to education, contained in Protocol No. 1 to the European Convention, was omitted from the American text.

The definitions of the American Convention are generally closer to those of the United Nations Covenant on Civil and Political Rights than to the European Convention, though there are several differences which are sometimes due to following the European model. As one would expect, many articles provoked long and lively discussion at the San José Conference, for example those on the right of property, the right of asylum, the rights of illegitimate children, and on the prohibition of propaganda for war, which is included, as an exception, in the article on freedom of expression. On a number of occasions delegates maintained that it would be better to follow the United Nations texts and so avoid conflicting definitions at the regional and universal levels. Generally, however, this argument was rejected, on the ground that since the American States had decided to go ahead with the conclusion of their own Convention after the UN Covenants had been completed, it was appropriate to introduce modifications in the light of circumstances in the American republics.

Two of the most important rights guaranteed in the UN Covenant and in the two regional Conventions are the right to liberty and security, including freedom from arbitrary arrest, and the right to a fair trial. The draft submitted to the San José Conference contained provisions defining these rights which gave less protection than Articles 9 and 14 of the UN Covenant and Articles 5 and 6 of the European Convention. The special advisers drew attention to these differences, and the Conference agreed to change the provisions concerned. As a result, Article 7(5) now provides that 'any detained person shall be brought promptly before a judge ... and shall be entitled to trial within a reasonable time,' and so on. In Article 8, on the right to a fair trial, the text submitted to the Conference provided for 'a fair hearing' without further definition. The Conference agreed to a proposal to strengthen this very important provision by adding the words 'by a competent, independent and impartial tribunal established by law' from the UN Covenant, together with the words 'within a reasonable time' from the European Convention.[6]

Another question which was discussed was how the Convention should deal with reservations. During the negotiations some delegations argued that reservations should be permitted only in respect of constitutional provisions which are in conflict with the provisions of the Convention, because if a State were permitted to make a reservation merely because a provision of domestic law was inconsistent with the Convention, the number of reservations would be excessive. On the other hand, some argued that too rigid an attitude on this point would make ratification more difficult, and probably slower, and might even prevent the Convention from coming into force. The first point of view had considerable support, but was not accepted by the plenary Conference. Agreement was finally reached on a proposal of Uruguay with the result that Article 75 permits reservations 'in conformity with the provisions of the Vienna Convention on the Law of Treaties signed on 23 May 1969'. In retrospect it seems that the fears on this issue were rather exaggerated. Although the

Inter-American Court has already had occasion to consider Article 75 in two of its advisory opinions,[7] of the numerous States which have ratified the Convention, an insignificant minority have made reservations.

It will be noted that the Convention contains no guarantees of economic, social and cultural rights like those to be found in the first UN Covenant and the European Social Charter. Instead, there is merely a general undertaking in Article 26 to adopt measures to achieve the full realisation of the rights implicit in the corresponding standards of the OAS Charter. Although this undertaking is supported by an obligation in Article 42 to send the Inter-American Commission copies of the annual reports which States prepare for the OAS bodies concerned with economic, social and cultural rights, this is a weak and unsatisfactory arrangement. In 1988 the Additional Protocol, known as the 'Protocol of San Salvador',[8] was therefore concluded with a view to improving matters. The new Protocol guarantees thirteen additional economic, social and cultural rights and has much in common with the first UN Covenant. As in the Covenant, the rights concerned are protected by a reporting system, but an important difference is that they are also subject to the jurisdiction of the Inter-American Commission and Court through the same system of individual petitions as the civil and political rights guaranteed in the original American Convention.

As already mentioned, in 1990 a further protocol was concluded which has the effect of prohibiting the States which are parties to it from using the death penalty.[9] This brings the American Convention into line with the European Convention on Human Rights and the Covenant on Civil and Political Rights, both of which, it will be recalled, also have protocols on this subject. As yet, however, neither this latest protocol nor the Protocol of San Salvador has been generally accepted.[10]

## III. The system of international control

The American Convention on Human Rights, like the European Convention, provides for two organs of control: a Commission and a Court. But there are important differences in the composition, functions and powers of the organs established under the two regional systems, as we shall see.

A problem which faced those who drafted the American Convention was that when they came to define the composition, functions and powers of the Inter-American Commission on Human Rights, they were not creating a new organ but conferring new functions and powers on an existing body. As already noted, the Inter-American Commission was created in 1959 by Resolution VIII of the meeting of consultation of the ministers for foreign affairs at Santiago. Originally a promotional organ, it was granted limited powers to consider individual complaints at the Rio Conference in 1965. Then, in 1967, the conference on the revision of the Charter transformed it into one of the statutory organs of the OAS, and decided that its structure and competence would be determined by the new Convention, which was being prepared.

As a result of this evolution the 1969 Convention was able to confer new functions and powers on the existing Inter-American Commission, but, of course, the new provisions would apply only to States which ratified the new Convention. It was therefore also necessary to provide that the existing functions and powers of the Commission would remain and continue to be exercised in relation to States which did not ratify the new Convention. In other words, the Inter-American Commission would have a double mandate: one resulting from the Convention in relation to States parties to the Convention; and the other resulting from the earlier decisions of 1959, 1965 and 1967 in relation to all members of the OAS, whether or not they ratified the Convention.

This was in fact what happened. And since the American Convention on Human Rights entered into force only on 18 July 1978, and some time had to elapse before the Commission's new functions could be effectively exercised, almost all its work during its first twenty years of existence was taken up with its 'old functions'. It is therefore useful to begin by considering the activities of the Commission outside the Convention.[11]

### 1. The 'old functions' of the Inter-American Commission

Following its creation in 1959, the Inter-American Commission drew up a Statute which was approved by the OAS Council in 1960. The Statute gave the Commission power to examine the human rights situation in OAS member States where flagrant and repeated violations were occurring; to request pertinent information of the governments concerned and, if necessary, to request their consent to visit their territory; to make such visits if the necessary consent was obtained; to put forward any recommendations it thought advisable; and to prepare reports. It was not competent to take decisions on individual complaints of violation of human rights, but it could take account of such complaints as sources of information on the state of human rights in the countries concerned.

The competence to consider individual complaints of violation of a limited number of specific rights was conferred on the Commission, as already mentioned, by the Rio Conference in 1965, and the Statute was amended accordingly. The new text empowered the Commission to examine communications submitted to it and any other available information, to request pertinent information from governments, to make appropriate recommendations, and to report on these activities to the Inter-American Conference. It will be noted that when the Commission utilises these procedures it can make recommendations and reports, but is still not authorised to take decisions.

Using these provisions the Inter-American Commission has examined the situation of human rights in a considerable number of the Latin American republics. Sometimes this has been on the basis of complaints received and evidence obtained outside the country concerned, but sometimes its examination has also included on-the-spot visits and hearing of witnesses, including both governmental representatives and individual complainants. The results of these investigations have been incorporated in a series of 'country reports'.

Examples of the first category are a series of reports on the situation of human rights in Cuba which began in 1962. Regrettably, the Cuban government did not co-operate with the Commission when it was preparing these studies. A particularly striking case of visits on the spot, on the other hand, concerned the Dominican Republic when civil war was raging in 1965. Members of the Commission spent several months there and were able to intervene on behalf of detained persons and secure the release of prisoners on both sides as well as observance of other humanitarian measures. Another sort of humanitarian mission was undertaken by the Commission in 1980, when about twenty diplomats attending a reception at the Dominican embassy in Bogotá were held hostage by a group of terrorists. As the result of an agreement negotiated with the government of Colombia, the Inter-American Commission supervised the release of the hostages and the evacuation of the terrorists and also undertook to monitor the trials of certain political prisoners.

Other 'country reports' produced by the Inter-American Commission concern the human rights situation in Haiti (1980, after a visit in 1978); Uruguay (1977); Chile (annual reviews from 1974 to 1980, one resulting from a visit in 1974); Panama (1978, after a visit during the previous year); Nicaragua (visit and report in 1978); El Salvador (visit in 1978, report in 1979); and Argentina (visit in 1979 followed by a report in 1980). In all these countries serious violations of human rights were found.[12]

The Commission's report on Argentina precipitated a major crisis in the OAS. It was considered by the General Assembly of the OAS, meeting in Washington in November 1980. The report was highly critical of the Argentine government and the United States proposed a resolution condemning the violations of human rights in that country. Argentina threatened to leave the Organisation if this was adopted, and was supported by Bolivia, Chile, Paraguay and Uruguay. The agenda of the conference included not only the special report on Argentina, but also the annual report of the Commission, which recounted serious violations of human rights in Chile, El Salvador, Paraguay and Uruguay. In the end the conference adopted a resolution in which it took note of the reports and made a general condemnation of countries which violate human rights but without naming any of them specifically.[13] At the same time, several member States expressed their support for the Inter-American Commission and the conference requested it to undertake an investigation on the human rights situation in Bolivia.

As regards the complaints which it receives from individuals and groups, the Commission seems to be struggling with an uphill – some would say an impossible – task. A large number of complaints are received, yet the Commission is a part-time body with only seven members, all with other occupations, to cope with the volume of work. An even greater obstacle is the lack of effective co-operation from the governments concerned, for in the great majority of cases they reply to the Commission's inquiries with a minimum of information and are evidently seeking to cover up, rather than investigate, the violations brought to their attention.

In this difficult situation the Commission has adopted a rule to the effect that once a communication has been declared admissible, the facts alleged will be presumed to be confirmed if the government concerned fails to bring forward convincing evidence in rebuttal. It is on the basis of this presumption, which is entirely reasonable in the circumstances, that the majority of the decisions of the Commission are reached on individual complaints. The results of the Commission's work can be seen in its annual reports to the General Assembly of the OAS, which present a depressing picture of arbitrary arrest, detention without trial, interrogation accompanied by torture, exile without judicial process and a variety of similar violations. Co-operation of governments in investigating the complaints is generally minimal and in nearly all cases serious violations are established.

From this brief summary two conclusions may be drawn. First, a large part of the Commission's contribution to human rights has stemmed from its 'old functions', which antedate the entry into force of the American Convention on Human Rights in 1978. Indeed, the Permanent Council of the Organisation recognised as much when it decided in 1978 that the Commission should continue to apply its existing Statute and regulations without change to those member States which are not parties to the Convention, and should apply any new Statute and regulations that might be approved only to States that have ratified the Convention. Matters were taken a stage further at the ninth regular session of the General Assembly of the OAS in October 1979, when a new Statute of the Commission was approved. This contained three separate articles on the functions and powers of the Commission. Article 18 deals with its powers with respect to all members of the OAS, which are mainly promotional, while Article 19 deals with its powers in relation to States which have ratified the Convention. The latter powers, as we shall see shortly, are principally concerned with its action on petitions and communications under the terms of the Convention and its relations with the Inter-American Court of Human Rights. Article 20 then sets out its powers in relation to States which have not yet ratified the Convention and authorises the Commission to continue to act in accordance with the old procedures.[14]

Our second conclusion is prompted by a comparison of the work of the Inter-American Commission on Human Rights with that of the European Commission of Human Rights, described in Chapter 4. It is plain that they are radically different. The two Commissions operate in quite different circumstances, one might almost say at quite different levels. The European Commission has, with very rare exceptions, been concerned with what might be called the finer points of human rights law – questions, for example, such as what is a reasonable time in detention pending trial, what is the precise content of the right to a fair trial, what limitations may be placed on freedom of expression, and what exactly are the implications of the right of freedom of association? Furthermore, when dealing with such problems the European Commission has almost always had the full co-operation of the governments concerned and the full support of its parent organisation, the Council of Europe.

The Inter-American Commission, on the other hand, has had to deal with problems of a quite different order: arbitrary arrests on a massive scale, systematic use of torture, scores or hundreds of 'disappeared persons', total absence of judicial remedies, and other flagrant violations of civilised standards. In dealing with such cases it has found the governments concerned more like antagonists than willing partners, while at the General Assembly of the OAS the lip service paid to its work, and the genuine support of some governments, have not prevented others from expressing violent and destructive criticism.

When studying the development of international techniques for the protection of human rights, it is therefore necessary to appreciate that the problems confronting the Inter-American Commission are far graver than those in Europe, and give due recognition to the efforts of the Commission to expose the serious violations which occur and seek justice for the victims.

## 2. The 'new functions' of the Inter-American Commission

First, a few words about the organisation of the Commission, which is covered in Articles 34–40 of the Convention.

When the Convention was drawn up in 1969, it was decided to keep the number of members at seven, as in the original decision of 1959. They must be persons of high moral character and recognised competence in the field of human rights (Article 34). A proposal was made at the San José Conference that the General Assembly of the OAS should have the power to enlarge the membership of the Commission when this was considered to be necessary. However, the proposal was rejected, apparently because it was feared that the possibility of such action by a political body might affect the independence of the Commission. While this is a real enough point, the fact remains that the burden of work falling on the seven members of the Commission under the present arrangements is excessive.

The Commission represents all the member countries of the OAS (Article 35). However, the members of the Commission sit in a personal capacity (Article 36) and this is, of course, essential to guarantee their independence.

There was a long discussion during the drafting of the Convention as to whether all member States of the Organisation or only contracting parties should have the right (1) to propose candidates, (2) to elect members, and (3) to have their nationals sit as members of the Commission. On the one hand, it was argued that if only a limited number of member States ratified the Convention, it was they who should decide on the membership of the organ whose full jurisdiction only they accept. On the other hand, it was pointed out that the Commission is an organ of the OAS as a whole (as a result of the 1967 Protocol of Buenos Aires)[15] and that, consequently, all member States ought to participate in the election and be eligible to have their nationals sit as members. It was the second argument which prevailed. As a result, all member States may propose candidates and vote in the election by the General Assembly of the OAS. They may propose up to three candidates, with the unusual proviso that if they do, at least one must be of another nationality. The term of office of members of the Commission is four years. However, they may be re-elected, but only once (Article 37). The necessary services are furnished by a specialised unit in the General Secretariat of the OAS (Article 40). The first election under the terms of the Convention took place at the ninth regular session of the General Assembly of the OAS, in October 1979.

Articles 41–43 of the Convention relate to the functions of the Commission. They repeat the 'old functions' of a promotional character conferred on the original Commission in 1959, which include the making of recommendations to member governments and requesting information from member governments on human rights matters, and the submission of an annual report to the General Assembly (Article 41). There is a provision which we noticed earlier for the examination by the Commission of governments' reports on compliance with the economic, social and cultural standards established by the OAS Charter (Article 42) and an undertaking by States parties to provide the Commission with information which it may request as to the manner in which their domestic law complies with the Convention (Article 43).

The new functions of the Commission are set out in Articles 44–47. It is competent to consider petitions from individuals, groups of individuals or NGOs alleging violation of the Convention by States parties (Article 44). But in contrast to Article 25 of the European Convention, acceptance of this competence by States ratifying the treaty is not optional but obligatory. In terms of the provision of effective international procedures for protecting human rights, the compulsory jurisdiction of the Commission under Article 44 is the outstanding feature of the American Convention.

Needless to say, the Commission's competence to receive individual petitions was not achieved without much discussion. When Article 44 was being examined in Commission II of the San José Conference, Argentina proposed that the right of individual petition should be made optional and was supported by the delegate from Panama (who quoted the European Convention) and those from Nicaragua and the Dominican Republic. However, Chile, supported by Uruguay, the United States and others, and followed by Mexico, argued in favour of an obligatory provision. This view was accepted in the Commission by ten votes to none, with five abstentions, and subsequently in the plenary meeting.

Article 45 then deals with inter-State complaints. The working party of Commission II recommended by a majority that this should also be made an obligatory procedure. But in the plenary Commission Argentina and Mexico opposed it, supported by Nicaragua, while Brazil, Panama, Paraguay and the Dominican

Republic abstained, with the result that the proposal was not carried. As a consequence, the procedure for inter-State complaints is optional. A declaration accepting the competence of the Commission may be made at any time and may be for a limited or unlimited period of time and a number of States have made such declarations.[16] A suggestion was made that it should also be possible for a State to make such a declaration accepting the competence of the Commission *ad hoc* for a particular case, and this also was accepted.

It is therefore evident that, as regards the competence of the Commission, the American Convention is the exact opposite of the European Convention. Acceptance of the right of individual petition follows automatically from ratification, whereas the procedure for inter-State complaints is optional. This is undoubtedly a major advance in establishing an effective system of international control, bearing in mind that a compulsory system of inter-State complaints could be politically explosive in the Latin American context.

The rules on admissibility (Articles 46 and 47) are generally similar to those contained in the European Convention. They include the requirement of exhaustion of domestic remedies and require that the petition should be filed within six months of the notification of the final domestic decision. In order to resolve the question of whether an applicant may bring a case successively before the UN Committee and the regional Commission, the suggestion was made that a petition should be declared inadmissible if at an earlier stage it had been submitted to another procedure of international settlement. This was accepted and incorporated as Article 47(d).

Once the Commission has decided that a case is admissible, its first task is to establish the facts. It may undertake an investigation, for which the States concerned will furnish all necessary facilities (Article 48(1)(d)). An urgent procedure for emergency cases is set out in Article 48(2). The Commission then has the task of trying to bring about a friendly settlement. The procedure (Articles 48(1)(f) and 49) is broadly similar to that of the European Convention. If no friendly settlement is achieved, the Commission is required to draw up a report setting out the facts and stating its conclusions and may make such proposals and recommendations as it thinks fit (Article 50).

There was much discussion as to what should happen at the next stage. The draft submitted to the Conference proposed that, if the case was not submitted to the Court within three months, the Commission should take a final decision on the question of violation. However, this did not meet with general agreement, because many States were not willing to grant the Commission such extensive powers. Consequently the article was redrafted so as to provide that if, within three months, the matter is not settled or submitted to the Court, the Commission may, by an absolute majority of its members, 'set forth its opinion and conclusions concerning the question submitted for its consideration'. It may also 'make pertinent recommendations' and fix a period of time within which the State concerned is to take the measures needed to remedy the situation. At the end of that period the Commission decides whether the State has taken adequate measures, and whether to publish its report (Article 51).

From the political point of view this was no doubt a wise compromise. From a lawyer's perspective, however, it must be noted that the American Convention still does not provide for a definite decision on the question of violation if a case does not go to the Court. Nevertheless, it does go a good deal further than the UN Covenant in this respect. Indeed, if the Commission expresses the opinion that a State has violated the Convention and sets a period of time within which remedial measures should be taken, then decides that adequate measures have not been taken and publishes its report with the reasons for its action, to all intents and purposes there is a decision on violation.

### 3. *The Inter-American Court of Human Rights*

The draft Convention submitted to the San José Conference provided for the creation of an Inter-American Court of Human Rights, with the power to give a decision if a contracting party referred a case to it after the Commission had examined the matter and expressed its opinion. The jurisdiction of the Court, however, would be optional.

The first question the Conference had to decide was whether a Court of Human Rights was desirable in the American context. The Mexican representative suggested that it would be premature, and stated that his government could not agree that such a body should be in a position to pass judgement on the legality of the acts of a State. He therefore urged that the Court should be omitted from the Convention altogether. However, many delegations took the opposite view and considered that a judicial organ was indispensable. The representative of Chile, for example, maintained that this would be the logical culmination of the process which had begun in 1948 with the proclamation of the American Declaration of the Rights and Duties of Man and continued with the establishment of the Inter-American Commission on Human Rights in 1959. The United States also favoured the creation of the Court and pointed out that if its jurisdiction was optional, there would be no difficulty in accommodating States which were unwilling to accept it. At the end of the general discussion, it was agreed to establish an Inter-American Court of Human Rights with optional jurisdiction.[17]

The Court consists of seven judges, elected in an individual capacity from among jurists of the highest moral authority and recognised competence, and who possess the qualifications required for the highest judicial office (Article 52). In contrast with the procedure for the election of the members of the Commission, only the parties to the Convention may propose candidates and take part in the election. However, candidates may be of the nationality of any member State of the OAS, and, as with the Commission, the lists of three candidates put forward by the parties must include at least one who is not a national of the proposing State (Article 53).

The right to participate in the election of the judges is not limited to the States which have accepted the jurisdiction of the Court. Moreover, unlike the European Convention, there is no provision requiring a stated number of acceptances of the jurisdiction of the Court before the first election. As a result, it was possible to begin the procedure for setting up the Court shortly after the entry into force of the Convention in 1978. In fact the election took place in the course of the meeting of the General Assembly of the OAS in May 1979.

The judges are elected for a term of six years, and may be re-elected, but only once (Article 54). Article 58 left the choice of the seat of the Court to be determined by the General Assembly of the OAS. In July 1978, when it was known that the entry into force of the Convention was imminent, the General Assembly recommended that the Court should be based in Costa Rica. This was subsequently confirmed by the States parties and was appropriate recognition of the fact that that country had acted as host to the Conference which had drafted the Convention in 1969, was the first State to ratify the Convention in April 1970, and the first to accept the compulsory jurisdiction of the Court. It also called to mind that Costa Rica was the seat of the Central American Court of Justice when it was set up in 1907.

Article 55 deals with the question of the 'national judge', that is, whether a judge who is a national of a party to a case should have the right to sit in a case in which his or her own country is involved. This involves as a corollary the question whether, if there is no 'national judge', the State concerned may appoint an *ad hoc* judge. This is the arrangement in both the International Court of Justice and the European Court of Human Rights. The Inter-American Commission on Human Rights had proposed that a judge who is a national of a party to a dispute should stand down and not participate in the proceedings. The Brazilian representative argued that this would be a more progressive arrangement and more likely to assure impartiality in the composition of the Court. This view, however, did not prevail. The final text therefore follows the traditional system of national and *ad hoc* judges (Article 55).

When the special advisers had explained the role of the European Commission in the proceedings of the European Court of Human Rights, it was decided to include an article in the American Convention providing that 'the Commission shall appear in all cases before the Court' (Article 57).

The Court appoints its own Secretary (Article 58). Article 59 provides that the Court shall establish its own secretariat, which functions under the direction of the Secretary of the Court, but in accordance with the administrative regulations of the General Secretariat of the OAS to the extent that they are not incompatible with the Court's independence. The importance attached to such independence, a vital element in any system of judicial supervision, is therefore clear.

## 4. *The competence of the Court*

Only States parties and the Commission may submit cases to the Court (Article 61). Consideration was given to the idea of allowing individual applicants to refer a case to the Court if they were dissatisfied with the opinion of the Commission, and the example of the Central American Court was mentioned as a precedent. Predictably, however, the system established by the European Convention was quoted on the other side, and several delegates stated that their governments would be unwilling to accept the right of individuals to activate the Court. A proposal to confer such a right was therefore rejected by a majority vote.

Under Article 62 of the Convention contracting parties may declare that they accept the jurisdiction of the Court unconditionally or on condition of reciprocity, and for an indefinite or for a limited period of time.[18] The suggestion was made, and accepted, that this should also be possible *ad hoc* and so the words 'or for specific cases' were added.

The delegate of Costa Rica proposed the insertion of an article authorising the Court to order interim measures 'in cases of extreme seriousness and urgency, and when it is necessary to avoid irreparable damage...'. When this was accepted it was incorporated as paragraph 1 of Article 63 and, as we shall see, has proved very important in practice.

The powers of the Inter-American Court are very wide and much more extensive than those of the European Court. If it finds that there has been a violation, it may order that the rights of the injured party be reinstated and, where appropriate, can also order that the consequences of a violation should be remedied and damages paid (Article 63). Moreover, the contracting parties undertake to abide by the judgement of the Court, and an order for damages will be directly enforceable in the State concerned (Article 68). This last provision has no counterpart in the European Convention, but is comparable to the effect of judgements of the European Court of Justice under the Treaty of Maastricht.

What is the ultimate sanction if a State refuses to comply with a judgement of the Court? Although there is not, and perhaps cannot be, any indefeasible sanction, the Inter-American Court is required to submit an annual report to the General Assembly of the OAS, indicating, in particular, cases in which a State has not complied with its judgements and making 'the pertinent recommendations' (Article 85). Producing an annual report is an unusual procedure for a judicial body, and it may not always be

easy for the Court to know whether a State has fully complied
with a judgement. However, Article 65 was introduced to provide
at least some form of sanction. Being reported for non-
compliance to the General Assembly, which will be attended by
several hundred delegates and receive wide publicity, is no doubt
a procedure which most governments would prefer to avoid.

Article 64 of the Convention invests the Inter-American Court
with wide powers to give advisory opinions.[19] Requests for
advisory opinions may relate not only to the American Convention on Human Rights, but also to other treaties concerning
the protection of human rights in the American States. All the
organs of the OAS listed in Chapter X of the Charter (as
amended by the Protocol of Buenos Aires) may consult the Court
on matters within their competence.[20] In addition, under Article
64(2) any member State of the OAS may request and receive an
opinion on the compatibility of any of its domestic laws with the
American Convention on Human Rights or any other treaty
relating to human rights in the American States. It is interesting
that the right to request such advisory opinions is not limited to
contracting parties to the American Convention. The thinking
here was that this would enable a State which is considering
ratification to obtain an authoritative opinion on whether a
particular domestic law might be incompatible with the
Convention. In practice, as we shall see, Article 64(2) has not yet
been used by a non-party, but the possibility remains for the
future.

### IV. The work of the Court

#### 1. *Advisory opinions*

When the Inter-American Court was given the authority to issue
advisory opinions, it was hoped that this would enable it to play
an active part in the Convention system, whether or not a
substantial number of States accepted its jurisdiction and
regardless of the Commission's readiness to refer cases to it. The
wisdom of providing the Court with wide powers under Article
64 is now apparent, for not only has the Court handed down a
number of important advisory opinions, but until quite recently
this aspect of its activity was much more significant in practice
than its contentious jurisdiction.

The Court's first advisory opinion was given in 1982 and others have followed at an average of just over one per year. The Court, it must be remembered, has no control over the volume of business, which depends entirely on the readiness of the States and the relevant organs of the OAS to refer cases to it. It is therefore interesting to note that of the fourteen advisory opinions requested to date, nine were asked for by States, while five were requested by the Inter-American Commission.

The cases to date, though relatively few in number, have already taken the Court into several quite different areas of the Convention. In its first case, which we shall call the *Other Treaties case*,[21] the question was the actual scope of the advisory jurisdiction and, in particular, the meaning of the reference in Article 64(1) to 'other treaties concerning the protection of human rights in the American States'. The request was made by the government of Peru, which asked specifically whether 'other treaties' meant treaties adopted within the framework of the Inter-American system, or was more general and included, for example, the United Nations Covenants, or other human rights treaties to which American and non-American States may be parties.

The Court held that the broader view was correct, so that in principle any human rights treaty to which American States are parties can be the subject of an advisory opinion. The Court qualified this a little by pointing out that its advisory jurisdiction is permissive, and that there might be circumstances in which it would be proper to deny a request, for example if the issue in the case involved an obligation assumed by a non-American State. However, the Court also stated that the purpose of the Court's advisory role is 'to assist the American States in fulfilling their international human rights obligations'[22] and that the object of the American Convention is to integrate the regional and the universal systems of human rights protection. In the light of this reasoning and the Court's conclusion, it is possible that the advisory opinions of the American Court may one day provide a most valuable guide to the interpretation of a wide range of human rights treaties.

The Court's second case, also in 1982, again concerned the scope of its advisory jurisdiction, although not as the main issue. In the *Effect of Reservations case*,[23] the Commission asked the

Court to say when a State becomes a party to the American Convention if it ratifies or adheres to the Convention with one or more reservations. Before answering this question, however, the Court made the important jurisdictional ruling that the Commission was competent not only to request the present opinion but generally, since by virtue of its functions it enjoys 'an absolute right to request advisory opinions within the framework of Article 64(1) of the Convention'.[24]

The main issue, which raised a technical but very practical issue in the law of treaties, turned on whether reservations to the Convention are subject to acceptance by the other parties. The crucial article of the American Convention (Article 75) is unclear on the point, but the Court interpreted it as meaning that reservations are not subject to the acceptance of the other parties. It supported this conclusion by explaining that human rights treaties are not in the nature of bargains between States, involving a reciprocal exchange of rights and obligations, but have as their object and purpose:

> the protection of the basic rights of individual human beings, irrespective of their nationality, both against the State of their nationality and all other contracting States.... [T]he States [Parties] can be deemed to submit themselves to a legal order within which they, for the common good, assume various obligations, not in relation to other States, but towards all individuals within their jurisdiction.[25]

It is interesting to note that the character of the American Convention was an essential element in the Court's reasoning, and that in emphasising the special character of human rights treaties, the Court drew heavily on the earlier reasoning of both the International Court and the European Commission.[26]

The *Restrictions to the Death Penalty case*[27] in 1983 was another case with a double aspect. The case arose because the Commission had a disagreement with Guatemala over the scope of a reservation which the latter had made to Article 4(4) of the Convention, which concerns the imposition of the death penalty for political crimes. When the Commission asked the Court for an advisory opinion on the point, Guatemala argued that because the request related to a dispute involving Guatemala, and Guatemala had not accepted the jurisdiction of the Court in contentious cases, the question could not be answered by means of an advisory opinion.

This is a type of argument which the International Court of Justice has considered on several occasions[28] and which its predecessor, the Permanent Court, discussed as long ago as 1923.[29] The American Court referred to several of these cases in its opinion and held that since the request clearly fell within the sphere of competence of the Commission, the Court had jurisdiction to give the opinion requested.

Having established that it was competent, the Court had to consider the main issue in the case, which was the effect of Guatemala's obligations under Article 4(2). In dealing with these questions the Court emphasised the primacy of the text when interpreting both Article 4 of the Convention and the reservation, but also held that 'in interpreting reservations, account must be taken of the object and purpose of the relevant treaty'.[30] Bearing in mind that the Convention is a human rights treaty, the Court concluded that Guatemala's reservation should be construed in a way that was compatible with the object and purpose of the Convention, and (and this was the whole point of the case) which also left Guatemala's obligations under Article 4(2) intact.

The first case in which the Court was requested to determine the compatibility of a particular law with the Convention was the *Proposed Amendments case*[31] in 1984. Here Costa Rica asked the Court if certain amendments which were proposed to the naturalisation provisions of the constitution would be compatible with Articles 17, 20, and 24, dealing with, respectively, the rights of the family, the right to a nationality, and the right to equal protection. Sensibly deciding that the case fell under Article 64(2) even though the proposed amendments were not yet 'laws', the Court found that in most respects the new arrangements would be compatible with the Convention, but ruled that one provision, which concerned naturalisation and discriminated between spouses, would contravene Articles 17(4) and 24.

The *Licensing of Journalism case*[32] in 1985 raised both a general question under Article 64(1) and a specific issue under Article 64(2). The general question was how far the compulsory licensing of journalists, a common practice in Latin America, is compatible with Article 13 of the Convention, which protects freedom of expression. The specific issue was whether the law regulating this matter in Costa Rica could be approved. In a long opinion reviewing the scope of freedom of expression, and making extensive use of case law from the European Convention, the Court concluded that the compulsory licensing of journalists is incompatible with Article 13 if it denies any person access to the full use of the news media as a means of expressing opinions or imparting information. In the light of this principle it then ruled that the particular law was not compatible with the Convention.

The next three cases were all referred under Article 64(1) and raised general issues of varying importance. In the *Interpretation of 'Laws' case*[33] in 1986, Uruguay asked for an interpretation of Article 30 of the Convention, which provides that restrictions on the enjoyment or exercise of its rights and freedoms may only be applied 'in accordance with laws enacted for reasons of general interest'. The point on which the Court was asked to rule was whether the word 'laws' in this provision refers to laws in the formal sense, that is, to legal norms passed by the legislature and promulgated in the way prescribed by the constitution, or to laws in the material sense, that is, as a synonym for the entire body of law, without reference to the procedure followed in the creation of the norm, or to the rank assigned to it in the particular system.

The Court held that the first view was correct and took the opportunity to explain both the link between human rights and democracy and the special significance of these concepts in the Americas. Explaining that the Convention 'has its own philosophy under which the American States "require the political organisation of these States on the basis of the effective exercise of democracy",'[34] the Court concluded that the word 'laws' in Article 30 'means a general legal norm, tied to the general welfare, passed by democratically elected legislative bodies established by the Constitution and formulated according to the procedures set forth by the constitutions of the States parties for that purpose'.[35]

The *Right of Reply case*[36] in the same year raised a narrower point. Here Costa Rica asked about the scope of Article 14, which guarantees the right of reply, and the Court gave a short opinion in which it explained the relation between this part of the Convention and the domestic law of the parties. Then in the *Habeas Corpus case*[37] in 1987 the Commission asked the Court

for an opinion on a more basic issue which, like the question in
the *Interpretation of 'Laws' case*, concerned the scope of
permissible limitations to the rights protected by the Convention.

Article 27(1) of the American Convention authorises suspension of its guarantees in emergency situations and thus
corresponds to Article 15 of the European Convention. However,
Article 27(2) provides that the articles guaranteeing certain rights
may not be suspended, and goes on to prohibit suspension 'of the
judicial guarantees essential for the protection of such rights'. The
Commission's question was whether, in view of its importance,
the writ of *habeas corpus* is one such non-suspendable guarantee.
The Court concluded that it is, and supported this with reference
to both the 'inseparable bond between the principle of legality,
democratic institutions and the rule of law',[38] which it had
identified in the *Interpretation of 'Laws' case*, and to the special
position of emergency powers.

In the *Judicial Guarantees case*[39] the Court had a further
opportunity to examine the scope of Article 27(2) when Uruguay
asked for an opinion on the general question of the meaning of
the 'essential' guarantees which that provision refers to. The
Court replied that guarantees not subject to derogation include
*habeas corpus*, *amparo* and any other judicial remedy designed to
guarantee respect for rights and freedoms which may not be
suspended, and that guarantees not subject to suspension include
those judicial procedures inherent in representative democracy as
a form of government and provided for in the laws of the States
parties to secure the rights referred to in Article 27(2). This
opinion thus considerably expanded the review of emergency
powers which the Court had begun in the *Habeas Corpus case*.

It is interesting to note that in the *Habeas Corpus case* the
Court referred to 'the realities that have been the experience of
some of the peoples of this hemisphere in recent decades,
particularly disappearances, torture, and murder committed or
tolerated by some governments'.[40] As the Court recognised,
political conditions in many of the States which are parties to the
American Convention make the scope of emergency powers an
especially vital issue. In the advisory opinions on Article 27(2),
therefore, as in the *Licensing of Journalism* and *Interpretation of
'Laws' cases*, the Court's advisory opinions were able to develop
and clarify the law on a matter of particular regional interest.

The Court's next opinion, in 1990, dealt with another issue of the same kind. In the *Interpretation of the American Declaration case*[41] Colombia asked for an opinion on whether the American Declaration of the Rights and Duties of Man qualified as a treaty for the purposes of Article 64(1) of the Convention. In an earlier case the Commission had implied that it did, by holding that it created binding obligations for all OAS member States.[42] The Court, however, disagreed and held that the Declaration could not be regarded as a treaty. However, it went on to state that the Declaration is an authoritative interpretation of the human rights provisions of the OAS Charter and as such is indeed a source of international obligation. This is particularly important for countries such as the United States which are not parties to the American Convention on Human Rights, as it entitles the Commission to measure their practice against the Declaration. Like the *Other Treaties case*, which raised an analogous point, this case therefore shows how the Court can use the opportunity presented by an advisory opinion to deal with much broader issues.

As noted earlier, Article 46 of the Convention lays down the conditions of admissibility of a claim, which include in Article 46(1)(a) the usual requirement of exhaustion of domestic remedies. In the *Domestic Remedies case*,[43] the Commission asked for an opinion on the relation between this provision and Article 46(2), which allows for certain exceptions. In its advisory opinion in 1990 the Court indicated that exhaustion of domestic remedies is not required if a claimant has been unable to obtain legal representation on account of poverty or fear in the legal community. It added, however, that once the State party has proved that domestic remedies were available, the onus is on the claimant to show that the case falls within Article 46(2) and that legal representation was necessary. As arguments about domestic remedies bulk large in the work of any human rights tribunal, this is a useful clarification. In a more general way, the *Domestic Remedies case* shows the value of the advisory jurisdiction in enabling such basic issues to be dealt with in the abstract, instead of through individual cases.

In 1991 Costa Rica asked the Court for an advisory opinion on whether a bill which would establish a Superior Court of Criminal Appeal was compatible with Article 8(2)(h) of the

Convention, which guarantees the right to appeal in criminal cases. As in the *Proposed Amendments case*, the intention was to use Article 64(2) of the Convention to test certain legislative proposals. On this occasion, however, Costa Rica was unsuccessful, for in its ruling in this *Compatibility of Draft Legislation case*[44] the Court decided not to respond to the request on the ground that to do so would demean its contentious jurisdiction and prejudice the rights of those with cases against Costa Rica currently before the Commission. This is the first and so far the only occasion on which the Court has declined to give an advisory opinion, which is clearly not a step to be taken lightly. On the other hand, as the *Restrictions to the Death Penalty case* had already demonstrated, the relation between the Court's advisory and contentious jurisdiction raises important issues and so sometimes such a refusal will be justified.

The *Certain Attributes case*[45] in 1993 raised a very different kind of issue. Here Argentina and Uruguay requested an advisory opinion under Article 64(1) on a whole series of questions relating to the powers of the Commission, including its authority to interpret the Convention and its procedure. The Court held that the Commission is competent to determine the scope of a State's obligations, but not to apply its internal law; that the Commission is prohibited from considering the merits of cases it declares inadmissible; and that when reports are produced under Articles 50 and 51 only the latter may be published. These issues had all arisen in concrete cases before the Commission, but the Court held that this was not an objection because the request for an advisory opinion was not an attempt to raise a contentious case in disguise. Instead, the Court treated the request as an opportunity to clarify the powers of one of the Convention organs, which is, of course, one of the functions of advisory opinions.

Finally, in the *International Responsibility case*[46] in 1994 the Commission asked the Court to determine the legal effects of a law that manifestly violates the obligations of a State under the Convention and to indicate the nature and responsibilities of State agents who comply with such a law. The Court replied that a law which violates the Convention and affects protected rights and liberties engages the State's international responsibility and that if enforcement of the law constitutes an international crime, it also creates individual responsibility. The request in this case was prompted by Peru's promulgation of a new constitution which extended the death penalty, thereby contravening Article 4(2) of the Convention. Peru opposed the request on the ground that the Commission has no power to seek an advisory opinion under Article 64(2), but the Court rejected this objection, pointing out that as the request was framed in abstract terms, it came within Article 64(1). Thus, as in the *Restrictions to the Death Penalty case* and nearly all the other advisory opinions, the request raised a general issue of interpretation, and as such lay within the Commission's competence.

## 2. Contentious cases

The regular use which has been made of the Court's advisory jurisdiction stands in sharp contrast to its activity with regard to contentious cases, which has developed more slowly. In 1981 the government of Costa Rica referred the *Gallardo case*[47] to the Court in circumstances which were unusual because the case had not been considered by the Commission. The government argued that it was entitled to waive this first stage of the proceedings, but the Court disagreed. In an important review of the role of the Convention organs the Court emphasised that the processing of a case by the Commission is more than a matter of convenience for the respondent, and constitutes an integral part of the Convention system. Since the Commission fulfils a vital and independent function, it was not open to a State to dispense with the first stage of the proceedings and refer a matter directly to the Court. The decision was undoubtedly correct, but the effect, of course, was to render the case inadmissible, with the result that the substantive point, which involved the murder of a person while in prison, was never examined.

Following the unsuccessful attempt to refer the *Gallardo case*, several years elapsed before the contentious procedure was used again. In its opinion in the *Licensing of Journalism case* in 1985 the Court indicated that the Commission could have raised the relevant point in contentious proceedings and stated that it should have done so, instead of leaving Costa Rica to seek an advisory opinion. Stung by the criticism that its neglect of the Court had damaged the delicate balance of the working of the Convention, in April 1986 the Commission referred three cases to the Court.[48]

The cases, *Velásquez Rodríguez, Garbi and Corrales* and *Cruz,* were all very similar and concerned people who had disappeared in Honduras. Early in 1988 the Court was informed that one person who had given evidence and another who was due to do so had been murdered and that the lives of other witnesses were in danger. It therefore issued two orders under Article 63(2) of the Convention requiring the government of Honduras to adopt measures to protect the rights of witnesses and investigate the killings.[49] The problem of 'disappeared persons' is one with which the Inter-American Commission is all too familiar and the events just described are a reminder, if one is needed, of the problems confronting the Convention institutions.

In its decision on the merits in the *Velásquez Rodríguez case*[50] in 1988 the Court found that Honduras had violated its obligations to respect and ensure the right to personal liberty contained in Article 7 of the Convention, the right to humane treatment in Article 5 and the right to life in Article 4. It also decided that Honduras was required to pay compensation to the next of kin of the victims. In this case, unlike the Court's advisory opinions, factual as well as legal issues were significant and the judgement contains important material on the treatment of evidence in human rights cases. As this was the Court's first contentious case, it was encouraging that the judgement was able to cover so much ground and that the decision of the Court was unanimous.

In its judgement in the *Cruz case*, in 1989, the Court reached a similar conclusion, but in *Garbi and Corrales* decided that the Commission had failed to prove its case.[51] In further judgements in the same year the Court made assessments of the compensation due in the claims which had been successful.[52] Those decisions too raise points of general legal interest, as the Court decided that compensation must be paid not only for the victims' loss of earnings, but also for the emotional and moral harm to their next of kin. As regards the victims' children, the Court held that a trust fund should be created to administer the sums awarded. This part of the judgement led the Commission to seek guidance from the Court as to how the fund might be protected from inflation and this point was clarified by a further decision in 1990 in which the Court exercised its power to interpret its judgement of 1989 in accordance with Article 67 of the Convention.[53]

Since this first group of cases, the Court has decided several other cases, almost all involving serious violations of the American Convention. In the *Aloeboetoe case*, for example, Surinam admitted responsibility for the detention, abuse and murder of seven unarmed Bush negroes who were suspected by soldiers of belonging to a subversive group. Because liability was admitted, the main issue in this case was damages, which the Court dealt with fully in a judgement in 1993.[54] Like the corresponding stage of the *Velásquez Rodríguez case*, this provided the Court with an opportunity to explore an issue on which there is relatively little case law and the present case is particularly interesting for the way in which the Court identified the victims' successors by applying tribal customary law and dealt with the question of moral damage. As in the earlier case, the Court ordered the creation of trust funds to administer the compensation.

Surinam was also the respondent in the *Gangaram Panday case* (1994)[55], in which the Court decided that the petitioner had suffered a violation of his right to personal liberty contrary to Article 7 of the Convention, but rejected claims based on various other articles, including Article 4, which protects the right to life. This was a controversial case because the victim had died while in detention in suspicious circumstances and there was evidence indicating that he might have been tortured. The Commission accepted this conjecture and upheld the claim on all counts, but the Court, making its own assessment of the facts, adopted a more cautious approach. Three judges dissented on the issue of Article 4, arguing that if the prisoner had committed suicide, as the respondent alleged, the State had brought this about by detaining him illegally. For the violation of Article 7 the Court ordered Surinam to pay $10,000 to the victim's dependants.

Two cases decided in 1995 involved situations resembling those in earlier cases. The *Neira-Alegría case*,[56] like the *Velásquez Rodríguez case*, involved disappearance and the *El Amparo case*,[57] like the *Aloeboetoe case*, concerned murders by the military. In the former the Court unanimously found that Peru had violated Article 4 and a number of other provisions of the Convention when a cell block in which the three victims were being held was destroyed; and in the latter the Court unanimously held Venezuela responsible for the death of fourteen fishermen who were massacred by a commando patrol. In both

cases the Court decided that the respondent must pay compensation, to be fixed by agreement with the Commission, reserving
the right to review and approve the agreement and, if no
agreement could be reached, to determine the amount of
reparation and costs itself.

Although the main work of the Court in contentious cases
involves applying the substantive guarantees of the American
Convention, it may also be required to perform various incidental
functions. As already noted, these can include determining
compensation, which sometimes requires further proceedings,
and, where necessary, interpreting a judgement, as in the
*Velásquez Rodríguez case*. Before dealing with the merits the
Court must, of course, consider any objections to the admissibility of a case or to its jurisdiction which are raised by the
respondent and these too will usually be addressed in a separate
judgement.[58] Likewise, if a case is referred to the Court and a
friendly settlement is concluded before the merits can be
considered, it will be necessary for the Court to approve the
settlement in a judgement. This happened in the *Maqueda case*
(1995),[59] where the victim was sentenced to ten years' imprisonment for taking part in a demonstration, but subsequently had his
sentence commuted in an agreement for a friendly settlement
between Mr Maqueda's representatives and the government of
Argentina, which the Court then endorsed.

Of all these incidental functions the most important in practice
is unquestionably the Court's power to adopt provisional
measures under Article 63(2) of the Convention. It will be
recalled that this was first exercised in the *Velásquez Rodríguez
case* and requests for similar action have been made in many later
cases. Such requests are not automatically granted, as the Court
must first establish that the various conditions laid down in the
Convention have been fulfilled.[60] In appropriate circumstances,
however, the power will be used and the Court has adopted
provisional measures as a means of protecting witnesses, as well
as for other purposes on a number of occasions. Thus in both the
*Colotenango case*,[61] where the respondent was Guatemala, and
the *Caballero Delgado and Santana case*,[62] which concerned
Colombia, cases involving allegations of murder and other serious
violations, provisional measures to protect witnesses were
ordered.

From this survey of some of the leading cases it is evident that, after a very slow start, the Court has begun to develop a significant contentious jurisprudence. It is also evident that the subject matter of this case law mirrors the work of the Commission in the sense that nearly all the cases which the Court has considered to date have involved allegations of extremely serious violations of human rights, which are all too prevalent in Latin America. While it is excellent that such abuses are now being given judicial scrutiny, the work of the Court, like that of the Commission, is inevitably affected by the regional environment. Where governments rule by terror, victims may be too frightened to come forward, witnesses may need protection, and when decisions are handed down, it may be difficult to make them effective. Like the Commission, however, the Court is doing its best to address these problems, and now that contentious cases are regularly being referred to it, further developments in this aspect of its jurisprudence can be expected.

## V. Other regional developments

Although the American Convention on Human Rights is by far the most important contribution of the OAS to the protection of human rights in the region, it was not the first initiative of this kind. We have already seen that the Inter-American Commission began its work in 1959, ten years before the Convention was concluded, and regional conventions dealing with specific aspects of human rights had been produced even earlier. Between 1928 and 1954, for example, the OAS sponsored no less than four conventions on different aspects of asylum,[63] and conventions dealing with the nationality and civil and political rights of women were drawn up in 1933 and 1948.[64]

In recent years a number of further conventions of this type have been negotiated. The Inter-American Convention to Prevent and Punish Torture[65] was concluded in 1985, one year after the United Nations Convention on the subject, which was described in Chapter 3. Like the UN Convention, the Inter-American Convention commits the parties to preventing and punishing torture, defines the concept of torture and includes provisions relating to the training of the police and others responsible for custody, to the trial of those accused of torture and to the extradition of offenders. Unlike the UN Convention, however, this Convention deals only with torture and does not cover other forms of ill-treatment. The supervisory arrangements are also more limited, as no new organ is created for this purpose. Instead, States merely undertake to keep the Inter-American Commission informed of the measures they have adopted to apply the Convention, while the Commission, for its part, must 'endeavour' to reflect the current situation in its annual report (Article 17). The Convention came into force in 1987 and has now been ratified by about half the parties to the American Convention on Human Rights.[66]

In 1994 two further conventions were concluded. The Inter-American Convention on the Prevention, Punishment and Eradication of Violence against Women,[67] as the title indicates, deals with the same subject as the UN General Assembly Declaration of February 1994,[68] but as it does so in treaty form, creates binding obligations. The Convention defines violence against women as including physical, sexual and psychological violence (Article 2), lists key rights of women and imposes a range of duties on the States parties, intended to eliminate violence against women and its causes. A threefold mechanism of protection is envisaged. In the first place, States undertake to report to the Inter-American Commission of Women on their measures to implement the Convention (Article 10); secondly, the States parties and the Inter-American Commission of Women are authorised to seek advisory opinions from the Inter-American Court (Article 11); and thirdly, individuals and NGOs may lodge petitions with the Inter-American Commission concerning those obligations which require immediate implementation.[69] The new Convention came into force in March 1995, when it had been ratified by two States.[70]

The other recent convention is the Inter-American Convention on the Forced Disappearance of Persons.[71] Here too there is an earlier General Assembly Declaration on the subject, which dates from 1992,[72] and the new Convention reinforces this commitment. It contains an undertaking by the States parties to eliminate and punish the practice of forced disappearances, to co-operate with each other in eradicating it, and to adopt the measures needed to implement these objectives. 'Forced disappearance' is defined (Article 2) and there are the necessary provisions dealing

with the extradition and prosecution of offenders. Of particular
note are the provisions excluding the defence of superior orders
(Article 8), forbidding the use of special courts (Article 9) and
prohibiting derogation (Article 10). Supervision is through the
same procedure as the Convention on Human Rights, that is to
say, the Inter-American Commission and Court (Article 13), and
the former also is authorised to seek urgent information from the
government concerned, when it receives a petition. Forced
disappearances are, of course, already a violation of international
human rights law, as cases like *Velásquez Rodríguez* demonstrate.
The new Convention reinforces this point and should soon receive
wide endorsement.[73]

The developments just described are symptomatic of a renewed
emphasis on human rights in the OAS, following the replacement
of the military regimes which were responsible for so many of the
abuses described in this chapter with governments of a more
democratic character in a significant number of member States.
This change, which still has far to go, began in the 1980s and has
led not only to the adoption of new conventions and a general
improvement in the human rights situation in Latin America, but
also to changes in the OAS. At the beginning of this chapter we
mentioned that protocols to amend the OAS Charter have
recently been adopted and it is appropriate to conclude by saying
a further word about this development, as both protocols are
directly concerned with human rights.

The Protocol of Washington,[74] adopted in 1992, has two
objectives. First, it adds a completely new article to the OAS
Charter, laying down that a member of the OAS with a
democratically constituted government which has been overthrown may be suspended from participating in all OAS
activities. Suspension requires a decision by two-thirds of the
member States and can be effected only when diplomatic
initiatives have been exhausted. Secondly, the Protocol amends
several provisions of the Charter so as to add eradication of
extreme poverty to the essential purposes of the OAS listed in
Article 2, and to give prominence to the issue of extreme poverty
in other relevant articles. This Protocol thus seeks to buttress civil
and political rights by supporting democracy, while at the same
time emphasising economic and social rights by encouraging
action against poverty.

The other Protocol, the Protocol of Managua,[75] is intended to promote further the issue of economic rights by streamlining the process through which technical co-operation can be delivered to the member States. It therefore restructures the relevant sections of the Charter to create a single Inter-American Council for Economic Development to replace the existing Inter-American Economic and Social Council and Inter-American Council for Education, Science and Culture. This has been described as 'tantamount to a fundamental redefinition by OAS Member States of a regional approach to development problems in the hemisphere'.[76]

Both the Protocol of Washington and the Protocol of Managua require acceptance by two-thirds of the members of OAS and are not yet in force. However, in a continent in which both democracy and development have been conspicuously lacking in the past, they unquestionably represent a significant step forward.

## Notes

1 The decisions of the Third Special Inter-American Conference are summarised in A. H. Robertson, 'Revision of the Charter of the O.A.S.', *International and Comparative Law Quarterly*, XVII, 1968, p. 346. For the text of the Protocol of Buenos Aires, which effected these changes, see *International Legal Materials*, VI, 1967, p. 310.
2 The three special advisers were M. René Cassin, President of the European Court of Human Rights, Professor Balladore-Pallieri, judge of the European Court and subsequently its President, and Professor A. H. Robertson, the author of the first edition this book.
3 Text in I. Brownlie, *Basic Documents on Human Rights*, third edition, Oxford, 1992, p. 495, and P. R. Ghandhi, *International Human Rights Documents*, London, 1995, p. 147.
4 On 1 January 1995 twenty-five States were parties to the Convention.
5 Text in *International Legal Materials*, XXV, 1986, p. 527.
6 For a comparison of the rights protected by the two regional instruments see J. Frowein, 'The European and American Conventions – a comparison', *Human Rights Law Journal*, I, 1980, p. 44.
7 The *Effect of Reservations case* and the *Restrictions to the Death Penalty case*, see notes 23 and 27 below.
8 Text in Brownlie, *Basic Documents*, p. 521, and Ghandhi, *Human Rights Documents*, p. 164.
9 Text in Ghandhi, *ibid.*, p. 170.
10 On 1 January 1995, both protocols had received only three ratifications and only the 1990 protocol was in force.
11 See L. R. Scheman, 'The Inter-American Commission on Human Rights',

American *Journal of International Law*, LIX, 1965, p. 335, and D. L. Shelton, 'The Inter-American human rights system', in H. Hannum, *Guide to International Human Rights Practice*, second edition, Philadelphia, 1992, p. 119.

12　The conclusions of the Inter-American Commission were also communicated to the Commission on Human Rights of the United Nations under the procedure established by ECOSOC Resolution 1159 (XLI) of 1967 – see, for example, document E/CN.4/1333/Add.1 of 15 February 1979. On the practice of the Inter-American Commission see Robert E. Norris, 'Observations in loco; practice and procedure of the Inter-American Commission of Human Rights', *Texas International Law Journal*, XV, 1980, p. 46.

13　General Assembly of the OAS, Tenth Regular Session, AG/document 1348/80 of 27 November 1980.

14　The old procedures were the basis of the Commission's jurisdiction in the *Baby Boy case*; see *Human Rights Law Journal*, II, 1981, p. 110, and for discussion Shelton, *Human Rights Law Journal*, II, 1981, p. 309. Subsequently, the same procedures were used in the *Application of Death Penalty on Juveniles case*, which contains an interesting discussion of customary international law and *ius cogens*, see *Human Rights Law Journal*, VIII, 1987, p. 345, and D. T. Fox, *American Journal of International Law*, LXXXII, 1988, p. 601.

15　See note 1.

16　On 1 January 1995 ten States had made declarations under Article 45.

17　See T. Buergenthal, 'The Inter-American Court of Human Rights', *American Journal of International Law*, LXXVI, 1982, p. 231. For excellent general reviews see S. Davidson, *The Inter-American Court of Human Rights*, Aldershot, 1992, and C. M. Cerna, 'The structure and functioning of the Inter-American Court of Human Rights (1979–1992)', *British Year Book of International Law*, LXIII, 1992, p. 135.

18　On 1 January 1995 the jurisdiction of the Court had been accepted by sixteen States.

19　See T. Buergenthal, 'The advisory practice of the Inter-American Human Rights Court', *American Journal of International Law*, LXXIX, 1985, p. 1.

20　The organs concerned are the General Assembly, the meeting of consultation of the ministers of foreign affairs, the Councils, the Juridical Committee, the Commission on Human Rights, the General Secretariat, and the specialised organisations.

21　*'Other Treaties' Subject to the Advisory Jurisdiction of the Court*, Advisory Opinion No. OC-1/82 of 24 September 1982, ACHR, Series A, No. 1. Text in *Human Rights Law Journal*, III, 1982, p. 140.

22　*Ibid.*, para. 25.

23　*The Effect of Reservations on the Entry into Force of the American Convention*, Advisory Opinion No. OC-2/82 of 24 September 1982, Series A, No. 2. Text in *Human Rights Law Journal*, III, 1982, p. 153.

24　*Ibid.*, para. 16.

25　*Ibid.*, para. 29.

26　See the *Reservations to the Convention on the Prevention and Punishment of the Crime of Genocide*, Advisory Opinion, 1951, ICJ Reports, p. 15, and *Austria v. Italy*, European Yearbook of Human Rights, IV, 1960, p. 140.

27 *Restrictions to the Death Penalty*, Advisory Opinion No. OC-3/83 of 8 September 1983, Series A, No. 3. Text in *Human Rights Law Journal*, IV, 1983, p. 339.

28 See, for example, the *Western Sahara*, Advisory Opinion, 1975, ICJ Reports p. 12.

29 See the *Status of Eastern Carelia*, Advisory Opinion, 1923, PCIJ, Series B, No. 5.

30 *Restrictions to the Death Penalty case*, para. 65.

31 *Proposed Amendments to the Naturalization Provisions of the Constitution of Costa Rica*, Advisory Opinion No. OC-4/84 of 19 January 1984, Series A, No. 4. Text in *Human Rights Law Journal*, V, 1984, p. 161.

32 *Compulsory Membership in an Association Prescribed by Law for the Practice of Journalism*, Advisory Opinion No. OC-5/85 of 13 November 1985, Series A, No. 5. Text in *Human Rights Law Journal*, VII, 1986, p. 74.

33 *The Word 'Laws' in Article 30 of the American Convention on Human Rights*, Advisory Opinion No. OC-6/86 of 9 May 1986, Series A, No. 6. Text in *Human Rights Law Journal*, VII, 1986, p. 231.

34 *Ibid.*, para. 30.

35 *Ibid.*, para. 38.

36 *Character and Scope of the Right of Reply or Correction Recognised in the American Convention*, Advisory Opinion No. OC-7/85 of 29 August 1986, Series A, No. 7. Text in *Human Rights Law Journal*, VII, 1986, p. 238.

37 *Habeas Corpus in Emergency Situations*, Advisory Opinion No. OC-8/87 of 30 January 1987, Series A, No. 8. Text in *Human Rights Law Journal*, IX, 1988, p. 94.

38 *Ibid.*, para. 24.

39 *Judicial Guarantees in States of Emergency*, Advisory Opinion No. OC-9/87 of 6 October 1987, Series A, No. 9. Text in *Human Rights Law Journal*, IX, 1988, p. 204.

40 *Habeas Corpus case*, para. 36.

41 *Interpretation of the American Declaration of the Rights and Duties of Man within the Framework of Article 64 of the American Convention on Human Rights*, Advisory Opinion No. OC-10/89 of 14 July 1989, Series A, No. 10. Text in *Human Rights Law Journal*, XI, 1990, p. 118.

42 See the *Baby Boy case*, note 14.

43 *Exceptions to the Exhaustion of Domestic Remedies in Articles 46(2)(a) and 46(2)(b) of the American Convention on Human Rights*. Advisory Opinion No. OC-11/90 of 10 August 1990, Series A, No. 11. Text in *Human Rights Law Journal*, XII, 1991, p. 20.

44 *Compatibility of Draft Legislation with Article 8(2)(h) of the American Convention on Human Rights*, Advisory Opinion No. OC-12/91 of 6 December 1991, Series A, No. 12. Text in *Human Rights Law Journal*, XIII, 1992, p. 149.

45 *Certain Attributes of the Inter-American Commission on Human Rights*, Advisory Opinion No. OC-13/93 of 16 July 1993, Series A, No. 13. Text in *International Human Rights Reports*, I(2), 1994, p. 196.

46 *International Responsibility for the Promulgation and Enforcement of Laws in Violation of the Convention (Arts. 1 and 2 of the American Convention on Human Rights)*, Advisory Opinion No. OC-14/94 of 9 December 1994, Series A, No. 14. Text in *International Human Rights Reports*, II, 1995, p. 380.

47  *Decision on the Application of the Government of Costa Rica with Regard to Viviana Gallardo et al.*, decision of 13 November 1981, No. G 101/81. Text in *Human Rights Law Journal*, II, 1981, p. 328. For the Court's preliminary decision and for its decision closing the case see *ibid.*, II, p. 108, and V, p. 77, respectively.

48  See Resolutions 22/86, 23/86 and 24/86, all of 18 April 1986. Texts in *Human Rights Law Journal*, VII, 1986, pp. 424, 427 and 428.

49  Orders of 15 January and 19 January 1988. Texts in *Human Rights Law Journal*, IX, 1988, pp. 104 and 105.

50  *Velásquez Rodríguez case*, judgement of 29 July 1988. Text in *Human Rights Law Journal*, IX, 1988, p. 212.

51  See judgement of 20 January 1989, Series C, No. 5 (*Cruz*), and judgement of 15 March 1989, Series C, No. 6 (*Garbi and Corrales*).

52  *Velásquez Rodríguez – Compensatory Damages Judgment of July 21, 1989*. Text in *Human Rights Law Journal*, XI, 1990, p. 127. For the *Cruz* judgement, see Series C, No. 8.

53  *Velásquez Rodríguez – Interpretation of the Court's Judgment of July 21, 1989*. Text in *Human Rights Law Journal*, XII, 1991, p. 14.

54  *Aloeboetoe et al. Case Reparations*, judgement of 10 September 1993. Text in *International Human Rights Reports*, I(2), 1994, p. 208. For discussion see S. Davidson, 'Remedies for violations of the American Convention on Human Rights', *International and Comparative Law Quarterly*, XXXXIV, 1995, p. 405.

55  *Gangaram Panday case*, judgement of 21 January 1994. Text in *International Human Rights Reports*, II, 1995, p. 360.

56  See American Society of International Law, *Human Rights Interest Group Newsletter*, V(1), 1995, p. 30.

57  *Ibid.*, p. 29.

58  See, for example, the *Caballero Delgado and Santana case, Preliminary Objections*, judgement of 21 January 1994. Text in *International Human Rights Reports*, II, 1995, p. 393.

59  See American Society of International Law, *Human Rights Interest Group Newsletter*, V(1), 1995, p. 29.

60  See, for example, the *Reggiardo-Tolosa case*, Order of 19 January 1994. Text in *International Human Rights Reports*, II, 1995, p. 411.

61  *Colotenango case*, Order of 22 June 1994 and decision of 1 December 1994. Texts in *International Human Rights Reports*, II, 1995, pp. 414 and 421.

62  *Caballero Delgado and Santana case*, decision of 7 December 1994. Text in *International Human Rights Reports*, II, 1995, p. 425.

63  See the OAS Conventions on Asylum (1928); on Political Asylum (1933); on Diplomatic Asylum (1954); and on Territorial Asylum (1954).

64  See the OAS Conventions on the Nationality of Women (1933); on the Granting of Political Rights to Women (1948); and on the Granting of Civil Rights to Women (1948).

65  Text in Brownlie, *Basic Documents*, p. 531, and Ghandhi, *Human Rights Documents*, p. 171,

66  On 1 January 1995 the Convention had been ratified by thirteen States.

67  Text in *International Legal Materials*, XXXIII, 1994, p. 1534.

68  Text, *ibid.*, p. 1049.

69  The obligations in Article 7 of the Convention require immediate implement-
    ation; those of Article 8 only progressive implementation.

70  Bolivia and Venezuela.

71  Text in *International Legal Materials*, XXXIII, 1994, p. 1529.

72  Text in *International Legal Materials*, XXXII, 1993, p. 903.

73  The Convention requires two ratifications to come into force. On 1 January
    1995 there were no ratifications.

74  Text in *International Legal Materials*, XXXIII, 1994, p. 1005.

75  Text *ibid.*, p. 1009. The integrated text of the OAS Charter, as amended by
    these and earlier protocols, can be found *ibid.*, p. 981.

76  The quotation is from the Acting Secretary of State's report on the two
    protocols to the President of the United States. Text in *American Journal of
    International Law*, LXXXVIII, 1994, p. 720.

# CHAPTER 7

# *Regional co-operation on human rights elsewhere*

## I. Introduction

The American Convention, as we have just seen, has shown that a regional human rights treaty can function and be effective in a difficult environment, just as the European Convention has demonstrated the value of such an arrangement in more propitious circumstances. In the light of this experience it would be natural to expect attention to be given to the possibility of creating similar systems in other parts of the world and this has indeed occurred. Progress, however, has so far been rather patchy. While there have been calls for the creation of regional systems in Asia and the Pacific,[1] no agreements or institutions have resulted. In Africa, on the other hand, there is a functioning regional system, based on the African Charter on Human and Peoples' Rights, while in the Arab world there is a Commission with limited powers and a regional Convention which is not yet in force. In this chapter we shall begin with a review of the latter developments, then examine the African Charter in some detail and conclude with some general thoughts on the relation between regional and universal arrangements.

## II. The Permanent Arab Commission on Human Rights

The League of Arab States was founded in March 1945, shortly before the end of the Second World War.[2] Originally, it had no concern with human rights, becoming interested in these matters only two decades later as a result of three related developments.

The first arose out of the League's practice of co-operation with the United Nations. In August 1966 the Economic and Social

Council invited four regional organisations, the Council of Europe, the Organisation of American States, the Organisation of African Unity, and the League of Arab States, to attend sessions of the UN Commission on Human Rights in order to discuss their respective human rights activities.[3] At about the same time, the four regional organisations were urged to support the initiative of the United Nations in celebrating 1968 as International Human Rights Year and, as a corollary, were invited to attend the International Conference on Human Rights in Tehran, the Year's main event.[4] While the Council of Europe and the Organisation of American States already had their own human rights programmes, the Arab League had not, but now had an incentive to consider establishing one. In September 1966 the Council of the League decided to accept the invitation to participate in International Human Rights Year and soon appointed a committee of governmental representatives to consider how it should implement the decision.[5]

The second development was that early in 1967 the UN Commission on Human Rights decided to study the possibility of setting up regional commissions in areas where they did not already exist.[6] Later that year the Arab League, like other regional organisations, was asked for its views on this proposal. Its reply made the following points:

1    The field of human rights is a vital one for strengthening links among countries which belong to a regional area.
2    As for the procedure of establishing regional commissions on human rights and specifying their functions, the League of Arab States believes that the proper foundations for setting up such regional commissions are the foundations on which a regional intergovernmental organisation is based. Thus the regional commissions should be established within the framework of international or regional intergovernmental organisations.

Having expressed these views to the United Nations, it was no surprise when the League subsequently gave further attention to the idea of establishing its own regional Commission on Human Rights.

The third development occurred at the International Conference on Human Rights at Tehran in 1968. A number of Arab countries sought to include on the Conference agenda the question of 'respect and implementation of human rights in occupied territories', meaning the territories occupied by Israel during the war of June 1967. Whatever view may be taken about that war, there is no doubt that one result was that many thousands of people found themselves living under foreign occupation with some of their basic rights severely restricted. As a result, the problem was included on the agenda of the Tehran Conference, with the support of the majority of delegations. The concerted action of the Arab States at the Conference, assisted by the Secretariat of the Arab League, thus demonstrated that it was possible to use human rights as a means of censuring Israel over its treatment of the inhabitants of the occupied territories.

These various developments led the Arab League to conclude that the time was ripe to set up its own Commission on Human Rights. The Council of the League decided to organise an Arab regional Conference on Human Rights in Beirut in December 1968, as part of its contribution to International Human Rights Year, and used it to announce that it had decided to set up a Permanent Arab Commission on Human Rights.[7]

The rules of procedure which the League established for the Commission cover both procedural matters and its composition and functions. Each member State of the League is represented on the Commission, which means that its members are government officials, as in the UN Commission, and not independent persons serving in a personal capacity, as in the European and Inter-American Commissions. Other Arab States may be invited to attend, and representatives of the Gulf Emirates are invited as observers. The Council of the League appoints the chairperson of the Commission for a term of office of two years, which is renewable, and the Secretary-General of the League appoints the Commission's Secretary.

The functions of the Commission, like those of other Commissions of the League, are essentially to prepare draft agreements or other proposals for the Council. However, it has a power of initiative and may submit its own recommendations and suggestions to the Council. In accordance with this power, the Commission prepared a plan of action, which was approved by the Council of the League at its session in September 1969. This programme is based on the principle that all matters relating to human rights in the Arab world fall within the competence of the

Commission, particularly the co-ordination of joint action, the protection of the rights of the individual, and promoting respect for human rights in Arab countries in general. As one would expect, the Commission has given priority to the question of the rights of Arabs living in the occupied territories.

The programme is in two parts, relating respectively to action at the national level and action at the international level. As regards national action, it includes the creation of national commissions on human rights, which would be linked to the Permanent Commission of the League; receiving reports from member States on their activities in the field of human rights and making recommendations; and, perhaps most important of all, undertaking preparatory work for a proposed Arab Charter on Human Rights. At the international level, the Commission has concentrated on assisting the League and the delegations of member States at various conferences, including sessions of the UN Commission on Human Rights and the Working Group set up to investigate Israel's conduct in the occupied territories. The Commission also sends an annual report on its activities to the United Nations Commission, and its representatives played an active part in the UN seminar on the establishment of regional commissions on human rights with special reference to Africa, which was held in Cairo in 1969.

Information about the results achieved by the Commission is rather sparse. Its activities appear to have been mainly concerned with the situation in the occupied territories, which has now greatly improved as a result of recent political developments. The Commission's terms of reference, like those of the UN Commission, are essentially to promote human rights, rather than to protect them, in contrast with the European Commission. Work was also done on the proposed Arab Charter on Human Rights, which has resulted in action at the intergovernmental level. At a conference in Baghdad in 1979 the Union of Arab Lawyers proposed the conclusion of an Arab Convention on Human Rights which would guarantee fundamental rights as they are understood in an Islamic context. Subsequently, Arab jurists meeting at Syracuse approved the text of a Draft Charter of Human and Peoples' Rights in the Arab World.[8] This document, which was envisaged as the basis for an Arab treaty, set out civil and political rights, economic and social rights, and a list of

'Collective Rights of the Arab People'. It also contained comprehensive arrangements for supervision and implementation, including both a new Commission on Human Rights and a Court. Like the earlier proposal for an Arab Convention, this document had no official status but in September 1994 the Council of the League of Arab States approved an Arab Charter on Human Rights, which, when it comes into force, will provide the Arab world with a regional arrangement comparable to those which already exist in Europe, the Americas and Africa.[9] It is clear then that much remains to be done to bring into operation an Arab regional system, which is greatly needed, but significant evidence of progress is now discernible.

### III. The African Charter on Human and Peoples' Rights

#### 1. *The origin and history of the Charter*

The advances which led to the establishment of regional organisations in Europe and America have also produced results in Africa. Between 1958 and 1962 the independent African States held a series of conferences. The conference in Lagos in 1962 approved a proposal for permanent machinery for economic and technical co-operation and Liberia suggested additional arrangements of a political character, including annual meetings of the foreign ministers and the appointment of a permanent secretariat. The following year a summit conference of heads of State and government held in Addis Ababa adopted the Charter of the Organisation of African Unity (OAU). Article II of the Charter includes among the aims of the OAU 'to promote the unity and solidarity of the African States', 'to eradicate all forms of colonialism from Africa' and 'to promote international co-operation, having due regard to the Charter of the United Nations and the Universal Declaration of Human Rights'.

Although many national constitutions refer to, and sometimes incorporate, the provisions of the Universal Declaration, this was the first time that the constituent instrument of a new international organisation had done so. Article III of the Charter then proclaims a number of principles which all member States accept. These include the sovereign equality of all member States and non-interference in their internal affairs, and also 'absolute dedication to the total emancipation of the African territories which are still dependent' and 'a policy of non-alignment with regard to all blocs'. Membership of the OAU is open to 'each independent, sovereign African State' (Article IV). South Africa, which was not a member in the apartheid era, joined the Organisation in 1994, following its first free elections.

The organs of the OAU are the Assembly of Heads of State and Government, which is the supreme organ and meets at least once a year; the Council of Foreign Ministers, which meets at least twice a year and whose principal function is to prepare or execute decisions of the Assembly; the General Secretariat; and a body called the Commission of Mediation, Conciliation and Arbitration. Article XIX of the Charter contains a specific undertaking about peaceful settlement of disputes and provided for the creation of the above Commission by a separate protocol. This instrument was concluded in 1964 and is considered an integral part of the Charter. The creation of this specifically African machinery represents an attempt to settle disputes on a regional basis without referring them to the Security Council, which is, of course, consistent with Articles 52 and 53 of the UN Charter.[10]

The headquarters of the OAU is at Addis Ababa, and this is also the seat of the Economic Commission for Africa of the United Nations, which naturally encourages contacts between them.

The formation of an African Commission on Human Rights was first proposed at the African Conference on the Rule of Law, organised by the International Commission of Jurists in Lagos in 1961. The Conference adopted the 'Law of Lagos', in which it declared that: 'in order to give full effect to the Universal Declaration of Human Rights, this Conference invites the African Governments to study the possibility of adopting an African Convention on Human Rights'. This was the first step in a process which extended over the next twenty years, and culminated in the adoption of the African Charter on Human and Peoples' Rights in 1981. To see the delicate issues inseparable from human rights law making, it is interesting to trace the way in which this was achieved.

At the twenty-third session of the United Nations Commission on Human Rights in 1967 a proposal was tabled with the aim of encouraging the creation of regional Commissions on Human

Rights in those parts of the world where they did not already exist.[11] The most significant aspect of this proposal was that it was signed by the representatives of five African States[12] and clearly envisaged the creation of a Human Rights Commission in Africa.

The United Nations Commission decided to set up an *ad hoc* study group to consider the proposal and the group met in New York early in 1968. Its members were sharply divided on the question whether it was desirable to create regional Commissions, with the East European members expressing their traditional view that such bodies were likely to interfere with matters which fall within the domestic jurisdiction of States, contrary to the principle of national sovereignty and in violation of Article 2(7) of the Charter. The contrary view, of course, was that once States have assumed international obligations to promote and respect human rights, as they had done in the Charter and were soon to do much more explicitly in the Covenants, these matters can no longer be regarded as exclusively within their domestic jurisdiction.

The report of the study group was largely a record of dissenting views, but there was agreement on one point. This was that if further regional Commissions were to be created, it should be on the initiative of the States in the region and not imposed by the United Nations.[13] In March 1968 the report was considered by the UN Commission, which referred it for comment to the member governments and the regional organisations. In the reply which he sent to this request, the Secretary-General of the Council of Europe stated that, while it was not for him to say what advantages would be gained from the establishment of regional Commissions in other parts of the world, the European experience had shown that it was possible for a group of States in one region 'which have a common heritage of political traditions, ideals, freedom and the rule of law' to set up a more effective system for the protection of human rights than appeared to be possible on a worldwide basis.

By the time that the UN Commission came back to the matter at its twenty-fifth session, in March 1969, two things had happened to change the situation and create a more favourable climate. The League of Arab States had set up the Permanent Arab Commission on Human Rights, which showed that the idea of regional Commissions was gaining ground and had met with the support of a number of governments in Asia and North Africa. Furthermore, the government of the United Arab Republic had invited the United Nations to hold a seminar in Cairo as part of its programme of advisory services, to discuss the question of regional Commissions, with special reference to Africa.

This seminar took place in September 1969[14] and was attended by participants from twenty African countries, as well as representatives of the Council of Europe and the Arab League. There was a surprising amount of agreement on the desirability of establishing a regional Commission on Human Rights for Africa. The lead was taken by the delegation of the United Arab Republic, whose positive stance was generally supported. If this was due in part to the desire to achieve a greater respect for human rights throughout the African continent, it was probably also significant that human rights had now become an accepted basis in the UN for attacking political opponents, whether over the Israeli-occupied territories, the practice of apartheid, the situation in Namibia, or other international controversies. Whatever the reasons, there was soon general agreement that an African Commission should be created.

The type of Commission which most of the participants had in mind was not one in the same mould as the European Commission, with its quasi-judicial functions, but rather a Commission for the promotion of human rights, more on the lines of the UN Commission, or the Inter-American Commission in its original form. The agenda drawn up by the UN Secretariat listed the following possible functions for the new Commission:

1    education and information activities;
2    undertaking research and studies;
3    performance of advisory services;
4    holding seminars and awarding fellowships;
5    fact finding and conciliation;
6    consideration of communications from States, individuals and groups of individuals and the kind of action to be taken in response.

By the end of the discussion on the competence of the African Commission, it had been agreed to include the functions set out under points (1) to (4) above without reservation, and points (5) and (6) as optional provisions.

The other item for consideration was the means of establishing a regional Commission for Africa, and its geographical extent. On the second point, it was agreed that the Commission should include all African countries sharing the same political ideas, in other words that it should cover the whole of Africa except those countries tainted with apartheid and colonialism. It was also agreed that the African Commission should be created by resolution of the OAU, rather than by the conclusion of a Convention. To this end it was decided to invite the Secretary-General of the UN to send the report of the seminar to the Secretary-General of the OAU with a request that he should communicate it to his member governments and place the question on the agenda of a forthcoming meeting of the OAU. At the same time the hope was expressed that the UN, interested Specialised Agencies and regional organisations would all lend their advice and assistance to the OAU if it decided to proceed with the project.

The report on the Cairo seminar was duly communicated to the UN Commission on Human Rights at its twenty-sixth session, in 1970, and, as the participants had requested, to the Secretary-General of the OAU. The OAU, however, took no action at this stage.

The next step was a conference held in Addis Ababa in 1971 under the auspices of the United Nations Economic Commission for Africa and with the participation of the OAU. The matters discussed, which were the African legal process and the individual, related more to substantive issues of human rights than to the issue of new institutions, but the conference had been planned as a follow-up to the Cairo seminar, and repeated the recommendation for the establishment of a regional Commission on Human Rights for Africa.

Though this conference also was not followed by any practical action, the idea was kept alive at various subsequent meetings. One of these was the UN Seminar on the Study of New Ways and Means for Promoting Human Rights with Special Attention to the Problems and Needs of Africa, held in Dar-es-Salaam in 1973.[15] Two unofficial meetings which also discussed the question were the Third Biennial Conference of the African Bar Association in Freetown (Sierra Leone) in 1978, and a Seminar on Development and Human Rights organised by the International Commission of Jurists in Dakar in the same year.

An important step forward was taken by the OAU when the Assembly of Heads of State and Government adopted a 'Decision on Human Rights and Peoples' Rights in Africa', at the Assembly's sixteenth Ordinary Session, held in Monrovia in July 1979. As part of that decision the Assembly called on the Secretary-General of the OAU to 'organise as soon as possible in an African capital a restricted meeting of highly qualified experts to prepare a preliminary draft of an African Charter on Human Rights providing, *inter alia*, for the establishment of bodies to promote and protect human rights'.[16] The decision stated that human rights 'are not confined to civil and political rights but cover economic, social and cultural problems', that special attention must be given to the latter, and that 'economic and social development is a human right'. The decision also called on the OAU Secretary-General to draw the attention of member States to 'certain international conventions whose ratification would help to strengthen Africa's struggle against certain scourges, especially against apartheid and racial discrimination, trade imbalance and mercenarism'.

Two months later the United Nations organised a further seminar on the establishment of regional Commissions on Human Rights, with particular reference to Africa, which was also held in Monrovia. This was attended by participants from thirty African countries, as well as observers from Specialised Agencies, regional organisations and NGOs.[17] It was naturally encouraged by the OAU decision taken in July concerning the preparation of an African Charter on Human Rights. Widespread support was expressed for the idea of establishing an African Commission on Human Rights, but it was also suggested that the member States of the OAU lacked the political homogeneity which characterised the members of certain other regional organisations. The point was also made that they were primarily concerned with improving the living conditions and basic education of their peoples and that recommendations would only be made within the framework of the OAU decision adopted earlier by the heads of State.

It was accepted that the principle of non-interference in the internal affairs of a sovereign State should not exclude international action when human rights were violated in a particular State, but it was also considered that the functions of an African Commission on Human Rights should, in the beginning, be primarily promotional. As regards functions of protection, some participants stated that the Commission could be authorised to investigate alleged gross violations of human rights and to act as a mediator, but the majority maintained that it would be premature to admit individual petitions. At this first stage the priority was seen as to inform people and make them aware of their individual human rights, and the suggestion was made that here a useful role could be played by national and local institutions, as well as NGOs. Emphasis was also placed on the need to take account of the size of the African continent, the great number of African States, their cultural diversity, and the poor state of communications in many parts of Africa.

The seminar worked out a 'Monrovia proposal' for establishing an African Commission on Human Rights of sixteen members, elected by the Assembly of Heads of State and Government of the OAU, to serve in their personal capacity. Its functions would be 'to promote and protect human rights in Africa'. It would apply 'the international law of human rights', and the relevant international texts. While the functions of the Commission would be mainly promotional, it could also study alleged violations, propose its good offices and make reports and recommendations to the OAU. The seminar asked its chairman, the Minister of Justice of Liberia, to submit the Monrovia proposal to the Chairman of the OAU, President Tolbert of Liberia. The intention was obviously that the proposal should be considered by the meeting of experts which the OAU had already decided to convene with the task of preparing an African Charter on Human Rights.

Matters were not helped by the fact that President Tolbert and his government were overthrown a few months later in a military coup d'état. Nevertheless, the OAU meeting took place in the form of a ministerial conference held in Bangui (Gambia) in June 1980. It was presented with a draft African Charter on Human and Peoples' Rights which had been prepared by a meeting of experts held in Dakar in 1979. This was a draft for an international Convention of sixty articles, containing both substantive and procedural provisions. However, the ministerial conference in 1980 was able to examine only the first seven articles, with the result that a further meeting was needed in

January 1981. This completed work on the draft Charter, which was then submitted to the eighteenth summit meeting of the OAU, held in Nairobi in June 1981.

The summit meeting approved the Charter and opened it for signature on 26 June 1981. The Charter, which required ratification by a simple majority of the member States of the OAU, came into force in October 1986 and has now been ratified by more than forty States, making it the most widely accepted regional convention.[18]

## 2. *The rights protected*

In Article 1 of the African Charter the parties agree to recognise the rights, duties and freedoms which it contains and 'to adopt legislative or other measures to give effect to them'. This is followed by a non-discrimination provision (Article 2) and a list of substantive articles with several unusual features. The first is that the Charter covers economic, social and cultural rights, as well as civil and political rights. This clearly distinguishes it from the European and American Conventions with their more traditional approach and reflects the importance which the African States attach to these issues. Secondly, as the title of the Charter indicates, its provisions are not limited to human rights in the sense of individual rights of both categories, but extend also to 'peoples' rights', that is, to collective or 'third-generation' human rights, as they are sometimes called. Here too the desire to move beyond the conceptual framework of the other regional conventions is apparent. Thirdly, the African Charter, again in contrast to the earlier instruments, includes provisions which express the idea that human beings can only realise their potential fully as a member of a group. While this is plainly linked to the idea of collective rights, its consequence is held to be that a person has duties, as well as rights, in the community, so provisions to this effect are also included in the Charter.

(a) **Civil and political rights**   The provisions relating to these rights are to be found in Articles 3–16 of the Charter, which guarantee the following rights and freedoms:

1   the right to equality before the law;
2   the right to respect for life and the integrity of the person;

3  freedom from exploitation and degradation, including slavery, torture and cruel, inhuman or degrading punishment;
4  the right to liberty and security of the person;
5  the right to a fair trial;
6  freedom from retrospective punishment;
7  freedom of conscience, including religious freedom;
8  the right to receive information and to express opinions;
9  freedom of association;
10  freedom of assembly;
11  freedom of movement, including the right to asylum;
12  prohibition of mass expulsion;
13  the right to participate in government;
14  the right of equal access to the public service;
15  the right of equal access to public property and to public services;
16  the right to property.

The list bears an obvious resemblance to the corresponding parts of the other regional conventions, as well as to the Covenant on Civil and Political Rights, and, of course, this is not accidental. It would be wrong to suppose, however, that the treatment of civil and political rights in the African Charter is identical to that in the earlier instruments. While a detailed comparison must be sought elsewhere,[19] two general observations, one commending the Charter's approach, the other critical, may be made.

In support of the Charter it can be seen that its list of civil and political rights includes all the rights covered by the original European Convention – except, rather curiously, the right to marry[20] – some rights which were added by subsequent protocols, for example the right to participate in government and the right to property, and others such as the right of equal access to the public service, which have still to be recognised. Although the omitted rights are sometimes found in other conventions, there is no doubt that as regards the ground covered, the treatment of civil and political rights in the African Convention is quite extensive.

The criticism is that a comparison between the definition of certain rights in the African Charter and the equivalent provisions of other instruments reveals the Charter to be drafted in a way that seems bound to produce difficulties. One problem is that in several cases the right concerned is defined inadequately. Article 4, for example, guarantees respect for life and the integrity of the person, then states vaguely 'No one may be arbitrarily deprived of this right'. Similarly, Article 6, potentially one of the most important provisions of the Charter, guarantees the right to liberty and security of the person, and concludes 'no one may be arbitrarily arrested or detained'. The question which springs to mind, but which is not answered in the Charter, is what does the word 'arbitrarily' mean in these provisions?

A related difficulty is that the Charter, like other human rights instruments, permits limitation of the rights guaranteed, but does so in terms which are again terse and often appear to emasculate the main provision. Thus, Article 9(2) provides that 'Every individual shall have the right to express and disseminate his opinions *within the law*', while Article 10(1) lays down that 'Every individual shall have the right to free association *provided he abides by the law*' (emphasis added). If the qualifying words are compared with the corresponding provisions of the other regional conventions the contrast is striking. Whereas they permit the limitation of rights only in carefully defined circumstances, the African Charter appears to define the right by reference to national law. Since the main purpose of human rights treaties is to supply a standard against which national law can be measured, the problem with the language of the Charter is apparent.

Must we conclude then that the protection afforded by the extensive provisions of the African Charter is largely illusory? In the absence of case law applying its provisions, this cannot be answered. However, a suggestion as to how some of the less satisfactory provisions of the Charter might be amplified can be based on Article 60. This provides:

> The Commission shall draw inspiration from international law on human and peoples' rights, particularly from the provisions of various African instruments on human and peoples' rights, the Charter of the United Nations, the Charter of the Organization of African Unity, the Universal Declaration of Human Rights, other instruments adopted by the United Nations and by African countries in the field of human and peoples' rights as well as from the provisions of various instruments adopted within the Specialised Agencies of the United Nations of which the parties to the present Charter are members.

In relation to the problem under discussion, the wide range of source material which this article makes available suggests that when the Commission needs to fill out the more enigmatic parts of the Charter and keep its limiting provisions within sensible bounds, it may be able to derive valuable assistance from practice elsewhere.[21] For example, in determining what constitutes an 'arbitrary' deprivation of liberty, the African Commission could usefully refer to the detailed list of permissible actions set out in Article 5 of the European Convention. Similarly, the Strasbourg organs already have an extensive jurisprudence on the question of what is needed for an action to be in accordance with the law,[22] and the fact that Article 12 of the European Convention recognises the right to marry subject 'to the national laws governing the exercise of this right' has not prevented the Court and the Commission from ruling that such laws are acceptable only insofar as they do not interfere with the 'substance' of the Convention right.[23] How far the African Commission may be prepared to adopt this kind of approach remains to be seen, but if the Commission is prepared to look for it, material to support the dynamic interpretation which the Charter needs will not be hard to find.

(b) **Economic, social and cultural rights**   The African Charter deals with these rights in Articles 17 and 18, but the two provisions cover a total of seven aspects of economic, social and cultural rights, as follows:

1  the right to education;
2  the right to participate in the cultural life of one's community;
3  the duty of the State to promote and protect morals and traditional values;
4  the duty of the State to take care of the physical and moral health of the family;
5  the duty of the State to assist the family as the custodian of morals and traditional values;
6  the duty of the State to eliminate discrimination against women and ensure the protection of the internationally recognised rights of women and children;
7  the right of the aged and disabled to special measures of protection;

The right to education is guaranteed in the American Convention and in the First Protocol to the European Convention. The other rights are unique to the African Charter.[24] The place of economic, social and cultural rights in international law will be considered in the next chapter and so a detailed discussion of this part of the Charter would be inappropriate at this stage. However, since the inclusion of rights of this kind in a regional treaty is so unusual, it is worth briefly considering the way they are dealt with and the implications of their inclusion.

A comparison between the provisions of the African Charter and those of the Covenant on Economic, Social and Cultural Rights indicates that the latter is more comprehensive in the sense that it covers more rights. It is also more detailed, because rights which are merely stated in the Charter are usually elaborated in the Covenant. The right to education, for example, which appears in Article 7(1) of the Charter in the simple form 'Every individual shall have the right to education', is covered by Article 13 of the Covenant, which runs to 400 words and is actually longer than the treatment of economic and social rights in the whole of the Charter. Comparison between the terms of the African Charter and those of the European Social Charter reveals a similar contrast.

The conclusion to be drawn from this is not that support for economic and social rights by the African States is lukewarm or a sham. Many, after all, are parties to the United Nations Covenant, while Article 17(3) of the Charter, which makes the promotion and protection of morals and traditional values a duty of the State, goes much further than any other treaty.[25] Moreover, as we shall see shortly, in evaluating the Charter's treatment of economic and social rights, account must be taken of its later articles, on duties. It remains true, however, that the Charter is not a detailed treatment of economic and social rights. The reason, it is suggested, is that the intention of the framers was simply to emphasise the importance of economic and social rights and especially their close relationship with civil and political rights, which could be done without a full elaboration. This conclusion, which is consistent with the background to the Charter considered earlier, is supported by the fact that since many African States were already parties to the Covenant on Economic, Social and Cultural Rights, an exhaustive treatment of these matters at the regional level was hardly necessary. Looked at in this way, as a symbolic affirmation of the place of economic and social rights in the thinking of the African States, the inclusion of a relatively small number of rights, set out in a broad and unparticularised way, becomes easier to understand and justify.

(c) **Peoples' rights**   These rights are contained in Articles 19–24 of the Charter, which cover the following collective rights:

1    the right to equality of peoples;
2    the right to self-determination;
3    the right to dispose of wealth and natural resources;
4    the right to economic, social and cultural development;
5    the right to national and international peace and security;
6    the right to 'a general satisfactory environment' favourable to development.

It is perhaps worth emphasising that although all the rights in this part of the Charter are collective rights, two appear elsewhere as individual rights. These are the right to equality, which is covered in Articles 2 and 3, and the right to cultural development, which, as we have just seen, is included in the articles on economic, social and cultural rights (Article 17(2)). What the later articles of the Charter are dealing with, however, is not the individual's rights to equality and cultural development, but the corresponding rights of peoples.

In our earlier discussion of the right of self-determination we saw that the impulse to use international law to further human rights came originally from the idea that rights inhere in individuals, and this is still the basis of modern thinking. It follows that the concept of collective rights introduces a quite new element into the law which may sometimes be hard to reconcile with the traditional approach.[26] Some of the difficulties were touched on earlier and will be further explored in Chapter 8. For the moment, therefore, we shall concentrate on the specific features of the African Charter.

The Charter is the first international agreement to list collective rights in such detail, but it is not the first to mention them. Moreover, as we shall see, some of the ideas which are presented here as collective rights are to be found in other instruments in a different form. Thus, as in the case of economic and social rights and the provisions we shall consider shortly on duties, the treatment of collective rights, though a new departure in one sense, is also an extension of contemporary ideas.

Articles 19 and 20, which cover the rights to equality and self-determination, were clearly inspired by Article 1(1) of the two United Nations Covenants. In the light of their historical experience it is hardly surprising that the African States wished to include these provisions, nor that they chose to elaborate the right to self-determination by recognising the right of colonised or oppressed people to free themselves 'by resorting to any means recognised by the international community' (Article 22(2)) and proclaiming a people's right to assistance from other parties 'in their liberation struggle against foreign domination, be it political, economic or cultural' (Article 22(3)).

The Covenants also inspired Article 21 of the Charter, which deals with the right to dispose of wealth and natural resources. It will be recalled that this is covered in Article 1(2) of the Covenants, but the Charter is again more elaborate. Article 21(2) provides that 'In case of spoliation the dispossessed people shall have the right to lawful recovery of its property as well as to an adequate compensation'. Article 24(4) lays down that the parties shall exercise the right to dispose of wealth and natural resources 'with a view to strengthening African unity and solidarity'. And Article 24(5) contains an undertaking by the parties 'to eliminate all forms of foreign economic exploitation' in order to benefit their peoples. These details have no counterpart in the Covenants.

Article 23 deals with 'the right to national and international peace and security' and has a number of links with other instruments. Although no other instrument guarantees the right explicitly, the Universal Declaration comes close in its Article 28, which provides, 'Everyone is entitled to a social and international order in which the rights and freedoms set forth in this Declaration can be fully realised'. Moreover, both the Covenant on Civil and Political Rights and the American Convention contain an undertaking to prohibit propaganda for war, which is a means to the same end. In addition to the general statement of the right in Article 23(1), the Charter provides that States will ensure that an individual enjoying the right of asylum 'shall not engage in subversive activities against his country of origin or any other State party to the Charter' (Article 23(2)(a)) and also that 'their territories shall not be used as bases for subversive or terrorist activities against the people of any State party to the present Charter' (Article 23(2)(b)). These provisions have no equivalent in other human rights treaties, but the first qualifies the right of asylum under Article 12 in a way which is easy to justify and could perhaps be implied, while the second is a statement in terms of peoples' rights of a duty of all States under general international law.

Two provisions of the African Charter which have no equivalent at all in other international instruments are Article 22, on the right to development, and Article 24, which states 'All peoples shall have the right to a general satisfactory environment favourable to their development'. These articles are typical third-generation rights, which will be discussed later. It is worth noting that since both articles refer to 'development' they are related. Neither this concept nor the key terms of Article 24 are defined, which has prompted the Commission to take steps to clarify matters.[27] Even so, establishing the scope of these rights will be difficult.

A problem which arises in relation to all the articles in this part of the Charter is to decide what constitutes a 'people'. The general issue here, which occurs whenever collective rights are being considered, has been discussed in our earlier review of the United Nations Covenants and need not be reiterated. In relation to the situation in Africa, however, several points are particularly worth bearing in mind.

The emphasis which the African States have given to the maintenance of stable frontiers in the continent, and their equally strong anxiety to maintain the integrity of existing States despite the fissiparous tendencies of tribalism, make it likely that for most, if not all, of the parties to the Charter the concept of 'a people' is identified with the African nation State. If, however, 'peoples' and States came to be thought of as identical in all respects, the concept of peoples' rights will fail to achieve its potential. It is therefore pleasing to see that the African Commission has indicated that it regards these provisions of the Charter as protecting 'the different sections of the national community'.[28] Because so many African States contain diverse indigenous groups, the concept of peoples' rights, treated in this way as relevant to tribalism and similar problems, could mark a real advance in the promotion of human rights in Africa. Thus, while a desire to avoid its more destructive consequences is understandable, if used constructively the concept of human and peoples' rights could be an interesting and useful innovation.

(d) **Duties** The subject of duties is dealt with in Articles 27–29, which form Chapter II of the Charter. It begins with three general principles: every individual has duties towards his or her family and society, the State, 'other legally recognised communities', and the international community; rights and freedoms must be exercised with due regard to the rights of others, collective security, morality, and common interest; and every individual has a duty to respect and consider others without discrimination and to promote mutual respect and tolerance. We then find a list of eight specific duties, which are set out in Article 29, as follows:

1     the duty to the family;
2     the duty to use one's physical and intellectual abilities for the benefit of the State;
3     the duty to avoid compromising the security of the State;
4     the duty to preserve and strengthen social and national solidarity;
5     the duty to preserve and strengthen the national independence and territorial integrity of one's country and to contribute to its defence;
6     the duty to work to the best of one's ability and to pay taxes;
7     the duty to preserve and strengthen 'positive African cultural values' and to promote the moral well-being of society;
8     the duty to do one's best to promote African unity.

Although the African Charter is the first human rights treaty to prescribe the individual's duties in such an elaborate way, the inspiration for some of these provisions can be traced back to earlier instruments. Thus, Article 27, which sets out the principle of duties towards others and the obligation to respect others' rights, is similar to Article 32 of the American Convention, and Article 29(6), which makes work a duty as well as a right and also establishes the obligation to pay taxes, has a direct counterpart in Articles 36 and 37 of the American Declaration of the Rights and Duties of Man.

Certain other provisions in this part of the Charter, though lacking a precise equivalent elsewhere, can be seen as a sequel to some of the rights laid down in earlier articles. Thus, Article 28, which establishes the duty not to discriminate, is the corollary of

Article 2, which establishes the right not to be discriminated against, while Article 29(1), laying down the individual's duty to the family, is complementary to Article 18, which ascribes a similar duty to the State. Although therefore the Charter is unusual in prescribing these duties expressly, the provisions concerned are in a sense implicit in its earlier content.

Where the Charter breaks entirely new ground is in its elaborate statement of the individual's political duties in Article 29. Since these, like the earlier references to peoples' rights, are something new in human rights law, it is worth pausing to consider why it was thought necessary to include such provisions and what their effect is likely to be.

We may dismiss at once the idea that the articles in question were included so that the Charter could be used to force individuals to do their duties, as well as to enable them to protect their rights. In other words, there seems no prospect of claims being brought against individuals on the basis of these provisions. As we shall see shortly, the institutional arrangements of the Charter are completely unsuitable for this purpose, and in any case a human rights treaty is not a criminal code.

What then is their purpose? The duties set out in Article 29 are collectively referred to in Article 10 as 'the obligation of solidarity' and this, perhaps, is a clue to the answer. The Charter includes a section on duties for the same reason as it includes a group of articles on economic and social rights and peoples' rights. It includes these articles because the States concerned wished to put forward a distinctive conception of human rights in which civil and political rights are seen to be counterbalanced by duties of social solidarity, just as they are complemented by economic and social rights and supplemented by peoples' rights. There is, it may be recalled, one other text which adopts the same approach, the American Declaration on the Rights and Duties of Man of 1948, which lists ten duties of the individual, though in rather different terms from those of the African Charter. When the American Convention was drawn up almost all the references to duties were omitted. The African States, on the other hand, needing a treaty which would perform the functions of both the Declaration and the Convention, included references to duties, economic and social rights and peoples' rights so that one document would contain the complete picture.

Although the articles on duties are unlikely to be enforced against individuals, they will have an effect. Indeed, if, as we have suggested and their content confirms, they reflect a distinctive attitude towards human rights in Africa, their effect is likely to be substantial. In the first place, the Commission has indicated that it expects States to describe the programmes they have established to ensure the performance of these duties in the reports they submit under Article 62 of the Charter.[29] Secondly, the fact that the Charter contains such a categorical statement of the duties of the individual seems bound to colour the interpretation of its other provisions. Suppose, for example, someone objects to military service on religious or moral grounds and argues that Article 8, which guarantees freedom of conscience, requires that he should be recognised as a conscientious objector. Article 29(5) requires the individual to contribute to the defence of his country and must inevitably have an important bearing on his claim. Similarly, if a doctor is required to work in an unpopular part of the country and argues that this constitutes 'exploitation' contrary to Article 4, or an interference with the right to freedom of movement under Article 12, the contrary argument is very likely to rest on the duty to serve the national community by placing one's 'physical and intellectual abilities at its service', according to Article 29(2).

The point is not that these cases would necessarily be decided against the individual, for there is no reason in principle why duties should be regarded as any more absolute than rights. It is rather that, in a treaty which places so much weight on duties, provisions dealing with rights cannot be interpreted as if they stood alone. It is worth noting here that the other regional conventions recognise the issue of social solidarity but deal with it by using a different drafting technique. First, they define the rights which they protect in some detail, then they employ both general and specific provisions to restrict their scope by reference to the interests of others. This largely avoids the need to refer in the text to the individual's duties, or the claims of community and society.[30] The African Charter, with its briefer treatment of rights and limitations, perhaps needs the concept of duties to make up for earlier omissions. It remains to be seen whether the distinctive approach of the African Charter is just a matter of technique – a different path leading to the same destination – or whether, as seems more likely, an emphasis on personal duties will lead to a narrower conception of the individual's rights.

## 3. *The system of international control*

Implementation of the Charter is entrusted to a Commission of eleven members appointed by the Conference of Heads of State of the OAU. They sit in a personal and independent capacity and, in conformity with the general practice, no two members of the Commission may be nationals of the same State.

The functions of the Commission fall into two parts. In accordance with the thinking which provided much of the inspiration for the Charter, the Commission has important promotional functions. However, it is not, as once seemed likely, only a promotional body, for the Commission also has the task of ensuring that the rights laid down by the Charter are protected, and for this purpose is equipped with powers comparable, though not identical, to those of the European and American Commissions.

The promotional role of the Commission is set out in Article 45(1) of the Charter, which requires it to collect documents, undertake studies and research on African problems in the field of human and peoples' rights, organise seminars, symposia and conferences, disseminate information, encourage national and local institutions concerned with human rights, and, where necessary, give its views or make recommendations to governments. As part of the same process the Commission is 'to formulate and lay down rules aimed at solving legal problems relating to human and peoples' rights', so as to provide a basis for national legislation. It is also to co-operate with other African and international institutions on human rights issues.

Turning now to the functions of the Commission in protecting human rights, we find that the Charter contains a reporting procedure, a procedure for inter-State complaints and a procedure for individual complaints. It is therefore similar in this respect to the UN Covenant on Civil and Political Rights and its First Optional Protocol, although there are some important differences of detail. The reporting procedure is laid down in Article 62, which provides for States to submit reports every two years describing the steps they have taken to implement the Charter.

Surprisingly, there is no indication of who is to receive the reports, but the obvious inference is that the Commission should perform this function and this is what happens in practice. As in the Covenant, all parties must submit reports.

Inter-State complaints are likewise provided for in a mandatory procedure. Under Article 48 if one State claims that another is violating its obligations under the Charter, either may refer the matter to the Commission for investigation. The Charter makes it clear, however, that the primary objective in such situations is to secure a friendly settlement. Not only is this the first aim of the Commission when a case is referred to it, but under Article 47 a State with a complaint is encouraged to approach the other party directly, with a view to settling the matter without involving the Commission at all.[31] Arrangements for friendly settlement are, it will be recalled, a feature of both the European and American Conventions, but Article 47, which reflects the African States' preference for informal methods of dispute settlement, is unique to the African Charter.

A matter which is referred to the Commission can be dealt with only if all local remedies have been exhausted, unless it is obvious that this process would be unduly prolonged. For issues within its competence the Commission has wide powers of investigation. It can ask the States concerned to provide it with information and they are entitled to appear before it and submit oral or written representations. Article 52 provides that when the Commission has obtained from the States concerned 'and from other sources' all the information it deems necessary, and has attempted to reach an amicable solution, it must prepare a report containing the facts and its findings. The report is sent to the States concerned and to the Assembly of Heads of State and Government, to whom the Commission may also make 'such recommendations as it deems useful' (Article 53). In addition to its reports on individual cases, the Commission, as might be expected, is required to submit a general report on its activities to each ordinary session of the Assembly.

Articles 55–59 of the Charter set out the arrangements for dealing with individual complaints. Article 55 provides for the Secretary of the Commission to prepare 'a list of the communications other than those of States' and to transmit it to the Commission, which decides by a simple majority if a communication is to be considered. The significant points about this provision are, first, that there seems to be no restriction as to who may file a communication. There is therefore nothing corresponding to the requirement in Article 25 of the European Convention that the applicant must claim to be the 'victim' of a violation. A second point of interest is that the powers of the Commission under Article 55 are again mandatory. It will be recalled that acceptance of the right of individual petition under the European Convention is optional. In contrast, the African Commission's competence to deal with individual or other non-State communications is accepted automatically, as soon as a State ratifies the African Charter.

Before a communication can be investigated it must satisfy certain conditions of admissibility, which are laid down in Article 56. In most respects these follow the usual pattern: a communication must not be anonymous or insulting, local remedies must have been exhausted, if available, and the communication must not be out of time. An unusual condition is that communications must not be 'based exclusively on news disseminated through the mass media'.[32] This is clearly designed to limit the opportunities for an *actio popularis* suggested by Article 55, a restriction which, if other evidence is hard to find, may be regrettable. On the other hand, the treatment of the problem of the applicant who tries to use several procedures simultaneously is unusually generous, as the Charter only prevents the Commission from considering cases which have actually been settled by the use of another procedure.

Prior to the Commission's consideration of a communication on the merits, it must be brought to the attention of the State concerned (Article 57). Then, if it appears to the Commission 'that one or more communications apparently relate to special cases which reveal the existence of a series of serious or massive violations of human and peoples' rights', the Commission must draw the matter to the attention of the Heads of State and Government. The Assembly may then request the Commission to undertake 'an in-depth study of these cases and make a factual report accompanied by its findings and recommendations' (Article 58(2)). In addition, under Article 58(3) the chairperson of the Assembly is authorised to request an in-depth study in all cases of emergency.

What, then, is the function of the Commission in relation to communications which are not special cases? Here, unfortunately, the Charter is vague and two views of its meaning are possible. One view is that the Commission has no function at all in such cases. In other words, its only job is to identify 'special cases' and refer them to the Assembly in the hope that they will be passed back for further investigation. Any case which does not fall into this category would thus be rather like a case which is declared inadmissible: the Commission would scan it but proceed no further. The other view is that for cases outside the special category the Commission has the same functions as under the inter-State procedure. In other words, it must conduct an investigation, attempt conciliation, and report its conclusions to the Assembly.

It need hardly be pointed out that if the first view were to be accepted the Commission's role in relation to individual communications would be insignificant by comparison with its European and American counterparts. As a body without independent authority, the Commission would scarcely be in a position to 'ensure the protection of human and peoples' rights' as Article 45 requires it to do. For these reasons, and because, as we have seen, individual rights are best protected by procedures which the individual can activate, it is a matter for satisfaction that when it met in 1988 to establish a procedure for receiving and considering communications, the Commission decided to interpret its powers in the wider way.[33]

As well as having the power to deal with reports and communications from States and individuals, the Commission is authorised to issue what are in effect advisory opinions. Article 45(3) permits it to 'interpret all the provisions of the present Charter at the request of a State party, an institution of the OAU or an African Organisation recognised by the OAU'. This power, which bears an obvious resemblance to that provided for in Article 65 of the American Convention, could be very important in practice. Straddling, as it does, the boundary between the Commission's promotional functions and its work in protecting human rights, Article 45(3) creates a possibility for cases to be referred to the Commission without the political problems which complicate and can sometimes inhibit inter-State complaints. As we saw in Chapter 6, the advisory jurisprudence of the Inter-American Court is making a major contribution to the elucidation of obligations under the American Convention, and it is quite possible that one day the African Charter may see a similar development.

## 4. *The work of the Commission*

The first election of the members of the African Commission took place in August 1987 and the first meeting in November, when the Commission elected its President and Vice-President. Subsequent elections have resulted in various changes in the Commission's composition. The Charter lays down that members serve in their individual capacity; however, it is noticeable that most of those elected so far have been senior government officials. At its second session, in 1988, the Commission adopted its Rules of Procedure.[34] Since then the Commission has normally held two sessions every year, each of about two weeks, although in some years additional extraordinary sessions have been held.[35]

The bulk of the Commission's work to date has been taken up with promotional activities of various kinds. These are extremely important in view of the generally poor state of human rights education in Africa and, as noted earlier, are duly emphasised in Article 45 of the Charter. To discharge these obligations individual members of the Commission have been assigned responsibility for the promotion of human rights in specific countries and have attended seminars, while the Commission as a whole has made recommendations to the States parties on human rights education and has sought to publicise its activities. Two particularly important initiatives are the close co-operation which the Commission has sought to develop with NGOs, more than one hundred of which have been granted observer status, and the development of an infrastructure to support the Commission's activities, including the creation of an Information and Documentation Centre and a strengthened Secretariat.[36] The Commission has also undertaken studies of specific rights which are guaranteed in the Charter, and recently accepted in principle the idea of establishing an African Human Rights Court.[37]

Although the Commission's promotional work has so far been the main element in its activity, its role in protecting human rights has not been neglected. In relation to the reporting obligation laid down in Article 62, at its third session, in 1988, the Commission sought a mandate from the OAU to receive and process such reports, and when this was given, adopted guidelines relating to the form and content of reports at its fourth session, in the same year.[38] The guidelines are very detailed and suggest that in addition to describing how they are implementing the Charter, States should report on their implementation of the 1966 United Nations Convention on the Elimination of All Forms of Racial Discrimination, the 1973 Convention on the Suppression and Punishment of the Crime of Apartheid, and the 1979 Convention on the Elimination of All Forms of Discrimination against Women.

As the three UN Conventions already have their own reporting arrangements, this attempt to extend the functions of the Commission seems unnecessary and, together with the intimidating nature of the main guidelines, may have contributed to States' reluctance to provide it with reports. Whatever the reason, the parties to the Charter have been slow to discharge their obligations under Article 62, and when reports have been produced, they have been of variable quality.[39] Like the UN treaty bodies, the African Commission invites the representatives of the State concerned to discuss the report and answer questions, but observers have noted that compared with UN practice the ensuing debates are rather superficial.[40] This, of course, is a criticism which was also made of the UN bodies until quite recently and the situation may therefore improve as the Commission gains experience and confidence.

So far there have been no reports of inter-State complaints under Article 48, but individual complaints, submitted in accordance with Article 55, present a different picture and here the Commission appears to have been quite active. At its fifteenth session, in 1994, for example, the Commission indicated that it had examined eight new communications and seventy which were already under consideration, while at its two sessions in the previous year, it had reviewed a total of ninety-four existing and twenty-one new communications.[41] On the basis of the complaints received the Commission has expressed its concern at the violation of human rights in a number of African countries and is reported on occasion to have secured the release of detainees.[42] Unfortunately, however, the significance of the Commission's practice in relation to individual communications is impossible to assess, as its interpretation of the obligation of confidentiality laid down in Article 59(2) has made it slow to release detailed information.[43]

The Commission indeed has published very little document-ation on its work, not only because of confidentiality, but also through a lack of resources. This has been a major constraint on its activities. Thus in its crucial early years the Commission lacked an effective Secretariat and was unable, for example, to maintain proper records of its sessions, or to translate and copy its documentation. No human rights organ, however dedicated and well intentioned, can function effectively without resources. Providing the Commission with the necessary support should therefore be a high priority for all who are concerned for its future.

Despite its many limitations, the African Charter on Human and Peoples' Rights is a very significant step in international human rights law. Not only does the Charter itself contain many innovative provisions, but the system it creates is by a considerable margin the largest regional human rights system in terms of the number of States concerned, as well as the only functioning arrangement in the Afro-Asian world. The Commission has not been in operation for very long and how it develops rests on what the members of the OAU want, or will allow, it to do. The African Charter of Human and Peoples' Rights is nevertheless already a milestone in a continent where underdevelopment and undemocratic government are endemic, and progress on human rights an urgent and pressing need.[44]

## IV. Regionalism and universalism

The existence of three regional systems for the protection of human rights – the European, the American, and the African – and the prospect of others elsewhere, raise the question whether regional arrangements are compatible with the universal system of the United Nations, or whether they are likely to diminish the value of the human rights work of the UN and perhaps even undermine its effectiveness.

The issue has been much discussed. An early instance was the lively debate at the second International Colloquy on the

European Convention, organised by the University of Vienna and the Council of Europe in 1965. The report on this subject presented by M. Jean-Flavien Lalive of Geneva argued in favour of the establishment of regional arrangements and regional commissions, while the statement made by Mr Egon Schwelb, in the light of his long experience of the work of the United Nations Commission, took the contrary view.[45] More recently, as noted in Chapter 1, there has been debate as to whether standards of human rights are truly universal, or so bound up with culture as only to be realisable locally, which might be seen as another argument in favour of regionalism.

There is naturally a good deal to be said on both sides of the question. On the one hand, experience has shown that in Europe it was possible to conclude a Convention containing binding obligations and setting up new international machinery at a time when this was not possible in the world at large. Though the UN Covenants have now been widely ratified, the number of States which have accepted their optional provisions is still limited, so that for the foreseeable future the European system is likely to provide far more effective guarantees than the universal system. If a regional system can be justified in this way in one part of the world, logic requires the same view as regards regional systems elsewhere.

On the other hand, it can be argued that human rights belong to human beings by virtue of their humanity and should be guaranteed to everyone on a basis of equality and without distinction, wherever they may live. Discrimination on grounds of race, sex, religion, or nationality is forbidden both in the United Nations texts and in the regional Conventions. Equally, it might be said, there should be no distinction based on regionalism. The Arab and the Asian should have the same human rights as the European or the American. In our view this last principle is incontrovertible. How then are we to reconcile the two points of view?

A possible answer is as follows. Human rights should indeed be the same for all persons, everywhere, at all times. In other words, the normative content of different international instruments should in principle be the same. There may, of course, be variations in formulation, due to differences in drafting or legal traditions, but the basic rights and fundamental freedoms should be the same for all. Here the touchstone is the Universal Declaration, which sets out, as the preamble puts it, 'a common standard of achievement for all peoples and all nations'. Hence, no regional system can be regarded as acceptable unless it is consistent with the norms and principles set out in the Universal Declaration.

When we come to measures of implementation, however, the position is different. While it is desirable that the most effective system possible should be established everywhere, it is plain that at present the same system is not acceptable in all parts of the world. Even within Europe this was for many years the position, because several members of the Council of Europe were slow to accept the optional provisions of the European Convention. If this was the case inside one regional organisation, how much more is it true of different regions of the world, one of which – Asia – has so far shown no signs of willingness to accept any form of international control at all.

It is therefore reasonable, on practical grounds, to set up regional arrangements for the protection of human rights which may differ from each other, provided that the rights to be protected are essentially the same and are substantially those laid down in the Universal Declaration. We saw in Chapter 4 that this is the approach adopted by the European Convention, in which the contracting parties expressed their determination 'to take the first steps for the collective enforcement of certain of the rights stated in the Universal Declaration'. Other regional systems are therefore equally legitimate if they too set up procedures which can be accepted by a group of States in a particular area, as a way of enforcing some or all of the rights proclaimed in the Universal Declaration.

This reasoning is supported by two other arguments. First, given the diversity of the modern State system, it is natural that regional systems of enforcement should be more readily accepted than universal arrangements. A State cannot be forced to submit itself to a system of international control and will do so only if it has confidence in it. It is much more likely to have such confidence if the international machinery has been set up by a group of like-minded countries, which are already its partners in a regional organisation, than if this is not the case. Moreover, it will be willing to give greater powers to a regional organ of restricted membership, in which the other members are its friends and neighbours, than to a worldwide organ in which it and its associates play a relatively small part.

The second supporting argument is the purely practical one of distance. To take Europe as an example, it is obviously easier and more convenient for all concerned when a complaint by one State against another, and *a fortiori* an individual application against a State, can be heard in Strasbourg rather than New York. The same applies to other regions of the world, insofar as their regional commissions have competence to consider inter-State complaints or individual applications.

A third point to be borne in mind is that the concept of regionalism and the principle of regional settlement are perfectly consistent with the Charter of the United Nations. Articles 33 and 52 of the Charter expressly recognise the principle of regional settlement of disputes threatening international peace and security. The same principle can properly be extended to disputes about the violation of human rights. Indeed, this is explicitly recognised in Article 44 of the Covenant on Civil and Political Rights, which acknowledges the legitimacy of other arrangements.

In principle, then, regional systems for the promotion and protection of human rights are not inconsistent with the ideal of a worldwide United Nations system, provided that they constitute local arrangements to secure greater respect for the norms established by the United Nations in the Universal Declaration. However, it would be wrong to leave this topic without recalling that reconciling regional with universal schemes for human rights protection presents practical, as well as theoretical, problems.[46] The more regional systems are developed, the more applicants will be in a position to try to pursue their claims at the universal and regional levels simultaneously. Whether this is possible, and if so the conditions under which it may be done, will therefore become increasingly important issues. Indeed, cases of this kind now crop up quite regularly and the organs concerned are in process of working out ways of dealing with them. But the issues here are difficult and will continue to demand attention as the separate human rights systems are developed.

A different sort of problem arises from the application of the various human rights conventions. Here, the need is to find a way of ensuring that the guarantees which form the substance of human rights law are applied in different places in a broadly uniform way. The reason for this was put forward earlier. In principle human rights should be the same for all, and this is clearly a matter not just of texts, but also of interpretation. Notice, however, that the stipulation is for rights to be interpreted in a broadly uniform way, not identically. Since the texts themselves are often different, some differences in interpretation are inevitable. More significantly, since there is not in fact a uniform world culture, we have to recognise that differences in the way that rights are interpreted are a legitimate result of cultural diversity.[47] Which rights should be regarded as basic and immutable and which secondary and open to different interpretations is, of course, a matter for debate.

The fact that human rights are not viewed identically in different parts of the world is reflected in the language of the various instruments, as we have seen. This leads to our final point about the relation between the various systems, which is that the practical problems which stem from having two levels of protection would be significantly eased if there were more similarity between the different human rights treaties. Certainly the effect of cultural diversity must again be taken into account, and no one should underestimate the difficulty of securing even relatively minor additions to treaty obligations. If the will is there, however, the harmonisation of human rights provisions is by no means a fantasy, as the conclusion of recent protocols to the European Convention demonstrates. While some differences between human rights treaties will no doubt always exist, the goal of ensuring that regional and universal arrangements reflect a common standard makes efforts to bring them closer together well worth pursuing.

## Notes

1  For an excellent survey of current thinking see J. T. H. Tang (ed.), *Human Rights and International Relations in the Asia Pacific Region*, London, 1995. As Tang notes (pp. 194–200), although there is no regional system of protection, Asian NGOs are now extremely active.

2  Further information on the history and structure of the League of Arab States was given in the first edition of this book at pp. 140–3. See also B. Boutros-Ghali, 'The Arab League (1945–1970)', *Revue Egyptienne de Droit International*, XXV, 1969, p. 67.

3  ECOSOC Resolution 1159 (XLI) of 5 August 1966.

4  General Assembly Resolution 2081 (XX) of 20 December 1965.

5  Arab League Council Resolution 2304 (XLVII) of 18 March 1967.

6  Recommendation 6 (XXIII) of 23 March 1967.

7  See Arab League Council Resolution 2443 of 3 September 1968. The creation of the Commission and the decisions of the Conference were reported to the UN Commission on Human Rights at its twenty-fifth session (document E/CN.4/L1042 of 18 February 1969). For further discussion, see S. P. Marks, 'La Commission Permanente Arabe des Droits de l'Homme', *Human Rights Review*, III, 1970, p. 101.

8  See Council of Europe, *Human Rights Information Sheet*, No. 21, Strasbourg, 1988, p. 122. The text of the Draft Charter will be found *ibid.*, p. 243.

9  See Council of the League of Arab States, 102nd session, Resolution 5437, 15 September 1994. As of 1 January 1995 no States had yet ratified the Arab Charter.

10  See J. G. Merrills, *International Dispute Settlement*, Cambridge, 1991, Chapter 6, and also T. O. Elias, 'The Commission of Mediation, Conciliation and Arbitration of the Organisation of African Unity', *British Year Book of International Law*, XL, 1964, p. 336, and T. Maluwa, 'The peaceful settlement of disputes among African States 1963–1983', *International and Comparative Law Quarterly*, XXXVIII, 1989, p. 299. On the OAU in general, see T. O. Elias, 'The Charter of the Organisation of African Unity', *American Journal of International Law*, LIX, 1965, p. 243.

11  UN document E/CN 4/L 940, draft Recommendation II, *Report of the Twenty-Third Session* (E/4322), pp. 109–25.

12  The States concerned were the Congo, Dahomey, Nigeria, Senegal, and Tanzania.

13  UN document E/CN 4/966 and addendum (*Report of the UN ad hoc Study Group Established under Resolution 6 (XXIII) of the Commission on Human Rights*).

14  The official report of the session is contained in UN document ST/TAO/HR/38, 1969. Part of this account was published in *Human Rights Law Journal*, II, 1969, pp. 696–702. A further account of the Cairo seminar was given in the first edition of this book at pp. 151–7.

15  Report in UN document ST/TAO/HR/48.

16  OAU document AHG/115 (XVI).

17  UN, *Bulletin of Human Rights*, No. 25 (July–September 1979), pp. 23–5.

18  On 1 January 1995 the African Charter had been ratified by forty-nine States. For the text of the Charter see I. Brownlie, *Basic Documents on Human Rights*, third edition, Oxford, 1992, p. 551, and P. R. Ghandhi, *International Human Rights Documents*, London, 1995, p. 175. For discussion of the Charter see R. Gittleman, 'The African Charter on Human and Peoples' Rights: a legal analysis', *Virginia Journal of International Law*, XXII, 1981–82, p. 667, and U. O. Umozurike, 'The African Charter on Human and Peoples' Rights', *American Journal of International Law*, LXXVII, 1983, p. 902.

19  See, for example, B. O. Okere, 'The protection of human rights in Africa and the African Charter on Human and Peoples' Rights: A comparative analysis with the European and American systems', *Human Rights Quarterly*, VI, 1984, p. 141.

20  However, the African Commission has indicated that it regards the right to marry as coming within Article 18, which deals with the protection of the family. See the Commission's Guidelines for National Periodic Reports (1988), Part II, para. 28(b), text in *Human Rights Law Journal*, XI, 1990, p. 403.

21  Also relevant in this connection is Article 61, which provides: 'The Commission shall also take into consideration, as subsidiary measures to determine the principles of law, other general or special international conventions, laying down rules expressly recognized by member states of the Organization of African Unity, African practices consistent with international norms on human and peoples' rights, customs generally accepted as law, general principles of law recognized by African states as well as legal precedents and doctrine.'

22  Thus, in the *Sunday Times case* the European Court held that the expression 'prescribed by law' in Article 10(2) of the European Convention must be interpreted as involving at least two requirements: 'Firstly the law must be adequately accessible: the citizen must be able to have an indication that is adequate in the circumstances of the legal rules applicable to a given case. Secondly, a norm cannot be regarded as a "law" unless it is formulated with sufficient precision to enable the citizen to regulate his conduct: he must be able – if need be with appropriate advice – to foresee to a degree that is reasonable in the circumstances, the consequences which a given action may entail' (ECHR, Series A, No. 30, para. 49). See further J. G. Merrills, *The Development of International Law by the European Court of Human Rights*, second edition, Melland Schill Monographs in International Law, Manchester, 1993, pp. 129–32.

23  See the *Rees case*, Series A, No. 106, para. 50.

24  It will be recalled, however, that Article 26 of the American Convention contains a general undertaking to take measures to secure the rights generated by the economic, social and cultural standards set out in the OAS Charter.

25  See also in this connection the 1990 African Charter on the Rights and Welfare of the Child. For discussion of this treaty, which is not yet in force, see B. Thompson, 'Africa's Charter on Children's Rights: A normative break with cultural traditionalism', *International and Comparative Law Quarterly*, XLI, 1992, p. 432.

26  For an interesting discussion of this question in the context of the African Charter, see S. C. Neff, 'Human rights in Africa: Thoughts on the African Charter on Human and Peoples' Rights in the light of case-law from Botswana, Lesotho and Swaziland', *International and Comparative Law Quarterly*, XXXIII, 1984, p. 331.

27  See the Commission's Guidelines for National Periodic Reports, note 20, Part III, paras 6–13.

28  *Ibid.*, Part III, para. 2. See also R. N. Kiwanuka, 'The meaning of "People" in the African Charter on Human and Peoples' Rights', *American Journal of International Law*, LXXXII, 1988, p. 80.

29  *Ibid.*, Part IV, paras 1–8.

30  See P. Sieghart, *The International Law of Human Rights*, Oxford, 1983, p. 42.

31  It should be noted, however, that under Article 49 a State which considers that another State has violated the Charter is entitled to refer the matter directly to the Commission by addressing a communication to the chairperson, to the Secretary-General of the OAU, and to the State concerned.

32 The UN Commission on Human Rights has a similar requirement when considering communications under the Resolution 1503 procedure (see Chapter 3), as does UNESCO when utilising the procedure for considering human rights complaints described in Chapter 8. See further Sieghart, *International Law of Human Rights*, pp. 426, 435.

33 See Rules of Procedure of the African Commission on Human and Peoples' Rights, adopted on 13 February 1988, Rules 101–118, text in *Human Rights Law Journal*, IX, 1988, p. 333.

34 See previous note.

35 The Commission's first four Activity Reports, covering the work of the nine sessions held between November 1987 and March 1991, can be found in *Human Rights Law Journal*, IX, 1988, p. 326; XI, 1990, pp. 390 and 432; and XII, 1991, p. 278.

36 See the Activity Reports referred to in the previous note and W. Benedek, 'The 9th Session of the African Commission on Human and Peoples' Rights', *Human Rights Law Journal*, XII, 1991, p. 216, E. V. O. Dankwa, 'Conference on regional systems of human rights protection in Africa, the Americas and Europe', *Human Rights Law Journal*, XIII, 1992, p. 314, and C. Flinterman and E. Ankumah, 'The African Charter on Human and Peoples' Rights', in H. Hannum (ed.), *Guide to International Human Rights Practice*, second edition, Philadelphia, 1992, p. 159.

37 See Council of Europe, *Human Rights Information Sheet*, No. 35, Strasbourg, 1995, p. 141, noting that the Commission has also recently appointed a special rapporteur on extrajudicial executions.

38 Text in *Human Rights Law Journal*, XI, 1990, p. 403.

39 See Benedek, 'The 9th Session', p. 217.

40 See *Human Rights Monitor*, XIX, 1992, p. 19.

41 See Council of Europe, *Human Rights Information Sheet*, No. 35, Strasbourg, 1995, p. 141.

42 See Dankwa, 'Conference on regional systems', p. 315.

43 However, in two recent cases involving Nigeria, the Commission found violations of Articles 6, 7, 10 and 26 of the Charter, and issued its first reasoned decisions. See *International Human Rights Reports*, II, 1995, pp. 616 and 619.

44 For further discussion of human rights in Africa, with particular reference to the political context, see M. Haile, 'Human rights, stability and development in Africa', *Virginia Journal of International Law*, XXIV, 1983–84, p. 575.

45 See A. H. Robertson (ed.), *Human Rights in National and International Law*, Manchester, 1967, pp. 330–42 and 355–6.

46 For discussion of this problem and related aspects of the same issue see T. Meron, 'Norm making and supervision in international human rights: reflections on institutional order', *American Journal of International Law*, LXVI, 1982, p. 754.

47 For illustration of this point in the context of the African Charter see Neff, 'Human rights in Africa'.

# CHAPTER 8

# *Economic, social and cultural rights*

'All human rights are universal, indivisible and interdependent and interrelated'.[1] This concept of human rights, which is to be found in the Vienna Declaration and Programme of Action, adopted at the 1993 World Conference on Human Rights, in philosophical terms is a complex one, and much ink could be expended on examining its implications. For present purposes, however, two aspects of the statement are significant.

First, it reminds us that there are different sorts of human rights – not only the civil and political rights we have been mainly concerned with so far, but also economic, social and cultural rights, which have already been mentioned in various contexts, and possibly others we have yet to consider. Secondly, the words quoted emphasise that whatever type of right we are dealing with, because rights are 'indivisible and interdependent' we must not treat some as more important than others. In particular, economic, social and cultural rights are not subordinate to civil and political rights, or vice versa.

Economic, social and cultural rights are protected by a variety of instruments at the regional and universal levels. The regional measures concerned, namely the European Social Charter, the recent protocol to the American Convention on Human Rights and relevant articles of the African Charter on Human and Peoples' Rights, have been examined in the previous three chapters. Accordingly, the focus of this chapter will be on the treatment of economic, social and cultural rights in the United Nations and its Specialised Agencies, along with certain related developments.

# I. The International Covenant on Economic, Social and Cultural Rights

In 1950 the General Assembly of the United Nations decided that economic, social and cultural rights should be included in the single international Covenant which was then projected. Two years later, however, it changed its mind and decided that there should be separate Covenants dealing with the two categories of rights, but that they should be prepared simultaneously and contain as many similar provisions as possible. The Commission on Human Rights followed these instructions, with the result that the General Assembly was able to approve the International Covenant on Economic, Social and Cultural Rights on 16 December 1966, at the same time as the Covenant on Civil and Political Rights.[2]

## 1. *The rights guaranteed*

In the event, the wish that the two Covenants should contain as many similar provisions as possible could not be realised to any significant extent. Of course, the rights protected are different, with the exception of the right of all peoples to self-determination, which forms Article 1 of both Covenants. In addition, however, the obligations assumed by the States parties and the two systems of international control are also very different in character, as we shall see.

Articles 2–5 of both Covenants set out the general provisions on the obligations of the States parties. But whereas the obligation assumed by contracting parties in the Covenant on Civil and Political Rights is intended to be of immediate application, the general obligation assumed by contracting parties in the Covenant on Economic, Social and Cultural Rights is not, and in this way reflects the nature of the rights secured. Paragraph 1 of Article 2 reads as follows:

Each State Party to the present Covenant undertakes to take steps, individually and through international assistance and co-operation, especially economic and technical, to the maximum of its available resources, with a view to achieving progressively the full realization of the rights recognized in the present Covenant by all appropriate means, including particularly the adoption of legislative measures.

It is thus quite clear that this is what is known as a promotional convention, that is to say, it does not set out rights which the parties are required to implement immediately, but rather lists standards which they undertake to promote and which they pledge themselves to secure progressively, to the greatest extent possible, having regard to their resources. As already indicated, this difference in the obligation results from the very nature of the rights recognised in this Covenant.

Of the remaining general provisions in the Covenant on Economic, Social and Cultural Rights, the non-discrimination clause (Article 2(2)) is similar to that in the other Covenant, as are also the proclamation of the equal rights of men and women (Article 3) and the provisions in Article 5 designed to prevent abuse of the rights secured, together with a general saving clause. Article 4 relates to limitations on the rights protected. Limitations are permissible only 'as determined by law ... and solely for the purpose of promoting the general welfare in a democratic society'. However, there is no provision for derogations in a state of emergency, as in the other Covenant.

Finally, paragraph 3 of Article 2 contains the following unusual provision, designed to protect developing countries from economic exploitation by their more powerful neighbours: 'Developing countries, with due regard to human rights and their national economy, may determine to what extent they would guarantee the economic rights recognized in the present Covenant to non-nationals.' Plainly this paragraph introduces the principle of discrimination since it explicitly permits developing countries to discriminate against foreigners with regard to the enjoyment of certain economic rights. It was perhaps included to make the point that the Covenant cannot be used to protect foreign investments in developing countries. However, neither Covenant protects the right of property, and so this provision has little relevance to that problem.

When we come to the particular rights protected in the Covenant on Economic, Social and Cultural Rights, we find a longer list and more detailed definitions than those contained in the Universal Declaration. The latter included only six articles relating to these rights in 1948; by the time the Covenants were concluded in 1966 the number had increased to ten. This illustrates a tendency, which has been continued, to pay increasing attention to economic and social rights. This tendency, which came about mainly as a result of the admission to the UN of a large number of developing countries as new members, has been accompanied by a corresponding reduction in emphasis on those rights of a civil and political character. It is perhaps indicative that in the General Assembly resolution approving the new Covenants, the Covenant on Economic, Social and Cultural Rights was placed before the Covenant on Civil and Political Rights.

The economic, social and cultural rights protected by the Covenant are the following:

*Article* 6 the right to work;
7 the right to just and favourable conditions of work including fair wages, equal pay for equal work and holidays with pay;
8 the right to form and join trade unions, including the right to strike;
9 the right to social security;
10 protection of the family, including special assistance for mothers and children;
11 the right to an adequate standard of living, including adequate food, clothing and housing and the continuous improvement of living conditions;
12 the right to the highest attainable standard of physical and mental health;
13 the right to education, primary education being compulsory and free for all, and secondary and higher education generally accessible to all (Article 14 permits the progressive implementation of this right);
15 the right to participate in cultural life and enjoy the benefits of scientific progress.

There is a substantial amount of common ground between this list and that contained in the 1961 European Social Charter. As we saw in Chapter 5, the Charter proclaims nineteen economic and social rights, but often formulates as two or three separate rights provisions which are grouped together in one article of the Covenant.

Comparing the two UN Covenants reveals a major difference in the way their respective provisions are formulated. The rights contained in the Covenant on Civil and Political Rights are stated in the classic form 'Everyone has the right to ...' or 'No one shall be subject to ...'. In the Economic and Social Covenant, on the other hand, the normative articles adopt a different formulation, usually 'The States Parties to the present Covenant recognise the right ...'[3] or 'The States Parties to the present Covenant undertake to ensure ...'.[4] In other words, we find an undertaking or a recognition by States rather than the affirmation of a right inherent in the individual as such. When it is recalled that the undertaking of the contracting parties in Article 2 of the Covenant is 'to take steps ... with a view to achieving progressively the full realization of the rights recognized in the present Covenant', the promotional character of the instrument is plain.

## 2. The system of international control

For the implementation of the Covenant on Economic, Social and Cultural Rights, Articles 16–25 provide for a system of periodic reports by States detailing the measures adopted and the progress made in achieving the observance of the rights concerned. The scheme as laid down provided for these reports to be considered by the Economic and Social Council (ECOSOC), which was then itself to follow a complex procedure involving consultations and reporting to other organs.[5]

It is therefore clear that the Economic and Social Council is ostensibly the keystone in the system of implementation of this Covenant. This is really no surprise, given that the object is the implementation of economic and social rights. Nevertheless, two comments must be made. The principle that the organ responsible for supervision should be independent, which is respected in the other Covenant, was jettisoned here, since ECOSOC consists of representatives of governments and not individuals acting in a personal capacity. The other point is that the tasks conferred on ECOSOC by the Covenant are very extensive, and the amount of paperwork involved in obtaining, receiving and analysing reports from more than 100 governments, consulting the Commission on Human Rights and appropriate Specialised Agencies, making and transmitting general recommendations to governments and obtaining their comments, and finally reporting on all this to the General Assembly, would be formidable. In view of the length and complexity of the agenda of ECOSOC, and the difficulty which the Council experiences in coping with its numerous other tasks, it must be doubtful whether, as a practical matter, it was the most appropriate choice to serve as the organ of im-plementation of the Covenant.

How its supervisory functions were to be reconciled with its other work was a question which ECOSOC considered as soon as the Covenant came into force in 1976. The solution adopted was to establish a Sessional Working Group to assist it in its new task. At the same time it established a programme for the periodic reports, requiring their presentation in biennial stages. The Sessional Working Group, which was formally set up in 1978, consisted of fifteen members of the Council who were also representatives of States parties to the Covenant, and from 1979 to 1986 met annually for three weeks during the first regular session of ECOSOC. It was not a success. Not only were the sessions too short for it to give proper consideration to the reports which States submitted, but the composition of the group meant that much of the time available was wasted in wrangling over the scope of its supervisory role. Here, as so often, the root of the problem was that while many governments wished to see an effective system of supervision, a minority, including the Soviet Union and East Europeans, did not. With some members determined to prevent any questioning of parties' performance of their obligations, and a bitter controversy over the role of the Specialised Agencies, the Working Group's reports were merely a description of its activity, without conclusions or recommend-ations.[6]

In 1985 ECOSOC, recognising the inadequacy of the Working Group procedure, decided to make a fresh start. To assist it in supervising the Covenant it set up a new committee, consisting of eighteen experts elected in their personal capacities and on the basis of equitable geographical distribution. The new body, which is known as the United Nations Committee on Economic, Social and Cultural Rights, held its first session in March 1987.[7] As a result of this development the system of supervision is now very different from what a reading of the Covenant would suggest and the arrangements set out in Articles 16–22, aptly described by one commentator as envisaging 'a rather constipated form of paper warfare',[8] have been replaced by a far more effective system.

The Committee on Economic, Social and Cultural Rights has the task of supervising the reporting procedure provided for in the Covenant, which means that in this respect its functions are like those performed by the Human Rights Committee, the Committee on the Elimination of Racial Discrimination and the other treaty bodies. It normally holds one or two sessions annually, each of three weeks, which enables it to consider about ten reports. States are expected to submit their initial report within two years of becoming a party to the Covenant and thereafter to provide a report every five years. As there are now more than 130 parties to the Covenant,[9] it is clear that the Committee requires more time to do its supervisory work adequately, although, as with the other treaty bodies, the fact that many States fail to submit reports, or produce them late, relieves the pressure.

To assist governments in preparing their reports the Committee has adopted the consolidated guidelines prepared by the chairpersons of the treaty bodies and, following the standard practice, invites the government concerned to send a representative to answer questions when its report is being reviewed. However, since 1993 the Committee has also allowed NGOs to make oral presentations at the beginning of each session. This gives them an opportunity to comment on the reports which the Committee is about the consider and is a valuable innovation. For, as we saw in Chapter 2, ensuring that those responsible for supervising a treaty have independent sources of information is essential if a reporting procedure is to be effective.

Another point made earlier was that a treaty body should be able to evaluate States' reports, pointing out strengths and weaknesses and making recommendations to the government concerned. In its early years the Committee was unable to do this owing to internal disagreement, but now follows the practice of the Human Rights Committee and adopts Concluding Observations on each report.[10] To encourage co-operation, the Committee has recently adopted the practice of considering the situation in States which have failed to produce a report.[11] Moreover, as a way of reinforcing the system of periodic reports and enabling it to respond to particular problems, the Committee regularly invites governments to provide it with supplementary information and to engage in dialogue on the issue. In 1994, for example, following the expression of concern by the Committee on the issue of housing rights and forced evictions in Panama, the Dominican Republic and the Philippines, it received information from the States concerned and discussed this question with their representatives.[12]

Like other treaty bodies, the Committee on Economic, Social and Cultural Rights not only responds to the reports it receives from States, but also makes General Comments, addressed to all parties to the Covenant, in which it elucidates their obligations. Its first such comment, in 1989, contains an excellent review of the aims of the reporting system and its third, in the following year, clarifies the nature of States' obligation under Article 2(1) of the Covenant to 'take steps' to realize the rights it contains. General Comment No. 2, also in 1990, examined another basic issue, namely the role of the Committee in advising ECOSOC on how best to promote co-operation with other UN bodies in accordance with Article 22 of the Covenant, while General Comment No. 4 in 1991, the first to deal with substantive matters, reviews the right to adequate housing, which forms part of Article 11(1).[13]

In addition to the activities just described, the Committee has undertaken a number of initiatives related to its monitoring of the Covenant. One day in each session is normally reserved for a general discussion of a specific issue in which NGOs and Specialised Agencies can participate. In 1994, for example, the Committee discussed the role of social security measures with particular reference to the transition to a market economy and human rights education. The Committee also seeks to co-ordinate its work with other UN agencies. Thus in 1993 it was addressed by the special rapporteur on the issue of impunity of the Sub-Commission on Prevention of Discrimination and Protection of Minorities and in the following year by a representative of the World Health Organisation (WHO), who spoke about human rights in relation to HIV/AIDS. And the Committee itself prepared a submission for the World Summit for Social Development in 1995.[14]

At present, as we have seen, the Committee can only supervise the Covenant through the reporting procedure as there is no provision for individual communications. For some time, however, the Committee has been examining the possibility of providing for such communications in an optional protocol and was given encouragement to continue this work at the 1993 World Conference on Human Rights.[15] Setting up an arrangement for individual communications in respect of economic, social and cultural rights will not be entirely straightforward, and the Committee has already indicated that if such a protocol can be devised, only a few States are likely to accept it. Such a development would, nevertheless, significantly strengthen the Covenant's system of control and so, as a way of improving the protection of economic, social and cultural rights, should be welcomed.

## II. Economic and social rights: the ILO

The International Labour Organisation (ILO) was established by the Treaty of Versailles in 1919. Its constitution, which forms Part XIII of the Treaty, does not refer to human rights as such, but confers important functions on the Organisation in the field of what we now call economic and social rights. So, for example, such matters as the regulation of the hours of work, the prevention of unemployment, the provision of adequate wages, social security, equal pay for equal work, and freedom of association all come within its scope.[16]

The Declaration of Philadelphia of 1944, which was incorporated in the Constitution of the ILO two years later, made more specific references to freedom of expression and association and continued: 'All human beings, irrespective of race, creed or sex, have the right to pursue both their material well-being and their spiritual development in conditions of freedom and dignity, of economic security and equal opportunity.' Here then we have a direct link with the conception of human rights as generally understood today.

In discharging the functions for which it was established, the ILO has been a pioneer in the international protection of economic and social rights and has an impressive record of achievement in this field. As with other international organisations, there are two principal aspects of this work: standard setting and measures of implementation or international control. Although the two aspects are intimately and necessarily linked, it is convenient, at least initially, to consider them separately.

As regards standard setting, the ILO employs two principal methods: the conclusion of international conventions and the adoption of recommendations. The conventions, of course, are binding only on the States which ratify them, but under Article 19 of the ILO Constitution the member States are required to submit conventions to the competent authority (normally the legislature) with a view to their ratification within twelve or eighteen months. This provision is designed to avoid the situation which so often occurs elsewhere, when a text is approved in an international organisation but no action is taken at the national level. Recommendations of the ILO, on the other hand, do not create legal obligations for States. Their purpose is rather to set standards which are intended to provide guidance for governments in their national legislation or administrative practice.

Since its creation more than seventy years ago the ILO has adopted more that 170 international conventions, which constitutes an unparalleled body of 'international legislation', with more than 5,500 ratifications. The number of recommendations addressed to governments is even larger than the number of conventions. It is clearly impossible to list all the ILO conventions here, but the following may be noted as among the most important from the point of view of human rights: the Convention on Freedom of Association and Protection of the Right to Organise (1948), the Convention on the Right to Organise and Collective Bargaining (1949), the Equal Remuneration Convention (1951), the Abolition of Forced Labour Convention (1957), the Discrimination (Employment and Occupation) Convention of 1958 and the Employment Policy Convention of 1964. Subsequent instruments of note include: the Workers with Family Responsibilities Convention (1983); the Vocational Rehabilitation and Employment Convention (1983); and, most recently, the Indigenous and Tribal Peoples Convention (1989).[17]

Other matters dealt with in ILO conventions and recommendations are social security, various aspects of the right to work (employment agencies, and vocational training, for example), conditions of work (minimum wages, reduction of hours of work, a weekly rest period, holidays with pay), and the protection of migrants, children and young workers. The rights of women as regards maternity leave, night work and other matters are a subject which has always been treated as important and in recent years has been given particular attention. In 1990, for example, the ILO adopted a protocol to the Night Work (Women) Convention (Revised) of 1948, as well as adopting a new Night Work Convention and Recommendation.

Of special interest from the standpoint of human rights is the system of international control operated by the ILO, for, as we shall see, this is considerably more effective than that provided in the United Nations Covenants.[18]

In the first place, there is the ILO reporting system. This system is not the product of a specific convention, which would naturally apply only to States which had ratified that convention. It is provided for in the ILO Constitution itself, and therefore automatically applies to all members of the Organisation. Under Articles 19 and 22 of the Constitution, member States are required to report to the ILO on the measures they have taken to bring conventions and recommendations to the attention of the competent national authorities with a view to ratification or other suitable action. As regards conventions which they have ratified, States report on their implementation. As regards conventions which they have not ratified, they report on their intentions for giving them effect and any difficulties which impede ratification. About 3,000 reports a year are sent to the ILO in accordance with these provisions, which create a most effective form of supervision.

A particularly important stipulation is that governments must send copies of their reports to national organisations of employers and workers, who thus have the opportunity of commenting on them if they wish. Their observations must then be communicated by the governments to the ILO. It is clear, therefore, that one of the key features of an effective reporting system, the availability of critical information from other responsible sources, which until recently was a weak point in the International Covenant on Economic, Social and Cultural Rights, has always been fully provided for in the procedures of the ILO.

Another important element is the examination of the governments' reports by an independent organ, made up of people who are not government officials. This is secured in the ILO system at two stages. First, there is the Committee of Experts on the Application of Conventions and Recommendations. This consists of twenty members who are appointed, not by governments, but by the Governing Body of the ILO on the recommendation of the Director-General. They are persons who are experts in legal and social matters, such as judges and university professors, whose task is to examine in complete independence and objectivity whether the situation revealed in the national reports and the comments of the professional organisations corresponds in all respects to the obligations which the State concerned has assumed. The Committee of Experts can make 'observations' on any situation which it regards as not in conformity with those obligations and these form part of its annual report to the International Labour Conference. More frequently, the Committee makes 'requests' direct to governments, which permit the latter to explain or rectify certain discrepancies without the matter becoming public. Like the friendly settlement procedure under the European Convention on Human Rights, this discreet means of dealing with problems can be just as effective as more spectacular methods. Several hundred observations and requests are made each year.

The second stage of supervision takes place at the International Labour Conference, which each year appoints a Committee on the Application of Conventions and Recommendations. This body, being a committee of the Conference, has the tripartite structure which is the distinctive feature of the ILO, and so consists of representatives of governments, employers and workers, about two hundred members in all. It examines the reports of the Committee of Experts, particularly the observations about discrepancies between obligations and national practice, and asks the governments concerned for explanations. The presence of representatives of both sides of industry means that the discussions are well informed. They may, and often do, lead to vigorous criticism of governments whose record is defective. In due course the Committee itself reports to the plenary Conference.

This is therefore a system of international control which, with the scrutiny of independent experts and the participation of organisations with separate sources of information, is far more effective than if it were operated exclusively by governments. Research has demonstrated that over one fourteen-year period more than 1,000 improvements in national practice resulted from the use of these procedures, and in the sphere of freedom of association alone there were fifty-five cases in which discrepancies were eliminated.[19]

In addition to these reporting procedures, the ILO Constitution also provides for a complaints procedure, and a 'representations' procedure through which investigations can be initiated.[20] One State may bring a 'complaint' against another if it considers that the latter is not complying with the obligations of a convention by which both are bound. In such a case the Governing Body of the ILO sets up a Commission of Enquiry to hear the evidence. The Commission, which consists of three members, follows a judicial procedure and can hear witnesses or make an on-the-spot investigation. This formal procedure has, however, rarely been used and the cases concerned have generally had political overtones. *Ghana v. Portugal*, for example, in 1961, concerned allegations of forced labour in the Portuguese colonies and *Portugal v. Liberia*, in the same year, raised similar issues. In 1968 complaints were made about freedom of association under the military regime in Greece and in 1974 about working conditions in Chile. More recent cases have involved Poland, the Dominican Republic, the Federal Republic of Germany, Nicaragua and Romania.[21] In each case the Commission of Enquiry established the facts and made various recommendations, which the government concerned has usually accepted.

Under the 'representations' procedure a trade union or an employers' organisation can claim that a convention is not being observed and the matter will be investigated by a special committee appointed by the Governing Body of the ILO. There were few cases of this kind before 1970, but the procedure has been more widely used since. In 1991, for example, represent-ations relating to five countries[22] were considered and so the potential of this method of supervision is beginning to be exploited. It should be noted, however, that, like other ILO procedures, a 'representation' must come from within the Organisation. Unlike the UN treaty procedures, it can therefore not be activated by a private individual.

One of the economic and social rights to which the ILO rightly attaches special importance is freedom of association, because this right is the basis of all trade union activities. Apart from the two Conventions on Freedom of Association (1948) and the Right to Organise and Collective Bargaining (1949), the ILO has set up special procedures to protect freedom of association which apply not only to the parties to those conventions, but, by virtue of the

Constitution, to all members of the Organisation. The procedures in question were established in 1950 and have been formally recognised by the Economic and Social Council of the United Nations.[23]

First, there is the Committee on Freedom of Association, which consists of nine members of the Governing Body, three from each group in the tripartite membership. A complaint may be referred to the Committee either by a government or by one of the professional organisations. Naturally it is the workers' organisations which most frequently start proceedings. The examination of a complaint is normally conducted on the basis of documents alone, but an on-the-spot investigation is sometimes undertaken on the Committee's behalf. Detailed reports containing proposed recommendations to the governments concerned are then submitted to the Governing Body, which almost invariably approves them.

More than 1,600 cases have been handled by this procedure, relating to many aspects of freedom of association, including dissolution of trade unions, the arrest of union leaders, and interference by governments in trade union affairs. An assessment of the results indicates that in a number of cases governments have acted on the Committee's recommendations, though regrettably this is not always so. However, a substantial body of case law has been built up, the principle of accountability is being progressively developed, and other organs of the ILO can now be brought into play when appropriate.

The second organ concerned with freedom of association is the Fact-finding and Conciliation Commission, which consists of independent persons appointed by the Governing Body on the proposal of the Director-General. As its name implies, the Commission has the primary task of establishing the facts concerning a particular situation and attempting to achieve an amicable solution. But it can examine a problem only with the consent of the government concerned. As a result it has dealt with far fewer cases than the Committee on Freedom of Association, although in several cases it did important work, including those involving Japan (1964), Greece (1965), and Chile (1974).[24]

Summarising the position, we can therefore say that in the particular field of economic and social rights the ILO has established a number of different methods, some based on reporting by governments, others on complaints procedures, which taken together constitute a highly developed system of international control over the performance of human rights obligations. This system, impressive and effective though it is, is unfortunately too little known outside a limited group of specialists. It is a pity that more account was not taken of the ILO system when the measures of implementation of the Covenant on Economic, Social and Cultural Rights were worked out. Quite possibly a number of governments were unwilling to see arrangements as effective as the ILO system included in the Covenant precisely because they would have involved a greater measure of international control. The creation of the Committee on Economic, Social and Cultural Rights has, of course, now gone a long way towards rectifying the deficiencies in the arrangements for supervising the Covenant. There could, nevertheless, still be room for ECOSOC, acting in accordance with Article 18 of the Covenant, to profit from the experience of the ILO and so render more effective the protection of the economic and social rights which it enshrines.

### III. Cultural rights: UNESCO

Several of the Specialised Agencies of the United Nations are concerned with the promotion, in a broad sense, of economic and social rights. For example, the Food and Agriculture Organisation (FAO) does important work in helping governments to improve and increase food supplies, so helping to combat under-nourishment and starvation. These activities were carried on long before – and quite independently of – the adoption of the UN Covenants in 1966, but nevertheless are directly relevant to the obligations assumed by States in Article 11 of the Covenant on Economic, Social and Cultural Rights, which recognises the right of everyone to an adequate standard of living, including adequate food, clothing and housing, and the fundamental right of everyone to be free from hunger.

Similarly, the work of the WHO is directly relevant to the right of everyone to the enjoyment of the highest attainable standard of physical and mental health, recognised in Article 12 of the same Covenant. The World Bank is likewise concerned, though less directly, with the right of all peoples freely to pursue their economic development, which is recognised in Article 1, on the right of self-determination. However, the FAO, WHO and the World Bank have not, and almost certainly could not, establish international systems for the protection of these rights, which is the subject matter of this book. It is therefore sufficient for our purpose to note in passing that their work is both relevant to, and designed to promote, the rights we have mentioned, without going into details of their respective programmes. This relevance is already recognised in Article 18 of the Covenant on Economic, Social and Cultural Rights, which, as we have seen, provides that ECOSOC may make arrangements for the Specialised Agencies to report on progress in achieving implementation of those provisions of the Covenant falling within their scope.

Of more immediate interest is the work of UNESCO in the promotion and protection of cultural rights. Article 1 of the Constitution of UNESCO states that the purpose of the Organisation is:

> to contribute to peace and security by promoting collaboration among the nations through education, science and culture in order to further universal respect for justice, for the rule of law and for the human rights and fundamental freedoms which are affirmed for the peoples of the world, without distinction of race, sex, language or religion, by the Charter of the United Nations.

The promotion of human rights and fundamental freedoms is thus expressly affirmed as one of UNESCO's aims when undertaking activities in the fields of education, science and culture.

As in the case of the FAO and WHO, these activities began long before the General Assembly approved the two Covenants; but the fact that the first Covenant is concerned with economic, social *and cultural* rights plainly demonstrates a field of common interest. Article 13 of this Covenant, it will be recalled, establishes the right of everyone to education, and continues by providing that primary education shall be compulsory and free for all, while secondary education, including technical and vocational training, and higher education shall be made generally accessible, through the progressive introduction of free education. Furthermore, Article 15 concerns the right to take part in cultural life and to enjoy the benefits of scientific progress and its applications. It is therefore evident that UNESCO should be able, in accordance with Article 18 of the Covenant, to make a significant contribution to the work of ECOSOC and the Committee on Economic, Social and Cultural Rights in supervising its implementation.

While the Covenants were still being negotiated, UNESCO produced the Convention against Discrimination in Education, adopted by the General Conference in December 1960.[25] This Convention, which is comparatively short and simple, contains undertakings to eliminate and prevent discrimination in education based on race, colour, sex, language, religion, and other grounds. It provides that primary education shall be free and compulsory and secondary and higher education generally available and accessible. These provisions correspond closely to Article 13 of the Covenant on Economic, Social and Cultural Rights, which already existed in draft form. The Convention itself does not provide for measures of implementation in the generally accepted sense, although there is a provision for information to be communicated to UNESCO in periodic reports and for disputes about its interpretation or application to be referred to the International Court of Justice. To supervise the reporting procedure a special committee to examine the reports of member States, consisting of twelve members, was established in 1965.

Two years after the conclusion of the Convention, a protocol was approved and opened for signature in December 1962. This provides for a Conciliation and Good Offices Commission, to which any State party can refer a dispute if it considers that another State party is not respecting its obligations. The Commission, which consists of eleven members serving in their personal capacity, has the task of ascertaining the facts, offering its good offices, and seeking a friendly settlement of the matter. It may make recommendations, although it has no judicial function. The Commission has been set up, but has not yet been called on to deal with a dispute.

Like the United Nations though on a smaller scale, UNESCO receives numerous complaints about the violation of human rights in the educational and cultural fields. Initially, again like the United Nations, it considered that it had no competence to deal with such communications. However, as UN practice changed, and after the Optional Protocol had been approved by the General Assembly in 1966, UNESCO's policy changed too. In

April 1978, after various preliminary decisions of the Executive Board and consideration of a detailed study by the UNESCO Secretariat, the Executive Board took a decision on the procedures which should be followed in the examination of cases and questions which might be submitted to UNESCO concerning the exercise of human rights within its spheres of competence.[26]

This decision recognised that UNESCO may be called upon to examine two types of communications: those concerning individual and specific cases and those concerning massive, systematic or flagrant violations forming a consistent pattern. The main feature of the new procedure is that communications of both types are referred to the committee which was originally established to consider the reports of States on the implementation of the Convention against Discrimination in Education. The name of this body had been changed in 1971 to 'Committee on Conventions and Recommendations in Education' and its membership increased to fourteen. In 1978 it was given the revised title of 'Committee on Conventions and Recommendations', and as a result of successive enlargements now has thirty members.

The resolution of the Executive Board requires that, provided the author agrees, communications should be transmitted to the government concerned and to the Committee, which will examine them in private sessions, which representatives of the government concerned may attend. The Committee must first decide whether the communication is admissible. Here the usual rules apply: the matter must be within the competence of UNESCO, applicants must indicate whether they have attempted to exhaust domestic remedies, and so on. The task of the Committee is then to try to bring about a friendly solution of the matter. It is required to submit confidential reports on these activities to the Executive Board, which considers them in private session and decides what further action is necessary. But questions of massive, systematic or flagrant violations, which include the consequences of aggression, colonialism, genocide, and apartheid, must be considered by the Executive Board and the General Conference, in public meetings.[27]

Because individual complaints are dealt with confidentially, the value and effectiveness of this aspect of UNESCO's work is not easy to assess. It appears that about thirty-five communications are examined at each session. Some, naturally, are rejected as inadmissible and consideration of others may be deferred. The remainder are examined on the merits, when the Committee may decide to request further information from the author, the relevant government or both, or recommend other action. The Committee may, for example, request the Executive Board to invite the Director-General to address an appeal to the government concerned for clemency or the release of a detained person.

It is clear that as a way of dealing with individual complaints, the procedure just described emphasises informality and conciliation, which may sometimes be more effective than more confrontational methods. Such an assessment would certainly seem to be borne out by the success rate, which according to a recent report is better than fifty per cent.[28] This is all the more remarkable when it is recalled that the basis of the procedure is a progressive interpretation of UNESCO's constitutional responsibilities and not a human rights treaty in the normal sense. As such, the activity of the Committee on Conventions and Recommendations, already a striking example of the relevance of human rights to the work of a Specialised Agency, suggests interesting possibilities for the future.

## IV. Some other proposals: 'new human rights'

In recent years a good deal of thought has been given to the question of extending the scope of human rights beyond those to be found in the Universal Declaration and the two International Covenants. An indication of this tendency has been an emphasis on the role of development, which was mentioned in Chapter 1. The thinking here is that, quite apart from moral considerations, the economic development of the poorer countries of the world is essential to their social well-being and political stability and that without it they are in no position to guarantee the civil, political, economic, social and cultural rights prescribed in the major international texts. As a consequence, the 'right to development' has been asserted as a human right.[29]

In a similar way, the concern felt in many countries and international organisations about the need for the protection of the environment, particularly against the pollution generated by modern industrial societies, has led some to the conclusion that there is a human right to a clean and healthy environment. Others maintain that there is a human right to peace and a human right to share in the 'common heritage of humankind', that is, the natural resources of the deep sea bed and other areas not subject to territorial sovereignty. Indeed, some writers and governments suggest that the so-called 'new human rights', including those just mentioned, constitute the 'third generation of human rights' which should receive international recognition after the two first 'generations' or categories protected by the UN Covenants of 1966.[30]

A distinct but related question, which has been much discussed in the United Nations, is the establishment of a new international economic order. The developing countries constitute seventy per cent of the world's population but possess only thirty per cent of the world's income. With decolonisation, virtually all became members of the United Nations, with a consequent increase in their political influence, especially when they act together. The group of non-aligned developing countries established at Bandung in 1955 with seventy-seven members now comprises well over 100, and constitutes two-thirds of the total membership of the General Assembly. It has been pressing vigorously for concerted new measures to redress the existing inequalities between the richer and poorer nations, and for this purpose adopted as its slogan the concept of a 'new international economic order' (NIEO).

The United Nations has held a series of special sessions largely devoted to these issues and has announced successive 'development decades'. In May 1974 the Sixth Special Session of the General Assembly adopted a Declaration and Programme of Action on the Establishment of a New International Economic Order,[31] which was followed in December that year by the Charter of Economic Rights and Duties of States.[32] Detailed examination of these important texts is not possible here, but in any study of human rights they cannot be ignored. They proclaim twenty principles on which the new economic order should be founded. These include the broadest co-operation of all States in fighting inequality, better prices for raw materials and primary commodities, active assistance to developing countries by the whole international community, free of political conditions, the use of a reformed international monetary system for the better promotion of development, and many others. This ambitious programme has recently been scaled down,[33] but even in its revised form, if carried out, would make an important contribution to the realisation of economic and social rights in the Third World.

Some would go further and claim that the establishment of the new economic order is a precondition of respect for human rights in many countries. But this is very dangerous. It is evident that many economic and social rights, including freedom from hunger, the right to an adequate standard of living and to the enjoyment of physical and mental health, cannot be secured in countries where the majority of the population are living on or below the poverty line. It is also right that the developed countries should be frequently reminded of this. The danger, however, is that this may be used as an excuse for the non-observance of other rights which have little or nothing to do with underdevelopment. Economic circumstances are never a justification for arbitrary arrest, State-sponsored murder, or detention without trial. Without waiting for the achievement of a new international economic order, we can acknowledge that better economic conditions are often essential for the realisation of economic and social rights, yet insist that their absence is no justification for the abuse of civil and political rights.

This brings us back to the so-called 'new rights': the right to development, the right to the environment, the right to share in the common heritage of mankind, the right to peace, and so on. Are these concepts human rights in any meaningful sense of that term? To deal with this question fully would require a review of different theories of human rights, which is beyond the scope of this book. However, thinking about the issue of 'third-generation rights' may be easier if the following factors are borne in mind.

In the first place, the word 'human' in the expression 'human rights' has a specific meaning. It indicates that the rights under consideration are rights pertaining to human beings by virtue of their humanity. As stated in both the UN Covenants, 'these rights derive from the inherent dignity of the human person'. In our view this means that the rights which can properly be called 'human rights' are rights of individual human beings stemming from their nature as human beings, and not rights of groups, associations, or other collectivities. This is borne out by the wording repeatedly used in the Universal Declaration and in the Covenant on Civil and Political Rights, 'Everyone has the right ...'; while the Covenant on Economic, Social and Cultural Rights repeatedly stipulates that 'the States Parties ... recognise the right of everyone to' the different rights protected. It is quite clear from this language that what the Universal Declaration and the Covenants are concerned with are the rights of individual human beings. This being so, is it accurate to designate as 'human rights' so-called rights which pertain not to individuals but to groups or collectivities? To avoid misunderstanding, the point being made here is not that collective rights are a contradiction in terms, or are incapable of existing. Such a view would plainly be untenable. The Covenants themselves recognise one collective right, namely the right of self-determination, in Article 1 and, as we saw in Chapter 7, the African Charter sets out a number of others in the form of 'peoples' rights'. Collective rights therefore undoubtedly exist and, although not free from conceptual problems,[34] can certainly be added to in the future. The question, then, is not about the possibility of collective rights, but about whether they should be regarded as human rights. There is, of course, room for more than one view as to what is appropriate here. Our suggestion, however, is that language and thinking will be clearer if we use the expression 'human rights' to designate individual rights and 'collective rights' to designate the rights of groups and collectivities.

The second consideration relates to the use of the word 'rights' in the expression 'new human rights'. Economic development, the protection of the environment, the common heritage of mankind and peace: are these concepts 'rights' in any meaningful sense? They can, and should, be objectives of social policy. They may be items in a political programme; however, they cannot yet be said to be legally enforceable claims. Most people no doubt prefer peace. But if one's country is at war, it is certain that there is no legally enforceable 'right to peace'. Naturally it would be possible to define 'rights' in such a way as to include all desirable objectives of social policy, and in that event the 'new human rights' would become 'rights' by virtue of the definition. But this would be to distort the ordinary meaning given to the term 'human rights' and, more seriously, would run together goals which enlightened humanity ought to pursue with claims which are already protected by international law. The trouble arises, then, because advocates of 'new human rights' tend to confuse objectives of social policy with rights in the lawyers' sense. If one wishes to see some objective achieved – a clean and healthy environment, for example – it is tempting to say that this is a right to which we are all entitled. But it is not a good idea to take wishes for reality.

The last point to be borne in mind is that there is a crucial distinction between legal rights and moral rights. We may consider that we have a moral right to something – consideration from others, perhaps – when we have no legal right to it at all; everyone will be able to think of other examples. If advocates of the 'new human rights' assert that we have a moral right to peace, to the environment, and so on, then many will be inclined to agree. But there is all the difference in the world between these and other moral rights, on the one hand, and, on the other, rights, whether civil and political or economic and social, which have been incorporated in international treaties. While it is true that moral ideas provide both an incentive to create new law and a yardstick for its interpretation, only when the process of law making has taken place can any 'new human right' move from the realm of aspiration.[35]

## Notes

1 See *International Human Rights Reports*, I(1), 1994, p. 240. The words quoted are from para. 5 of Part I.

2 For the text of the Covenant see I. Brownlie, *Basic Documents on Human Rights*, third edition, Oxford, 1992, p. 114, and P. R. Ghandhi, *International Human Rights Documents*, London, 1995, p. 68. For discussion see M. Craven, *The International Covenant on Economic, Social and Cultural Rights*, Oxford, 1995.

3 See Articles 6, 7, 9, 11, 12, 13 and 15.

4 See Article 8.

5 For discussion of these provisions see E. Schwelb, 'Some aspects of the measures of implementation of the Covenant on Economic, Social and Cultural Rights', *Human Rights Law Journal*, I, 1968, p. 363.

6 See P. Alston, 'The Committee on Economic, Social and Cultural Rights', in P. Alston (ed.), *The United Nations and Human Rights. A Critical Appraisal*, Oxford, 1992, pp. 479–81.

7 See P. Alston and B. Simma, 'First session of the U.N. Committee on Economic, Social and Cultural Rights', *American Journal of International Law*, LXXXI,

1987, p. 747. The second session of the Committee is described in volume LXXXII, 1988, p. 603. For excellent accounts of the Committee's subsequent evolution see Alston, 'The Committee on Economic, Social and Cultural Rights', and Craven, *The International Covenant.*

8 See Alston, 'The Committee on Economic, Social and Cultural Rights', p. 475.

9 On 1 January 1995, 131 States were parties to the Covenant.

10 See, for example, the Committee's Concluding Observations of May 1994 on the reports submitted by Uruguay, Romania, Morocco, Iraq and Belgium. Texts in *International Human Rights Reports*, I(3), 1994, pp. 142–54.

11 See, for example, the Committee's Concluding Observations of May 1994 on the state of implementation of the Covenant by Mauritius and The Gambia. Texts *ibid.*, pp. 154 and 158.

12 See *Human Rights Monitor*, XXV/XXVI, 1994, p. 41, and XXVII, 1994, p. 17. In 1995 Panama agreed to receive a fact-finding mission, which reported back to the Committee in the same year.

13 For the texts of General Comments Nos 1–4 see *International Human Rights Reports*, I(1), 1994, p. 1. The latest General Comment is No. 5 of 1994, which deals with persons with disabilities; text *ibid.*, II, 1995, p. 261. As Alston points out, this aspect of the Committee's work is particularly important in view of the very general terms in which the Covenant is drafted. See Alston, 'The Committee on Economic, Social and Cultural Rights', p. 490.

14 See *Human Rights Monitor*, XXIII, 1993, p. 15.

15 See the Vienna Declaration and Programme of Action of 25 June 1993, Part II, para. 75, text in *International Human Rights Reports*, I(1), 1994, p. 240, *Human Rights Monitor*, XXVII, 1994, p. 18, and XXVIII, 1995, p. 17.

16 A great deal has been written about the work of the ILO in protecting the social rights with which it is especially concerned. The following are particularly useful: C. W. Jenks, *Human Rights and International Labour Standards*, London, 1960; *idem*, 'Economic and social change in the law of nations', *Hague Recueil des Cours*, 138, 1973, p. 455; F. Wolf, 'Human rights and the ILO', in T. Meron (ed.), *Human Rights in International Law*, Oxford, 1984, pp. 273–306; and V. A. Leary, 'Lessons from the experience of the International Labour Organisation', in Alston, *The United Nations*, p. 580.

17 The texts of many of these conventions can be found in Brownlie, *Basic Documents*, pp. 243–318, and Ghandhi, *Human Rights Documents*, 1–119.

18 See N. M. Poulantzas, 'International protection of human rights: implementation procedures within the framework of the ILO', *Revue Hellenique de Droit International*, XXV, 1972, p. 110, and F. Wolf, 'ILO experience in the implementation of human rights', *Journal of Law and Economics*, X, 1975, p. 599.

19 See N. Valticos in K. Vasak (ed.), *Les Dimensions Internationales des Droits de l'Homme*, UNESCO, Paris, 1978, p. 457.

20 See L. Swepston, 'Human rights complaint procedures of the ILO', in H. Hannum (ed.), *Guide to International Human Rights Practice*, second edition, Philadelphia, 1992, p. 99.

21 See Leary, 'Lessons', p. 608.

22 Leary, *ibid.* The countries concerned were: Turkey, Argentina, Mauritania, Iraq and Libya.

23 See ECOSOC Resolution 277(X). For discussion of this aspect of the work of the ILO, see K. Yokota, 'International standards of freedom of association for trade union purposes', *Hague Recueil des Cours*, 144, 1975, p. 309.

24 For discussion of these cases and the 1975 case involving Lesotho, see T. M. Franck and H. S. Fairley, 'Procedural due process in human rights: fact-finding by international agencies', *American Journal of International Law*, LXXIV, 1980, pp. 340–4. On the Chile case see also Leary, 'Lessons', pp. 605–6.

25 The text of this treaty can be found in Brownlie, *Basic Documents*, p. 318. By 1 January 1995 eighty-four States had ratified this Convention.

26 Decision of the Executive Board 104 Ex/Decision 3.3 of 28 April 1978. The relevant part of this text is set out in P. Sieghart, *The International Law of Human Rights*, Oxford, 1983, pp. 434–6. See also P. Alston, 'UNESCO's procedure for dealing with human rights violations', *Santa Clara Law Review*, XX, 1980, p. 665.

27 See further S. P. Marks, 'The complaint procedure of the United Nations Educational, Scientific and Cultural Organisation', in Hannum, *Guide*, p. 86, and D. Weissbrodt and R. Farley, 'The UNESCO human rights procedure: an evaluation', *Human Rights Quarterly*, XVI, 1994, p. 391.

28 See Marks, *ibid.*, p. 97, citing a report produced by UNESCO in 1990.

29 In addition to the references in Chapter 1, see R. Y. Rich, 'The right to development as an emerging human right', *Virginia Journal of International Law*, XXIII, 1982–83, p. 287; J. Donnelly, 'In search of the unicorn: the jurisprudence and politics of the right to development', *California Western International Law Journal*, XV, 1985, p. 473; V. P. Nanda, 'Development as an emerging human right under international law', *Denver Journal of International Law and Policy*, XIII, 1985, p. 431; R. J. Vincent, *Human Rights and International Relations*, Cambridge, 1986, Chapter 5; and R. Y. Rich, 'The right to development: a right of peoples?', in J. Crawford (ed.), *The Rights of Peoples*, Oxford, 1988, p. 39.

30 An excellent bibliography on these and other 'new human rights' can be found in the volume edited by Crawford, *The Rights of Peoples*. See also P. Alston, 'A third generation of solidarity rights: progressive development or obfuscation of human rights law?', *Netherlands International Law Review*, XXIX, 1982, p. 307.

31 Resolutions 3201 (S-VI) and 3202 (S-VI). See also Resolution 3362 (S-VII) of the Seventh Special Session.

32 Resolution 3281 (XXIX).

33 See R. L. Barsh, 'A Special Session of the UN General Assembly rethinks the economic rights and duties of states', *American Journal of International Law*, LXXXV, 1991, p. 192.

34 For an account of these problems, see Crawford, *The Rights of Peoples*, *passim*.

35 For an excellent discussion of the practical issues raised by the question of the new human rights, see P. Alston, 'Conjuring up new human rights: a proposal for quality control', *American Journal of International Law*, LXXXV, 1991, p. 192.

# CHAPTER 9

# *Humanitarian law*

## I. The legal foundations

The origins of humanitarian law[1] were outlined in Chapter 1, where we noted various developments during the nineteenth century relating to the first matters of concern to the Red Cross: the condition of the sick and wounded in the field, the condition of the sick and wounded and shipwrecked at sea, and the care and exchange of prisoners of war. These early measures culminated in the international recognition given to the Red Cross in 1919 by Article 25 of the Covenant of the League of Nations. During the decade which followed various steps were taken to establish a constitutional structure for the Red Cross. The League of Red Cross Societies was founded in 1919 as the 'parent body' of the various national societies. And not long afterwards the eighteenth international conference of the Red Cross, meeting at The Hague in 1928, approved statutes which established the following structure: the International Committee of the Red Cross (ICRC) in Geneva, the League of Red Cross Societies, originally in Paris, but transferred to Geneva during the Second World War, and the national societies themselves. The last took the title of the Red Crescent in Moslem countries, and the Red Lion in Iran.[2]

A further strand in the development of humanitarian law concerns the rules which regulate the weapons which may be used in warfare. At the Hague Peace Conference in 1899, a declaration concerning asphyxiating gases was adopted which contained an undertaking not to use projectiles for the diffusion of such substances. The Hague Convention of 1907 went further and contained a general prohibition on the use of poison or poisonous weapons in land warfare. This, however, did not prevent the extensive use of poisonous gases on the western front during the war of 1914–18. Matters were taken a stage further by the Geneva Protocol of 1925, which prohibited the use in war of asphyxiating, poisonous or other gases and also extended the prohibition to the use of bacteriological methods of warfare, prohibitions which were respected during the Second World War.

How far is it possible to employ humanitarian law to limit the use of weapons in a situation which is itself in flat contradiction of the basic concepts of humanity? Or, as Professor Draper once put it, how is an essentially inhumane activity to be conducted, even in part, in a humane manner?[3] The problem which arose earlier this century in relation to poisonous gases and bacteria became much more acute in 1940 with the indiscriminate bombing of cities, and in 1945 with the development of atomic weapons. These developments show how the horizons of humanitarian law have widened during the course of this century. A hundred years ago humanitarian law was concerned with combatants who, through sickness or injury, could no longer take part in the combat. It was extended to prisoners of war, that is, combatants who, on account of their capture, can no longer fight. It is now concerned with whole sectors of the population consisting of persons, including women, children and the aged, who are not and cannot be combatants, but are plainly threatened by the methods of warfare now available.

This leads us to another concern of humanitarian law: the protection of the civilian population. Until recent times a clear distinction could be, and usually was, made between the armed forces and the civilian population, although the latter was often the victim of appalling atrocities, as in the religious wars of the sixteenth and seventeenth centuries. But the distinction was easy to make, even if the proper conclusion was not always drawn. Consequently, in the eighteenth century it was not unknown for civilians to travel without difficulty in countries with which their own State was at war because, being civilians, they were not concerned with the hostilities and their status as non-combatants was respected.

In the twentieth century things have changed for the worse. Quite apart from the question of weapons of mass destruction, the concept of total war involves the fate of the civilian population as never before. This applies with particular force in occupied territories. The taking of hostages, reprisals on the civilian population, the treatment of resistance groups ('patriots' to one side, 'terrorists' to the other), the conscription of labour, and many other problems present themselves. These matters were largely outside the treaty framework of humanitarian law in its early years, but formed the subject of one of the Geneva Conventions in 1949.

The cataclysm of the Second World War led to a fundamental reappraisal of humanitarian law. The War had produced suffering and desolation on a scale never before imagined. It is estimated that the First World War was responsible for 10 million deaths, but the Second for 50 million. This included 26 million combatants and 24 million civilians, of whom 1½ million were civilians killed in air raids.[4] Appalled by this calamity, the League of Red Cross Societies, the International Committee and the national governments agreed to undertake a revision of humanitarian law. The result was the four Geneva Conventions of 1949, which amount to a codification of existing law, plus a marked development in the light of recent history.

The Geneva Conventions of 1949 relate to:

1   the amelioration of the condition of the sick and wounded in the field;
2   the amelioration of the condition of the wounded, sick and shipwrecked members of armed forces at sea;
3   the treatment of prisoners of war;
4   the protection of the civilian population in time of war.

The first three Conventions deal with what might be called the traditional functions of the Red Cross. The fourth was quite new and represents the first attempt to draw up a treaty to deal with the problems mentioned earlier. The question of chemical and bacteriological warfare remained regulated by the Geneva Protocol of 1925.

At the time of writing the Geneva Conventions of 1949 have been ratified by more than 180 States.[5] While it is beyond the scope of this chapter to analyse them in detail, particular topics will be discussed in the following section. The following general points may also be noted. Article 1, common to all four Conventions, provides that the parties 'undertake to respect and to ensure respect for the present Convention in all circumstances'.

Human rights in the world

In other words, the obligation is general and absolute and does not depend upon reciprocal respect for its obligations by the other party or parties to the conflict. Article 1, in addition, requires States to use their best endeavours to secure respect for the Conventions by non-governmental organisations under their control and also, significantly, by other contracting States.

Article 2 of all four Conventions lays down that they shall apply to 'all cases of declared war or of any other armed conflict', so that a legal state of war is no longer essential for the application of humanitarian rules.

Article 7 of the first three Conventions, and Article 8 of the fourth, provide that a beneficiary of their provisions may in no circumstances renounce his or her rights. In other words, the rules established by the humanitarian conventions are rules of *ordre public*. Offenders who violate their provisions incur obligations under international law, although the obligations concerned must be enforced by the national courts to whose jurisdiction the offenders are subject. Should there also be an international organ before which they are responsible? Likewise, should the individual beneficiary have an international remedy if his or her rights are violated? As yet there is no international body to enforce the Conventions and no corresponding remedy for the individual. As we shall see, however, this is a matter on which there have been important recent developments.

## II. The Geneva Protocols

In 1977 two protocols to the Geneva Conventions of 1949 were concluded, representing a significant further step in the development of humanitarian law. To see why they are important a word or two is needed about two problems which have been the subject of a great deal of discussion since 1949: the situation which arises in cases of undeclared war or civil strife, and the problem of the use of weapons of mass destruction.[6]

### 1. *Undeclared war or civil strife*

The typical situation which gave rise to the application of the rules of humanitarian law in the past was a war as generally understood, that is, an international conflict between two or more States. Traditionally this occurred after a declaration of war, although, especially today, international conflicts can and do take place without such a declaration. Even so, there is normally no difficulty in establishing the existence of a conflict of an international character. Article 2 of the Conventions of 1949, as we have seen, makes it clear that they apply to 'all cases of declared war or of any other armed conflict'.

In the twentieth century, however, there has been an increasing number of conflicts of a very different nature. Do the rules of humanitarian law apply when the conflict is national rather than international? How is such a situation to be defined? There are marked differences between a full-scale civil war, such as those in Spain between 1936 and 1939, in the Congo in the early 1960s, in the Yemen in 1965, or in Nigeria in 1968–69, on the one hand, and, on the other, various situations of rebellion or civil strife in which an established government maintains that it is simply suppressing a local insurrection, but other States give support to the insurgents on the ground that they are a national liberation movement. Such situations, moreover, arouse particularly strong feelings and, as the disintegration of Yugoslavia has recently demonstrated, can lead to appalling atrocities. While most soldiers will respect the integrity, and therefore the human rights, of a member of the armed forces of an enemy State, they may feel and behave very differently to one whom they consider a traitor or murderous criminal. Thus, the application of humanitarian law becomes particularly difficult in situations of civil strife, especially when insurgents receive assistance from a sympathetic foreign power, with the result that the conflict is in some respects international, even though the armed forces of two countries are not directly involved.

Article 3 of the four Conventions of 1949 represents the first attempt to deal with this problem. It sets out rules which apply to 'armed conflict not of an international character occurring in the territory of one of the High Contracting Parties'. In such cases 'persons taking no part in the hostilities, including members of armed forces who have laid down their arms and those placed *hors de combat* by sickness, wounds or any other means ... are, in all circumstances, to be treated humanely, without any distinction founded on race, colour, religion or faith, sex, birth or wealth, or any other similar criteria'. Article 3 also prohibits specifically:

(a) Violence to life and person, in particular, murder of all kinds, mutilation, cruel treatment and torture.
(b) Taking of hostages.
(c) Outrages upon personal dignity, in particular, humiliating and degrading treatment.
(d) The passing of sentences and the carrying out of executions without previous judgment pronounced by a regularly constituted court affording all the judicial guarantees which are recognized as indispensable by civilized peoples.

Article 3 marked an important advance in international humanitarian law and has aptly been described as 'an audacious and paradoxical provision which aims at applying international law to a national phenomenon'.[7] Nevertheless, there has been considerable difficulty in ensuring its effective application. This is largely because States are reluctant to admit the existence of 'an armed conflict not of an international character', perhaps through fear of the construction that may be put on such an admission, even though the same article states that 'the application of the preceding provisions shall not affect the legal status of the parties to the conflict'.

An illustration of the problem is provided by the Algerian war, in which France had about 400,000 troops engaged and the insurgent National Liberation Front had a well developed organisation of its own. It was, however only at a late stage in the fighting that the French government admitted that Article 3 was applicable. Indeed, the applicability of Article 3 has been recognised in only a few of the cases of internal conflict which have occurred since 1949. The need for further international action on this subject was therefore plain.

## 2. Weapons of mass destruction

The problem raised by modern methods of mass destruction, whether bombing with conventional weapons, as in the Second World War, or by nuclear devices, is obvious. Whereas humanitarian law as it has developed over the last hundred years has sought to distinguish between combatants and non-combatants, such methods of warfare by their very nature do not, and cannot, make such a distinction.

In 1965 the twentieth Red Cross conference at Vienna attempted to tackle this problem, and adopted its Resolution XXVIII, which contained the following declaration:

> The Conference,
>
> ... solemnly declares that all Governments and other authorities responsible for action in armed conflicts should conform at least to the following principles:
>> that the right of the parties to a conflict to adopt means of injuring the enemy is not unlimited;
>> that it is prohibited to launch attacks against the civilian populations as such;
>> that distinction must be made at all times between persons taking part in the hostilities and members of the civilian population to the effect that the latter be spared as much as possible;
>> that the general principles of the law of war apply to nuclear and similar weapons.

The same matter was discussed, together with other aspects of humanitarian law, by the International Conference on Human Rights at Tehran in 1968. In its Resolution XXIII the Conference noted that the provisions of the Geneva Protocol of 1925 had not been universally accepted or applied and might need revision in the light of modern developments. Then, in the operative part of the Resolution, the Conference requested the UN General Assembly to invite the Secretary-General to study:

(a)  Steps which could be taken to secure the better application of existing humanitarian international conventions and rules in all armed conflicts.

(b)  The need for additional humanitarian international Conventions or for possible revision of existing Conventions to ensure the better protection of civilians, prisoners and combatants in all armed conflicts and the prohibition and limitation of the use of certain methods and means of warfare.

The Conference also requested the Secretary-General, in consultation with the International Committee of the Red Cross, to take steps to bring the subject to the attention of all members of the United Nations.

There was a great deal of discussion of these problems during the next few years, both in the General Assembly[8] and at the twenty-first international conference of the Red Cross at Istanbul in 1969. Resolution XIV of the Istanbul conference related to weapons of mass destruction, and read in part as follows:

> The twenty-first International Conference of the Red Cross, Considering that the first and basic aim of the Red Cross is to protect mankind from the terrible suffering caused by armed conflicts, Taking into account the danger threatening mankind in the form of new techniques of warfare, particularly weapons of mass destruction, ... Requests the United Nations to pursue its efforts in this field, Requests the International Committee of the Red Cross to continue to devote great attention to this question, consistent with its work for the reaffirmation and development of humanitarian law and to take every step it deems possible,
>
> Renews its appeal to the Governments of States which have not yet done so to accede to the 1925 Geneva Protocol and to comply strictly with its provisions,
>
> Urges Governments to conclude as rapidly as possible an agreement banning the production and stock-piling of chemical and bacteriological weapons.

In addition, the conference, in its Resolution XIII, encouraged the ICRC to maintain and develop its co-operation with the United Nations and to pursue its efforts with a view to proposing rules to supplement existing humanitarian law and arranging a diplomatic conference for the purpose.

As a result of these and other developments the Swiss government convened the Diplomatic Conference on the Reaffirmation and Development of International Humanitarian Law Applicable in Armed Conflicts. This held four sessions in Geneva from 1974 to 1977, which were attended by the representatives of more than a hundred governments, and produced two protocols to the Geneva Conventions of 1949. The success of international conferences often depends on proper preparation, and the groundwork for this Conference was laid by two sessions of a Conference of Government Experts in 1971 and 1972. Thus, when the protocols finally emerged, they were the result of seven years' work by some of the world's leading specialists on the subject of humanitarian law.

## 3. *The Protocols of 1977*

The First Protocol relates to the protection of victims of international armed conflicts and was intended to bring the provisions of the 1949 Conventions up to date, especially as regards the use of weapons of mass destruction and the protection of the civilian population. The Second Protocol relates to the protection of victims of non-international armed conflicts and develops the rules in Article 3 of the four Geneva Conventions, which has already been quoted.[9]

Before agreement was reached on the Protocols there was a sharp difference of opinion as to whether humanitarian law can properly equate what is essentially an internal, national conflict with an international conflict. As already noted, since 1945 there has been an increasing number of conflicts which involve national liberation movements but which are not wars in the traditional sense. When discussing these conflicts at the United Nations many developing countries advocated the recognition of what they saw as struggles against colonial and alien domination and racist regimes, in pursuit of the right to self-determination and independence. Moreover, in December 1973, on the eve of the Diplomatic Conference, the General Assembly adopted a resolution in which it declared that such conflicts should be regarded as international armed conflicts in the sense of the Geneva Conventions of 1949 and that the participants in such conflicts should be accorded the same legal status as that granted to participants in international conflicts by the Conventions of 1949. Whether the Protocols should reflect this policy was then the subject of intense debate by the Diplomatic Conference in 1974. There, as in the UN General Assembly, there was a majority in favour, and as a result paragraph 4 of Article 1 of the First Protocol states explicitly that it applies to 'armed conflicts in which peoples are fighting against colonial domination and alien occupation and against racist regimes in the exercise of their right to self-determination...'. The principle is thus expressly recognised in the text, but it raises numerous problems,[10] and may account for the fact that many governments have still to ratify this Protocol.

Other important provisions of the First Protocol are to be found in Part III, section 1 (Articles 35–42), concerning 'Methods and Means of Warfare', and Part IV (Articles 48–79), relating to the civilian population. Both concern the problems raised by modern weapons of mass destruction. Article 35 sets out three basic rules:

1   In any armed conflict, the right of the parties to the conflict to choose methods or means of warfare is not unlimited.
2   It is prohibited to employ weapons, projectiles and material and methods of warfare of a nature to cause superfluous injury or unnecessary suffering.
3   It is prohibited to employ methods or means of warfare which are intended, or may be expected, to cause widespread, long-term and severe damage to the natural environment.[11]

The next article relates to the development of new weapons and provides that in developing or acquiring them contracting parties are under an obligation to determine whether their use would violate the Protocol or any other rule of international law. The remaining articles of this section deal with other rules of general application, including the prohibition of killing, injuring or capturing an adversary by resort to perfidy; the prohibition of the improper use of the emblems of the Red Cross and the United Nations, the prohibition of giving no quarter, and the prohibition of attacking a person *hors de combat*. Section 2 of Part III then sets out a number of rules on combatant and prisoner-of-war status.

Part IV of the First Protocol contains more than thirty articles on the protection of the civilian population during hostilities, which are designed to develop and bring up to date the principles established in the Fourth Convention of 1949. Article 48 sets out the basic rule requiring that the parties to a conflict 'shall at all times distinguish between the civilian population and combatants and between civilian objects and military objectives and accordingly shall direct their operations only against military objectives'. Article 51 takes this further by providing that 'the civilian population as such, as well as individual civilians, shall not be the object of the attack' and by prohibiting indiscriminate attacks, including indiscriminate bombardment of a city, town or village, even if it contains a military objective.

Many other prohibitions are set out in the following articles, including prohibitions of attacks on civilian objects, on historic

monuments and works of art; of the starvation of civilians or
destruction of their food supplies; and of attacks on the natural
environment. Reprisals against the civilian population are also
prohibited. There are separate and detailed provisions (Articles
61–7) about respect for civil defence organisations and services
and about humanitarian relief measures (Articles 68–71). It is
plain that these provisions are based on humane considerations
and, to the extent that they are observed in practice, go far
towards mitigating the effect of hostilities on the non-combatant
population.

The Second Protocol of 1977 relates to the protection of
victims of non-international armed conflicts.[12] It must be
remembered, however, that wars of national liberation and armed
struggle against racist regimes, as already explained, have been
promoted by the First Protocol to the status of international
conflicts. The Second Protocol is therefore concerned with other
forms of internal conflict, that is to say, with civil wars as
generally understood.

The main object of this Protocol is to secure the humane
treatment of those threatened by, but not directly involved in,
such conflicts. This is stated in Article 4, of Part II, which is
devoted to 'Humane Treatment':

1. All persons who do not take a direct part or who have ceased to
take part in hostilities, whether or not their liberty has been
restricted, are entitled to respect for their person, honour and
convictions and religious practices. They shall in all circumstances be
treated humanely, without any adverse distinction. It is prohibited to
order that there shall be no survivors.
2. Without prejudice to the generality of the foregoing, the
following acts against the persons referred to in paragraph 1 are and
shall remain prohibited at any time and in any place whatsoever:
(a)  violence to the life, health and physical or mental well-being of
persons, in particular murder as well as cruel treatment such as
torture, mutilation or any form of corporal punishment;
(b)  collective punishments;
(c)  taking hostages;
(d)  acts of terrorism;
(e)  outrages upon personal dignity, in particular humiliating and
degrading treatment, rape, enforced prostitution and any form
of indecent assault;
(f)  slavery and the slave trade in all their forms;

(g)  pillage;
(h)  threats to commit any of the foregoing acts.

The Second Protocol, with twenty-eight articles, is much shorter than the First Protocol (102 articles). Part III contains five articles on the treatment of the wounded, sick and shipwrecked, which recall the first two Conventions of 1949. Part IV then sets out in Articles 13–18 provisions concerning the protection of the civilian population. These rules are broadly similar to, though less detailed than, the corresponding provisions of the First Protocol. They prohibit attacks on the civilian population, starvation and destruction of food stocks, attacks on historic monuments and works of art, and the displacement of the civilian population, and also contain rules protecting the personnel of relief organisations. The last ten articles are Final Provisions of a technical nature.

The two Protocols of 1977 represent the culmination of many years' work by the representatives of more than a hundred governments. It was especially significant that many States from the Third World, which were not independent when the Conventions of 1949 were drafted, were able to play their part in the development of humanitarian law nearly thirty years later. There is no doubt that the substantive provisions of the Protocols were conceived in a liberal and humanitarian spirit which is to be encouraged. The Protocols, which were opened for signature in June 1977, both came into force in December 1978. Although not yet as widely accepted as the 1949 Conventions, both Protocols now have well over a hundred ratifications.[13]

### III. Human rights and humanitarian law

Having considered the evolution of humanitarian law, this seems a convenient point to raise a general issue which for the human rights lawyer is the heart of the matter: the relationship between human rights and humanitarian law.[14]

M. Jean Pictet has written: 'Humanitarian law comprises two branches: the law of war and the law of human rights.'[15] While recognising the force of this view, the approach we have adopted is quite different. The contention of this book is that humanitarian law is one branch of the law of human rights, and that human rights provide the basis and underlying rationale for humanitarian law.

It is not difficult to see why the opposite view is held. Humanitarian law was conceived before human rights law: the former has developed over more than a hundred years, while the latter has been the concern of international law for only half a century. The United Nations Charter in 1945 contained brief, if numerous, references to human rights and it was only in 1948 that the Universal Declaration was adopted in Paris, just a year before humanitarian law, already highly developed, was codified in the Geneva Conventions of 1949.

When we look at the substance of the two disciplines, however, it is apparent that human rights law is the genus of which humanitarian law is a species. The basic texts relating to human rights, notably the Universal Declaration and the United Nations Covenants, lay down standards of general application to all human beings, by reason of their humanity. Those standards ideally should apply at all times and in all circumstances. Unfortunately, some of them are suspended in time of war, which is in many ways a contradiction of the whole idea of human rights. But even in time of war certain rights must be respected by combatants towards their enemies and, precisely because war is a time when many rights are suspended, it becomes all the more necessary to define and protect those rights which must still be respected. They constitute what might be called 'core human rights', from which no derogation is permitted, even in times of armed conflict.

Thus the major human rights treaties are all based on the principle that some human rights are so fundamental that they must be respected at all times, even in periods of armed conflict. This, of course, is one of the foundations of humanitarian law. But it is not sufficient. The effective protection of the victims of armed conflict requires not only that they should enjoy certain of the basic rights which belong to everyone, but also that they should benefit from certain supplementary rights which are necessary precisely because they are victims of armed conflict, such as medical care, the right of prisoners to correspond with their families, the right of repatriation in certain circumstances, and so on. These are the matters on which the provisions of humanitarian law for the particular situation of armed conflict go beyond the requirements of human rights law. It is evident nevertheless that a number of the rights which humanitarian law seeks to guarantee to the victims of armed conflict are also included in human rights treaties as rights which should be guaranteed to everyone. To see this interaction more clearly, it is worth looking at these non-derogable standards in a little more detail.[16] Which humanitarian rights are secured by the UN Covenant on Civil and Political Rights even in times of war?

The first of the rights from which no derogation may be made is the right to life (Article 6). The text permitting derogations (Article 4) does not indicate that any are permissible in time of war, no doubt on account of the reluctance of the General Assembly to admit that war can ever be lawful, but the phrase 'in time of public emergency which threatens the life of the nation' is clearly wide enough to include a time of war. It should be noted, however, that in order for a derogation to be lawful, the public emergency must be 'officially proclaimed'. This means that in situations of undeclared war or civil strife no derogation is permissible in the absence of an official proclamation of a state of emergency, with the result that in this kind of situation all the rights proclaimed in the Covenant must continue to be respected.

The special protection of the right to life means that even in time of armed conflict acts such as the killing of prisoners and the execution of hostages are unlawful. Article 15 of the European Convention also treats the right to life as sacrosanct, but adds the limitation 'except in respect of deaths resulting from lawful acts of war'. However, acts such as the killing of prisoners and the execution of hostages are never 'lawful acts of war', so the result is the same. Does this article also prohibit the killing of civilians by weapons of mass destruction? It would seem difficult to maintain that it does not.

The second sacrosanct article in the UN Covenant is of supreme importance: 'No one shall be subjected to torture or to cruel, inhuman or degrading treatment or punishment. In particular, no one shall be subjected without his free consent to medical or scientific experimentation' (Article 7). This prohibition of inhuman treatment is far reaching and covers many of the rights protected by humanitarian law. Admittedly, it would be better to have a positive formulation, such as 'all persons shall be treated with humanity and with respect for the inherent dignity of the human person'. Such a positive formulation is to be found in Article 10 of the Covenant, where it relates to 'all persons deprived of their liberty', which would, of course, include prisoners of war. But this is a less effective guarantee, because Article 10 is not one of the articles from which no derogation may be made.

Article 8 is also important in the present context. Its first two paragraphs prohibit slavery and servitude and are not subject to derogation. Unfortunately, paragraph 3, containing the prohibition of forced or compulsory labour, is subject to derogation, with the result that this guarantee does not necessarily apply at a time of public emergency which is officially proclaimed. Nevertheless, the right of derogation is not absolute. Article 4 permits States to take measures derogating from their obligations under the Covenant only 'to the extent strictly required by the exigencies of the situation' and 'provided that such measures are not inconsistent with their other obligations under international law and do not involve discrimination'. Consequently, there are many circumstances in which the prohibition of forced or compulsory labour will still apply, and so it seems fair to regard this also as a humanitarian right which is, as a general rule, protected by Article 8(3).

Four other rights protected by the Covenant are specially protected and not subject to derogation. These are: freedom from imprisonment for debt, prohibition of retrospective criminal law, the right to recognition as a person before the law, and freedom of thought, conscience and religion. However, these are perhaps less relevant to our present investigation of the relationship between humanitarian law and the law of human rights.

Drawing attention to the fact that a number of important humanitarian rights are protected by the UN Covenant, and also of course by the various regional conventions, is not meant in any way to disparage or to undervalue the humanitarian conventions. Our object is simply to show that the two disciplines share a number of areas of common concern and that although humanitarian law was developed earlier, human rights law already covers some of the same ground and is likely to continue to expand. This has consequences we shall consider below.

That there is now a growing measure of convergence between the two subjects has been amply demonstrated at international conferences. One of the more important texts adopted by the 1968 World Conference on Human Rights was its Resolution

XXIII, which carried the title 'Human Rights in Armed Conflict'. This was based on the fundamental precept that 'peace is the underlying condition for the full observance of human rights and war is their negation'. Resolution 2444(XXIII) of the General Assembly, adopted later in the same year, is a resolution 'on respect for human rights in armed conflicts', and the same title was given to the report prepared by the Secretary-General following the adoption of this resolution. There are likewise numerous references to international humanitarian law in the Vienna Declaration and Programme of Action of the 1993 World Conference.[17] Even more significant is the fact that at its special sessions on former Yugoslavia in 1992 and on Rwanda in 1994 the Commission on Human Rights treated issues of human rights and humanitarian law together and gave its special rapporteurs mandates covering both. It is therefore clear that humanitarian law is now increasingly recognised as the particular branch of human rights law applicable in times of armed conflict.

What is the practical effect of this convergence and inter-penetration of the two disciplines? The Covenant on Civil and Political Rights, as we have seen, provides a new legal basis for the protection of several humanitarian rights. Moreover, it has a number of other important consequences. The widespread ratification of the Covenant means that over a hundred States are now under an obligation to report to the United Nations on the measures they have adopted to give effect to the rights which the Covenant guarantees. As noted earlier, in accordance with Article 40 the procedure involves examination by the Human Rights Committee of the reports of governments, comments on each report by the Committee and, under Article 45, an annual report by the Human Rights Committee to the General Assembly, via ECOSOC, on the work it has accomplished. This therefore establishes a modest system of international supervision as regards certain humanitarian rights.

Another consequence is that if the States concerned have accepted the optional procedure for inter-State complaints under Article 41 of the Covenant, other States may bring a violation before the UN Committee. Moreover, it will be recalled that if they are parties to the Optional Protocol to the Covenant, they accept that the Human Rights Committee can 'receive and consider communications from individuals subject to its jurisdiction who claim to be victims of a violation of any of the rights set forth in the Covenant'. This clearly amounts to a further step in the direction of international supervision.

A final consequence is that acceptance of the Covenant, with or without the optional arrangements, involves accepting that respect for its provisions is a matter of concern to international law and the international community. It follows that a party to the Covenant cannot properly object that the question of respect for the rights protected is a matter 'essentially within the domestic jurisdiction of the State' within the meaning of Article 2(7) of the Charter. It can therefore be seen that the inclusion of certain humanitarian rights in the UN Covenant is extremely significant because as part of the Covenant they are subject to a greater measure of international control than under the specific humanitarian conventions.

## IV. Recent developments

### 1. *Means and methods of warfare*

Humanitarian restrictions upon the means and methods of warfare were, as we have seen, addressed at the Hague Peace Conferences in 1899 and 1907 and subsequently developed, first in the 1925 Geneva Protocol, and then in the First Geneva Protocol of 1977. These measures alone would justify the conclusion that such restrictions occupy a significant place in international humanitarian law, but are by no means the end of story. To bring our treatment of this topic up to date three further conventions must now be mentioned, dealing with matters inadequately covered in earlier instruments.

The first convention is the 1977 UN Convention on the Prohibition of Military or Any Other Hostile Use of Environmental Modification Techniques.[18] As the title indicates, this convention is concerned with environmental modification as a method of warfare, an issue which aroused particular concern in the early 1970s, following the extensive use of defoliant agents by the United States in Vietnam. Although attacks upon the environment are partly covered by the First Geneva Protocol of 1977, the new convention is more comprehensive, providing as it does both a wide-ranging definition of 'environmental modification techniques', and a prohibition on the military or hostile use of such techniques 'having widespread, long lasting or severe effects' on another party (Article 1). This convention, which is the first to be exclusively concerned with environmental modification, has been widely accepted, and both the United States and Russia are parties to it.

The second convention is the 1981 UN Convention on Prohibitions or Restrictions on the Use of Certain Conventional Weapons which may be deemed to be Excessively Injurious or to have Indiscriminate Effects.[19] This was originally intended to form part of the 1977 Geneva Protocols, but when inclusion proved impossible owing to lack of time, it emerged as a separate convention. The 1981 Weapons Convention is essentially an application of the principle that the right to choose means and methods of warfare is not unlimited, and the principle that weapons which cause superfluous injury or unnecessary suffering are prohibited. As already noted, these principles of customary law are set out in Article 35 of the 1977 First Protocol. The 1981 Convention in its three substantive protocols shows their effect in three contexts.

Protocol I, which is mainly directed at plastic land mines, prohibits the use of any weapon 'the primary effect of which is to injure by fragments which in the human body escape detection by x-rays'. Protocol II contains an elaborate series of prohibitions or restrictions on the use of mines, booby traps and certain other devices; and Protocol III is concerned with incendiary weapons. It should be noted that while Protocol I contains a complete prohibition, Protocols II and III are concerned with the protection of civilians rather than combatants, attempts to negotiate a ban on the use of specific weapons in combat having been unsuccessful. As an extension of the 1977 Geneva Protocols, the 1981 Convention is, however, a useful step forward.

The third, and most recent, convention is the 1993 Chemical Weapons Convention.[20] The problem of chemical weapons was under discussion for a long time, but it was only with the collapse of the Warsaw Pact and the end of Soviet hegemony in Eastern Europe that the political obstacles to agreement were removed. The new convention is a complex document which cannot be examined in detail here. Its main features are that it contains a comprehensive prohibition on the production, development, transfer or use of chemical weapons, accompanied by an obligation to destroy any weapons the parties already possess and the facilities for their production. The use of riot control agents is permitted, though not in warfare, and there is an extremely comprehensive system of verification and control to monitor compliance.

To be fully effective the 1993 Convention must be supported not only by the industrialised countries of the northern hemisphere, but also by every State with the capacity to make chemical weapons. Although the new convention is a relatively recent instrument, a large number of States have already signed it. If the momentum can be maintained and general ratification achieved, an issue which humanitarian law has had on its agenda for most of the twentieth century will at last have been resolved.

### 2. *Security Council initiatives*

The United Nations Charter lays down that the Security Council has primary responsibility for the maintenance of international peace and security (Article 24) and to that end invests the Council with certain powers with regard to both the pacific settlement of disputes (Chapter VI) and action with respect to threats to the peace, breaches of the peace and acts of aggression (Chapter VII). As is well known, for the first forty years of the UN's existence the exercise of these powers was always inhibited, and often actually prevented, by the Soviet–American rivalry which was the defining feature of the Cold War. With the collapse of communism, however, the situation changed and in the new and more constructive atmosphere which has ensued, a reinvigorated Security Council has been able to adopt measures which would have been unthinkable only a few years ago.

Most of the Security Council's recent activity is, of course, concerned with issues of peace and security rather than with human rights and therefore outside the scope of this book. On some occasions, however, the Council has found itself dealing with humanitarian issues as part of its wider functions. An illustration, which will be examined in the next section, is its creation of special tribunals in order that those who offend against humanitarian law can be prosecuted. Other examples are discussed below. As many of the conflicts in which the Security Council is called upon to act, including civil conflicts, have a humanitarian dimension, this kind of involvement is likely to continue.[21]

What activities of this type have been undertaken? In 1991, following Iraq's ejection from Kuwait, there were rebellions in Iraq by the Kurds in the north and the Shias in the south, which the government sought to suppress. In Resolution 688 the Security Council characterised Iraq's measures as a threat to international peace and security and this resolution was relied on by Western States to justify the despatch of a large military force to northern Iraq to prevent further repression and ensure the distribution of humanitarian aid.[22] At about the same time Iraq agreed to a permanent cease-fire, in Resolution 687, and as a consequence became subject to elaborate UN fact-finding missions intended *inter alia* to monitor the destruction of its chemical weapons capability.[23]

In 1992 the Security Council became involved in humanitarian activities in Somalia. In Resolution 751 it established the UN Operation in Somalia (UNOSOM), which was later expanded and had as one of its main tasks the provision of humanitarian assistance to the starving population.[24] This also became one of the major functions performed by the UN Protection Force (UNPROFOR) in Bosnia, created by Security Council Resolution 743 in February 1992 and subsequently expanded. A further task assigned to UNPROFOR was the supervision of the 'safe areas' in Bosnia, which were created by Resolutions 819, 824, 836 and 844 between April and June 1993.[25] These resolutions, unlike Resolutions 743 and 751, were all adopted under Chapter VII of the Charter.

No doubt there is an element of artificiality in discussing resolutions in which the Security Council addressed humanitarian issues in isolation from the numerous resolutions which were passed dealing with other aspects of these situations. Likewise, it would be wholly wrong to mention these humanitarian resolutions without at the same time referring to the wider political context and pointing out that, of the various resolutions cited, only Resolution 687 can be said to have fully achieved its objective. Since Security Council action was never directed to the overthrow of Sadam Hussein, attempts to deal with repression in Iraq could be no more than a palliative, while the UN's inability to control events in Somalia and Bosnia meant that here too

Security Council resolutions promised more than they ultimately achieved. But if the measures in question were limited in their effects, all represented attempts to use the new situation in the Security Council for humanitarian ends. As such they hold many lessons for the future and consequently deserve attention in a review of recent developments.

### 3. *International prosecution of offenders*

In May 1993 the Security Council created an international tribunal to prosecute persons responsible for violations of international humanitarian law in former Yugoslavia. This is the first time since the Nuremberg and Tokyo tribunals that an international tribunal has been established to enforce international humanitarian law and its creation reflected mounting alarm in both the Security Council and the United Nations as a whole at reports of mass killings, so-called 'ethnic cleansing' and other outrages in the chaos of Yugoslavia's disintegration. In Resolution 780 (1992) the Council had established a Commission of Experts to investigate such violations[26] and in Resolution 808 (1993) approved in principle the idea of a tribunal to oversee prosecutions. The Secretary-General was asked to report on how this might be established and it was his report, containing a draft statute for the tribunal, which the Council adopted in May 1993 by Resolution 827.[27]

In 1994 the Security Council used a very similar procedure to create an international criminal tribunal for Rwanda. Again the move was prompted by alarming reports of widespread atrocities from, among others, the special rapporteur for Rwanda appointed by the UN Commission on Human Rights, and again the Council by Resolution 935 (1994) had earlier appointed a Commission of Experts on the country. The tribunal for Rwanda was created by Resolution 955 (1994),[28] which not surprisingly is modelled on Resolution 827. Thus, while there are certain differences between the two tribunals which reflect their particular functions, for present purposes they can be discussed together.

The new tribunals are now beginning to function[29] and have already been the subject of detailed analysis. It would not be appropriate to repeat that exercise here, but it is perhaps worth making some general points about their significance.[30] In the first place, it should be noted that in both cases the Security Council was acting under Chapter VII of the Charter, having determined that the situation in the territory concerned constituted a threat to international peace and security and that an international tribunal would contribute to the restoration of peace. These decisions clearly provide a precedent for taking similar action in the future. Secondly, the Statutes of the two tribunals support the view that important components of humanitarian law have become part of custom and as such are binding on all States. Likewise, when the tribunals begin to decide cases their application of the law will have significant weight as precedents, particularly as regards common Article 3 of the Geneva Conventions.[31] Thirdly, and finally, it is worth noting that both Statutes contain due process provisions which follow Article 14 of the Covenant on Civil and Political Rights and are designed to safeguard the rights of the accused. These are a reminder that enforcing the law is not just about securing convictions, but itself requires respect for human rights, if the trial process is to be legitimate.[32]

The creation of tribunals to deal with criminal behaviour in particular places is one way of trying to make humanitarian law effective and is not inappropriate in situations, like those in Rwanda and former Yugoslavia, where widespread atrocities have occurred and there is a general desire to bring the perpetrators to account. However, an alternative and possibly more satisfactory approach would be to set up an international criminal court with general jurisdiction to which such cases could be referred. This would remove the need to set up special tribunals, which may not always be politically feasible, and at the same time would enhance the status of humanitarian law by providing it with a permanent tribunal comparable to the International Court of Justice. There is, of course, no international criminal court at present, but as one has recently been proposed by the International Law Commission (ILC), it is worth considering what the creation of such a tribunal would entail.

In the draft statute which the ILC finalised in 1994[33] it proposed that a court of eighteen judges be created by treaty and that it should have jurisdiction in two subject areas. The first covers crimes under general international law, which are listed as: genocide; aggression; serious violations of the laws and customs applicable in armed conflict; and crimes against humanity. Before there could be a prosecution in relation to aggression, however, the Security Council would first have to determine that an act of aggression had been committed by a State. The second area consists of crimes under treaties. The latter are listed and include, for example, conventions dealing with hijacking and trafficking in drugs, as well as the 1984 UN Convention against Torture, which was outlined in Chapter 3.

The detailed arrangements on the new court's jurisdiction are rather complex and cannot be examined here. It should be noted, however, that proceedings would be initiated through a 'complaint', which could be brought only by States which had accepted the court's jurisdiction, or by the Security Council. Unlike the special tribunals considered earlier, there would thus be no independent power in the prosecutor to initiate proceedings. A particularly difficult problem arises over the surrender of the accused, as it is unlikely that all States will accept the jurisdiction of the court, and many, in any case, have constitutional provisions which prevent the extradition of nationals. The ILC draft deals with this by somewhat technical provisions which require surrender in certain circumstances, unless the accused is already being prosecuted before the national courts. But a State which does not accept the court's jurisdiction would merely be under an obligation to co-operate and consult.

Once it is accepted that humanitarian law should, as a matter of principle, be enforceable in international courts, the choice is effectively between *ad hoc* tribunals, like those created for Yugoslavia and Rwanda, and a court of general jurisdiction, as proposed by the ILC. It is clearly not possible at this early stage to predict which, if either, model will be preferred in the future, but it seems safe to predict that when deciding their reactions to the ILC's proposal, governments will be influenced by the record which the two special tribunals are already beginning to develop. As that record will also be influential if decisions have to be made about the creation of further *ad hoc* tribunals, the experience of the next few years is likely to be crucial for humanitarian law and the prospects of international enforcement.

## Notes

1 Of the many works dealing with humanitarian law and the Red Cross the following merit particular attention: G. I. A. D. Draper, 'The Geneva

Conventions of 1949', *Hague Recueil des Cours*, 114, 1965, p. 63, and *idem*, 'The implementation and enforcement of the Geneva Conventions of 1949 and of the two additional Protocols of 1978', *Hague Recueil des Cours*, 164, 1979, p. 1; H. McCoubrey, *International Humanitarian Law*, Aldershot, 1990; G. Best, *Humanity in Warfare*, London, 1980, and *idem*, *War and Law since 1945*, Oxford, 1994.

2  See S. Rosenne, 'The Red Cross, Red Crescent, Red Lion and Sun and the Red Shield of David', *Israel Yearbook of Human Rights*, V, 1975, p. 9.

3  Draper, 'The Geneva Conventions', p. 66.

4  The figures are from J. S. Pictet, 'Armed conflicts – laws and customs', *ICJ Review*, 1969, p. 30.

5  On 1 January 1995 all four Conventions had been ratified by 185 States. For discussion of the effects of such widespread adherence, see T. Meron 'The Geneva Conventions as customary international law', *American Journal of International Law*, LXXXI, 1987, p. 348.

6  Another issue which was considered in 1977 was the role of the protecting power, addressed in Article 5 of the First Protocol. For discussion of this issue see the third edition of this book at pp. 274–6.

7  J. S. Pictet, 'The twentieth International Conference of the Red Cross', *ICJ Journal*, VII, 1966, p. 15.

8  See particularly Resolution 2444(XXIII) of 1968, reaffirming that it is prohibited to launch attacks against the civilian population as such; the Secretary-General's report on *Respect for Human Rights in Armed Conflict*, UN document A/7720, 1969; Resolution 2597(XXIV) of 1969, requesting the Secretary-General to consult the International Committee of the Red Cross about further action; Resolution 2603(XXIV) of 1969, declaring the use of chemical and bacteriological weapons contrary to international law; and the discussions in the Commission on Human Rights in 1970, document E/CN 4/1039, pp. 24–6.

9  For the text of the two Protocols see A. Roberts and R. Guelff, *Documents on the Laws of War*, second edition, Oxford, 1989, pp. 387 and 447. For discussion in addition to the references in note 1, see G. H. Aldrich, 'New life for the laws of war', *American Journal of International Law*, LXXV, 1981, p. 764, and B. A. Wortley, 'Observations on the revision of the 1949 Geneva "Red Cross" Conventions', *British Year Book of International Law*, LIV, 1983, p. 143.

10  See further W. V. O'Brien, 'The *jus in bello* in revolutionary war and counterinsurgency', *Virginia Journal of International Law*, XVIII, 1977–78, p. 193; D. Schindler, 'The different types of armed conflicts according to the Geneva Conventions and Protocols', *Hague Recueil des Cours*, 163, 1979, p. 117; and G. Abi-Saab, 'Wars of national liberation in the Geneva Conventions and Protocols', *Hague Recueil des Cours*, 165, 1979, p. 353.

11  When signing the Protocols the United Kingdom and the United States declared that they interpreted the First Protocol as not relating to the prohibition or use of nuclear weapons. Their view was (and is) that such questions should be settled at other meetings and not in the framework of humanitarian law. In 1993 the World Health Organisation and the UN General Assembly both asked the International Court of Justice for advisory opinions on the legality of nuclear weapons.

12 For discussion of this Protocol, see D. P. Forsythe, 'Legal management of internal war: the 1977 Protocol on Non-International Armed Conflict', *American Journal of International Law*, LXXII, 1978, p. 272; A. Cassese, 'The status of rebels under the 1977 Geneva Protocol on Non-International Armed Conflicts', *International and Comparative Law Quarterly*, XXX, 1981, p. 416; and D. P. Forsythe, 'Human rights and internal conflicts: trends and recent developments', *California Western Journal of International Law*, XII, 1982, p. 287.

13 On 1 January 1995 the First Protocol had been ratified by 135 States and the Second Protocol by 125 States.

14 On this subject in addition to the references in note 1, see Pictet, 'Conference of the Red Cross', and M. Mushkat, 'The development of international humanitarian law and the law of human rights', *German Yearbook of International Law*, XXI, 1978, p. 150.

15 Pictet, 'Conference of the Red Cross', p. 22.

16 See also on this issue the 1994 decision of the UN Sub-Commission on Prevention of Discrimination and Protection of Minorities to transmit to the Commission on Human Rights a Declaration of International Minimum Standards. See A. Eide, A. Rosas and T. Meron, 'Combating lawlessness in gray zone conflicts through minimum humanitarian standards', *American Journal of International Law*, LXXXIX, 1995, p. 215.

17 For the text of the Declaration see *International Human Rights Reports*, I(1), 1994, p. 240.

18 Text in *International Legal Materials*, XVI, 1977, p. 88, and Roberts and Guelff, *Documents*, p. 379. See also McCoubrey, *International Humanitarian Law*, pp. 162–4.

19 Text in *International Legal Materials*, XIX, 1980, p. 1523, and Roberts and Guelff, *Documents*, p. 473. See also F. Kalshoven, 'Conventional weaponry: the law from St. Petersburg to Lucerne and beyond', in M. A. Meyer (ed.), *Armed Conflict and the New Law*, London, 1989, p. 251.

20 Text in *International Legal Materials*, XXXII, 1993, p. 800. See also T. Taylor, 'The Chemical Weapons Convention and prospects for implementation', *International and Comparative Law Quarterly*, XXXXII, 1993, p. 912.

21 For a good general survey see P. Taylor, 'The role of the United Nations in the provision of humanitarian assistance: new problems and new responses', in J. T. H. Tang (ed.), *Human Rights and International Relations in the Asia Pacific Region*, London, 1995, p. 139, and for more detailed treatment of particular issues, N. S. Rodley (ed.), *To Loose the Bands of Wickedness: International Intervention in Defence of Human Rights*, London, 1992.

22 See L. Freedman and D. Boren, '"Safe havens" for Kurds in post-war Iraq', in Rodley, *To Loose the Bands of Wickedness*, pp. 43–99.

23 See H. McCoubrey and N. D. White, *International Organizations and Civil Wars*, Aldershot, 1995, p. 84.

24 *Ibid.*, pp. 242–5.

25 *Ibid.*, pp. 180–3.

26 See M. C. Bassiouni, 'The United Nations Commission of Experts established pursuant to Security Council resolution 780 (1992)', *American Journal of International Law*, LXXXVIII, 1994, p. 784.

27 Text in *International Legal Materials*, XXXII, 1993, p. 1203. The report of the Secretary-General is *ibid.*, p. 1159. The Statute of the International Tribunal can also be found in *International Human Rights Reports*, II, 1995, p. 510. For general discussion see J. C. O'Brien, 'The International Tribunal for Violations of International Humanitarian Law in the Former Yugoslavia', *American Journal of International Law*, LXXXVII, 1993, p. 639.

28 Text in *International Legal Materials*, XXXIII, 1994, p. 1598, and *International Human Rights Reports*, II, 1995, p. 521.

29 For relevant documentation see *International Legal Materials*, XXXIII, 1994, pp. 484, 1576 and 1590.

30 See further O'Brien, 'The International Tribunal', T. Meron, 'War crimes in Yugoslavia and the development of international law', *American Journal of International Law*, LXXXVIII, 1994, p. 78, and *idem.*, 'International criminalization of internal atrocities', *American Journal of International Law*, LXXXIX, 1995, p. 554.

31 See Meron, 'War crimes', pp. 80–3.

32 It is interesting to note that the ILC revised its statute for a proposed international criminal court to provide greater safeguards for the accused, using the statutes of the two special tribunals as a model. See the latest article by J. Crawford, 'The ILC adopts a Statute for an International Criminal Court', *American Journal of International Law*, LXXXIX, 1995, p. 404.

33 See Crawford, *ibid.*, and *idem.*, 'The ILC's draft statute for an international criminal tribunal', *American Journal of International Law*, LXXXVIII, 1994, p. 140.

# CHAPTER 10

# *International human rights law today and tomorrow*

Having reviewed the position in human rights law by examining the various instruments and procedures individually, we are now in a position to stand back a little and consider what this extensive and varied range of material can tell us about the present state of human rights law and the factors which will determine its future.

## I. The growth of human rights law

No one reading the material set out in the preceding chapters can fail to be struck by the dramatic development of this part of international law over the last fifty years. As we have seen, the Universal Declaration of 1948 was the first international text to list human rights as such, although the United Nations Charter, three years earlier, had already indicated that these were likely to be a prominent issue in the post-war world. From such early beginnings developed the elaborate network of treaties which form the basis of the modern law.

Among these treaties it is not difficult to identify some which can be considered as of key significance. Of the regional instruments, pride of place must be granted to the European Convention of 1950, the first, and in terms of effectiveness still the most important, of the regional instruments, and the instrument which, by demonstrating the feasibility and value of regional arrangements, set the pattern for the subsequent American Convention of 1969 and the African Charter of 1981. At the universal level the most significant treaties are, of course, the two United Nations Covenants of 1966. The outcome of a long period of gestation, the Covenant on Civil and Political Rights enables any State which wishes to do so to assume obligations not unlike those of the European Convention, while the Covenant on Economic, Social and Cultural Rights reflects the desire of many members of the United Nations to broaden the human rights agenda to include matters of social and economic policy.

The instruments just mentioned are rightly regarded as landmarks in the evolution of the modern law. However, the contribution of agreements dealing with more specific aspects of human rights should not be forgotten. Although it has not been possible to discuss these in detail, we have tried to show that the general obligations created by the regional Conventions and the Covenants have not only been refined by a more detailed treatment in other treaties, but in many cases have been supplemented by the creation of entirely new obligations and procedures. It will be recalled, for example, that the 1966 Convention on the Elimination of All Forms of Racial Discrimination and the 1979 Convention on the Elimination of All Forms of Discrimination against Women have each made an important contribution to the developing law on discrimination, and in the field of economic and social rights, the treaties and recommendations emanating from the ILO have generated an enormous and effective code of international labour law.

Treaties dealing with individual issues are especially important where their subject matter falls outside the mainstream of human rights law. In this respect the various agreements relating to humanitarian law are particularly noteworthy. While torture and a number of other issues which arise in this field are already covered by other treaties, humanitarian law is a subject which is sufficiently specialised to have acquired its own set of rules and principles. As we saw in the previous chapter, after this need was recognised at the end of the last century, such a system soon began to evolve and, following one major revision in the four Geneva Conventions of 1949, has been further developed in the two Protocols of 1977.

The Protocols and subsequent additions to humanitarian law are a reminder that the treaties which form the basis of the modern law are constantly being modified and added to. New law may take the form of more or less elaborate arrangements to supplement existing conventions, as with the Geneva Protocols and the various protocols to the European Convention, or entirely new agreements, as with the recent UN, European and American Conventions on torture. The form depends largely on the subject matter and is of secondary importance.[1] The vital point is that the number of human rights treaties is not static, but is constantly being increased.

The conclusion of a treaty is usually a sign of progress, but, to create new obligations, the products of so much diplomatic effort must be accepted by States. The real test of legal progress is therefore not the number of new agreements, but the extent to which human rights treaties are being ratified. To put the point in a slightly different way, even if no new human rights treaties were to be concluded, we could still speak of human rights law developing if those already agreed were being more widely accepted.

Applying the test of ratification, we find that the present position gives considerable cause for satisfaction. There is, naturally, often an interval of several years between the conclusion of a treaty and its entry into force, but some recent conventions have been ratified very quickly – the European Convention on Torture, for example – and others have come into force sooner than expected – the African Charter, for example – while agreements such as the UN Covenants, which have been in force for some time, continue to attract a steady stream of adherents. This is encouraging because it shows that the network of obligations is continuing to develop. It is worth remembering, however, that a great many members of the United Nations have yet to accept either of the Covenants.

As these and other conventions receive progressively wider adherence, the absence of this or that State will become less important since the obligations concerned can become binding on all States by virtue of customary international law. However, this cannot happen in relation to instruments, such as the First Optional Protocol, which deal with important procedural matters, and in any case States are more likely to respect a commitment which has been accepted specifically rather than one which arises by virtue of customary law. The wider ratification of human rights treaties must therefore be regarded as an objective at least as important as the conclusion of new treaties.[2]

If the growing network of treaty obligations is one measure of the growth of human rights law, the development of means of implementation is perhaps even more significant. An international lawyer from the pre-United Nations era would no doubt be surprised at the range of obligations which States have assumed in the field of human rights. However, he would be astounded by the range and number of international bodies which have been given the competence to supervise the performance of those obligations and whose powers of investigation may extend into every corner of domestic jurisdiction. As we have seen, these range from independent bodies such as the Human Rights Committee, to groups of governmental representatives such as the UN Commission; from courts, like the European and Inter-American Courts of Human Rights, to quasi-judicial and non-judicial bodies like the various regional commissions and the two UN bodies; and from bodies with a rather broad remit, like all of those just mentioned, to those with a very specific function, such as the UN Committee on the Elimination of Discrimination against Women and the European Committee for the Prevention of Torture. These are clearly very different kinds of organs. Yet they are all concerned in some sense with the implementation of human rights. As it is now rather unusual for a human rights treaty to be concluded without some form of supervisory machinery, the proliferation of such bodies, and the corresponding recognition that means of implementation are an essential complement to substantive obligations, must be regarded as a second element in the growth of human rights law.

No review of the developments which have taken place in recent years would be complete without reference to a third element which has contributed to the growth of the law and which seems likely to be even more important in the future. We refer to the practice of the bodies which have just been mentioned. Human rights law is more than the substantive and procedural obligations to be found in treaties or general international law; it is the process whereby the procedures are used to interpret and apply the substantive principles, the process, in short, through which law on paper becomes law in action.

It is easy to see that it is at the level of application that human rights law is at present least satisfactory. Although, as we have noted, the creation of means of implementation is in itself highly significant, the deficiencies of many of our current arrangements are all too obvious. The incompleteness which is evident when we study the substantive law is even more apparent when we consider the means of implementation, for where implementation procedures are optional, States often decline to accept them. Encouraging States to accept the competence of the Human Rights Committee, or the optional provisions of the regional conventions, is therefore a primary goal.

Similarly, the machinery itself is often not as good as it might be. In addition to the problems of possible conflicts of jurisdiction, many institutions need more powers than States have so far been prepared to give them, if they are to work effectively. Then there is the crucial issue of enforcement. Even an organ with the jurisdiction and powers to handle cases properly requires some form of institutional support to implement its decisions. However, such support is rarely available. Greece, as we have seen in Chapter 4, was effectively expelled from the Council of Europe for violating its undertakings, but in most situations, even when violations of human rights are gross and persistent, sanctions of this kind are simply not available.

But there is also another side to the picture. Institutions to supervise the application of human rights conventions exist and are used. Individuals are released from detention, claimants are compensated, laws and administrative practices are exposed and changed, all as a result of proceedings before international bodies. Moreover, although the primary purpose of such proceedings is to vindicate the rights of the individual, in many cases the decisions which are handed down also develop the law. Much of the work we have described has had this effect and, as the institutions set up by the various treaties continue their work, this source of law is likely to grow.

How this process occurs is a subject we have discussed elsewhere and which need not be considered here.[3] That it occurs, and sometimes in ways that might not be expected, is sufficiently demonstrated by the work of the European Court of Justice, which has held that fundamental rights and general principles of law analogous to fundamental rights are part of Community law.[4] In reaching this conclusion the Court relied on the European Convention, which, as we have seen, has itself already generated a substantial jurisprudence. Now, it would be wrong to equate the work of the Court of Justice, which is mainly concerned with other matters, with that of the Strasbourg institutions, which are wholly concerned with human rights. It would similarly be wrong to suggest that all bodies concerned with human rights questions have made, or are likely to make, equally important contributions to legal development. Together, however, they make a contribution which is too important to ignore, giving life to each human rights text and materiality to its ideals.

## II. The reality of human rights law

What has been said so far is enough to demonstrate that at the United Nations, through the work of the Specialised Agencies and in the various regional systems, there have come into being a number of schemes of human rights protection, all of which are being both developed and added to. The question which must now be considered is whether, as a result of this activity, it is correct to speak of a developing international law of human rights. We must first consider what this question means. If we are content to regard 'the international law of human rights' as simply the sum total of the various treaties, procedures, principles of customary law and case law, the answer is obviously 'yes'. If, on the other hand, what we mean is whether in the light of current practice the different human rights schemes now exhibit a degree of convergence which makes it inappropriate to think of them as entirely separate phenomena, then our question is more interesting, and the answer more complex.

There is, of course, no doubt that historically the law of human rights grew up in a number of separate compartments. We saw in Chapter 1 that international concern for human rights can be traced to the movement to abolish slavery in the early years of the nineteenth century and the beginnings of the movement to humanise warfare later in the century. Though both sprang from a similar humanitarian impulse, as legal developments they had little in common, and this was also true of the next step, the attempt to provide minorities with protection through the League of Nations. As this was another quite separate issue, it was dealt with through its own treaties and procedures.

The signing of the United Nations Charter brought about a fundamental change. For the first time 'human rights' were referred to in the constitution of an international organisation. It is true that the reference was in general terms, but the very mention was significant because it suggested that here was a concept of universal application. As we have seen, the Universal Declaration in 1948 then sought to define what was meant. The process of defining human rights was carried further by the United Nations Covenants and the various regional and other instruments.

Now, although each new development was influenced by what had gone before, and in turn influenced its successors, this process did not produce a series of identical conventions. As we have noted, the various regional conventions differ to a considerable extent in the ground they cover, and even when they are concerned with the same right – the right to a fair trial, for example – they are frequently couched in different terms. In the same way, although there are important areas of overlap between the various regional conventions and the United Nations Covenants, there are again many important differences between them.

The result is a complex pattern of obligations, so that while it is certainly possible to think in terms of what the Inter-American Court of Human Rights has called 'the common core of basic human rights standards',[5] generalisation is difficult and each right or concept should be considered separately. It is obviously beyond the scope of the present work to undertake this kind of investigation.[6] However, a glance at some of the recent case law of human rights tribunals will perhaps be enough to show how treaty provisions can have a significance beyond their immediate context, and how human rights law is being progressively developed.

Human rights conventions often divide their articles into two parts: first, a statement of the right concerned, then a qualifying provision defining the circumstances under which a derogation, or limitation, of the right is permitted. Probably the best known is the phrase to be found in several articles of the European Convention that any limitations on a right shall be 'prescribed by law' and 'necessary in a democratic society' for the attainment of certain objectives. The meaning of these words has been an issue in a number of cases in the European Court. In the *Malone case*,[7] for example, the Court emphasised that to be 'in accordance with law' an interference must not only have some basis in the domestic law, but the law in question must also be accessible and formulated with sufficient precision to enable citizens to regulate their conduct. This interpretation has also been adopted in other cases.

Other human rights instruments, as one would expect, contain some very similar qualifications. For example, Article 15 of the American Convention provides for the right of peaceful assembly subject only to restrictions which are 'imposed in conforming with the law and necessary in a democratic society'[8] and Article 16 deals with freedom of association in similar terms. Likewise, Article 8 of the African Charter on freedom of conscience and religion and Article 9 on freedom of assembly[9] are in the same vein as Article 4 of the United Nations Covenant on Economic, Social and Cultural Rights, which provides that:

> in the enjoyment of those rights provided by the State in conformity with the present Covenant, the State may subject such rights only to such limitations *as are determined by law only in so far as this may be compatible with the nature of these rights and solely for the purpose of promoting the general welfare in a democratic society.*[10]

In view of this very similar terminology it would seem that we are justified in speaking here of an international law of human rights and in suggesting that the approach which is adopted towards these common provisions in one system is likely to be important generally. If that is correct, then in view of the extensive practice which is now on record under the European Convention and which is clearly influencing the Inter-American Court,[11] we already have a significant jurisprudence in which the scope and meaning of some key concepts in human rights law have been considered.

The point just made about the transferability, so to speak, of interpretations of general concepts applies with equal force to many substantive provisions. Again, the essential requirement is that the right is dealt with in substantially similar terms.

In the provisions concerning a fair trial, for instance, there is an important difference in the treatment of civil rights and obligations, but the reference to a 'criminal charge' is substantially similar in the European Convention, the American

Convention and the International Covenant on Civil and Political Rights.[12] The question of what constitutes a 'criminal charge' has generated almost as much case law for the European Court as the meaning of civil rights and obligations. The Court has had to consider, for instance, how far disciplinary proceedings in prison involve criminal charges,[13] how the article applies to military discipline,[14] and whether it is open to a State to avoid Article 6 by classifying road traffic offences as 'administrative offences'.[15] The reasoning of the European Court in these cases is naturally very helpful as and when similar questions arise in other international bodies. Here, then, because we are dealing with a right couched in broadly similar terms in the various conventions, we can certainly speak of the development of a truly international human rights law.

The meaning of 'criminal charge' is just one example and there are many others. For example, the meaning of 'discrimination' was considered by the European Court in the *Belgian Linguistics case*[16] in a judgement which was referred to by the Inter-American Court in the *Proposed Amendments case*.[17] The meaning of 'forced labour' in Article 4 of the European Convention is another instructive example. When interpreting this term in the *Van der Mussele case*,[18] the Court treated the concept of forced labour as a general one by making use of an ILO Convention on the subject.[19] Likewise, there is the requirement in Article 6 of the European Convention that the tribunal hearing a case be 'independent and impartial' and that its judgement and proceedings shall be public. These requirements have all been subject to extensive interpretation in cases raising issues which are bound to arise in other tribunals. Finally, it is interesting to note that when considering the requirement of publicity for a domestic court's judgement, the European Court referred to the corresponding provision of the International Covenant on Civil and Political Rights.[20] Although the Covenant uses slightly different terms, the Court's decision in this case had the effect of assimilating the two provisions.

Before leaving this topic there is one important qualification which should be made. This relates to the way in which human rights law is applied in various systems. There is, as we have seen, already a good deal of overlap among the various human rights instruments as regards both general concepts and the rights which are to be protected. As a consequence, even if there is no further harmonisation, it seems reasonable to speak here of 'international human rights law' and to expect that where a particular right is common to, say, the European Convention and the American Convention, the interpretation and application of a provision by the European institutions will influence the decisions of the American institutions and vice versa. This influence is, however, something which will vary a good deal from case to case, not just because there is no formal obligation to follow the rulings under another Convention, but also because, as we pointed out when discussing the merits of regionalism, in some situations it would be unreasonable to do so.

An example which springs to mind is the right to a hearing 'within a reasonable time'. This is common to all three regional Conventions. However, it is very unlikely that this requirement will be applied in exactly the same way in Europe, in Latin America, and in Africa, and in view of the very different conditions in which the legal systems function in those regions, such uniformity would hardly be appropriate.

Another example might be the prohibition on inhuman or degrading treatment or punishment, which is common to all three of the regional Conventions, as well as to the International Covenant on Civil and Political Rights. In a case in 1978, as noted in Chapter 4, the European Court held that this prohibition (which is in Article 3 of the European Convention) was contravened by the birching of a juvenile in the Isle of Man.[21] The decision was somewhat controversial in the European context and, although it has already been influential,[22] would not necessarily always be followed elsewhere. Torture, which is also prohibited by Article 3, is a concept on which there is likely to be a large measure of agreement. Inhuman or degrading treatment or punishment, on the other hand, particularly in the field of penal policy, is a matter on which one can expect to see greater differences of view.

So the qualification is that while interpretation of human rights obligations under one set of institutional arrangements may be significant and influential, it will not always be enough to produce this effect for provisions to be couched in similar terms, because the cultural or other factors which determine the interpretation and application of human rights in one setting may have no relevant counterpart elsewhere.

## III. The politics of human rights

When asked about their attitudes towards human rights, individuals, and for that matter government officials, will normally say that they are in favour. Conversely, it is very difficult to find anyone who will deny that human rights law is a good thing, or that the degree of protection available to those under threat is excessive and ought to be reduced. With so much apparent agreement about the importance of human rights, it is easy to think of this aspect of international law as somehow outside, or even above, politics and to imagine it continuing to develop in a similar apolitical way. This would, however, be a serious mistake. Human rights issues are unavoidably political, and unless this is appreciated, neither the development of the law to date nor the possibilities for growth in the future can be properly understood.

The political aspect of human rights can clearly be seen in the historic formulations of civil and political rights on which so many of the texts we have been considering are based. When Locke wrote his *Second Treatise on Civil Government*, and Rousseau his *Social Contract*, they were well aware that they were not just discussing the moral relationship between ruler and ruled, but dealing with issues of the utmost political importance. In a similar way, when governments subscribe to human rights treaties, they know that they are endorsing a certain set of political values and will be expected to implement them. Ratifying a human rights treaty is therefore more than a moral gesture. It is a recognition of the special status of certain ideals, with the political expectations which that creates.

Since the acceptance of legal obligations in this, as in other fields, changes the contours of the political landscape, it is not surprising that governments approach the negotiation of a human rights treaty with these considerations firmly in mind. When dealing with the background to the various conventions, we have described, at what may have seemed tedious length, some intricate and extended processes of drafting and negotiation. No apology is made for this because understanding that human rights texts do not spring into existence overnight, but are the outcome of political assessment and bargaining, is a major step to appreciating their real significance.

The political importance of the decision to treat a matter as an issue of human rights is something we have encountered throughout this book. The inclusion in the United Nations Covenants of the right to self-determination and the right to dispose of natural wealth and resources was part of the campaign which the developing States had been pursuing on these issues for many years. Likewise, the omission from the Covenant on Civil and Political Rights of any mention of a right to property stemmed from the unwillingness of many of the same States to see this right guaranteed. The European Convention, on the other hand, does protect the right to property in its Protocol No. 1, but contains no guarantees as regards the right to divorce, or the right of access to the civil service. As in the case of the Covenant, these omissions are deliberate.[23]

The political content of human rights is also apparent in the way particular rights are defined. Although the European Convention recognises the right of property, it does so in terms which provide the State with a far greater measure of control than Locke would have thought acceptable. This is because in the 300 years since Locke, ideas about the role of the State and the sanctity of property have changed. This change is reflected in the Convention, which permits States to make compulsory purchase orders, establish programmes of nationalisation, or restrict property rights in other ways, so long as certain safeguards are observed.

So far we have been indicating the political content of the substantive guarantees to be found in human rights treaties. If we turn to another feature of such instruments, their means of implementation, the political aspect of human rights is even more conspicuous. Providing a treaty with means of implementation acknowledges that human rights are a matter on which the State is accountable to an outside body. As such, the decision is one with major political implications, as is apparent in the way governments have often resisted the creation of implementation machinery by invoking the concepts of domestic jurisdiction and national sovereignty.

Assuming means of implementation are acceptable in principle, the next question is the form which they should take. Here the political issue is the extent to which governments are prepared to have their laws and practices subjected to independent scrutiny.

The variety of means of implementation which we have encountered demonstrates the range of attitudes on this question. It is significant, for example, that none of the many human rights treaties sponsored by the United Nations provides for the independent judicial supervision which we find in both the European and American Conventions. To be sure, judicial supervision is not always appropriate, but another feature of United Nations procedures is a marked preference for entrusting supervision to bodies such as the Commission on Human Rights, composed of the representatives of States and consequently lacking independence. This is not an invariable practice of course. The Human Rights Committee, the Committee on the Elimination of Discrimination against Women, and the more recent Committee on Economic, Social and Cultural Rights are, it will be recalled, all independent bodies. We have seen, however, that their powers are severely circumscribed, which confirms States' reluctance to submit themselves to independent scrutiny.

The contrast, it should be emphasised, is not between arrangements for supervision which have been influenced by political considerations and those which have not, for all arrangements for implementing human rights are, like the rights themselves, the reflection of political decisions. Rather, the contrast is between means of implementation which are structured in a way calculated to further the protection of human rights and those which are not. The European Convention, with its optional provisions relating to individual petitions and the jurisdiction of the Court, its filtering of applications by the Commission and its provisions for friendly settlement, points very clearly to the political factors which governments have in mind when devising implementation machinery. Unlike most States, however, the members of the Council of Europe were fully committed to protecting rights and therefore prepared to set up an effective system.

If politics is a prominent consideration when rights are being formulated and procedures for implementation being devised, it might also be expected to be relevant at the level of practice. This is so, and in a wider way than might be anticipated. The influence of politics on the application and interpretation of human rights by organs made up of the representatives of States scarcely needs reiteration. As we saw in Chapter 3, the work of the Commission on Human Rights, whether under the Resolution 1503 procedure or in its other activities, is to a large extent conditioned by political considerations. States with political influence, or with powerful friends, can use this to avoid investigation or, if this has already started, can try to bring it to a halt before anything has been achieved. By the same token States which are politically isolated can be the object of both investigation and political pressure. Although in this second case the effect is to promote human rights, and is therefore to be encouraged, no one would pretend that a forum in which some States are more equal than others is anything other than a political body.

What is perhaps not so obvious is that there is a sense in which organs like the European Court of Human Rights and the Human Rights Committee, though independent, also act politically. We do not, of course, mean that the individuals who sit on these bodies normally take instructions from governments, or are influenced in their decisions by the identity of the respondent. Nor do we mean simply that they act politically in the sense that everyone who is part of a legal order can be said to act politically in carrying out his or her official functions. While that is certainly true, there is a more specific sense in which human rights organs act politically, which derives from the functions they are required to perform.

Becoming a party to a treaty like the European Convention is rather like adopting a written constitution with judicial supervision. The effect is to give judges, or their equivalent, the final word on many highly political issues. It is therefore no longer enough for the legislature or executive to believe that a certain measure is desirable or necessary. If the measure can be challenged as an invasion of rights, it is for the judges to rule on whether it is permitted. This, it need hardly be pointed out, is to transfer political power from one set of institutions to another. As such, it invests the courts with a role very different from that which they have under a system of parliamentary sovereignty and, as controversies over appointments to the Supreme Court of the United States regularly remind us, places them very firmly on the political stage.

The relevance of all this to the work of human rights tribunals can readily be demonstrated by considering some of their more controversial cases. Issues such as telephone tapping, the control of immigration, the detention of suspected terrorists, and the regulation of homosexuality pose sensitive and highly controversial questions. In entrusting the final decision on these matters to international bodies, the parties to instruments like the European Convention are relinquishing an important part of their political sovereignty.

Appreciating the political role which bodies such as the European Court of Human Rights are required to play not only helps us to understand why States are often reluctant to entrust international bodies with such powers, but also enables us to see what such bodies are doing in better perspective. One example must suffice. Consider the scope of the margin of appreciation doctrine under the European Convention on Human Rights. Here the issue is often debated in terms of a wider or a narrower interpretation of the individual's rights. Since most commentators are in favour of extending individual rights, decisions are praised or condemned according to whether they grant the respondent a narrow or a broad margin of appreciation. This, however, overlooks what is also at stake in these cases, namely the question of how much power the Strasbourg organs should have vis-à-vis the member States. This is a political issue which must be registered before the margin of appreciation question can be properly evaluated. There is actually no contradiction between believing, on the one hand, that individual rights are important, and, on the other, that national parliaments enjoy a legitimate area of political authority which international institutions should respect. There can, of course, be differences of opinion about what the precise roles of national and international bodies are, but to see this as the question, rather than the scope of individual rights, one first needs to recognise the political significance of the European Court.[24]

A final word about the political dimension of human rights may be useful to avoid misunderstanding. Nothing which has been said here is intended to suggest that the moral dimension of human rights is unimportant. Similarly, we are not suggesting that because human rights have a political aspect, they do not also have a distinct legal aspect. Our point is simply that in studying human rights the legal, the moral, and the political aspects are all important. Like an apprentice steeplejack, we shall not get far if we concentrate on the first and second, and ignore the third dimension.

## IV. The theory of human rights

In our discussion so far we have seen how international action relating to human rights has grown and is continuing to develop, how one result of these processes has been the emergence of something which can truly be described as international human rights law, and how all of this has been shaped by, and at the same time influences, international and domestic politics. The point which must now be considered, and the question with which it is perhaps appropriate to conclude this survey, is the role of theory in relation to this part of international law.

Is theory important? Some will say that it is, because until we have a proper theory there can be no plan and until we have a plan there can be no action, or at least no rational action. On this view a coherent theory is an indispensable prerequisite of measures to protect human rights internationally or, for that matter, at the domestic level. Others, however, will maintain that action comes first and theory later. On this view theory is not important because its function is merely to rationalise what is already happening. Needless to say, those who adopt this approach are not much interested in theory and, viewing the subject as of minor importance, may regard it as wholly academic, or a waste of time.

If it were necessary to choose between these two ways of thinking about theory, or more accurately between a way of thinking about theory and a way of not thinking about it, our choice would be impossible. For though neither is wholly correct, each is making a point about the relation between action and its justification, which is important generally and has a direct bearing on the development and future of the law.

The idea that human rights law should develop in accordance with a theoretical plan, from which presumably it follows that nothing should be done until such a plan has been formulated, in present circumstances is clearly a prescription for total inaction. There are, as we have seen, different ways of thinking about human rights in theoretical terms which reflect different historical traditions, different cultural perspectives, and different political priorities.[25] If it had been necessary to accommodate these differences within a grand theoretical framework as a pre-condition of formulating legal texts, then the instruments described in earlier chapters would never have appeared. In this sense it is true that action can, and does, precede theoretical explanation and that, to a degree, theory stems from practice and not the other way round.

It is, however, one thing to say that theory is shaped by practice and another matter entirely to imagine that practice occurs in a theoretical vacuum. On the contrary, since the actions of governments, committees, commissions and courts are shaped by beliefs, the theories which people hold on human rights have a major effect on the way the law develops. Sometimes this will be obvious as when, for instance, a text emerges from a clash of opposing views. Sometimes, on the other hand, the significance of beliefs will be hidden because they are so widely shared as to be taken for granted. In the second case, however, the beliefs are still important and can usually be exposed with an appropriate strategy. Thus, the theoretical assumptions behind the European Convention on Human Rights stand out sharply when we compare it with an instrument such as the African Charter, which reflects a different theory. The theory behind the European Convention is, of course, that of the Western democratic tradition. In fact, however, all human rights texts reflect theoretical assumptions of some description. Just as individuals who profess themselves uninterested in theory nevertheless have a set of beliefs which influence their behaviour, so human rights texts may not always have as clear and coherent a theoretical base as the European Convention, but could not have been devised without theoretical assumptions of some kind in the minds of the negotiators.

In studying human rights law, then, we are necessarily studying legal theory. While we can describe what has been done without having first developed a comprehensive theoretical framework, we certainly cannot claim to understand it unless we appreciate that at each stage of its development the law of human rights has reflected ideas about what should be done, which rest either explicitly or implicitly on theories about human rights.

Although this book is primarily concerned with the practice of human rights, many theoretical issues have been touched on in the previous pages. Thus, we have considered the relation between civil and political rights on the one hand, and economic, social and cultural rights on the other. At various points we have also discussed the relation between individual rights, which are where the theory of human rights began, and the idea of collective rights, which originated with the concept of self-determination and has now been extended in the African Charter to include a number of other 'peoples' rights'. It will be recalled that the African Charter also introduces the concept of duties, an idea which is, of course, a familiar one in political and moral philosophy, but which had not hitherto been prominent in a human rights text. The questions posed by the concept of duties are a reminder that even in a field where the theoretical ground is well trodden, there can be room for a fresh analysis.

The development of the law poses further theoretical problems. As we have explained, recognising rights of one type may not be compatible with recognising rights of another type. Thus, steps to eliminate discrimination based on sex may transgress religious or cultural precepts, respect for which is also guaranteed. Since it is impossible to ensure both, which is to be preferred? Is the answer here the concept of a hierarchy of human rights,[26] a concept which, besides resolving the conflict between different rights, might also explain why some rights cannot be limited, even in a public emergency, while others can?

Finally, there is the issue touched on in Chapter 8, namely the question of when a matter of international concern can appropriately be treated as an issue of human rights. Rights are a vital concept, but even when supplemented by the concept of duties, are not a suitable vehicle for handling every issue. If we insist on translating all issues into the language of human rights, we not only trivialise this language, but also fail to use the resources of the law to their full potential. While there is therefore no reason to regard the scope of human rights law as fixed for all time in its present configuration, before adding new rights we should be clear about what we are doing because the price of failure to do so – of failure, that is, to think clearly about theoretical issues – is likely to be high. For here, as elsewhere, although the issues are theoretical, they must not be thought of as academic or inconsequential. On the contrary, because ideas about human rights influence the way the law develops,

theoretical assumptions have immediate and practical consequences and are a critical influence on its future.

## V. Conclusion

As we said at the beginning of this book, our aim has been, while
recognising the lamentable state of human rights in many parts of
the world, to show that more and more people are aware of this
situation and are endeavouring to do something about it. The
period over which this new edition was in preparation has
provided ample confirmation of both assertions. Reports
presented to the Commission on Human Rights and the General
Assembly of the United Nations, the investigations of the Inter-
American Commission on Human Rights into the situation in
certain countries of Latin America, evidence produced to the
Conference on Security and Co-operation in Europe about the
treatment of ethnic and national minorities in Eastern Europe and
the reports of Amnesty International all confirm the picture of
systematic and repeated violations in many countries. On the
other hand, the fact that these reports are made and widely
publicised, the debates and discussions which follow their
publication, and the number of people concerned with these
problems in international organisations, national and international parliamentary bodies and non-governmental organisations
demonstrate that people do care about human rights.

The mounting pressure of public opinion in the years to come
will continue to have an effect in persuading or shaming
governments which systematically violate human rights to
improve their behaviour. In this struggle international organisations and international lawyers have a particularly important
role to play, one might say a special responsibility. The Universal
Declaration called on every individual and every organ of society
to 'strive by teaching and education to promote respect for these
rights and freedoms and ... to secure their universal and effective
recognition and observance'. If this book can make a modest
contribution in helping them to do so, by explaining the
international arrangements which exist, the factors which
influence the development of human rights law and the
deficiencies which should be remedied, then it will have achieved
its object.

## Notes

1 However, it is important that as regards both substantive and procedural issues the negotiation of new treaties takes place with sufficient attention to existing arrangements. Since the United Nations is the major source of new human rights instruments, its approach to international law-making is particularly critical. For an incisive appraisal of current practice in this regard, see T. Meron, *Human Rights Law-Making in the United Nations*, Oxford, 1986, and *idem*, 'Reform of lawmaking in the United Nations: the human rights instance', *American Journal of International Law*, LXXIX, 1985, p. 664.

2 For some valuable suggestions on this issue, see D. Weissbrodt, 'A new United Nations mechanism for encouraging the ratification of human rights treaties', *American Journal of International Law*, LXXVI, 1982, p. 418.

3 See J. G. Merrills, *The Development of International Law by the European Court of Human Rights*, second edition, Melland Schill Monographs in International Law, Manchester, 1993.

4 See P. Pescatore, 'The content and significance of fundamental rights in the law of the European Communities', *Human Rights Law Journal*, II, 1981, p. 295; M. Dauses, 'The protection of fundamental rights in the Community legal order', *European Law Review*, X, 1985, p. 398; and N. Foster, 'The European Court of Justice and the European Convention on Human Rights', *Human Rights Law Journal*, VIII, 1987, p. 245.

5 See the *Other Treaties case*, ACHR, Series A, No. 1, para. 40, text in *Human Rights Law Journal*, III, 1982, p. 140.

6 For comparison of the various texts, see P. Sieghart, *The International Law of Human Rights*, Oxford, 1983; for discussion of the judicial contribution to the process, see Merrills, *Development of International Law*, passim.

7 ECHR, Series A, No. 82.

8 The provision continues, 'in the interest of national security, public safety or public order, or to protect public health or morals or the rights or freedoms of others'.

9 These provide respectively that 'No one may, subject to law and order, be submitted to measures restricting the exercise of these freedoms', and that 'The exercise of this right shall be subject only to necessary restrictions provided for by law'. It will be recalled, however, that the restrictions permitted by certain other articles of the Charter appear to be more far reaching – see Chapter 7, section III, 2.

10 Emphasis added.

11 See the *Licensing of Journalism case*, ACHR, Series A, No. 5, para. 46 (the European Court's interpretation of 'necessary' is 'equally applicable' to the American Convention, though note the qualification in para. 50 concerning the scope of the right to freedom of expression under the two Conventions). Text in *Human Rights Law Journal*, VII, 1986, p. 74. See also the *Proposed Amendments case*, Series A, No. 4, para. 62, where the Court recognised the concept of the margin of appreciation. For text see *Human Rights Law Journal*, V, 1984, p. 161. For further examples, and relevant decisions of the Human Rights Committee, see Merrills, *Development of International Law*, pp. 18–19.

12 See Articles 8(1) and 14(1), respectively.

13 *Campbell and Fell case*, ECHR, Series A, No. 80.
14 *Engel case*, Series A, No. 22.
15 *Oztürk case*, Series A, No. 73.
16 Series A, No. 6.
17 ACHR, Series A, No. 4, para. 56. Note also the points made about some of the decisions of the Human Rights Committee in Chapter 2.
18 ECHR, Series A, No. 70.
19 See Merrills, *Development of International Law*, pp. 218–19.
20 *Pretto case*, Series A, No. 71. See Merrills, *ibid.*, p. 221. The corresponding provision of the Covenant is Article 14(1).
21 *Tyrer case*, Series A, No. 26.
22 See *Ncube, Tshuma and Ndhlovu v. The State* (1988), 2 *SAfrLRep*, p. 702, and *Juvenile v. The State*, judgement No. 64/89, Crim. App. No. 156/88, discussed in H. Hannum, Case note, *American Journal of International Law*, LXXXIV, 1990, p. 768.
23 See the Court's comment on these omissions in, respectively, the *Johnston case*, Series A, No. 112, para. 52, and the *Kosiek case*, Series A, No. 105, para. 34.
24 See further Merrills, *Development of International Law*, Chapter 7.
25 For further discussion of this issue, see J. J. Shestack, 'The jurisprudence of human rights', in T. Meron (ed.), *Human Rights in International Law*, Oxford, 1984, pp. 69–114, and E. Kamenka and A. E.-S. Tay, *Human Rights*, London, 1978.
26 See T. Meron, 'On a hierarchy of international human rights', *American Journal of International Law*, LXXX, 1986, p. 1.

# Index

R and MH v. Italy case, 58
racial discrimination, see discrimination
rape, 309
    see also violence against women
Rasmussen case, 158 n. 48
recognition as a person before the law,
    right to, 36, 38, 202, 313
Red Cross, 19, 20, 87, 166, 299, 301,
    305–6, 308
refugees, 77, 87
Reggiardo-Tolosa case, 236 n. 60
religious intolerance, 92–3
    see also freedom of thought,
        conscience and religion
reply, right of, 203, 222
reporting systems, 42–51, 95–102, 103,
    106–7, 109–12, 174–6, 260–1, 264–
    5, 280–1, 284–5
reservations, 49, 96, 104, 117 n. 40,
    204–5
    cases on, 157 n. 9, 219–21
Reservations to Genocide Convention
    case, 234 n. 26
Resolution 1235 procedure, 80, 83–9,
    114
Resolution 1503 procedure, 78–83, 86,
    114, 273 n. 32, 338
Restrictions to the Death Penalty case,
    220–1, 225–6
retrospective law, 3, 36, 125, 202, 250,
    313
Right of Reply case, 222
Rights of Minorities in Upper Silesia
    case, 22
Ringeisen case, 158 n. 27
Roosevelt, Mrs Eleanor, 7, 28
Rousseau, J. J., 6, 18, 335

Sakharov, Andrei, 181
Sara case, 58
Schiesser case, 143
security of person, see liberty and
    security of person,
self-determination, 30, 32, 34–5, 38, 49,
    73 n. 20, 121, 151, 180, 254, 275,
    295, 307, 336, 342
self-incrimination, protection against,
    38
sex discrimination, see discrimination

Sigurdur A. Sigurjónsson case, 144
slavery, 15–17, 22, 36, 77, 92–5, 125,
    202, 250, 309, 313, 330
social and medical assistance, right to,
    172
socialist States and human rights, 9–12
social security, right to, 124, 172–3,
    277, 281–3
Soering case, 64, 147
Solidarity, 181
Somersett's case, 15
Sophocles, 8
Sørensen, Max, 191
Specialised Agencies, 97, 111, 246–7,
    251, 274, 278, 281, 289, 330
Standard Minimum Rules for Prisoners,
    153
standard of living, 288, 294
statelessness, 77
    see also nationality
Status of Eastern Carelia case, 235 n.
    28
Suarez de Guerrero case, 60, 69
Sub-Commission on Prevention of
    Discrimination and Protection of
    Minorities, 79–94, 164, 281
Sunday Times case, 145, 272 n. 22
Sunday Times (No. 2) case, 145
Swedish Engine Drivers' Union case,
    158 n. 39

Tehran Conference on Human Rights
    (1968), 7, 14, 239–40, 305, 313
Teitgen Report, 122, 160
terrorism, 140, 163, 301, 309, 339
Thierry Trébutien case, 157 n. 9
Toonen case, 62
torture, 12, 36, 49, 62, 85, 87, 94–5,
    124, 156, 185, 202, 209–10, 250,
    304, 309, 312, 326, 334
    American Convention, 230–1, 327
    cases, 59, 60, 107, 136–41
    European Convention, 153, 162,
        165–8, 327
    UN Convention, 77, 91, 104–8, 165,
        168, 182, 230–1, 321, 327
    UN Declaration, 104–5
    UN special rapporteur, 91
    UN Voluntary Fund, 91